An OPUS book

Town, City, and Nation
England 1850–1914

OPUS General Editors

Keith Thomas
Alan Ryan
Peter Medawar

P. J. Waller

Town, City, and Nation
England 1850–1914

Oxford   New York

OXFORD UNIVERSITY PRESS

1983

Oxford University Press, Walton Street, Oxford OX2 6DP

London Glasgow New York Toronto
Delhi Bombay Calcutta Madras Karachi
Kuala Lumpur Singapore Hong Kong Tokyo
Nairobi Dar es Salaam Cape Town
Melbourne Auckland

and associates in
Beirut Berlin Ibadan Mexico City Nicosia

First published 1983 as an Oxford University Press paperback
and simultaneously in a hardback edition

British Library Cataloguing in Publication Data

Waller, P. J.
Town, city and nation: England 1850–1914.
1. Cities and town – England – History
I. Title
307.76'0942   HT133
ISBN 0-19-219176-4
ISBN 0-19-289163-4 Pbk

Printed in Great Britain by
The Thetford Press Ltd., Thetford, Norfolk

For Jane

Preface

Urban historians who address a general audience customarily start with some justification, even propaganda, for their work. The reason is that the study of towns and cities is mostly eccentric to the history taught in colleges and schools or submerged within other traditions of inquiry, such as the growth of industrialization or the rise of social and political democracy. Recent years have seen several ventures, with urban history courses or 'special subjects' provided by several universities; but entire omission or nodding condescension remains common. Some urban historians feel slighted by this. They mutter darkly about an unthinking conservatism gripping those who devise syllabuses. Others quietly acknowledge that there are problems in studying urban history.

A marriage of history with economics, geography, and sociology is not easily negotiated; but urbanists have difficulty foremost in convincing their historian colleagues of the value and coherence of towns and cities as an organizing principle of history. Except perhaps for the half-century before 1850, when rapid urbanization was manifestly novel and too shocking to be ignored, there seems little point in giving towns and cities especial prominence. In earlier times there was allegedly too little urbanization to warrant more than passing attention; in modern times too much to handle with proper dexterity.

The publications of Peter Clark and Paul Slack, *Crisis and Order in English Towns, 1500–1700* (1972), and *English Towns in Transition, 1500–1700* (1976), have dispelled the suspicion that urbanization in the centuries before the period of classic industrial revolution is too petty for study. The modern urban historian has never had to fight to establish the importance of his towns and cities. By the late nineteenth and early twentieth centuries the urban was the normal. Herein lies the challenge to the modern urban historian: how can the study of towns and cities supply a sharp focus for the discrimination of particular trends when the urban condition was common to most people at this time? Urban history allegedly is invertebrate, most like antiquarianism, a promiscuous jumble of items brought together on the poor pretext that these things have been found in or have occurred in towns.

Two kinds of retort may be devised. Upon their strength the organization of this book relies. One is that, if the post-1850 period witnessed the first comprehensive urban age, it is necessary to understand how far the urban was established in the cultural, economic and political fashions of society. Second, the urban historian might resist the flattery of his enemies and dispute their contention that urbanization by the late nineteenth century was hegemonic, all-conquering and all-pervasive. For it is an essential part of the urban historian's task to demonstrate that urban functions and dysfunctions, the urban experience and the urban influence, were very variable. Though towns and cities shared many characteristics they were not equal or alike. They may be separated like members of families, having individual weights and specific attributes as well as general resemblances. The aims of this book are to punctuate that urban series, to investigate inter-urban and intra-urban structures, both as distinct and connected units, and to illustrate the changing composition of the parts.

The first chapter begins by establishing the size of the urban mass, proceeds to explore some methodological difficulties, then indicates what were the important transformations of the late nineteenth and early twentieth centuries. The next four chapters descend the scale of urbanity, from most to least urbanized – London (chapter 2); the great cities and manufacturing towns of the conurbations (chapter 3); the new growths of pleasure resorts, suburbia, satellite towns, and planned communities (chapter 4); thence to country towns, and town and country (chapter 5). By degrees the reader will be moved from megalopolis to polis to a point, almost imperceptible, where the boundary between town and country was traversed. This theme of an urban–rural continuum is sound analytically only if it is understood to obtain *within* as well as *between* towns. All towns exhibit a mixture of 'rural' and 'urban' features, spatially, culturally, economically. There is, therefore, an internal and external hierarchy – the village inside every city, and vice versa. Finally, chapters 6 and 7 deal with problems of central and local government and arrive at an evaluation of public activity in respect of England's towns and cities.

This book is unashamedly a work of synthesis, constructed chiefly from the labours of many scholars. Some fresh material and ideas have been added, though it may be that their incunabula were suggested by others. If a pretension to originality has to be advanced, that will be found in the type of connections which are made here between the work of different scholars. I hope that none is offended by my use of his work. The borrowing is for the most part candidly acknowledged by a reference in the text or bibliography. Where it is not, a general apology may diminish the charge of burglary. Several friends and colleagues, Lord Briggs, Professor D. Fraser, Mr K. V. Thomas, and Dr R. I. McKibbin, read the typescript in an unrefined stage; and Mr J. H. Davis scrutinized the chapter on London. It gives me pleasure to record here the benefit I gained from their criticisms. Grateful acknowledgement, too, is made to T. W. Freeman and Manchester University Press for permission to use maps and figures from Professor Freeman's book, *The Conurbations of Great Britain*, 1959, revised 1966.

P. J. WALLER

Merton College, Oxford
July 1982

Contents

Tables

Figures

1 Outline of the urban mass

I

Growth in urban centres and urbanization are not synonymous. Towns may emerge or expand without upsetting the overall balance of urban and rural parts in a nation. Town size can increase in a context of shrinking urbanization, if the rural portion of the total population grows faster. Modern English history, however, displays both growing towns and growing urbanization.

A commonly observed turning-point is 1851. Then the census disclosed that the urban population comprised more than 50 per cent of the whole. In 1801 (the date of the first national census) the urban population constituted about 33 per cent; in the early eighteenth century 20–25 per cent. Now, in the mid-nineteenth century, it seemed that rural England was in absolute as well as relative decline. However, owing to the acknowledged chaos of local government areas, the interpretation of the census statistics is encumbered with problems. The 1851, 1861, and 1871 censuses included as urban areas most settlements of 2,000 or more inhabitants, whose lives were regulated by authorities as diverse as a county quarter session, municipal borough or parish vestry. But not all settlements of 2,000 inhabitants were designated 'towns' in these censuses. In 1851 the Census Commissioners followed local wisdom. Clerks to the county quarter sessions were 'consulted as to the places which are entitled to be deemed towns, and several places containing more than 2,000 inhabitants [were] omitted, because in the opinion of those officers, they could not in strictness be so designated'. In 1861 it was observed that many places on the borderlines of categories were small market towns; others were 'such aggregations of houses as are commonly called on that account towns, without having yet any other elements of union, except the ordinary parish organization. It is difficult to distinguish these small growing towns from villages and hamlets; and the line of separation cannot be drawn between them by any definite rule.' Since the areas of these small towns could be determined only approximately, the general distinction which the census observed in demarcating town from country was density of population. The 1872 Public Health Act furnished later census enumerators with a more consistent statistical codification, the 'urban sanitary district'. This may be taken to represent a minimal urban community, since the concentration of people was deemed to require certain sanitary regulations without which urban living could not be sustained. By 1881 the aggregate urban population of England and Wales constituted 70 per cent, in 1911 almost 80 per cent. Taking the early 1890s as a base point, we find that the number of urban districts was 1,012; but the distribution of population was extremely uneven between one urban district and another. London alone contained about 4,230,000 people in an area of 75,442 acres; the 64 county boroughs contained about 7,590,000 people in an area of 347,889 acres; the 238 municipal boroughs about 3,360,000 people in 667,529 acres; and the 709 mere urban districts about 5,710,000 people in 2,181,995 acres. According to the census the average population in urban districts was 4,068 persons to the square mile, compared with 154 in rural districts; but this average was a very crude measure of the urban condition when, at one end, 360 urban districts were towns of 10,000 or more inhabitants and, at the other end, 194 urban districts were gatherings of fewer than 3,000 inhabitants.

Whether the historian is correct to treat these last communities as towns is not simply a matter of statistical judgement. Clearly these communities lacked most of the distinguishing characteristics of great towns, but they cannot be abandoned altogether by the urban historian. There were no Manchesters in the making here, although it had been a remarkable feature of the early nineteenth century that villages could mushroom into sizeable towns in a matter of decades. Exceptional growth was achieved in the late nineteenth century chiefly by three types of community (see Table I).

One was the residential suburb or satellite town like Wallasey or Croydon. According to John Burns, President of the Local Government Board, 500,000 acres of agricultural land were developed for building between 1893 and 1908. Not all of this represented suburban settlement; but an indication of the scale of building will be gained by translating this sum into a graphic figure. Half a million built-up acres equalled a conurbation covering every square inch of Oxfordshire, with an overspill of 16,352 acres besides. The combined acreage of all urban areas, however, amounted to no more than 7 or 8 per cent of land use. Pastoral England was very visible still.

Table I Urban areas of exceptional growth, 1861–1911

This table lists those urban areas[1] of above 50,000 population in 1921 which had enjoyed at least one period of exceptional growth (defined as an intercensal growth of over 25 per cent) since 1861[2]. The urban areas are grouped according to the decade in which their growth rate was greatest.[3]

1861–71	Acton, Barrow-in-Furness, Battersea, Birkenhead, Bootle, Bradford, Chesterfield, Croydon, Darlington, Dewsbury, Ealing, Gateshead, Grimsby, Hackney, Hammersmith, Hampstead, Islington, Kensington, Lambeth, Leeds, Leicester, Lewisham, Middlesbrough, Northampton (same rate as 1871–81), Paddington, Poplar, Reading, Rotherham, Sheffield, Southport, Stockton on Tees, Swindon, West Hartlepool, Willesden, Wimbledon.
1871–81	Barnsley, Bournemouth, Burnley, Burton-upon-Trent, Camberwell, Deptford, Derby, Eastbourne, Hastings, Hull, Leyton, Lincoln, Luton, Nottingham, Oldham, St. Helens, Salford, Stoke Newington, Tottenham, Warrington, West Ham, Wigan.
1881–91	Doncaster, East Ham, Enfield, Fulham, Hornsey, Newcastle upon Tyne, Newport (Mon.), South Shields, Walthamstow, Wandsworth, Wood Green, Woolwich.
1891–1901	Blackpool, Edmonton, Gillingham (Kent), Ilford, Smethwick, Southampton, Wallasey.
1901–11	Coventry, Hendon, Southend on Sea.

Source: *Census of England and Wales 1921, General Tables (1925)*, Table 11, pp. 46–7.[4]

Notes: 1. According to local government parlance, county boroughs, municipal boroughs, metropolitan boroughs, and urban districts.

2. It is emphasized that this list indicates periods of exceptional growth between 1861 and 1911 only. This does not necessarily identify the period of greatest growth in a town's history, which may have occurred either before 1861 or after 1911. Bradford, for instance, grew by 52 per cent in 1831–41 and by 55 per cent in 1841–51. Nevertheless its growth by 34 per cent in 1861–71 was the highest decennial rate it experienced between 1861 and 1911.

3. Boundary revisions cast a doubt on how 'real' the growth of some towns was. On this see pp. 9–10 in respect of Liverpool and Nottingham.

4. The percentage increase of the total population of England:

1861–71	1871–81	1881–91	1891–1901	1901–11	1861–1911
13.75	14.21	11.62	12.15	10.48	79.69

Another set of growth spots consisted of the nodal points of the changing industrial economy: new iron- and steel-producing centres like Barrow, Middlesbrough, and Scunthorpe; new railway-workshop centres like Ashford, Crewe, Darlington, Derby, and Swindon; new shipbuilding centres like Birkenhead; new glass and chemicals towns like St. Helens and Widnes; new coal entrepôts like Cardiff; new fish-ports like Grimsby; new light-engineering (bicycles and motor cars) towns like Coventry. Several of these towns were not new, though the development which caused their extraordinary expansion was. Nowhere is this better illustrated than at Swindon, where the two parts were actually designated Old Swindon and New Swindon. Old Swindon stood atop a hill with a church spire and 'pepper-pot of a corn exchange'. On market days it was bustling with cattle, horses, and carts. New Swindon was down below, gathered around the Great Western Railway works and station, 'noisy, new, cheap, and Liberal, full of every accent', according to Edward Thomas's description in 1909. The same obtained about other old centres which experienced an unusual rate of growth or acquired sizeable industrial sectors: towns like Leicester, Luton, and Nottingham which sucked into factories industries which were formerly country-cottage based or Lincoln, Ipswich, and Gainsborough which manufactured new agricultural machinery. Some of the country's single largest employers were located in these places – Ransomes of Ipswich had 2,500 employees in 1911; Marshalls of Gainsborough had 5,000 in 1913; and in Lincoln Clayton and Shuttleworth employed 2,300, and Ruston's 5,500, in 1907 and 1912 respectively.

Lastly, there were the seaside and pleasure resorts. If the urban historian of mid-Victorian England neglects all centres of around 3,000 people as too puny for notice, then he has eliminated those towns which achieved the fastest growths between 1861 and 1911. Southend had 3,000 inhabitants in 1861, 63,000 in 1911, an increase of 2,000 per cent. By 1921 the town had passed the 100,000 mark. The same was true of Blackpool, with 4,000 citizens in 1861, 58,000 in 1911, and 100,000 by 1921. The growth of Bournemouth was even more spectacular, from 1,940 inhabitants in 1861 to 79,000 by 1911, until its exposed position on the south coast stunted any further development during the Great War.

But it is not the Southends, Blackpools, and Bournemouths which will be excluded by too rigorous a definition of 'town', because places which enjoyed a dramatic rise inevitably force themselves to the historian's notice. Rather it is places which remained small and relatively undeveloped, that nonetheless furnished for their dependent rural areas some urban services, primarily a market, additionally specific industrial or technical facilities. The ancient Berkshire borough, Wallingford, is an example. The historian of the early twentieth century may easily ignore Wallingford. Statistically unexciting, the town contained 2,808 inhabitants in 1901, 2,840 by 1931. There seems little to be gained by making sentimental allusions to Wallingford's status as the most important town in Berkshire at the time of Domesday. In modern times Reading was indubitably the principal town in the county, with 15,000 people in 1851, 84,000 in 1901. An important railway and river junction, with a significant trade in agricultural seeds and machinery, Reading was 'biscuitopolis' foremost, the town where the firm of Huntley and Palmer alone employed over 5,000 people by 1914, about double the entire population of Wallingford. Elsewhere in Berkshire Windsor, Newbury, Wokingham, Maidenhead, and Abingdon were all of greater size than Wallingford. But Wallingford was not civically destitute. True, its two Members of Parliament, a continuous privilege since 1295, had been reduced to one in 1832, and separate representation was lost by merger into the county following the 1885 redistribution. Wallingford's borough organization, however, continued. The original charter dated from Henry I and, after several revisions, a town council survived into the twentieth century in the shape of a mayor, four aldermen, and twelve councillors. The castle had been demolished during the Commonwealth; but a grammar school and town hall, which had arisen shortly afterwards, remained. If political traces of Wallingford's past importance lingered, both ceremonially and actually, the same applied to its economic role. In the larger regional or national economy Wallingford was doomed to insignificance from the early fifteenth century, when the main London–Gloucester road was diverted by new bridges across the Thames near Abingdon; but Wallingford's ancient markets and fairs persisted. The 1663 renewal of the borough charter provided for two markets and four annual fairs; by 1900 only the weekly Friday market and one annual fair continued, although a corn exchange had grown meantime.

Wallingford's surviving fair was the Michaelmas hiring fair or 'mop'. This was both labour exchange – for farm-hands and domestic servants – and occasion for festival. The traditional character was preserved as men seeking new positions sported emblems of their occupations in hats or hands – woven straw for the thatcher, a curl of wool and crook for the shepherd, cow-hair for the cowman, whipcord for the carter, and so on. The Great War finally put an end to the Wallingford hiring fair. Already mops in the rest of the country had died, as the agricultural sector contracted or changed from arable to pasture, as a more regular labour force farmed the land, and as newer techniques of hiring workers – through formal bureaux and newspaper advertisements – were preferred. Wallingford, however, provided other services which maintained its position in the economy of the north-west Berkshire and south-east Oxfordshire countryside. The town stood on the Thames and was the terminus of a branch line from the main Great Western Railway. There was an active grain trade and some malting; and carriers' carts linked Wallingford with nearby villages. These carts plied a regular two-way traffic of passengers and goods, fetching farm produce into the town and conveying outwards newspapers and shop wares. Wallingford was also the location of a steam-tackle firm whose engines were hired to work the fields of the district, ploughing, drilling, reaping, and threshing.

The purpose of this digression is plain. Statistically stagnant, Wallingford nevertheless had not surrendered its claims as a town. No urban historian can leave the Wallingfords of England out of account. Cumulatively these tiny towns mattered. There were 686 towns each with fewer than 10,000 inhabitants in 1901. Together they represented 11.4 per cent of the urban population of England and Wales. In other words, one of every nine urban dwellers lived a life bounded by small-town horizons.

It would be foolish, however, in a sketch of late-nineteenth- and early-twentieth-century urban history to squat in solitary places. No contemporary who addressed the theme of urbanization held Wallingford in mind. The Victorian thought in larger terms and, though the calculation is arbitrary, we may agree that a 'proper' town was of greater magnitude, over 10,000 people, and a large town over 50,000 people. Likewise, we may ignore the formal means by which a town became a city – by royal charter or by being the seat of a bishopric – and suggest that a 'proper' city would have over 100,000 inhabitants and a great city over 200,000 inhabitants. What, then, was the distribution of this 'proper' urban population? In 1901 there were 361 towns each with 10–50,000 people, 39 large towns each with 50–100,000 people, 23 cities each with 100–200,000 people, 14 large cities each with populations of between 200,000 and a million, and one, London, with a population greater than a million. Of the urban population, 23.2 per cent lived in towns of 10–50,000 inhabitants – that is, almost one of every four urban dwellers lived in small to medium-sized towns; 9.5 per cent of the urban population lived in towns of 50–100,000 inhabitants – that is, about one in every ten

Table II Changes in total and urban populations in England and Wales, 1851–1911

Year	England and Wales Total population '000s	% change	All urban Total population '000s	% change	Towns over 100,000 Total population '000s	% change	Towns of 50–100,000 Total population '000s	% change	Towns of 20–50,000 Total population '000s	% change	Towns of 10–20,000 Total population '000s	% change	Towns of 2,500–10,000 Total population '000s	% change
1851	17,928	12.6	9,688	25.9	4,450.7	34.8	1,037.3	17.9	1,262.9	17.0	1,154.7	37.4	1,782.4	12.0
1861	20,066	11.9	11,784	21.6	5,774.5	29.7	1,225.5	15.4	1,503.9	18.9	1,320.5	14.4	1,959.7	9.9
1871	22,712	13.2	14,802	25.6	7,404.1	28.2	1,260.5	2.8	2,173.0	44.4	1,501.6	13.7	2,462.8	25.6
1881	25,974	14.7	18,180	22.8	9,394.4	26.9	1,903.6	51.0	2,440.8	12.3	1,710.8	13.9	2,730.6	10.9
1891	29,003	11.6	21,601	18.8	11,433.3	21.7	2,487.9	30.7	2,647.4	8.4	2,062.1	20.5	2,970.4	8.8
1901	32,528	12.2	25,372	17.5	14,201.8	24.2	2,409.6	-3.1	3,235.7	22.2	2,641.7	28.1	2,883.1	-2.9
1911	36,070	10.9	28,467	12.2	15,811.9	11.3	2,887.1	19.8	3,750.2	15.9	2,840.2	7.5	3,178.1	10.2

Source: R. Lawton (ed.), The Census and Social Structure (1978), p. 97. Based on C. M. Law, 'The growth of urban population in England and Wales, 1801–1911', Trans. Inst. Brit. Geogr. 41 (1967), pp. 125–43.

Table III Percentage of urban population of England and Wales living in various sizes of town, 1851–1911

Year	Towns over 100,000	Towns of 50–100,000	Towns of 20–50,000	Towns of 10–20,000	Towns of 2,500–10,000
1851	45.9	10.7	13.0	11.9	18.4
1861	49.0	10.4	12.8	11.2	16.6
1871	50.0	8.5	14.7	10.1	16.6
1881	51.7	10.5	13.4	9.4	15.0
1891	52.9	11.5	12.3	9.5	13.8
1901	56.0	9.5	12.8	10.4	11.4
1911	55.5	10.1	13.2	10.0	11.2

Table IV Percentage of total population of England and Wales living in various sizes of town, 1851–1911

Year	Towns over 100,000	Towns of 50–100,000	Towns of 20–50,000	Towns of 10–20,000	Towns of 2,500–10,000	All urban
1851	24.8	5.8	7.0	6.4	9.9	54.0
1861	28.8	6.1	7.5	6.6	9.8	58.7
1871	32.6	5.5	9.6	6.6	10.8	65.2
1881	36.2	7.3	9.4	6.6	10.5	70.0
1891	39.4	8.6	9.1	7.1	10.2	74.5
1901	43.7	7.4	9.9	8.1	8.9	78.0
1911	43.8	8.0	10.4	7.9	8.8	78.9

urban dwellers lived in large towns; 17.9 per cent of the urban population lived in cities of 100–200,000 people, 20.1 per cent in great cities of between 200,000 and a million, and 17.9 per cent in London (LCC area) – that is, roughly, one of every five urban dwellers fell into each of these categories.

To slice the urban segment in this way establishes only one perspective, and it bears the disadvantage of being static. Another series of figures is required to glimpse change and movement (Tables II, III, IV). The urban impulse was overwhelming if we look at the entire nineteenth century. Between 1801 and 1901 the population of England and Wales increased by twenty-four millions, and about 80 per cent of these inhabited towns. If we pursue this analysis further, to consider the magnetic power of the greater towns, we find that in 1851 30.6 per cent of the population of England and Wales inhabited towns of over 50,000 people and, using the same town boundaries, about

45 per cent in 1901. Using the revised boundaries current in 1901, we find the tendency to agglomerate in towns of over 50,000 people stronger still, for then the proportion was 51.1 per cent. Now, however, there was not a regular progression in the growth rate of the various ranks of towns, that is, a tendency for the large to grow faster than the medium-sized, and the medium-sized faster than the small. On the contrary, a saturation point had been reached within the unreformed boundaries of certain large cities, which could not grow other than by borough extensions. The greatest city (after London), Liverpool, represents a clear case of this. There the central business area expanded at the expense of residence, and suburban movements beyond the municipal boundaries were pronounced. The 1891 census recorded a decennial *decrease* in Liverpool's population of over 6 per cent; but environs which were incorporated in Liverpool in the next decade increased by 53 per cent. By 1921 an average 28.66 per cent of the occupied populations of Great Crosby, Little Crosby, Hoylake, Seaforth, Waterloo, and Wallasey daily commuted to work in Liverpool. It is a nice question whether this suburban development foreshadowed the obsolescence and decay of the greatest cities or was simply a different dimension of growth. Historians should not permit their verdict to be constrained by the purely formal criteria of censuses which reflect politically determined municipal boundaries.

So far broad brushwork has been used to paint urban outlines. The main distinction has been quantity of population; but statistical bands do not make for coherent historical groupings of towns. Consider those provincial cities with over 200,000 population in 1861, of which there were four, Liverpool, Manchester, Birmingham, and Leeds. A bracket of Liverpool and Leeds seems manifestly amiss since Leeds, a city of 207,000 in 1861, barely passed by 1911 what Liverpool was in 1861, about 444,000. Liverpool in 1911 contained 746,000 people. The scales of development were entirely different. The growth of Leeds, 1861–1911, was 115.46 per cent, well above the growth rate for England (79.69 per cent), while Liverpool was below it, at 68.02 per cent. Quite evidently we must examine the special characteristics of these cities. Both were substantial commercial centres, but Liverpool was a port and distribution point, Leeds a manufacturing city of engineering, cloth, and leather goods.

Mismatches can be exposed in every order of town, ranked according to size only. Thus Exeter and Gateshead each had 34,000 inhabitants in 1861, 49,000 and 117,000 in 1911, growths of 44.12 and

244.12 per cent respectively. It was entirely adventitious that this pair of towns should have had the same size in 1861. Subsequent developments underlined that they were different types, placed in incomparable regional settings and performing dissimilar economic functions. We must be careful, therefore, to respect the cardinal law of comparing like with like, and always alert for traps and mines across the statistical path. Take Norwich and Nottingham. Here were two county capitals, with castles and bishoprics (Catholic, in Nottingham's case), lying on navigable rivers, and with main-line railway communications to London. Each had a tradition of textile manufacturing: Norwich for worsteds then for crape, Nottingham chiefly in lace and hosiery. There was engineering in both cities. Otherwise Norwich trades were dominated by boot and shoemaking, by breweries and tanneries, by Colman's mustard and starch manufacture. Nottingham had Boot's drugs, Player's tobacco, Raleigh's bicycles, and sundry leather manufacture. Each city had 75,000 inhabitants in 1861, but by 1911 there were 121,000 inhabitants of Norwich and 260,000 of Nottingham, crude growths of 61.33 and 246.67 per cent respectively. What accounts for this discrepancy? Neither county capital was unaffected by the national fortunes of its trades or by the regional economy of its shires. For example, the revolution in the organization of the Nottingham hosiery trade, from domestic to factory production, during the 1850s and 1860s acted as an economic spur to the entire area; while Norwich, as an agrarian capital, was set into a different pattern of performance. But another explanation is a statistical quirk, a reorganization of administrative boundaries in the case of Nottingham, which made it twice the size of Norwich by 1881.

There is, therefore, imprecision about most urban growth series distinguished by population size alone. Other criteria will better establish the hallmarks of different urban types. This preliminary emphasis upon town variety is essential before comment is made about modern town characteristics in general and about the special transformations of our period, for one school of thought – epitomized by Lewis Mumford, *The City in History* (1961) – asserts that all Victorian cities were really the same, simply the city at one stage of evolution in form. In *Victorian Cities* (1963) Asa Briggs rejected this proposition as insensitive:

The first effect of early industrialization was to differentiate English communities rather than to standardize them. However much the historian talks of common urban problems, he will find that one of his most interesting tasks is

to show in what respect cities differed from each other . . . Below the surface
. . . nineteenth-century cities not only had markedly different topography,
different economic and social structures, and quite different degrees of interest
in their surrounding regions, but they responded differently to the urban
problems which they shared in common. A study of English Victorian cities,
in particular, must necessarily be concerned with individual cases.

This is a substantive argument. It challenges the urban historian to
specify the particular in the context of the general. Briggs demonstrated his case by city biographies, of Manchester, Leeds, Birmingham, Middlesbrough, London, and, out on a flank, Melbourne.
Nevertheless in his Introduction and Epilogue, and in his chapter
'City and Society', Briggs examined generalized features, movements,
and responses. This book, though differently organized, endorses
Briggs's philosophy: that we have no monotony of appearance or
characteristics in towns, any more than we have a sameness among
townspeople. But we can discern similar entities, common functions,
and shared problems amid the singular histories.

II

Historians have not been alone in studying towns. Towns are administrative, legal, political, social, and economic constructs. Consequently, sociologists, geographers, economists, political scientists and
philosophers have all contributed much to our understanding of city
forms and city life. Sociologists have primarily made a study of urban
attitudes and community organization. Geographers have examined
spatial use within cities and the relationship of city and region. Economists have considered the city's role in manufacture and marketing
and in the distribution of wealth. Political scientists and philosophers
have taken stock of the city as the setting and spring of humanist and
democratic endeavour, simultaneously a place where man's highest
faculties can flourish and where man's corruption can be complete.
Historians in their eclectic way have tried to acknowledge all these
approaches, and to test the academic images against historical
evidence of particular times and places. But one obstacle in the way of
historians fully tapping the reservoir of other learning is obvious. No
more than the historians are the sociologists, geographers and the rest,
confident or harmonious in their explanations of the processes they
describe. Inter-disciplinary collaboration is a splendid ideal, but it
makes the business of judging results no easier.

Consider first the sociological analysis, particularly the attempted classification of rural–urban differences. Many of its main propositions derive from an American context, expounded in the big-city atmosphere of Chicago. Altogether America was less urbanized than England. In many states the rural–urban contrasts were stark. Still, no sociologist of any reputation asserts that rural–urban differences have mutually exclusive properties. Changes over time have reinforced this blending and shading of qualities. The extension of social and technological services has endowed previously impoverished country regions with the verisimilitude of urban sanitary, educational and medical facilities, with rail, road, gas, and electricity connections, and with common cultural points which are neither urban nor rural. Nonetheless, rural–urban models are worth spelling out, because they embrace assumptions which many held and still hold to have real foundation. They involve distinctions about occupation, environment, size and density of settlement, heterogeneity of population, and social stratification, mobility, and relationships.

Regarding occupation, the contrast is between agricultural and non-agricultural pursuits. Farm work is relatively unspecialized and unregulated; and work-place and home life are more closely tied. Town work is chiefly in manufacturing, commercial distribution, and the professions. The connection of work and family units is more tenuous or altogether snapped; and the classes of work are more numerous, more specialized, more controlled. Regarding environment, the countryman's living is shaped more by natural forces; in towns man-made factors predominate. As for size, only aggregation makes possible the reciprocal activities of urban living, in industrial and leisure pursuits. The gross density of population in towns is greater than in villages; the heterogeneity of the citizens is more marked, in origins, opinions, and behaviour; and the urban social stratification is more intricate and fluid. As for mobility, towns are characterized by movement, both to and within. There is not much contrary movement, from town to country, since the suburban and exurban movement is really an expansion of the town or urbanization of the countryside. Finally, with regard to social relationships, those of the country are more typically few, narrow, family-based, personal, and enduring; those of the town more numerous, extra-familial, impersonal, and casual.

The conclusion is that for most practical purposes town-dweller and country-dweller operate at different levels of cognition, summarized traditionally in a contrast of wit and naïvety, or deviousness and honesty. The mentality of the countryman is shaped by a culture that is chiefly oral, customary, and superstitious. The townsman's modes of thought are moulded by an environment that is chiefly literate, progressive, sceptical, or scientific. This is because secondary contacts predominate in the city, primary contacts in the country. Two important consequences stem from this. One is that though the townsmen's acquisitiveness or materialism is the sharper, as individuals townsmen are mostly futile. They are civilized but unhappy and repressed. Their effectualness emerges only through corporate organizations of the voluntary or official kind, in social, industrial, and political matters. Another consequence is that the reduction of the townsmen's sense of personal significance gives rise to sociopathic stresses which emerge in lunacy, suicide, crime, vice, corruption, riot, or in mere aimlessness, alienation, and anomie.

The trouble with this analysis is that it proceeds by antithesis. It is artificial to contrast rural and urban as traditional and modern. All societies contain hybrid systems whose cultural development and attributes are out of phase one with another. They coexist, overlap, intermingle or are superimposed on each other, within one community, within a single person. They are not clear-cut and pure in form. Thus towns contain economic activities in which the family unit and age-old skills and working practices are preserved, as well as businesses which are technologically advanced or structured in a highly specialized manner. Sections of each town are moribund or in a state of galloping progress. So too with individuals: the *Weltanschauung* of the old and young, rich and poor, is an immensely varied mixture. Superstition and reason wrestle in every mind. None is easy to categorize.

Take attitudes to folk and formal medicine, for instance. Recourse in illness or discomfort to herbalists and purveyors of traditional treatments ('wise' people) or new patent medicines (from Morison's to Beecham's pills) remained widespread in nineteenth-century towns as well as in the countryside, and was superseded only slowly by recourse to regular medical practitioners. But those who interpret the popularity of unorthodox medical practice as an example of surviving superstition are remarkable for their confidence more than their fine judgement. Was it so irrational to trust empirics and amateurs when many of their ritual cures were derived from natural observation or botanical experiment, and when the authority of the professionals was so shaky? Quacks may not have been much cheaper than regular doctors but they were more numerous and accessible and (compared with surgeons) no more dangerous. Quacks enchanted the rich and educated as well as the poor and ignorant; and the medical profession itself inspired speculative enterprise – homoeopathy, allopathy, hydropathy and the rest.

No broad contrast of town and country attitudes as 'advanced' and 'antediluvian', 'critical' and 'credulous', is tenable; and no sociologist allows these contrasts to remain unqualified. It will be emphasized in the course of this book how much town and country are organically interlocked rather than separate. Nonetheless, the persistence of these stereotypes of urban–rural attitudes and experiences was and is remarkable. We shall find that we are dealing not with easily eradicated error but with profoundly held and vestigially valid intellectual perspectives.

Consider the conceptual framework of B. S. Rowntree, whose investigation of conditions in York, *Poverty: a Study in Town Life* (1901), did much to establish the credentials of the English school of empirical urban sociology. Rowntree understood that urban problems could not be considered in isolation from rural problems. He went on to study the latter, with May Kendall, in *How the Labourer Lives* (1913). There were two chief reasons for Rowntree's emphasis. One was that, as the rural energies of England were sapped, the implications for the towns were dire, since the 'physique of the town population in the past has been maintained to some extent by constant reinforcement of the anaemic town dwellers by countrymen'. But, Rowntree went on,

there is another point of view from which the matter should be considered – that of the national character. Work on the land, in constant contact with natural objects and often in comparative isolation, produces a solid strength of character which our English nation can ill afford to lose. Town dwellers may call the countryman slow or stupid. Certainly he thinks slowly, but his opinions when formed are not infrequently shrewd and sensible, and based on personal observation. The town dweller, on the other hand, suffers from living too quickly and living in a crowd. His opinions are the opinions of the crowd – and a crowd is easily swayed, for evil as well as for good. Not only, then, from the point of view of physical deterioration, is it well that at last the British nation has awakened to the importance of recruiting and developing her rural districts.

Rowntree's opinions were unexceptional for his time. As Gareth Stedman Jones has shown in *Outcast London* (1971), belief in and fear of hereditary urban degeneration was widespread between 1860 and 1914. It emerged especially in debates about how best to dispose of the casual labour problems of the big cities; but it may be seen as a common reference in the fictional literature and ephemeral journalism of the period, in official inquiries, such as the Royal Commissions on Labour (1892–4) and on the Poor Laws (1905–9), and the Inter-Departmental Committee on Physical Deterioration (1904); in the analyses of poverty undertaken by Charles Booth or the Charity Organization Society; in the theoretical and applied economics of Alfred Marshall and William Beveridge; and in the policy prescriptions of the social imperialist schools of politicians.

The geographers' investigation of city form has been no less controversial than the sociologists'. Value systems are not so central to their framework; but a major debate concerns the validity of concepts of 'pre-industrial' and 'industrial' cities, in order to distinguish spatial form. In the classic pre-industrial city the rich hog the centre, the poor huddle about the periphery. In the classic industrial city this model is practically overturned. The rich own and do business in the centre but it is the poor who live there. Chiefly, however, the industrial city is broken up into broadly segregated neighbourhoods – central business area, slum district, transition zones, suburbia. This single-core city model was modified by taking into account transport axes which segmented the city circle, and by introducing the concept of the multi-nuclei city, having several sub-centres of either a concentric or radial type; but all involve one basic proposition, that proximity and accessibility to a central location is at a premium in an industrial urban economy because of transport savings. Relative distances and amenity values, therefore, chiefly inform the land usage and determine the rental structure of properties devoted to manufacturing, office, and retailing businesses, the multiple occupancy of central-city slums, and the dispersed single-family suburban dwelling. Random secular influences impose the idiosyncrasies which individuate each city. These are the dynamics of building cycles, the habits of local building firms and speculators, and the decisions of landlords to abet or prevent development of estates; the taxation policies, improvement schemes, and building regulations ordained by central and local government; and the particular topography of rail, road, and water communications.

Even though the mechanism can be distorted by private and public interventions and by unusual physical features, still the simple land-market model of a ratio between distance and rent underpins the operation. The industrial city is thus highly differentiated in its spatial organization, for economic and social purposes. How closely actual towns and cities fit this model is merely an index of how far they have progressed in the transition from 'pre-industrial' to 'industrial' form.

This is one problem set for historians by the urban geographers' work. Another is to resolve the tension between territory and culture. Is it the spatial relations which determine social relations, or the social relations which determine spatial relations? Geographers have also studied towns in relation to regions, plotting and measuring the radii of agricultural produce and retail and professional services. These studies have led to a complex hierarchy of urban areas, from small towns to metropolises, based upon marketing functions.

The economists' analysis of cities also concerns markets, with an emphasis on the location of industry and allocation of resources, their efficiency and equity. This involves consideration of the mechanisms, advantages, constraints, and costs of agglomeration economics, both financially and, more imprecisely, in terms of 'quality of life'. Location decisions comprise numerous internal and external cost gradients, relating to land, transport, access to labour, materials, markets, and ancillary business services; and these decisions vary between particular sectors of trade and industry, within different types of manufacturing industry, as well as between these and retail businesses or offices. The applicability of modern theories to the past is imperfect. Industrial mobility has been enhanced by motorized freight transport, national energy and power systems, by computerization, telephone and telex communications, and by the redistribution of population into suburban communities or satellite towns. Moreover, government has played a greater role in decisions, by financial incentives, by public trading services, and by intervention to determine land use, to supply education, housing, employment, and transport, and to safeguard the environment.

Not all these considerations are irrelevant to a study of late-nineteenth- and early-twentieth-century urban history; but the influences stemming from the pre-existing shape of urban industrial England need to be understood first. In the pre-railway age when water transport was superior to road haulage, that access was practically indispensable for a town's growth. The most advantaged towns were those situated at junctions or transport break-points. In 1660 there were 685 miles of navigable waterways in England, 1,160 miles by 1730, 2,200 miles by 1790, 3,875 miles by 1830, 4,000 miles by 1850. The regional redistribution of population and industry which took place in that period was congruent with this factor. The growth of the West Midlands, West Yorkshire, and South Lancashire are classic instances. By 1841, according to Charles Hadfield, *The Canal Age* (1968), only Luton among the seventy leading towns in Britain was land-locked, with no direct outlet by navigable river, canal, or sea. The railways' impact on this scene was not trifling, but to a considerable extent one system of transport merely superseded another. Certain canals in industrial areas retained some profitability from heavy traffic, especially in coal; but by 1888 no more than eleven were making annual profits of over £10,000. Many were obsolete and, argued the Royal Commission on Canals and Inland Navigations (1906–9), 'considered as a whole, the waterways have had no share in the enormous increase in the transport business which has taken place between the middle of the nineteenth century and the present time'.

Over half the canals' total traffic was moved on 984 miles of canal. Coal constituted 45 per cent of the tonnage but this amounted to less than 1 per cent of rail- and sea-borne coal. Moreover, most canal traffic was short-distance, under twenty miles. There were simply too many locks – 2,377 altogether, or an average of one every one and a half miles – to make through-running an efficient, paying proposition; and the cost of widening and deepening the system in order to carry larger vessels was prohibitive. For long-distance freight and for passengers, therefore, the canals offered the railways no real competition from the start. The measure of the railways' impact on the urban hierarchy, however, requires nice judgement. They expanded the range of raw material supply and market for finished goods, without which established activity in some areas might have been checked and new activities in other areas might never have arisen on an appreciable scale. But, though new towns were indeed generated by the railways, their substantial contribution was to strengthen connections between existing towns and to make continued urbanization feasible. Only indirectly, by encouraging concentrated and specialized activities, did the laying down of the railways make a material difference to the rank-order of the urban hierarchy.

Urban historians must have an interest in industrial location theory as well as in transport economics. The predominance of industry in town centres reflects the fact that people were more easily moved than goods when road haulage was inefficient and when most workers walked, bicycled, or were conveyed by inexpensive omnibuses, trams, and suburban trains. The legacy of primitive location decisions remained in the concentration of activities in certain regions and towns. The reason that Tyneside was a great shipbuilding region lay in the sixteenth century, when a timber-fuel shortage threatened London and encouraged increased domestic and industrial use of coal. The easily worked coal supplies near the Tyne were moved by river and sea. Both barge- and ship-building were directly stimulated; and other industries consuming coal – salt, glass, pottery, and iron manufacture – were attracted to the area. Later developments fastened and intensified this activity, especially after 1850 with the laying down of the railways and exploitation of the Cleveland ore field. In 1855 Cleveland produced 9.1 per cent of UK iron ore and 2.6 per cent of pig iron; forty years later the proportion was 42 and 37 per cent respectively. Though the Cleveland share of UK production fell from 1895, the volume continued to rise. At the same time more collieries were sunk, for steam-coals, coking-coals, and gas-coals as well as for household coals; shipbuilding converted to iron and steel; armaments and chemical manufacture appeared too. As a result the population in the north-east conurbations, around Tyneside and Wearside, grew from 200,000 to two million; and this region, which once contained under half the total population of the four northern counties (Durham, Northumberland, Cumberland, and Westmorland), now held over 80 per cent. Similarly, the population of Teesside (including Darlington) grew from 87,640 in 1851 to 458,809 in 1911.

Many another region and town could boast equal continuity in a line of work, given adequate and accessible resources. The nineteenth-century novelty derived from market developments or applied technologies. Thus the shoe trade of Northampton was centuries old, because of the town's central position as a distribution point for this common article, and because of the ready supply of its raw material, hides, from the rich pastoral farming in the area. Factory methods of production in the late nineteenth century simply confirmed this tradition. What was true of a good-sized town like Northampton was applicable in greater measure still to small-market and single-industry towns of long standing, like Witney in Oxfordshire. Its site on the edge of the Cotswolds sheep-farming area, with the river Windrush supplying power and clear water for blanket manufacture and dyeing, was combined with established communications on the London–

Oxford–Gloucester road. After the railway arrived in Witney in 1861 leading manufacturers such as Early's (who were substantial shareholders in the railway) began modernization, installing power-driven looms (which the big Yorkshire manufacturers, like Benjamin Gott and Sons, had been using for over twenty years), integrating their plant, and erecting new mills. Again, therefore, in this case of blanket-making at Witney the original *raison d'être* of site was reinforced by late-nineteenth-century technological and transport developments.

By contrast we should acknowledge cases where historical forces continued to exert an influence on industry even after some reasons for the original settlement had perished; for example, when local supplies of raw materials were exhausted or when transport technology changed. In the late nineteenth century, in the northern textile regions, many mills remained located on waterways, which still carried goods, received industrial waste, and even supplied the source of energy. A move to new sites closer to railway yards was attractive mostly to the bigger firms. Similarly in the twentieth century, factories remain by railway lines though their raw materials and finished products might be moved chiefly by road. There is inertia involved here; but, in many instances, transport access weighs less than other factors. One noticeable feature of old-established industries is a reluctance to move from cramped central-city sites. The conversion costs of settling elsewhere may be greater than those of a marginal plant extension on the original site; or overheads may be reduced by a domestic out-work system. Certainly the proximity of an experienced, plentiful, and pliant labour force may act as a drag, even if high property rates suggest that a move to a decentralized location might be financially sensible. External economies, derived from the regional concentration of particular industries, were apparent early on in the industrial revolution. Andrew Ure, in *The Philosophy of Manufactures* (1835), noticed the vital support given to the mills of Lancashire and Yorkshire by engineering firms which made and repaired textile machinery: 'the concentration of mechanical talent and activity in the districts of Manchester and Leeds is indescribable by the pen, and must be studied confidentially behind the scenes, in order to be duly understood or appreciated.'

Generally new industries have been more mobile, freer to colonize decentralized urban sites or even to establish entire communities from scratch. Where established firms evinced this tendency it was usually due to a philosophy of social improvement, as well as to a sense of business advantage – for example, the decision of Titus Salt to leave Bradford in 1850 and develop a site near Shipley, which he named Saltaire; or the planned Joseph Rowntree Village Trust at New Earswick, which became the home of the transplanted York cocoa factory after 1900. Still, new industries were not released from certain basic requirements in site allocation, even those like the motor industry which was not disposed to any particular area because of its raw materials. The William Morris who became Lord Nuffield no doubt had some sentimental attachment to Oxford, his birthplace; but we can observe in the success of his car firm the same forces as Ure noted about the northern textile industry. Morris copied American production methods, assembling components supplied on sub-contract rather than seeking to manufacture the complete vehicle himself. Without the concentration of light engineering and specialist component firms in the West Midlands, as a result of the bicycle boom of the 1890s, it is difficult to see that Morris could ever have succeeded in Oxford.

Considerations of site choice and technological and transport change, then, will recur in this book. So too will other concerns of economists, particularly public economy, the fiscal policies of central and local government. There are a range of connected issues here, but the most dramatic are public health, questions of employment and housing, and the first steps in modern town planning; the municipalization of services essential to the urban infrastructure, gas, water, electricity, and transport; and the agitation for land reform, to alter the incidence of taxation between owner and occupier and between different types of property, chiefly from developed to undeveloped urban land and from buildings to sites. It was through such movements, many believed, that the progress and attractiveness of towns would be ensured.

These questions are entwined with political and philosophical estimations. Historically towns have origins in five causes, from reasons of trade, recreation, defence, religion, and administration. Their physical symbols were market, fair, castle, church, and chamber. The towns' political assertion allegedly was an important agent in popular emancipation from monarchical and aristocratic bondage. Ceremonially and physically towns have perpetuated this idea in the ritual of self-government and in grand public buildings. Towns also rivalled each other, but this competition was held to be healthy, a manifestation of independence which enlarged civic well-being. In the late

Victorian period some still struggled to escape from suffocating aristocratic influences; but elsewhere was reconcilement. Towns solicited aristocratic mayors. There were many reasons for this -- aristocratic territorial influence in several towns was strong – but the most subtle was that, far from suggesting subservience, it signified the towns' confidence that aristocrats might lend glamour as civic figureheads without posing a threat to civic independence. By now many towns had their own dynasties. Some were generations old; all had a grip over business and property. Their embrace of a more ancient landed aristocracy symbolized their awareness of a different social and political menace, organized labour. In this perspective the past struggles of municipalities from Crown and aristocracy seemed bogus. These had brought only partial independence for the majority of citizens, transposed from rural feudal to urban oligarchical governance. Now the democratic movement was earnest, conducted within towns as much as extramurally.

This was a secular crusade. Many assumed that urbanization and secularization were twins. Originally, however, towns had furnished a base for the priesthood. The trend towards secularization in the late Victorian period reflected the cultural diversity of cities rather than proved that city life and religious observance were inimical. The quality of urban living preoccupied many, not only moralists. Their indices of measurement were always incomplete, for what scale could register the opportunities and restrictions in the lives of urban types as different as plutocrat and pauper? The English literary and intellectual tradition was rife with anti-urbanism. Now for some it was deepened as urban tentacles, choking rural life, multiplied in number. Witness the poet and visionary, William Morris, contemplating a 'cockneyised countryside' with 'no rest, no beauty, no leisure anywhere: all England become like the heart of Lancashire is now'.

Other writers and artists evinced a contrary movement, a cult of the city. Some judged this symptomatic of the decadence of town living, a perverse paradox in the preference for the artificial over the natural; but at least it indicated that some towns provided a scope for eccentricity which was prohibited by the country. 'My dear boy,' says Lord Henry Wotton in *The Picture of Dorian Gray* (1891), 'anybody can be good in the country. There are no temptations there. That is the reason why people who live out of town are so absolutely uncivilized. Civilization is not by any means an easy thing to attain to. There are only two ways by which man can reach it. One is by being cultured, the other by being corrupt. Country people have no opportunity of being either, so they stagnate.'

Urban culture, corrupt or not, seemed omnipotent. Even by mid-Victorian times the urban portion of the population was so preponderating that the nation seemed really one city with one mind. Bagehot pronounced that 'public opinion nowadays is the opinion of the bald-headed men at the back of the omnibus'. All were growing less motley in character and thought: 'London ideas shoot out every morning, and carry on the wings of the railroad, a uniform creed to each cranny of the kingdom, north and south, east and west . . . There is little oddity in country towns now: they are detached scraps of great places'. Bagehot described the direction of a tendency, not its fulfilment. There was variety still. And it is a moot point whether the trend signified the nationalization rather than the urbanization or metropolitanization of culture.

Similar complexity characterizes the relations of town governments with Westminster. The mid-Victorian debate about the merits of local government versus central government was inappropriate. They were not mutually exclusive. Many MPs and civil servants were anxious to cultivate local initiative and self-reliance. Conversely, many councillors and town-hall officials wanted central government to display greater drive in tackling local problems. Centralization proceeded concurrently with decentralization. The Tocquevillean charge against democracy was that its lust for equality engendered a loathing of diversity. This implied a centralized bureaucracy which extinguished local independence. Certainly, the nineteenth century witnessed an expanding official supervision of institutions as diverse as prisons and schools; and reforming groups agitated for imperial legislation to get public abuses remedied. Financially, central and local government were interlocked and it appeared, through the grant-in-aid system, that the whip-hand was increasingly held by central departments, enabling them to prescribe standards of practice. But permissive, discretionary, and private legislation was cherished still. Moreover, local self-government was paraded in borough councils, School Boards, Poor Law Boards, Highway and Sanitary Boards.

There was undoubted scope for distinctive expression by urban authorities; but, just as men perceived that the country was drawing together into one cultural unit, so politically the country seemed more alert to common challenges and experiences. The 'National Efficiency' school of politicians and thinkers, around 1900, wished to accelerate this process. They were disrespectful of local tradition and independence. To them local government was practically synonymous with inefficiency. No longer should the expert suffer the supremacy of the amateur for, the Webbs wrote in 1911, 'social reconstructions require as much specialized training and sustained study as the building of bridges and railways, the interpretation of the law, or technical improvements in machinery and mechanical processes'. Government should be professionalized; and, if local government had any future, it lay with the large municipalities and county councils, better still with regional tribunals dispensing and managing public services. Administrative areas should be determined upon scientific principles. Large units would produce not merely efficiency but a more inspiring level of citizenship. Small units meant waste, graft and petty place-hunting, the slough of parochialism. This argument masked a difficulty about regionalism, that it attracted two potentially incompatible types. One was primarily interested in provincial democracy, in encouraging popular participation in government, thus to decentralize power. The other was primarily concerned to promote more efficient public utilities and economic planning, by curbing the whimsicality of local representative institutions and by using regional machinery as a tool of central government.

There are then paradoxes about this period. As a consequence of the completeness of the urbanization of society almost everything that went on in towns affected society at large. The nation's future, it seemed, would be written in the towns. However, far from being permitted to be the authors of their own and the country's destiny, towns were subject to limitation and direction by national authorities. Hence, though society was increasingly shaped by city ways the city itself, as R. E. Pahl has written, was what society let it be. Because England was a preponderating urban nation the value of the diminishing rural portion was enhanced. That this preface to recent urban history should conclude by emphasizing the claims of rural England is not perverse. An observation of the Verney Committee on Land Settlement (1915–16) serves as a leitmotiv of the period: 'The stability and physical strength of a nation depend largely on those classes who have been born or brought up in the country or have had the advantage of country life.' Though in some respects the city had become the nation, a resistance to it was strongly felt. The nation's governing voice was not a city echo.

2 London

That the capital, London, should take a chapter to itself requires no lengthy defence. Between one-sixth and one-fifth of the total population of England lived there. It was the largest city in the world, a plural city which encompassed almost every type of city and was supreme in each. London contained the country's biggest concentration of industry – chiefly clothing, footwear, and furniture. The size of this industry was for the most part disguised, because parcelled out among many small workshops. According to the 1851 census, 86 per cent of London employers employed fewer than ten men. Some large establishments could be found. The Royal Arsenal at Woolwich employed about 12,000 during the Boer War; the main locomotive works of the Great Eastern Railway, at Stratford, employed about 7,000 around 1910; and the Army clothing factory at Pimlico was another substantial concern. There were sizeable gas and electricity power stations, brewing, soap-boiling, sugar-refining, candle-making, tanning, and engineering works elsewhere; still, London industry was mostly characterized by the absence of large-scale factory methods of production. On the other hand, the port of London was the country's largest and, as the epicentre of railways and roads, London was indisputably the chief emporium of Britain and its empire. Incontestably, too, London was the functional and ceremonial seat of politics and diplomacy, the first place of finance and the professions, the most important stage for the world of art, literature, and entertainment; in sum, the centre and magnet for all things from luxurious living and High Society to mendicancy and the criminal underworld.

I

London's agglomerating habit was centuries old. It is our business to try to measure the modern strength of this ancient ascendancy, to establish what changes were taking place both within London and in London's relations with provincial England. It is no simple matter to comprehend London's dimensions and organization. It meant one thing to the Metropolitan Board of Works (established 1855) or London County Council (1888–9) – an administrative province. It meant another thing to the City Corporation – a jealously guarded enclave of roughly one square mile and almost immeasurable wealth, preserved within the heart of the capital. And to the Registrar-General in charge of censuses London meant something else again – an over-spilling, almost indeterminate, urban area. Some statistical definition was given to the concept of a Greater London in 1875. This was made coterminous with the Metropolitan Police District, with a radius of fifteen miles from Charing Cross. The population within the LCC area reached a maximum around 1901. Nowadays it is smaller even than at its foundation in 1888–9. Overall from 1861 to 1911 the population of the administrative county grew 61 per cent, the Greater London conurbation 125 per cent, England as a whole 80 per cent. Thus the capital, taking its broadest area, was more than maintaining its primacy in the general population (Table V).

Table V Population in London, 1861–1921

(a) Absolute sums, in thousands

	1861	1871	1881	1891	1901	1911	1921
London County	2,808	3,261	3,830	4,228	4,536	4,522	4,485
Outer ring	414	624	936	1,406	2,045	2,730	2,996
Total: Greater London	3,222	3,885	4,766	5,634	6,581	7,252	7,481

(b) Percentage increase or decrease over preceding census

	1871	1881	1891	1901	1911	1921
London County	+16.1	+17.4	+10.4	+7.3	−0.3	−0.8
Outer ring	+50.7	+50.0	+50.1	+45.3	+33.5	+9.7
Total: Greater London	+20.6	+22.7	+18.2	+16.8	+10.2	+3.2
Total: England	+13.75	+14.21	+11.62	+12.15	+10.48	+4.78

(c) Percentage of total population of England living in London

	1861	1871	1881	1891	1901	1911	1921
London County	14.8	15.2	15.6	15.4	14.7	13.3	12.8
Greater London	17.0	18.1	19.4	20.5	21.4	21.3	21.0

Already, by comparing the administrative county with the conurbation, a sense of London's population structure is communicated.

Work by late-nineteenth-century statisticians, E. G. Ravenstein, H. Llewellyn Smith, and A. F. Weber, led to the identification of certain 'laws of migration' which could be evinced in the case of London. Perhaps 'laws of migration' – this was the title of Ravenstein's paper, delivered to the Statistical Society in 1885 – was too strong a term, since human behaviour was not strictly comparable to the seasonal flights of birds or to animal progresses. Nevertheless, several characteristics were so marked as to constitute a pattern, and no great intelligence was required to interpret it, according to the newspaper editor R. D. Blumenfeld, who wrote in his diary, 15 October 1900: 'Everybody wants to come to London; and little wonder, since the rural districts are all more or less dead, with no prospect of revival.'

More women than men were migrants. Domestic service and the prospect of marriage were the prevailing forces. In addition women's opportunity of field-work was reduced in the late nineteenth century, and a more scientific milk trade was eliminating the ordinary dairy-maid. The number of women returned in the censuses as agricultural workers fell from 229,000 in 1851 to 67,000 in 1901. The majority of in-migrants to London were aged between 15 and 30, a circumstance which compounded the over-supply of unskilled, casual labour in the capital. With so many young adults siphoned off, the country was left with an age structure different from the towns. Statistics presented to the Royal Commission on the Poor Laws (1905–9) showed that in London old people over 60 constituted 66.9 per 1,000 population. In other wholly or mainly urban districts they formed 67.3 per 1,000, in wholly or mainly rural districts 102 per 1,000. The sex ratio was different too, particularly in the 15–19 age group which (in 1911) amounted to 864 females per 1,000 males in rural districts and 1,044 in urban.

Another general feature of the migrations related to places of origin: the greater the city the wider the magnetic field of its attraction. In the case of London, this extended internationally in a powerful way. East European pogroms brought 100–150,000 Jewish settlers to England between 1881 and 1914. Leeds, Manchester, and to a lesser extent Liverpool, were the eventual destinations of many fugitive foreign Jews; but East London was subject to the heaviest concentration of both settlers and transmigrants. Whitechapel's population by 1901 was 31.8 per cent alien. The proportion of foreign-born in the total population of London at that time was 2.98 per cent; in 1881 it had been 1.57 per cent. In many respects the Irish had prefigured the foreign Jews in the cumulative scale of their migration and in the density of their settlement in certain districts. Although the number of Irish-born in the population of London was falling in the late nineteenth century, the Irish contributed around 14,000 immigrants to London in 1851–61, 7,000 in 1861–71, 19,000 in 1871–81, and 20,000 in 1881–91. The old East End – Whitechapel, Stepney, and St. George's-in-the-East – contained an unusually high percentage of Irish-born.

By contrast most migrants from the English countryside reached London from a short distance. H. Llewellyn Smith, in his statistical work for Charles Booth's *Life and Labour of the People in London*, confirmed Ravenstein's conclusions in this respect by presenting six concentric rings which showed that the English provinces contributed migrants to London more or less in proportion to their distance from the capital. It was also the case, as Gareth Stedman Jones has shown, that migrants from the English countryside tended to settle more in the London suburbs and avoid the inner industrial perimeter (particularly the old East End). The inner industrial perimeter contained 69.71 per cent London-born in 1861 and 73.04 per cent in 1881, while the rest of London was 58.28 per cent London-born in 1861 and 59.89 per cent in 1881.

Railways had increased the volume of migration without substantially altering its character. More people moved long distances than ever before, but more people moved some distance who in previous ages might not have moved at all. The prevalent form remained short-distance drift in cumulative stages, rather than a massive far-reaching wave. Moreover, within the city movement was ceaseless. People continued to shift, in Booth's simile, like fish in a river. In what he called 'a fairly representative district in Bethnal Green', he found over 40 per cent of families moved in a single year. The books of School Board visitors which were made available to Booth recorded numerous transfers. Again, this intramural mobility resembled the country-to-town pattern. It was mostly short-range, street to street, not area to area: 'people usually do not go far, and often cling from generation to generation to one vicinity, almost as if the set of streets which lie there were an isolated country village.'

This was not unique to London. Historians of provincial towns and cities have uncovered a similar condition. It is not surprising that casual workers were highly mobile, having few personal possessions.

Removals were inspired by a variety of causes – to match the changing size and ages of the family; to be closer to friends, kin, ethnic associates, or the job of the moment; to escape debts. Of course, it was not only the miserable who were mobile. Professional men, and the fluctuating ranks of the lower-middle class – teachers, small shopkeepers, foremen, clerks – were counted among the nomads too. But there was a difference. Unlike the classes above them, artisans and higher, the mobility of the urban unskilled was very confined. Beatrice Webb, one of Booth's researchers, put it thus: the city poor resembled 'the circle of suicides in Dante's Inferno; they go round and round within a certain area'. The causes of this persistent but restricted mobility were chiefly four: the chains of debt and credit which tied the poor to local landlords, shopkeepers, and publicans; the dependency on personal contacts which might lead to work; the necessity of walking to work; and the fact that wives, whose supplementary earnings were important, were trapped within a similarly irregular and localized labour market.

The proportion of migrants in London's population was falling in the nineteenth century. In the period 1851–91, 84.03 per cent of London's increase in population resulted from the surplus of births, 15.97 per cent from net immigration. This last figure is the difference between those living in London who were born outside (over a third of the population) and those born in London who subsequently moved elsewhere (about a fifth of the population). A greater percentage of London's increase was thus being derived naturally, from the excess of births over deaths in the established population. This feature radically distinguished London from major European cities, as A. F. Weber observed. Two causes were outstanding. One was the superior sanitary provision of England, which resulted in a falling death-rate. Another, not unconnected, was the outflow of population to suburbs. This was especially obvious in London (see Fig. 1). The one-square mile of the City had a resident or 'sleeping' population which peaked around mid-nineteenth century at just short of 130,000. This had dropped to 112,000 by 1861; then it fell to 51,000 by 1881, 27,000 by 1901 and 14,000 by about 1921. By contrast the daytime or working population of the City rose from 170,000 in the mid-1860s, to 261,000 in 1881, 301,000 in 1891, and 437,000 by 1921. Most of those poor people cleared from the City initially were jammed into the adjacent East End, which suffered terrible overcrowding; but the resident population of many parts of the LCC area showed substantial

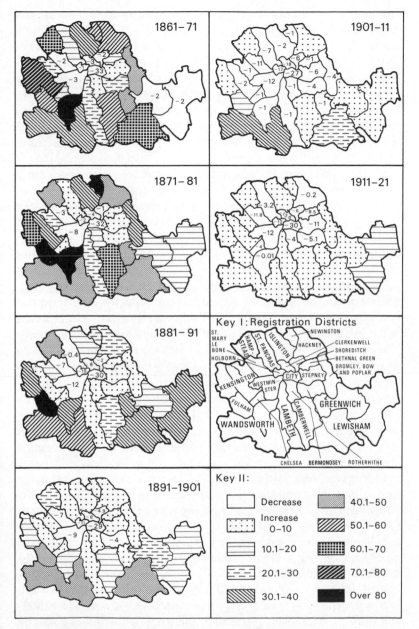

Fig. 1 London, increases and decreases per cent, 1861–1921

Source: T. W. Freeman, *The Conurbations of Great Britain,* Manchester University Press, 1959; second, revised, edition 1966, p. 49.

thinning by the 1890s, when eleven out of thirty districts of central London were revealing decreases in population regularly in each census. The outer ring of Greater London was expanding prodigiously. East and West Ham, Leyton, Tottenham, Hornsey, Willesden, Walthamstow, and Croydon were among the boom areas of the country. This trend was encouraged by government policy. An American expert on municipal government, Albert Shaw, reckoned that London's governors were investing more in surface and underground suburban transport (thus to decant population) than in health and housing matters directly.

Whether this comment deserves to be cast as a criticism is doubtful. The options available to the LCC (and, before 1889, the Metropolitan Board of Works) were unattractive. The freedom for manoeuvre was small. What in an average English town was the work of one or two sanitary and housing departments, in London was split between multiple bodies. The Housing of the Working Classes Committee of the LCC was chiefly concerned with clearance and improvement schemes under the 1890 Housing Act; but each of the twenty-eight Metropolitan Borough Councils (and, before them, the vestries) had concurrent powers with the LCC. Each was also a sanitary authority, and it was their duty to abate overcrowding and associated problems. The LCC made itself busy, providing by 1905 rooms for over 31,000 people; but council tenants were not generally displaced slum dwellers. Though some were unskilled labourers, more were from a superior class, clerks and artisans, even urban gentry like R. C. K. Ensor, barrister, journalist, and Labour-Progressive councillor. Higher rents, regulations which were thought irksome, and a preference for cottages over flats, deterred most working men from council housing.

This was a depressing conclusion; so too was the record of the LCC's part in establishing housing estates outside its own area, at Tottenham and elsewhere. By running trams to the out-districts the LCC was instrumental in inflating the value of once low-priced land; but, like any other local authority, it was without the legal ability to purchase land that was not immediately required for building. The difficulty of co-ordinating divided local government was thus highlighted. The LCC could build but it was the responsibility of other local authorities to provide tenants with services – drainage, hospitals and so forth. Moreover, restraining the whole of the LCC's activity was the high price of land in London. Generally, the LCC had to pay

35 per cent higher prices per acre than provincial local authorities. The fulfilment of local authority housing responsibilities was, therefore, fitful. Slum clearances or the enforcement of legislation against overcrowding, without providing cheap alternative accommodation, would exacerbate the housing famine. Low-cost travel from homes built on cheaper suburban land seemed the answer; but there was a substantial time-lag before needs and abilities in respect of transport, work, wages, and rents approached anything like a match. For the greater part of this period most of the inner-London poor were cramped in high-rented housing in order to remain within walking distance of their traditional employment. In the Edwardian period only eight of the twenty-eight boroughs recorded an amelioration in their statistics of overcrowding. 'Place a disused sentry-box upon any piece of waste ground in South or East London,' wrote C. F. G. Masterman in *From the Abyss* (1902), 'and in a few hours it will be occupied by a man and his wife and family, inundated by applications from would-be lodgers.'

Politicians were confronted with stern market forces in which casual labour could not compete with commerce for valuable space. For those poor people condemned to live in the heart of cities, cumulative deprivation clamped ever more tightly, as rising rents took a greater portion (sometimes over 20 per cent) of already inadequate incomes. The crude national level of overcrowding (defined as over two people per room) indicated improvement from 11.2 per cent of the population in 1891, 8.2 per cent in 1901, to 7.8 per cent in 1911; but the capital (with 19.7 per cent overcrowding in 1891) could show more than one black spot where the position was almost unyielding. In the central area 35.6 per cent of the population lived more than two per room in 1891. About 45 per cent were overcrowded if those living two per room were included. In 1901 the proportion living more than two per room in the central area was 29.6 per cent, in 1911 27.6 per cent; but the substantial decline had taken place on the northern and western sides of the central area. Only a meagre improvement had occurred on the south side, practically none whatever in the inner East End where the population had increased (chiefly from Jewish immigration) by 3.5 per cent.

The average rents of ordinary working-class homes in London, according to the Board of Trade's cost-of-living index in 1908, were 70 per cent higher than in Birmingham, and two or three times higher than in some medium-sized industrial towns of the north. The pressure was greatest in the East End, where rents had increased by an average 25.3 per cent between 1880 and 1900, compared with an average 11.2 per cent in the northern, southern, and western boroughs. From the mid-Victorian period a sense of crisis had agitated the inner-London authorities, as rising rents and accommodation shortages apparently spiralled out of control. The conclusion was forced from the London experience that the national exchequer could not permanently stand aside, for at the heart of the problem was the uneven distribution of wealth and resources. Graduated direct taxation and state subsidies to local council housing were the courses that were eventually adopted, though with bitter political controversy and incomplete conviction that this would effect the urban renewal which was earnestly sought.

This allusion to the housing difficulties of London serves to impress several points of general importance with regard to late-nineteenth and early-twentieth-century urban development. The first is that London, more than any city, was a living laboratory for experiment in the housing question, for individual and company philanthropy, for private enterprise, and for collective public action. From 1883 the exposures of the Revd Andrew Mearns, *The Bitter Cry of Outcast London*, and George Sims, *How the Poor Live*, stimulated a debate which led directly to the Royal Commission on the Housing of the Working Classes (1884–5). They also gave an impetus to investigative social work, in the Settlement Movement or Charles Booth's *Life and Labour of the People in London*. Some doubt was expressed about the importance which working people themselves placed on better housing. It was widely argued that working men would blow higher wages on immediate satisfactions rather than invest in better accommodation, though this could well reflect a want of confidence that wage improvements could be sustained for more than a brief period. Still, there seemed few bigger issues for politicians than those raised by London poverty and London government from the 1880s. Unregulated individualism was put on trial, for it was clear that greater numbers of Londoners lived in overcrowded conditions than amounted to the entire population of the second city in England, Liverpool. Here lay the stirrings against what Joseph Chamberlain denounced as 'the incurable timidity with which Parliament . . . is accustomed to deal with the sacred rights of property'.

II

By their declarations on London several statesmen defined their politics. By their liking or loathing of London life other men defined their characters and aspirations. The compulsion to experience London was commonly felt. Tennyson took his family there for a month or so annually, suppressing his dislike of the place, for the reason that he got 'so rusty' in the Isle of Wight; likewise Thomas Hardy, according to his own memoirs, believed that 'residence in or near a city tended to force mechanical and ordinary productions from his pen, concerning ordinary society-life and habits'. It may be that unless one regularly tastes what London offers one cannot appreciate the worth of the provinces. Until that initiation is performed the provinces will only strike their discontented residents with dispiriting dullness. Arnold Bennett's first novel, *A Man from the North* (1898), related of its hero, Richard Larch, that as a boy he 'learns to take a doleful pleasure in watching the exit of the London train from the railway station. He stands by the hot engine and envies the very stoker.' And in *Whom God hath Joined* (1906), Bennett remarked that the up-platform at Knype (Stoke) station, leading to London, always seemed more thrilling than the down-platform, leading to Manchester, Liverpool, and Scotland. None of these writers deprecated provincialism, as Matthew Arnold had done. Hardy spoke for all in a note of 1880: 'A certain provincialism of feeling is invaluable. It is of the essence of individuality, and is largely made up of that crude enthusiasm without which no great thoughts are thought, no great deeds done.' But the mediation of London was vital to release and to shape their energy. The metropolis was the midwife of provincial genius.

For men from the provinces on the brink of a career nothing was so heady as the prospect of metropolitan achievement. The artist son of a Bradford cloth-merchant, Will Rothenstein, was incapable of sleep during his first night in London, exhilarated by the romance of being in the same city as Watts and Leighton. Better still for conveying the thrill of London are the outpourings of that adventurer and amorist, Frank Harris, who burst upon London as editor of the *Evening News* in 1883. To be lionized in London was the summit of self-satisfaction though none remained on this perch for long. London's idolatry was notoriously transitory. Nonetheless London, Harris wrote,

made me drunk for years and in memory still the magic of those first years ennobles life for me and the later pains and sufferings, wrongs and insults, disdains and disappointments all vanish and are forgotten. I wonder if I can give an idea of what London was to me with the first draught of its intoxicating vintage on my hot lips and the perfumes of it in my greedy nostrils. London in the early eighties; London after years of solitary study and grim relentless effort; London when you are twenty-eight and have already won a place in its life; London when your mantelpiece has ten times as many invitations as you can accept, and there are two or three pretty girls that attract you; London when everyone you meet is courteous-kind and people of importance are beginning to speak about you; London with a foretaste of success in your mouth while your eyes are open wide to its myriad novelties and wonders; London with its round of receptions and court life, its theatres and shows, its amusements for the body, mind, and soul: enchanting hours at a burlesque prolonged by a boxing-match at the Sporting Club; or an evening in Parliament where world-famous men discuss important policies; or a quiet morning spent with a poet who will live in English literature with Keats or Shakespeare; or an afternoon with pictures of a master already consecrated by fame; London, who could give even an idea of its varied delights?

The 1880s and 1890s saw among certain sets 'quite a cult of London and its varied life, from costers to courtesans', Richard Le Gallienne, one of its devotees, remarked in 1926. Though called decadents, the poets and the rest were responding to the plenitude that modern cities, particularly London, could offer. Tawdriness and ephemerality were not really preferred to the substantial and enduring. These were celebrated simply as part of the unsleeping fecundity of modern cities, which released new angles of perception. Consider the hoardings decked with advertisements of mass-producing manufacturers, multiple retailers, and commercial theatres. *The Observer*, 5 October 1890, condemned their disfigurement of city streets; and the case for exercising restraint began to make headway from the Advertisement Regulation Act (1907). But Aubrey Beardsley had welcomed what to others were the worst, the new electric flashing-signs, as a foretaste of a London 'resplendent with advertisements [which] against a leaden sky will trace their formal arabesques'. The pastoral tradition was deliberately subverted in poems like Lionel Johnson's 'London Town', where 'the tumult of the street is no less music than the sweet surge of the wind among the wheat'; or in Le Gallienne's

> London, London, our delight,
> Great flower that opens but at night . . .

London was apostrophized because it was an achievement in itself, 'more wonderful', wrote Lionel Johnson, 'than Rome was, when the world was Rome'.

Perversity and artificiality, egoism, hedonism and eroticism, glibness and wayward invention, these have been advanced against the late-nineteenth-century belletrists. Yellow, the colour associated with the palettes of J. M. Whistler and Aubrey Beardsley, and dandyism, the dress of Oscar Wilde and Max Beerbohm, symbolize the sickliness and superficiality of thought. At their worst these writers and artists can be convicted of the charge. Lionel Johnson commemorated 'the haggard eyes of the absintheur, the pallid faces of "neurotic" sinners' in London's café society; and Wilde's assertion that 'The man who can dominate a London dinner-table can dominate the world' captured the insolence of a passing and unprincipled pose. The parodist, Beerbohm, represented urbanity at its most absurd when, in 1915, he and his wife rented a cottage in the Cotswolds. There Beerbohm took no exercise apart from a daily walk of 100 yards to the pub to buy cigarettes, attired scrupulously with stick and gloves.

Here was mere conceit, a studied unconventionality. This aspect actually passed quite quickly or was unimportant anyway. W. B. Yeats wrote dismissively in 1936 that after Wilde and Beardsley were gone, 'in 1900 everybody got down off his stilts; henceforth nobody drank absinthe with his black coffee; nobody went mad; nobody joined the Catholic Church; or if they did I have forgotten.' But the poseurs had not been all pose. Their city-cult was not uncritical. Wilde was sure that 'A modern city is the exact opposite of what everyone wants.' Beerbohm's champagne wit had a sober soundness. He was scornful of 'fool's prattle about *le fin de siècle*'. He went on: 'A phase of social evolution happens to coincide with a certain point in the kalendar.' Coincidence and spontaneity were apparent, external causes too. 'Épater le bourgeois', Flaubert had said. This was a widespread exploration and adventure. It invaded many spheres and took on many forms, from Baudelaire's poetry to Impressionist painting, from Nietzsche's philosophy to Ibsen's theatre, from Wilde's aestheticism to Arthur Morrison's social realism. The place of the city in these stirrings was clear. The city could not be bound by bourgeois convention. Middle-class morality must not be allowed to make facile judgements about city life, then pass it over, as the middle class was evidently doing in its fugitive progress from city to suburb. The city had to be confronted in its ambiguous aspects, the seamy side of its splendour, the splendour in its sickness. Both realists and romantics required that moralists in future adopt broader foundations for their judgements about city life. There was no heavier demand on writers and artists than to come to terms with London, epitome of urban life, the World City, in the imagination of their day.

Experiences had to be enlarged if understanding was to be real. In this pursuit such singular sorts as Richard Jefferies and Henry James joined the decadents. A confirmed countryman, Jefferies still placed himself among the front ranks of London's admirers. Its noise and dirt were admittedly repulsive, but its extravagance was irresistible, comparable to Nature itself. Hence, he wrote, 'I dream in London quite as much as in the woodlands'; 'I like the solitude of the hills and the hum of the most crowded city; I dislike little towns and villages.' Precious and polysyllabic, sophisticated and circumlocutory, Henry James was spellbound too. The London-lover, as he proclaimed himself in 1876, was not unconscious of the city's cruelties. *The Princess Casamassima* (1886) acknowledged the amount of ulcerated poverty; but this was the fault of social organization, a historic and widespread class inequality, not a recent and specific city vice. James's most considered estimation was an essay of 1888. There he observed that London's cruelties were excessive but inseparable from the 'general vibration' and immeasurable fullness that most appealed to the London-lover. London was 'the most complete compendium in the world'. 'We are far from liking London well enough till we like its defects', he advised; and 'if you learn to know your London you learn to know a great many things'. Especially London symbolized continuous culture and national vitality. It was 'the largest social incarnation of the language, of the tradition'.

In the first decades of the twentieth century a curious stage was reached in this relationship of artists and city. For writers like Dorothy Richardson or James Joyce, who worked in 'stream-of-consciousness' form, the city was both oasis of personal freedom and desert of social estrangement. In the interior world of these novelists, fugitive time makes other people unknowable but the familiar city offers security within which individuals may advance the exploration of self. *Portrait of the Artist as a Young Man* (1916) and *Ulysses* (1922) are biographies of Dublin as of Joyce. London occupied a similar role for Dorothy Richardson in her series, *Pilgrimage*, published from 1915. Thus the city itself had become a character, more companionable than people.

III

On the surface, release from past restrictions typified the literary and art world; but scrutiny reveals how its leading figures revered traditions of cultural coherence and community. Their provocativeness was in arguing that modern city life might extend and enhance this appreciation rather than reduce or destroy it. A similar tendency was evinced in High Society, which cautiously expanded its customary codes to admit more from the city into its circles. The nation's élite sojourned in London and was never fastened to it exclusively. Nonetheless at the season's height (from May to mid-July) society gathered there in a concentrated force that was unique. Mid-nineteenth-century society was organized by Grands Seigneurs and Grandes Dames. Five hundred members would be a generous estimate of London society then. Certain habits persisted: witness the influence wielded by the 'double duchess (Manchester and Devonshire), by Lady Londonderry, the Marchioness of Lansdowne, and Duchess of Portland. These sets represented traditions of landownership, Court politics, and diplomacy. Social barriers were upheld against individuals and groups who otherwise conformed to the norm of breeding or wealth. Thus Jews and those convicted of extramarital liaison had virtually no chance of appearing at Queen Victoria's Court. Curious patterns of specialization developed. Jews, for instance, succeeded in politics, law, medicine, and finance, but did not care to enter (or were excluded from) the armed services and the diplomatic service. A liberalization was apparent under King Edward but Establishment solidarity could crack from the heat of political partisanship. Home Rule in 1886, and the struggle over the House of Lords in 1909–11, brought ructions to the London season. Other circles intersected this establishment at certain points, encompassing the hunting and racing set, finance, the academic and clerical worlds, the law, and leaders of opinion in journals, the sciences and the arts.

The last to gain admission was the businessman. The Liverpool merchant, Samuel Smith, wrote in 1896 that 'the retired merchant or manufacturer enjoys more consideration in what are called the "upper circles" than an active man of business'. He wrote this after visiting America; but it was to that country that the aristocracy now looked to maintain an old habit, that of refuelling the established order by injections of new money. One such prize, the American-born Mrs Cornwallis-West (once Lady Randolph Churchill), contrasted the

London seasons of the 1870s and 1900s. Conspicuous was a greater relaxation and tolerance, in movement and behaviour, especially for women, with the decline of chaperonage, card-leaving and afternoon calls. Refugee French aristocratic ladies in the 1870s scandalized English society by smoking cigarettes; but this vice became general after the Egypt and Sudan campaigns of the 1880s and the popularity of cheap Virginia tobacco. Queen Victoria loathed the habit; but Edward and Alexandra succumbed, and smokers had breached most reserves by 1900, clubs and private houses, though not the cabinet until 1924.

Another invasion was by the press. This was abetted by the publicity-minded in society, so that 'even the most uninteresting must be interviewed; their houses, their tastes, their habits, photographs of themselves in their sanctum, all are given to the "man in the street"'. The revised *Who's Who*, issued under Douglas Sladen's editorship in 1897, is indicative of this change. Aristocrats appeared publicly stapled between the sheets with actresses. The success of the new *Who's Who* was due not simply to its expanded coverage but also to its inclusion of tittle-tattle, inviting the famous to describe their amusements. Mrs Cornwallis-West disapproved of this degree of familiarity (notwithstanding the sale of her own memoirs); but she had welcomed the dispersal of sabbatarian gloom from the late 1880s, when dinner-parties began to be given on Sundays. Likewise the growth of eating out: in the 1870s there were few restaurants where well-known couples could appear without an implication of impropriety. Finally, with the motor car, week-ending at a Home Counties' mansion became the fashion. London society was not abandoning the city so much as re-colonizing the country, having become larger, freer, more energetic.

Energy in abundance also distinguished the amusements of lesser society; but its robustness was increasingly curbed. *The Observer* in 1863 announced that London's music-halls were 'plentiful as blackberries'. There were said to be 500 in the capital in the 1880s. Many were simply public houses of the piano-in-the-parlour type, with or without singing and dancing licences. Among the established music-halls the East End naturally boasted the proletarian sort, like the Paragon, Mile End Road, the Foresters, Cambridge Road, or the Queen's, Poplar; but Charles Morton's Canterbury Hall (1851) in Lambeth, and his Oxford (opened 1861, destroyed by fire 1872) in Oxford Street, were remarkable for both their sumptuous fittings and the decorous behaviour of their clientele. In the West End the old London Pavilion and the Alhambra were 'simply the Haymarket and Regent-Street under cover', that is, a blind for prostitution. Both were taken over in the 1880s. The Alhambra was the first music-hall run by a limited liability company. Subsequently it developed a reputable orchestra.

Architecturally the music-hall soon ceased to be a distinctive type. From the 1870s, according to Roger Dixon and Stefan Muthesius in *Victorian Architecture* (1978), 'the large music halls were planned like theatres, with the bars separated from the auditorium'. By the 1890s the trend towards greater capitalization and commercialization had hardened. Entertainments empires and syndicates were formed. It was not in the shareholders' interest to provoke the authorities' censure and thus imperil investment by staging obscene shows before drunken audiences. Puritans like Mrs Ormiston Chant and the National Vigilance Committee, who agitated the LCC over the renewal of music-hall licences, would never be appeased; but impresarios and accountants now made slide-rule calculations to plot the lines between wholesome and profitable vulgarity and obnoxious and profitless indecency. 'Variety entertainment' was thus honed and perfected: the sing-song, stand-up comic, sentimental, melodramatic, or patriotic sketch, the conjuring or ventriloquist act, mind-reading, negro minstrelsy, step-dancing, gymnastics, performing animals and children. The extent of the clean-up was marked by the staging of the first Royal Command Variety show in 1912. Then the music-halls were past their peak of popularity. Moving pictures were the new craze. London had 90 cinemas in 1909, 400 in 1912.

The supply of entertainment was not restricted to music-halls, cinemas, and pubs. Regent's Park Zoo contained the world's largest collection of captive animals; and both the Government and private benefactors continued to expand the numerous museums and galleries, most notably in the 1880s and 1890s with the opening of the Kensington temples of science and the addition of the Tate Collection to the National Gallery. Theatres and concert-halls proliferated too; and mere spectacle was satisfied by Madame Tussaud's waxworks in Marylebone Road, by the shows of Barnum and Bailey or Edwin Cleary in the Olympia Hall, and by exhibitions and fireworks at the Crystal Palace and in Hyde Park. These facilities were designed not only for Londoners but for visitors from within and without the empire.

IV

That the tourists' London was different from the Londoners' London is an easy observation; but this for a time became a matter for political concern, that separate worlds should not impinge on each other. Until Asquith, as Home Secretary, in 1892 sanctioned the use of Trafalgar Square for public meetings on weekends and Bank Holidays, the right of assembly was curtailed. Campaigns to publicize the plight of the unemployed by demonstrations in the West End in 1886–7 raised the spectre of sansculottism in clubland. Shopkeepers petitioned the authorities to close the West End to demonstrators; and it was feared that American tourists would shy away from new hotels like the Grand (1880) and Metropole (1885).

There were so many Londons that even the Londoners' London was uncommon each to another. Broadly, men marked the difference of East and West End or dilated upon the character of north and south of the river; and the enclaves of Westminster and the City always caused special comment. To take a cab from Kensington to Stepney, with Sherlock Holmes and Dr Watson, was to pass 'in rapid succession . . . through the fringe of fashionable London, hotel London, theatrical London, literary London, commercial London, and, finally, maritime London, till we came to a river-side city of a hundred thousand souls, where the tenement houses swelter and reek with the outcasts of Europe.'

East London was not a separate city, though writers habitually treated it in this way. This was no novel discovery. It can be traced to Elizabethan times at least. The siting of the Court in the west had long attracted wealth and fashion. Subsequent decisions in estate development hardened this trend, as Dorothy George and Sir John Summerson have emphasized. Included in the East London of 1900 were the parishes east of Bishopsgate Street Without, stretching north of the Thames to the river Lea, that is Bethnal Green, Shoreditch, Poplar, Stepney, and Bow, now reaching up to Hackney, Clapton, and Stoke Newington. New industrial developments, the opening of the Royal Albert Dock, and the Great Eastern Railway's provision of workmen's train services, meant that East London also now comprised the working-class dormitories east of the Lea and south of Epping Forest: West Ham with 267,000 people by 1900, East Ham with 96,000, and Stratford, Walthamstow, Leyton and other inflated hamlets with another 200,000. Edgar Bateman's mordant lyrics capture the scene:

> Wiv a ladder and some glasses,
> You could see to 'Ackney Marshes,
> If it wasn't for the 'ouses in between.

By 1900 this swollen East London contained nearly two million people, a greater city than the capitals of Germany, Austria, and Russia. Unlike them, it was virtually a one-class community, a working-class city. Walter Besant emphasized the scantness of amenities. This city of two million contained no hotels and restaurants, no fashionable quarter, no private carriages seen in the streets, no public school, no university, no law courts except police courts, no public buildings except vestry or borough halls, no newspapers except local ones, no great libraries, no booksellers, no ancient sites, no civic patriotism. A city without history, a city without pride, a city of unparalleled meanness, a city first and last of joyless work: this was Besant's grim catalogue.

Readers of Besant's *East London* (1901) will be less startled if they turn to Besant's *South London* (1899). South London, Besant wrote,

is a city without a municipality, without a centre, without a civic history; it has no newspapers, magazines or journals; it has no university, it has no colleges, apart from the medical; it has no intellectual, artistic, scientific, musical, literary centre . . . its residents have no local patriotism or enthusiasm . . . it has no theatres except of a very popular or humble kind; it has no clubs, it has no public buildings . . .

Besant, it seemed, was capable of dismissing as of no account the greater part of London which was not the City or West End. Lumpenproletarian East London, artisan and petty-bourgeois South London, each was a travesty of urban civilization. Actually Besant was describing outward appearances before endeavouring to register the true character.

The work of East London displayed extraordinary variety but was mostly undertaken in small workshops rather than large factories. The conjunction of ancient and modern was epitomized by Bryant and May, the match company at Bow. Match-making was factory-based but matchbox-making employed more persons in domestic out-work, at crushingly low piece-rates. Each East End district had its flavour. Some metal work, but chiefly cheap clothing, cigar and food preparation, prevailed in Whitechapel where there was also the country's oldest church-bellmaking foundry. Furniture, silk, and toys predominated in Bethnal Green and Shoreditch; boots and shoes, with a little of everything (including Charrington's brewery) in Mile End; weaving and other trades in Spitalfields; cloaks, ties, cardboard-boxes, artificial flowers, printing and book-binding, watches and clocks in Clerkenwell; furs and feathers in Hoxton; all manner of workshops, mostly ship-repairing, on the Isle of Dogs; docks, warehouses, and railways in Stepney and Poplar; markets in Cheapside. The East End spanned the working-class spectrum – from the sweated trades, the casual and underemployed workers who predominated in the western part and along the waterfront, to the regularly employed and quietly respectable artisanate in the Poplar, Bow, and Bromley districts.

There was thus a seeming controlling intelligence in the hive of industry in the East End, just as in the West End and central London where there were streets of finance houses, streets of shipping companies, streets of newspapers, Inns of Court, squares of select residence, and zones for theatres, expensive shops, and hotels. Industrial districts south of the Thames also bore distinguishable characteristics. Again there was much domestic out-work, making hats, brushes, tennis balls, sacks, paper-bags and so forth. There was also the arsenal of Woolwich; the naval schools, engineering shops, chemical and electricity works of Greenwich; the marine engineering and foreign-cattle market of Deptford; Peak Frean's biscuits, the wharves and tanneries of Bermondsey; the grain and timber yards of Rotherhithe; the wharves, warehouses, and world's largest hop-market of Southwark; the potteries and engineering works of Lambeth.

East London contained technical invention in plenty, also a darker side – sub-contracting, sweating, irregularity of demand, and meagre remuneration. Craftsmanship survived but rarely in completeness. Watch-makers made only one bit of a watch. They were analogous to women in cigar-factories who methodically stripped ribs from tobacco leaves. A deadening vacuity hung over work and, for spiritual refreshment, workers (other than the Jews) did not look to religion. The vast part of the nominally Christian population of East London avoided the religious services of the churches and chapels, though they might exploit their secular services – charities, concerts, bazaars, and country trips. Employment was stupefying, but underemployment and unemployment were crushing. Here was the submerged tenth, in that loose phrase of the times which marked a contrast with the unoccupied at the other end of the social scale, the gentry, aristocracy, or upper ten thousand. But East London was not absolutely a city of the submerged, numerous though this class was. This was Besant's message: East London was 'not a city of slums, but of respectability'. How highly should we rate this evaluation? Besant was a popular writer. His novels resound, for all their pretended social realism, with shallowness. In contrast is George Gissing, dedicated, as Asa Briggs drily observes, to documenting failure as Samuel Smiles earlier documented success. Gissing was the most gifted novelist to employ late-nineteenth-century London as a backcloth to his fiction. In his novels the streets, whether of proletarian Clerkenwell and Hoxton (*Demos*, 1886; *The Nether World*, 1889) or of artisanal and petty-bourgeois Camberwell (*In the Year of Jubilee*, 1894), are drab and desolate. It was not just the slum-courts, those 'lurking-holes showing destitution at its ugliest', which unnerved Gissing. It was the housing for the better paid: 'To walk about a neighbourhood such as this [the Wilton Square district of Islington] is the dreariest exercise to which a man can betake himself; the heart is crushed by uniformity of decent squalor; one remembers that each of the dead-faced houses, often each separate blind window, represents a "home", and the associations of the word whisper blank despair'. Besant complained, too, of the wearisome uniformity and inadequacy of working-class and lower-middle-class work and housing. Where Gissing diverged was in his estimate of the impact. Gissing's London was the London of defeat, a nightmare region 'beyond the outmost limits of dread', 'a city of the damned'. Tenements, like the Farringdon Road Buildings – 'millions of tons of brute brick and mortar' piled up in unornamented 'vast, sheer walls' – epitomized to Gissing the prison-cage of the modern city within which the industrial army was barracked, 'an army fighting with itself, rank against rank, man against man, that the survivors might have whereon to feed. Pass by in the night, and strain imagination to picture the weltering mass of human weariness, of bestiality, of unmerited dolour, of hopeless hope, of crushed surrender, tumbled together within those forbidding walls.' Fogs and drizzle envelop the bodies of Gissing's men whose souls were equally unlit. His urban world was barren, barbaric, beyond amelioration.

Charles Booth once recommended Gissing's *Demos* as one of the few novels to give accurate glimpses of working-class life; but when Booth completed the *Life and Labour of the People in London* (1889–1902) he was disinclined to throw up his arms in horror and to make sensational statements about 'starving millions' and incipient anarchy. The Farringdon Road area, incidentally, was covered by Booth's investigators, who noted the mixed rather than uniform character of the population, as regards work and habits. There was a residuum of people in great poverty, through casual work and drink; also 'respectable' working people. Gissing's imagination had been seized by the tenement blocks. There were several here, Peabody Models and others. Inside them were comfortable tradesmen, artisans, warehousemen and the like, as well as ordinary labourers, not Gissing's savages about to deracinate society.

The same was true of East London as a whole. Before his investigation, Booth noted in 1892, East London

lay hidden from view behind a curtain on which were painted terrible pictures: – starving children, suffering women, overworked men; horrors of drunkenness and vice; monsters and demons of inhumanity; giants of disease and despair. Did these pictures truly represent what lay behind, or did they bear to the facts a relation similar to that which the pictures outside a booth at some country fair bear to the performance or show within?

Booth endeavoured to raise this curtain by a systematic classification of East London – an area defined by Booth, it should be said, as of about half the size taken by Besant –into eight classes, from A to H. Classes G and H, the lower-middle and upper-middle classes, hardly concern us here. Nevertheless, though proportionately fewer in East London than elsewhere, they constituted between 9 and 10 per cent of 400,000 East Londoners who came under Booth's scrutiny.

The lower classes spanned A to F. F comprised the higher artisan, about 13.5 per cent of the population, typically foremen, whom Booth was tempted to call 'the non-commissioned officers of the industrial army', without the sinister implications which Gissing derived from the same metaphor. Class E brought together most artisans and regular wage-earners, the largest category, over 42 per cent of the population. Class E was heterogeneous but, paid between 22s. and 30s. for regular work, most 'can, and do, lead independent lives, and possess fairly comfortable homes'. Independence, Booth stressed, was their leitmotiv. They and their wives exuded an almost caste-like pride: morally, intellectually, socially, the casuals were repugnant. They eschewed charity and conducted their lives providently, by competitive self-help, by co-operation and trade-union combination, or by both. This class, it was noted, 'owns a good deal of property in the aggregate'. Generally they remained above the poverty line; but the stealthy decline of the traditional London crafts, the vagaries of the industrial economy, and the inclination of the life-cycle could catapult them into misery. The most vulnerable were those earning closer to 22s. than 30s., those with large families, the aged, invalid and sick, and victims of periods of slump.

The struggling, those living sub-standard lives and in chronic want, were placed in categories B, C, and D. Altogether approaching 30 per cent of East Londoners, they were those with small regular earnings and intermittent earnings. These categories contained the irregular and seasonal workers and those pulled down from category E by personal habits or economic misfortunes. The lowest class, A, Booth estimated at 1.25 per cent of the population, comprising 'some occasional labourers, street-sellers, loafers, criminals and semi-criminals'. This was a degraded and incorrigible class which, together with the unemployable of class B, in Booth's view the state should remove, perhaps to penal labour colonies, in order to control their procreation and to prevent their contamination of the classes above. Booth was not seriously alarmed by class A: 'they are barbarians, but they are a handful, a small and decreasing percentage: a disgrace but not a danger'. He also protested against the bracketing together of the distressed classes, B, C, D, with the aspiring workers of category E, whose 'class ambition as well as their efforts to raise themselves as individuals' deserved encouragement and recognition.

The 'arithmetic of woe' thus required careful interpretation. Dickens's *Hard Times* (1854) had railed against Gradgrind's worship of facts, but much of the shock literature of the nineteenth century showed no respect for facts about the working classes, especially their heterogeneity. An important part of Booth's work was to render unsupportable generalizations about a tidal wave of wretchedness and viciousness, gaining on society and about to engulf it. Although the comfortable classes were shaken by the demonstrated scale of poverty, which was beyond repair by private philanthropy, Booth rejected the view that misery was all-pervasive and irremediable. That was why he embarked upon campaigns for old-age pensions and for a reconstruction of the casual labour market.

The case for each of these causes was clear. About 30 to 40 per cent of people aged over 65 were paupers. They had no margin to save during their working life. Low wages, sickness, and, perhaps, imprudent spending explained this. It might also be that few assumed they would reach or endure a long old age. The proportion of the population which was aged over 65 was only 4.6 per cent in 1861, rising to 5.2 per cent by 1911. The post-1945 proportion of elderly constitutes above 13 per cent. As for casual labour, Booth believed that 55 per cent of those whom he classed as poor were so because of insufficient wages. However prudently they spent those wages, cruel poverty would have been their fate.

Booth nonetheless was concerned to report that hard evidence, as well as impressionistic memory, indicated that the state of East London had been worse in the past than in the 1890s. This very miserable period was actually quite recent, the previous thirty years or so; and in some parts of the old East End it was at best faintly passing not absolutely past. This verdict is suggested by Gareth Stedman Jones in *Outcast London* (1971). Stedman Jones re-worked Booth's survey in conjunction with other sources to show how a chance combination of circumstances created a crisis in London's inner industrial areas. Civic improvements and the transition of the City into a largely non-residential district had shunted thousands into adjacent working-class parishes and engendered a cruel spiral of rising rents and increasing overcrowding. The housing problem deepened between 1860 and 1890 since most of the cleared and dispossessed could not contemplate a suburban alternative. There was insufficiently cheap, plentiful, or well-timed transport to, from, and within the suburbs; and there was insufficient dispersal of industry from the inner zones.

The casual labour of the old East End was trapped within an economy of declining trades. Conditions of employment deteriorated. Most London industries were subject to pressure because of scarce and expensive land, rising rents and fuel costs and, in the case of shipbuilding and heavy engineering, because of distance from raw materials as well. By the early 1870s Thames shipbuilding and ancillary trades had slumped beyond the point of recovery, and thenceforward were occupied mostly by repair work. By the 1880s most of London's heavy engineering, iron founding, and metal work had gone the same way, reduced to a repair basis or to supplying sundries to the building trade. On the other hand competition from provincial furniture, clothing, and footwear factories was met by the sweating and out-work system. This reduced capital-entry requirements and working overheads and dispensed with the need to enlarge floor space. Though the wage rates paid in London were above those in the provinces, much of this was absorbed by house rents; moreover, the irregular nature of most London trades prevented sustained high earnings. This condition of endemic underemployment could turn desperate in times of cyclical depression, in periods of exceptionally dense foreign and rural immigration, or during harsh winters when the discarded of the dockside and building trades swelled the ranks of casuals. Though some workers regularly switched occupations, the harmonization of seasonal demands was never perfect even in a general boom. In a tight market – and the period was mostly one of decline for the inner-London industries – two things tended to happen. On the one hand the disadvantages of the least skilled were cruelly exposed; on the other hand the 'respectable' working classes found themselves pushed down into competing for the same work and accommodation as the casuals. Thus that status distinction which Booth sought to uphold, that difference between the provident and respectable poor and the thriftless and disreputable poor, seemed close to extinction in the old East End.

Hence the substantial element of propaganda in Booth's story of improvement'. That improvement was not striking if material conditions alone were counted, though confidence was real that the dispersal of people and industry to suburbia would steadily bring relief. Booth measured 'improvement' more in attitudes, an improvement in people's expectations and in society's sentiments about what level of poverty and personal degeneracy was admissible. 'Limited socialism', or 'Socialism in the arms of Individualism', was Booth's prescription for an accelerated improvement in future. Individual responsibility would be clarified if the state would only sweep away the chronic failures along with 'the vicious and semi-criminal'. State-assisted emigration for the children and labour camps at home for the adults were the natural courses to follow. This would decontaminate the legitimate working classes; but to win them completely for capitalism selective state aid was required to mitigate blind market forces. Hence the following programme was evolved, by Booth and by others who took account of his findings: pensions (only to those who had not succumbed to poor relief); ill-health and unemployment insurance, funded by the state, the employer and the employee (the contributory principle to preserve self-respect and self-help); public works (only in times of general slump, to keep the respectable poor from the workhouse); education (chiefly in the form of technical instruction for boys and domestic science for girls); school medical inspection and free meals (to maintain physical standards); public parks and other facilities of recreation (to counter the public houses); council housing (where it was unprofitable for the private sector to meet deficiencies in accommodation); and slum clearance (to exterminate nests of corruption).

Booth redoubled his counsel after some of his optimism was shaken when he found a level of poverty in central and south London comparable to that in East London. These later parts of the survey were less comprehensive, but his anticipations about a much brighter state of affairs outside the East End were not fulfilled. The proportion of people in the LCC area who lived on or below a poverty line of about 18*s.* to 21*s.* per week (classes A, B, C, D) was placed finally at 30.7 per cent. Booth, however, was steadfast to his main theme: the resilience and vitality of the working classes, given proper encouragement and support from the state.

V

Booth's judgement countered a conventional middle-class picture: that of a foggy, malarial urban landscape in which there might grow a revolutionary temper to overturn society. To be sure there were fogs, and terrible ones too. The greatest London fog stretched from November 1879 to February 1880. London fogs were traditionally heavy. Hence the colloquialism, 'pea-souper', though Nathaniel Hawthorne thought London fog 'more like a distillation of mud than anything else; the ghost of mud – the spiritualised medium of departed mud, through which the dead citizens of London probably tread, in the Hades whither they are translated'. Incipient smoke controls meant that these visitations were losing severity in our period. One connoisseur, Arthur Machen, reckoned in 1924 that the 'last real fog was "presented" on or about December 23, 1904. It was not a fog of the first class, for it was pure white and rigorists might maintain that it was merely thick river mist.' But foggy, festering London retained a powerful hold over the middle-class imagination. It was an image for their fear of the streets, aversion from crowds, anxiety about impersonality.

Individuals from other classes might share this trepidation, newcomers to the city especially. The Oxfordshire stonemason, subsequently the first working man to hold junior ministerial office, Henry Broadhurst, recalled:

Like all country-bred lads, I was astounded at the life and movement of London. The teeming masses of humanity rushing in all directions, bent, as it appeared to me, on getting clear of their neighbours, yet never succeeding in shaking off their pursuers, the roar of the streets, the glare of the lamps at night-time, inspired in me a curious mingling of fascination and disgust. The same conditions were reproduced in the workshops. Above, below, and around me machines throbbed and whirled ceaselessly. The homely surroundings and social interests of country life had no existence here: life seemed a new thing, almost unearthly . . . A month's stay in modern Babylon was quite sufficient for me, and, gasping like a fish out of water, I set my face towards the open country.

But the persistence of this sense of alarming anonymity seems less typical of the lower than of the middle and upper classes. A few, the excessively self-contained, revelled in it. Lord Salisbury enjoyed London's impersonality because it protected him against recognition by loathsome Old Etonians. More general was the complaint which the Bishop of Oxford, Samuel Wilberforce, expressed in a talk about 'the London we live in' in 1864:

In London men and women were wonderfully insulated. In a village everybody knew everybody else. There was a great constraint in that. They lived under a continual observation. But a man came to London and no one knew about him. He [Wilberforce] recollected his first night in London. He looked out of the bedroom windows of the little inn in which he was staying, at the surging crowd which passed and re-passed beneath him; and he could have screamed for someone who knew him, or knew somebody he knew, or something about which he could talk to them. This feeling of isolation in the midst of a vast crowd was absolutely painful.

London's growth outstripped the individual's grasp. Dickens's knowledge of London was 'extensive and peculiar'; but London all the time was 'swelling wisibly' as his Sam Weller remarked. Macaulay reputedly walked most streets in London. No such claim could be made sensibly about anyone in the late nineteenth century, despite the prodigious pedestrians in that age. The watercolourist, Augustus J. C. Hare, commented in *Walks In London* (1878): 'Few indeed are the Londoners who see more than a small circuit around their homes, the main arteries of mercantile life, and some of the principal sights. It is very easy to live with eyes open, but it is more usual, and a great deal more fashionable, to live with eyes shut.'

The rapidity of London's growth startled the middle classes. No memoirs were complete without allusions to the green fields of boyhood which became the brickworks of middle or old age. That master platitudinarian, Martin Tupper, did not spare this reference in his autobiography in 1886. Devonshire Place, Marylebone, where he was born in 1810, had verged on the countryside; Regent's Park and Primrose Hill were then country proper; and Chalk Farm was notorious as a location for duels because of its rural seclusion. A sense of the country outside the city remained actual in mid-nineteenth-century London. George Godwin, in *Town Swamps and Social Bridges* (1859), reported that he had 'often distinctly identified, in Holborn and in parts of the City, the pleasant smell of the new hay from the meadows on the north of London'. North-east of Bethnal Green was indeed green and Cricklewood sylvan in the 1860s; but London grew at such a rate that many were inclined to agree with Samuel Smith MP in 1885, that 'by the end of the next century, London and the suburbs will contain 30,000,000 of people'.

Predictions like this aroused all sorts of fears. Contradictory speculations preyed upon minds simultaneously: a city of strangers and streets of solitary bemusement, or a city of covetous crowds and streets of din and strife? The common denominator, as Mandell Creighton felt upon becoming Bishop of London in 1897, was 'a great loss of the personal touch in everything one does', a vision of boxed-in people in boxed-in towns.

This spiritual oppression cannot be disregarded. Many reacted to London as Rudyard Kipling to Chicago: 'Having seen it, I urgently desire never to see it again.' At the same time there was a brightness in the bustle, 'the sociability and generous sharing of small means', which Beatrice Webb observed in 1886. This was noted generally but not always so generously commented upon. 'The incessant roar of carts, carriages and organs' Coventry Patmore found 'indescribably maddening'. A hatred of German street bands and Italian barrel-organists distinguished that tender poet and many besides. Carlyle and John Leech had petitioned against their noise pollution, and the Liberal MP, M. T. Bass, successfully moved a Bill to regulate street music within the metropolis in 1864. It was the only movement to draw out the crabbed inventor Charles Babbage, who reserved a special part of his misanthropy for street musicians. But, *The Observer* pointed out, street musicians were four times more common in Whitechapel than in Belgravia, and they made more money in poor areas than in rich. What significance historians might place on middle- and upper-class efforts to curb the menace is debatable. Personal taste and tolerance aside, it suggests an absolute increase of people forced to make a living from the streets – hawkers, costers, and prostitutes, as well as musicians, that expanding army of casuals and irregulars who were reported by Mayhew and others.

Street incident had an important place in the life of the poor. Booth recognized this in diverse aspects, the coster-mongers' commotion, Leather Lane, Petticoat Lane or Brick Lane markets, the demonstrations, pageants, showy funerals, gambling, dancing, chatting, and brawling. There was warmth and conviviality on the streets as well as in pubs and clubs. The poor displayed great resourcefulness in maximizing pleasures in the minimum of space. Booth's apophthegm was just: 'Destitution degrades, but poverty is certainly no bar to happiness.' It was notorious how urban space was filled in to build more houses or workshops; but the railway-travellers' attention was also drawn, as the train cut through working-class districts, to the 'small rough-roofed erections, interspersed with little glass houses' in the back-yards of many homes. 'These represent hobbies,' Booth wrote, 'pursuits of leisure hours – plants, flowers, fowls, pigeons, and there is room to sit out, when the weather is fine enough, with friend and pipe.' Renting accommodation in Nevill's court, Fetter Lane (off Fleet Street), Keir Hardie grew in a strip 'thirty inches wide and fifteen feet long' Welsh leeks, and primroses and daisies from Ayrshire.

City-dwellers made their own country. Window-gardening was fashionable. London anyhow was better supplied with greenery than any town in Europe. The gardens of West-End squares were railed; but Bethnal Green contained the 217-acre Victoria Park amid mean streets. By deliberate effort open spaces were spared. Hampstead Heath, Wimbledon Common, and Epping Forest were only the most famous trophies won by the Commons Preservation Society (founded 1866). By 1910 the Crown, City Corporation, LCC and Metropolitan Borough Councils controlled 18,700 acres of parks and open spaces in and around London. About a third lay within the county area. For the LCC alone, their 113 parks, gardens, or open spaces represented £2m. capital expenditure, £130,000 annual maintenance, and direct employment for 1,000 workers.

This one aspect of London government was sizeable but the subject of London's larger organization gave rise to bewildering figures and staggering images. In 1900 the 6,500,000 people of Greater London lived in 800,000 houses, traversing 17,800 streets, covering 7,000 miles in length, 688 square miles in area. Five hundred miles of railway track lay within a five-mile radius of Charing Cross; there were also 11,000 cabs moving about the capital. Provisioning London was a major industry. The capital was the chief centre for agricultural produce as well as for finance and commerce. Some provisions were internally generated: London's 750,000 cats thrived upon the vast rodent population and garbage accumulation, and from the 156,000 horses which died annually in the city and were butchered by cat's-meat men. Human dietaries required more complex calculation. This was a favourite Victorian pastime in marvelling at the wonder of their cities. To supply Londoners with food for a year, one enthusiastic numerator reckoned in the 1890s, would require 72 miles of neat cattle, 120 miles of sheep, 9 miles of swine, 7 miles of calves, 200 miles of hares and rabbits each ten abreast, 50 acres of poultry, a pyramid of bread 600 feet square at the base and three times the height of St. Paul's, a column of hogsheads of beer reaching a thousand miles above the heads of the tipplers, and a string of salmon stretching to Newfoundland. As for the common fish, vegetables and fruit, this seemed beyond the most determined hypothesizer; but among the retailers (not counting coster-mongers) were 250 pork butchers, 1,500 other butchers, 2,100 bakers, 650 fishmongers, 150 poultry dealers, 2,000 greengrocers, 2,500 grocers, 1,000 pastry-cooks, 2,400 chandlers, and 1,600 dairymen. The last, together with the slaughterers, remind us how much cattle remained within city precincts. Shippens and abattoirs were crammed against houses, rivals for scarce space, together with other malodorous trades dealing with animal fats and offals, from glue manufacturers to tripe merchants.

The number of cow-sheds and slaughter-houses gradually diminished as sanitary regulations became exacting. It was also the case that London's growing consumption rendered many of these urban producers uncompetitive with distant farmers who formed contracts with wholesale dairy companies. Cattle plague in 1865–6 had been an important turning-point when railway-carried milk supplied the deficiency caused by fatalities in the urban cow-sheds. Though London's cow-sheds still accounted for over 20 per cent of the capital's milk in the late 1880s, the rhythm of work in the countryside had become regulated by Londoners' needs. Richard Jefferies noted that the hour of milking, once pretty general, by the 1870s varied in places according to the times of milk-trains to London. Dairy farming became more scientific and mechanical. Stock was selected for its milk yield; thermometers, lactometers and refrigeration determined quality; and the milk was now contained in metal instead of wooden churns. Purity was far from perfect until the larger companies and local authority inspectors introduced controls against tubercular or adulterated milk. Nor was working-class consumption high by modern standards – averaging under 2 pints per family per week in 1905 – because few had the means to prevent milk from souring. The trend, however, was distinctly towards improvement, in the amount and quality of milk consumed. Altogether the drawing-power of the London market was enormous. It was boasted that vegetables and fruit which could be bought there were finer than at places where they were grown.

VI

The drawing-power of London was shown too in the quality of its governors, on the School Board between 1870 and 1904 and on the County Council from 1889. The former was an exemplar in many aspects of education; the latter stole some limelight in municipal enterprise from the provincial pace-setters of mid-Victorian times. Memorials of their work remain. Their architects – E. R. Robson, J. J. Stevenson and others – produced stylish school buildings, cottage estates and flats, influenced by the Arts and Crafts movement and by the red-brick Queen Anne vernacular revival. This exuberance indicated a striving beyond the humdrum and functional. Nevertheless, despite the glamour and ambition, London government frequently provoked disappointment. The editor of the Liberal *Daily News*, A. G. Gardiner, asseverated in 1911, 'the capital of the Empire is the worst governed city in the Empire'. The reason was not the vastness of London or the incompetence of its rulers (though they were then Conservative). The structure was inept. London's government was 'a thing of shreds and patches without form or design. The giant has grown, but his clothes have not grown with him.'

The City Corporation was one target for complaint. Separate from the rest of London government, the City Corporation governed those 673 acres which made up the commercial heart of the capital. The average rateable value of an acre of City property was about fifteen times the average for the rest of London by 1912. The City constitution, its privileges and procedures, were ancient survivals; but it would be wrong to conclude that the City was time-suspended. It is reckoned that a quarter of City buildings have been replaced every thirty years. One exceptionally active phase was between 1857 and 1877 when banks, the head offices of provincial firms, insurance houses, and railways jostled for new sites. Between 1861 and 1881 the rateable value of the City rose 161 per cent, from £1,332, 092 to £3,479,428. Between 1881 and 1901 it rose a further 40 per cent, to £4,858,312. The plutocracy erected mostly Italianate buildings as certificates of pedigree. Most great cities experienced renewal of their central business areas; but none rivalled the City as the cynosure of national and international finance.

The City, Joseph Chamberlain remarked, was 'the clearing-house of the world'. At a time when sectors of manufacturing industry groaned under competition from tariff-protected nations – the metals, glass, chemicals, and pottery trades complained most — the free-trade City flourished as the world's leading capital market. H. J. Mackinder predicted in 1899 that 'the financial importance of the City of London may continue to increase, while the industry, at any rate, of Britain, becomes *relatively* less'.

The City used its power to defend its privileged place in London government. It not only withstood absorption by the Metropolitan Board of Works or LCC; it actually stood inside these bodies, having representation on them, while resisting invasion of its own counsels. The City seemed to have an encyclopedic grasp of worldliness and to parade it shamelessly, from the 'gambling' of the Stock Market to the gluttony of Livery Company and Guildhall banquets. In satire of the feasting none surpassed Thackeray's *Greenwich-Whitebait*, an account of a dinner held by

the Right Worshipful Company of Chimney-Sweepers – it was in May, and a remarkably late pea-season. The hall was decorated with banners and escutcheons of deceased *chummies* – martial music resounded from the balconies as the Master of the Company and the great ones marched in. We sat down, grace was said, and the tureen-covers removed, and instantly a silence in the hall – a breathless silence – and then a great gurgle! grwlwlwlw it sounded like. The worshipful Company was sucking in the turtle! Then came the venison, and with it were two hundred quarts of peas, at five-and-twenty shillings a quart – oh, my heart sank within me, as we devoured the green ones! as the old waddling, trembling, winking citizens held out their plates quivering with anxiety, and, said Mr Jones, 'A little bit of the f-f-fat, another spoonful of the p-p-peas' – as they swallowed them down, the prematurely born children of the spring – and there were thousands in London that day without bread.

The City withstood Thackeray's pen in the 1840s as it was to survive every attack, up to and including Ernest Bevin's onslaught in 1923 against 'a cold and callous square mile of City without a soul'.

The causes were several. One was that the legendary gourmandizing and ceremonial had a place in the calendar of state ritual. The installation of a lord mayor annually saw the Crown's ministers dance attendance and make declarations of policy; in addition the state utilized City receptions to impress foreign potentates. When Sir Sydney Waterlow was Sheriff (1866–7) and Lord Mayor (1867–8) the Government entertained the Sultan of Turkey and Khedive of Egypt in the City. Afterwards Waterlow was dispatched to Paris, Constantinople, and Cairo in full state to complete the diplomatic *tournée*. Lord mayors received a salary of £10,000 but invariably drew upon private resources to cover expenses. Secondly, the City was not impervious to social change or civic responsibility. Money had no class, religion, or sex. The first Jew allowed to sit in Parliament, in 1859, a founder of the London and Westminster Bank, Sir David Salomons, was previously an alderman, sheriff, and lord mayor of the City. The first woman given the Freedom of the City, in 1872, was the grotesquely rich Angela Burdett-Coutts. She was celebrated as a philanthropist. In this duty the City was avid for prominence, observing a kind of civic equivalent of *noblesse oblige*. During the Boer War the City raised a regiment at its own expense.

The scale and deployment of City wealth aroused deep suspicions. In 1878 a Royal Commission investigated City charities. Some, like the 6s. 8d. a year for the burning of heretics, had ceased to apply; others, such as the educational trusts which now were used to maintain middle-class scholars and schools rather than the poor, had been misapplied. But the correct discharge of obligations required by ancient charities was an increasingly tricky business because the City as a residential quarter was fast losing significance. In some cases the very parishes and their churches had been extinguished. But forty-seven City churches remained, with a total benefice income of about £40,000. These expensive and underused buildings were a standing reminder of the obstructions across the path of Anglican modernization, as the London diocesan authorities sought to direct pastoral work towards the pagan parts of the proletarian East End and suburbia.

At the same time vast increases in property values inflated the endowments of City Companies. Fifteen million pounds was the estimated capital value of their property in 1880. There were seventy-six City Companies with 9,000 members. Until 1867 the liverymen enjoyed exclusively the right to elect the Common Council of the City Corporation. Thereafter their presence lost significance in

quantitative terms, by 1900 amounting to about a quarter of the electorate. Nevertheless, they retained the nomination of lord mayors,
sheriffs, and several other officers. Twelve companies were major,
according to civic precedence: Mercers, Grocers, Drapers, Fishmongers, Goldsmiths, Skinners, Merchant Taylors, Haberdashers,
Salters, Ironmongers, Vintners, and Clothworkers. By 1904 their
annual trust and corporate income was substantial: £111,000 in the
case of the Mercers, between £50,000 and £80,000 in the case of six
others. The wealthiest 'minor' companies, such as Leathersellers,
Brewers, Saddlers, and Carpenters, were practically equal to the lesser
of the major companies, with annual incomes of £10–£25,000.

It was imperative, for the City's reputation, to facilitate the diversion
of moneys to warrantable causes. One stimulus was the City of London
Parochial Charities Act (1883), through which numerous objects of
welfare were promoted, education (including professorial chairs and
closed scholarships at Oxford and Cambridge), free libraries, parks
and hospitals. By 1900, when the companies' annual corporate income
was £600,000, about one-third was devoted to charitable or trust purposes. Technical education naturally had strong appeal – the City and
Guilds of London Institute had been started in 1877 – and now grants
were made to several polytechnics, including Quintin Hogg's Regent
Street Polytechnic. Among other beneficiaries was the People's Palace
in East London. Walter Besant's inspiration to brighten ordinary
lives, this institution now fizzed with £60,000 from the Drapers. It
sprouted technical schools, swimming baths, gymnasia, libraries,
exhibitions, and concert-halls. Some lesser donations produced more
lasting monuments, like the £5,000 which the Goldsmiths gave in
1905 to subsidize volume VI of the *Oxford English Dictionary*.

It is hard to estimate the significance of this charitable work in preserving the City's freedoms, or of the practical philanthropy of individuals in the City, like Waterlow, Peabody, and the rest, in the model
dwellings movement. This was 'philanthropy plus five per cent',
charity for its own sake and charity which would reap a commercial
return. These housing societies did not solve the housing crisis, as one
of their partisans, Octavia Hill, admitted in 1875. Their combined
efforts over thirty years succeeded in housing only 26,000 people, or
just in excess of six months' growth in the capital's population. But
they established the possibilities of multi-storey dwellings and
widened the debate about working-class housing and its amenities.
There was an ulterior purpose too. Waterlow's biographer, George

Smalley, wrote in 1909, 'No man was farther than Waterlow from that pestilent nonsense which swaggers in the market-place under the name of Socialism.'

The City submitted to public inquiry occasionally but never lost control of its purse-strings. It was adept in surrendering the shadow to preserve the substance. Exempt from the 1835 Municipal Corporation Act, the City Corporation was not required to make financial returns to Parliament. It acted underhand in the 1880s, making corrupt payments to sham organizations like the Metropolitan Ratepayers' Defence Association, in order to defeat the Gladstone ministry's ambition to abolish the Corporation in a comprehensive Bill of London government reform. The City's malversations were exposed by Labouchere's journal, *Truth*, and by a Commons Select Committee in 1887; but it was spared the consequences. This introduces the most important cause of the City Corporation's survival: it had a corporate sense and was prepared to act, in a public and subterranean way. There seemed none to match it elsewhere in London.

Attempts were made to manufacture reform movements on the part of the rest of London. The two Liberal MPs for Chelsea, J. F. B. Firth and Sir Charles Dilke, exerted themselves in the early 1880s. Firth became first deputy-chairman of the LCC in 1889. Now he controlled the Municipal Reform League, engineering meetings and petitions as the City manipulated the Metropolitan Ratepayers' Defence Association; but they were less effective in scale and influence. Dilke, the President of the Local Government Board, was rather more successful on the Royal Commission on Working-Class Housing. He tarred all London vestries with the brush that blackened Clerkenwell as a den of slum-farmers. This had two objectives. One was to divert the housing controversy, raised by *The Bitter Cry of Outcast London*, into local government reform. The second was to deflect criticism of the ministry's London Government Bill, whose weakness was the absence of effective second-tier authorities to replace the vestries. Dilke's moral was clear. District councils could not be entrusted with responsibility. Slum landlords, Dilke alleged, controlled the vestries, were phoenix-like, and would quickly batten on any new body that was tiny and local. This opinion was most tendentious. Instead, it may be argued, Medical Officers of Health and their staff failed to enforce legislation against overcrowding less from the hostility of vested interests as from knowledge that it would intensify the housing crisis.

Dilke's efforts to achieve London government reform in this

parliament perished. The Gladstone ministry's programme was choked, especially by franchise matters in 1884–5; and the dispute between the Prime Minister and the Home Secretary, Harcourt, concerning control of the metropolitan police, delayed consideration of the London Bill. These were powerful factors; but ministers were able to procrastinate because of the absence of any sizeable and sustained movement for reform in the capital, and because of a division of opinion among the reformers who did announce themselves. Some wanted a strong centralized London authority; others wanted real powers, particularly independent rating power, for district councils.

The root problem was that inability to marshal London opinion which was at once the attraction of London socially and its curse politically. In 1841 Richard Cobden replied to a friend who complained of intolerance and bigotry in Scotland, that there was much in Manchester too. 'There is only one place in the kingdom', Cobden argued, 'in which a man can live with perfect freedom of thought and action, and that is London.' Cobden knew equally that Manchester was a better spring-board for the Anti-Corn Law League than London, where the free-traders' associations flopped. John Morley, whose *Life of Cobden* was written between 1879 and 1881, understood the relevance of the free-traders' disappointment: 'In London there is no effective unity; interests are too varied and dispersive; zeal loses its directness and edge amid the distracting play of so many miscellaneous social and intellectual elements.'

London ill suited conventional wisdom about the conditions for sparking effective local government. The Royal Commission which inquired into the City Corporation in 1853 observed that London was really a province. Hence its inhabitants had no 'minute local knowledge and community of interest', and a municipal authority for the whole of London was impossible. John Stuart Mill turned the argument round in 1861. The Londoners' indissolubility and hybridity was the result of subdivided administration. Londoners would co-operate for common objects, given proper arrangements. Prattle about the Londoners' supposed lack of civic-mindedness was only intended to maintain 'the fantastical trappings of that union of modern jobbing and antiquated foppery – the Corporation of the City of London'.

Mill's argument was apposite. Whatever corporate sense existed in London tended to flow from, rather than to create, the London County Council of 1889 and the Metropolitan Borough Councils of

1899. In *Local Government in England* (1875) George Brodrick held that an index of civic pride was a willingness to sanction expenditure on non-utilitarian objects. Manchester Corporation had established six free libraries, Birmingham five. By contrast only Westminster in London had adopted the Public Libraries Act. Civic pride in most London districts had to be contrived. One means was ceremonial ostentation. This came to be appreciated even by the London Labour party which, after the Great War, applauded George Lansbury's decision not to wear scarlet robes as mayor of Poplar. Herbert Morrison copied him in Hackney but changed his mind during his mayoralty in 1920–1, believing that people enjoyed seeing the trappings of office, and that resplendence served to focus borough affairs. The London boroughs' anonymity persisted, despite these efforts to generate awareness and enthusiasm. As Lena Jeger wrote in 1962, Londoners 'will tell you that they live in Kentish Town or Chalk Farm, rather than St. Pancras; in Limehouse or Mile End, rather than Stepney; in St. John's Wood, rather than Marylebone . . .'

Urgent trumpeting had greeted the LCC, established by the Local Government Act in 1888. *Reynolds' Newspaper*, 13 January 1889, proclaimed, 'The London County Council must be made to feel that its true function is not merely that of a huge administrative board but a genuine Parliament or Home Rule Legislature for the Metropolis.' A contrast with the Metropolitan Board of Works was implicit in *Reynolds'* hopes. The MBW ended its life in disgrace, with charges of corruption pressed against key officials. Its chairman for the last nineteen years, at a salary of £2,000, was Sir James MacNaghten McGarel Hogg, created Lord Magheramorne in 1887. A Conservative MP, Hogg was guiltless of stirring opinions in Parliament as in the metropolis. More gladiatorial leadership, however, would not have answered the Board's difficulties. It was constitutionally defective. It controlled main drainage and had abilities under building acts. Firefighting equipment and the ability to provide open spaces were added in the 1860s. But its relationship with the vestries and district boards remained uncomfortable, exhortatory not commanding. The amount surrendered to private enterprise – gas and water especially – contrasted with capable provincial councils. 'Why', asked the Progressive, John Benn, 'should Lord John Russell's glorious municipal charter of 1835 be available for Little Pedlington and denied to the five-millioned metropolis?'

Alternative plans of structural reform were canvassed: to transform the vestries or parliamentary boroughs into independent municipalities or to subordinate these to a metropolitan authority. The second seemed consonant with the significance of a capital. London, it was argued, 'is a kingdom, and must be treated as such before we can fairly grapple with its difficulties and use its exceptional privileges'. The prospect horrified conservative opinion. This would be devolution gone mad, creating a too-powerful engine of government, rich in resources, a rival to the national parliament. Vestries were not emasculated by the second Salisbury ministry which established the LCC in 1888. They survived until the third Salisbury ministry in 1899 raised metropolitan borough councils in their place. Thus the cramping of the LCC was perpetuated; moreover, the City Corporation was untouched.

Unlike the MBW's 46 members who were appointed by the vestries, district boards, and City Corporation, the LCC's 118 councillors were directly elected. More spontaneity than organization was conspicuous in the first election; nevertheless, expectations were raised. Goschen, Chancellor of the Exchequer, had long feared that democracy would be 'less faithful to political economy' and demand 'more government interference'. The Prime Minister, Salisbury, shared these fears, but not the conviction that all was lost. He sensed an advantage from the Radicals' anticipated capture of the LCC, writing to Goschen on 26 January 1889, 'I rather look to the new London County Council to play the drunken Helot for our benefit. Such a body at the outset must make some portentous blunders and I am not sorry that, as luck will have it, they will be carried to the account of the Radicals.'

Radical Liberals certainly proclaimed their possession of the LCC, especially after the first triennial election in 1892. Parties had been formed of Moderates and Progressives and victory went to the latter. The Moderates, subsequently the Municipal Reformers, were a vehicle for heterogeneous conservative opinion, the Progressives for an equally heterogeneous radical opinion. The LCC's first chairman, the Earl of Rosebery, had provided invaluable publicity and also the radical note by insisting on being addressed as Mr Chairman, not 'my Lord'. Rosebery was succeeded by Sir John Lubbock. Both represented the City but the banker polymath Lubbock was less acceptable to radical opinion, being a Unionist in imperial politics and antagonistic to municipal trading. Lubbock was discarded in 1892, but the Progressives were not markedly cohesive thereafter. On one hand was a socialist group whose ambition, described by John Benn, was 'to secure a millennium for London by return of post'. Among these could be counted John Burns. On the other hand were those like the Progressives' first leader, seventy-year-old Sir Thomas Farrer. Educated at Eton and Balliol, Farrer was a lawyer, the Board of Trade's permanent secretary between 1865 and 1886. He demanded a united London government, absorbing the City Corporation, for larger purposes; and he pressed this counsel as a member of the Royal Commission which considered the subject fruitlessly in 1893–4. In financial matters, however, Farrer was cautious. He was apt to regard any increase in public expenditure as 'extravagance'; and, during the course of Progressive rule, the voices of restraint, emanating from Farrer, Sir Algernon West, Lord Welby, Lord Hobhouse, and the rest, were far from hushed. Especially they dissented from the more extreme land-tax schemes espoused by those Progressives who had been influenced by Henry George or the Fabian Society.

It was difficult to place such temperamentally disparate horses between the same shafts. The carriage they pulled was of shoddy construction anyway, and the ground crudely defined. The new County of London was the old MBW area. This was not coterminous with the conurbation. A more rational basis would have been the metropolitan water and drainage area. Moreover, A. G. Gardiner emphasized, the 1888 Act gave to London county government where town government was required. Sidney Webb, in *The London Programme* (1891), accounted the LCC's powers as less than a provincial county borough's:

It had nothing to do with paving, cleansing or lighting the streets; waterworks, gasworks, markets, and tramways were completely outside its province; its police formed an army as alien as the Irish constabulary; it was functionless and almost powerless in valuation and assessment; it did not collect its own rates; it had no more control over the Thames than over the tides; it was neither the sanitary nor the burial authority; and it could not even prepare or supervise the registration of the voters who elected it. It was, in fact, simply a cross between the county justices and the Metropolitan Board of Works, and its chief occupations were a strange hotch-potch of lunatic asylums and the fire brigade, main drainage and industrial schools, bridges and baby-farms.

Lord Salisbury, however, castigated the Progressives' ambitions as 'megalomania'.

The history of the LCC from 1889 to 1914 can be divided into two phases, each representing a party domination, the Progressives between 1889 and 1907, the Municipal Reformers from 1907. In each period the party rule reached a perilous point. In 1895 and 1910 more or less equal numbers of Progressive and Moderate/Municipal Reform councillors were returned. Only the aldermanic majority of the established party preserved its rule intact. Another curiosity should be noticed. The ruling party of the LCC was the opposite to that of the state, except for 1892–5 and 1906–7. But we should not conclude that the political life of the capital was mostly autonomous or perverse. Of course, local issues animated the London electorate. Rising rates, the controversial Council steamboat service, and the spectre of socialist spending spreading from Poplar, these were thought the main causes of the Municipal Reformers' triumph in 1907. Local government elections, however, allow the release of discontent against the national government as well. The renewed Municipal Reformers' majority in the 1913 LCC elections was attributed by informed observers to the unpopularity of the Liberal Government's Insurance Act, as well as to satisfaction with 'skinflint' rule in London. Still, the turn-out of voters, different franchises, and the amount of uncontested returns, make judgements uncertain. For instance, the LCC polls in 1904, 1907, and 1910 were 20–30 per cent lower than London polls in the 1906 and 1910 general elections.

The story of the LCC is not told by the party outline. The party fortunes really represented ambition frustrated and disfigured, for government functioned within an inadequate structure. The LCC area became more constricted as Londoners progressively lived outside the administrative county. John Benn was one who denounced the badly made jigsaw of authorities, whose overlapping and uncoordinated activity was at once expensive, inefficient, and inequitable. Seven central bodies operated within the LCC area, spending £16m. per year: the LCC itself, the Metropolitan Water Board, Metropolitan Asylums Board, Central Unemployed Body, Thames Conservancy, Metropolitan Police (Home Office), and City Corporation (controlling markets, etc.). There were also 94 local bodies, spending £9m. per year: 28 Borough Councils, 31 Boards of Guardians, 4 School District Boards, 2 Sick Asylum Boards, and 29 Distress Committees. If we take Greater London, we find some 262 authorities spending about £34m. per annum: 6 County Councils, 38 Borough Councils, 61 Urban District Councils, 14 Rural District Councils, 50 Boards of Guardians, 54 Parish Councils, and 39 Distress Committees.

Those who wanted a centralized London government consequently clamoured as much after the LCC's foundation as before. Though the LCC became an education authority with the School Board's abolition in 1904, the day of the *ad hoc*, special authority was not passed. Fourteen of sixty-five members of the Metropolitan Water Board were LCC nominees; but the establishment of that body by the Conservative Government in 1902 represented a defeat of LCC ambitions to control London's water supply, previously managed by eight private companies. Another creation, in 1908, was the Port of London Authority. Its jurisdiction, from Teddington to the sea, covered sixty-nine miles and incorporated five dock systems. The belated fruit of a Royal Commission (1900–2), the PLA was a great advance in port management, previously subject to fifty-six authorities, some deriving from medieval times. The LCC was represented on the new authority, but its presence was barely tolerated, being allegedly inexpert. The City, Admiralty, Board of Trade, shipowning and trading interests, were ensconced. The City Corporation retained the sanitary supervision of shipping; Trinity House maintained lighting and buoying; the Metropolitan Police patrolled the river; and quays, wharves, and warehouses remained private enterprises. Democrats were offended by the flouting of direct election; and tidy minds were outraged by the duplicated staffs, wasted resources, and administrative friction. 'Hole and Corner Boards' Herbert Morrison called them. They were 'too much joint and not enough authority', choked with vested interests and unalert to London needs.

The chief bone of contention remained the LCC's restricted authority, even within its area. London's traffic chaos was blamed partly upon certain borough councils whose veto blocked through-services of trams. Comprehensive schemes – for gas, electricity, health, housing, transit, and town planning – were mutilated by the division of authority. Local interests had been empowered with ability, not to be constructive themselves so much as to prevent construction by others.

Liberals denounced the Bill which created the 28 metropolitan boroughs in 1899. Asquith argued that the Conservatives intended to neutralize the LCC and to 'buttress the unreformed City with a ring of sham municipalities'. T. J. MacNamara, a Progressive, was even more forthright: 'It was not so much to increase the dignity of local authorities as to enable the rich to shake off their obligations to the poor. The rich with their few needs want to cut themselves adrift from the poor parishes with their low rateable value and many needs.' That the wealthy areas would wriggle out had been indicated in 1897 when Kensington and Westminster petitioned to become autonomous boroughs under the Municipal Corporations Acts (1835 and 1882). But the uncertainty which pervaded Liberal–Radical opinion with regard to a central authority should not be forgotten. The author of the local government section of *The Radical Programme* (1885), T. H. S. Escott, expressly opposed the 'immense centralization' contemplated by the London Government Bill of 1884. His preference was to convert the London parliamentary boroughs into municipal boroughs. He would reserve for a central body (composed of borough council delegates, not directly elected representatives) only such questions as the main sewerage, lunatics, police, and possibly main roads, being 'essentially metropolitan' in nature. Proper borough councils, Escott believed, would 'obtain the services of better men . . . and the details would be more effectively looked after by persons conversant with the locality than if they were entrusted to a central body'.

As matters turned out, the LCC was not a great central authority. Neither were the metropolitan boroughs real decentralized authorities. In the 1900s inefficiency in administration and ineffectiveness in capability were the main drawbacks upon which reformers, like the London Reform Union, brooded. A single centralized control was their answer and, with regard to resources, a uniform rate was its complement. Inequality of burdens between the rich districts and poor was a repeated complaint. During the period of Progressive rule on the LCC (1889–1907) local rates increased between 30 and 50 per cent in every district; but the greatest increases, relative and absolute, occurred in the poorest districts.

A scheme of equalization would answer this and, it was believed, tend to diminish the borough councils and to promote the supremacy of the LCC. The Cities of London and Westminster together represented 40 per cent of the rateable value of London, the other twenty-seven boroughs the rest. Yet Westminster paid 6s. 6½d. in the £ in 1910–11, the City 6s. 7d. (under 33p), while the average rate in the others was 7s. 6d. (37½p). The revenues of the poorest boroughs were the lowest but their expenses, especially for sanitary and poor-law purposes, the highest. In poor Poplar ratepayers paid a combined rate of 12s. 1d. (60p), in prosperous Kensington 6s. 10d. (34p). Outside the LCC area the picture was the same: from comfortable Bromley at 6s. 8d. (33½p) to straitened Walthamstow at 10s. 8d. (53½p). Some of the administrative expenses of the metropolitan Poor Law had been equalized by the Common Poor Fund (established 1867), to which each poor-law union contributed on the scale of its rateable value; but for the rest the London (Equalization of Rates) Act 1894 afforded small satisfaction. Charges remained high and various. Alone, an equalization of rates would not satisfy the reformers or placate the electorate. Even if they managed to remove the immunities of the City and the inequalities between districts, the electors might still turn from the Progressives on the cry of 'high rates'. Hence the search for additional sources of revenue. This lighted upon the ground landlords, the Bedford, Grosvenor, and Portman estates and the like, which, it was alleged, pocketed an unearned increment from London land of nearly £300,000 p.a. and escaped the incidence of rates which fell on the occupiers of buildings. Thus metropolitan reform always was, as Sidney Webb remarked, a national if not an imperial question.

VII

A summary of London's influence results in a mixed account. Most socio-economic indices underlined Henry James's verdict, that all England was suburban to London. A century hence, H. G. Wells predicted in 1901, the Londoner might choose to live anywhere south of Nottingham and east of Exeter. In the post-railway age of motor vehicles and telecommunications, townsfolk would be dispersed in arterially-joined 'urban regions'. Wells probably underestimated the abiding attractions of density over dispersal. Most modern firms still require a nearby pool of labour and linked industries; travelling wastes time and money; and many social instincts are left unfulfilled without congregation, even given the compensating technology of telephones, radio, and television. Wells certainly overestimated the capacity of motor and air transport to relieve rather than further congest cities. But his central proposition was less controversial, that the ancient antithesis of town and country would dissolve – 'it will become . . . merely a question of more or less populous. There will be horticulture and agriculture going on within the "urban regions", and "urbanity" without them.' This anticipation was not far off realization. In 1902 the geographer, H. J. Mackinder, already considered London a region rather than a city:

In a manner all south-eastern England is a single urban community; for steam and electricity are changing our geographical conceptions. A city is no longer an area covered continuously with streets and houses. The wives and children of the merchants, even of the more prosperous of the artisans, live without – beyond green fields – where the men only sleep and pass the Sabbath. The metropolis in its largest meaning includes all the counties for whose inhabitants London is 'Town', whose men do habitual business there, whose women buy and spend there, whose morning paper is printed there, whose standard of thought is determined there.

The diary account of how Cynthia Asquith spent 16 April 1915 illustrates this. Reading an eighteenth-century novel, Samuel Richardson's *Pamela*, on the early-morning train to London, she reflected, 'One can hardly believe our habits and values will ever seem as incredibly quaint to our descendants as those of our ancestors, thus portrayed, do to us.' Her day included details which signal the class habits of a specific period; otherwise it passes as a fair summary of the saga of metropolitan shopping by well-to-do inhabitants of the Home Counties at any point in the twentieth century:

I got up to London just before twelve and had a hellish morning in pursuit of my summer tweed from Harrods. I went to Selfridge's first, took back a hat which made a trench in my forehead and found a pretty black-and-white one instead. Sharp skirmish with Harrods on telephone about my skirt. Had hair waved at Emile. Went to Harrods – found it closed and skirt just despatched to fictitious address in Conduit Street. Lunched in neighbouring A.B.C. shop off two poached eggs and rusks and butter. Returned to Harrods and finally ran down skirt. I caught the four-something train to Reigate at Charing Cross . . .

Here indeed was twentieth-century London, with mingled conveniences and frustrations, unequivocally the cardinal city.

The influence of London, throughout the south-east and further, was increasingly immeasurable. The indices are multifarious, in the style of dress and manner of speech, as well as in the pull of its business life. A contrasting picture emerges from political London. Increasingly controlling others in social and economic concerns, Londoners were incapable of controlling themselves politically, in the sense that the one big authority was unrealized. Had it been so, Londoners might not have found the governing machine they were promised, perfect in preparing for future needs as well as in providing for the present. One supreme authority might have raised a complaint similar to that levelled against the existing multiple authorities – government by committee, distant from direct election, cumbrous and uncoordinated, another Gulliver pegged down by a thousand tiny strings.

Already this was a headache. The LCC met weekly but its surveillance over the vast business conducted by its twenty-odd standing committees gave satisfaction to neither democrats nor professors of 'efficiency'. An informal cabinet system, comprising the leaders of the majority party, had developed as a means of giving direction to affairs; and a Special Committee of Procedure was appointed to consider the division and co-ordination of business. It reported in July 1913. The Finance Committee was advised to prepare estimates of annual expenditure and report these to the Council which would debate 'matters of principle'. These were strictly defined, and expressly emphasized tenders for public contracts and the size, conditions, and payment of staff. Still, numerous questions were explicitly delegated to committees, in relation to which the Council was mostly a rubber-stamp authority. This issue of how to combine effective government with democracy, responsibility, and accountability was advertised not only across late-nineteenth- and early-twentieth-century London but broadly across urban England.

In sum, the capital city had grown and spread to the point of virtual amorphousness, unorganized and unorganizable. The persistent feature of this period of London's history was the warning it gave about cities generally, their awesome power to defeat those who tried, tentatively or cockily, to control their overall movement, and the opportunities which they opened up to those content to be submerged in their vastness.

3 Great cities and manufacturing towns of the conurbations

A number of substantial cities in a country betokens an advanced economy. A simple agricultural state might need several small towns for educational, military, and administrative purposes, for market facilities and for basic industrial services; but rarely more than one great city, usually the capital, where political life, major industrial work and commercial organization are focused. It has been postulated that, as economies mature, specialization grows and a rank-size order among cities might be discerned. In an undeveloped country 'the law of the primate city' will obtain; in an advanced economy the several cities will be arranged in regular proportions, such that the second city will be about half the size of the largest, the third city a third the size of the largest, and so on.

This pleasing logic casts historical circumstances adrift; but self-evidently city size must have a relationship to the requirements of both regional and national economy. England by 1900 contained several ample cities. Liverpool and Birmingham were dwarfed by London, but each contained a larger population than that of thirty individual English counties or of every Welsh county except Glamorganshire. It was the great cities that Victorians contemplated when they weighed the urbanization of their society, because these were assumed to exhibit all the main features of urban living in fullest development.

This assumption needs explanation. Most towns are mixed in social composition and economically versatile. To label a town with one dominant characteristic usually proves exaggerated when detailed study is made. From other chapters in this book it will be seen that single classifications are insufficient. Pleasure resorts, dormitory suburbs, educational towns, cathedral cities, market towns, all contained communities who were engaged in other pursuits as well. C. A. Moser and W. Scott's *British Towns* (1961) applied above fifty criteria to towns of over 50,000 people; but while the criteria may be multiplied, the number also can be reduced in common sense. Broad classifications *are* useful to recognize semi-rural towns and fully fledged cities, or to differentiate industrial from commercial towns, principal cities from satellite towns, and so on. Specific classifications, too, are not inadmissible, so long as it is allowed that this is designed to capture the ethos of a place rather than to comprehend it with statistical strictness. It is right to call Burton-upon-Trent a brewery town, even though most nineteenth-century towns had a brewery and Burton contained miscellaneous concerns. Burton was not a one-industry town in that fireclay, plaster and cement were produced; but brewing in Burton had developed on a unique scale. Burton ales had had a reputation from the fourteenth century; but new techniques of manufacture and marketing account for their modern significance, when the river Trent was made fully navigable and the railways were laid. Out of 50,386 Burtonians in 1901, over 7,000 worked in some thirty breweries. The second largest occupation, engineering, was intimately tied to the brewing industry. Without brewing, Burton would not have been transformed from a small market and textile town. It was this which gave Burton its world-wide reputation. It was the capital of beer. Similarly, it can be observed of the great cities that, though they were, in modern parlance, multi-purpose or multi-functional, most to a marked degree specialized in one or two substantial activities. Their competitive positions as great cities were geared to the fortunes of particular trades.

I

Urbanization was not intensified simply because the country's population grew. It was the manner in which that population was industrially organized which made for greater urbanization. Historians take care both to distinguish between urbanization and industrialization *and* to emphasize that in certain circumstances they are intimately connected. This was never more so than in the sixty years from 1850. Then the proportion of people living in urban districts rose to 79 per cent; at the same time steam-power was extensively applied to manufacture. According to A. E. Musson and others, the combined steam horse-power in British industry was perhaps 35,000 h.p. in 1800, 300–400,000 h.p. in 1850, some 2 million in 1870, and 10 million when the first Census of Production was taken in 1907. Until 1870 most of the country's steam-power and 'self-acting' machinery was concentrated in textiles; and the average manufacturing unit comprised fewer than twenty hands.

The small workshop remained more prevalent than the large factory; nevertheless, the strategic importance of mechanization for the economy in general and for urbanization in particular is evident. Investment was greater; moreover, productivity was raised by technological and institutional improvements within manufacture and marketing and by complementary improvements in communications and public utilities. The economy underwent both sectoral and structural changes. Agriculture diminished in importance, building and mining expanded hugely. Among staple industries, shipbuilding enlarged its position (in 1913 building 60 per cent of the tonnage of the world's new ships) more than did textiles. Consumer-goods industries, like bicycles and confectionery, appeared for the first time. In terms of numbers employed, manufacturing grew less significantly than services of the menial, clerical, administrative, and professional kind. This was testimony that business was increasingly complex, a matter of co-ordinating a greater number of specialized contributions. At the overseas-trading ports companies which once acted as practically universal merchants were superseded by specialized traders, or forced to become the same, by the 1870s. Management was thus becoming departmentalized too, subject to the same pressure that was placed upon labour, so that separate skills might be exploited more effectively. In management's case the subdivision was most notable between technocracy, accountancy, and salesmanship. The trend from intimate firms towards bigger corporations was consonant with this momentum.

The proliferation of limited liability companies, following the 1855 and 1862 Companies Acts, was an outstanding feature of commercial and industrial life. Ultimately this imperilled the integrity and self-sufficiency of local life, as the expansion or contraction of employment in one town was determined at company headquarters, situated in another town or even country, regardless of sentiment and responsibility towards the local community. Labour was nudged in the same direction, via amalgamated trade unionism and the system of Labour Exchanges (1910). In advocating labour exchanges Churchill made the connection explicit. 'Modern industry', he said, 'has become national.' Therefore labour required equivalent organization, intelligence to increase its mobility nationwide. Another concern was the state of the law regarding company-promotion, as personages sold their reputations for sleeping-directors' fees. Thus Lords Dufferin and Loch were disgraced when their negligence was exposed in the fraudulent affairs of Whittaker Wright's companies, which crashed in 1901. This was not the sole instance of aristocratic puffing of company prospectuses which backfired. *The Economist* expressed qualms about guinea-pig directors as early as 1857.

In 1863 there were 360 limited liability companies; in 1900, 4,533; but our comment must be cautious. J. H. Clapham described the substantial areas of industry and commerce dominated by family firms in 1886–7:

all, or nearly all, the wool firms; outside Oldham, nearly all the cotton firms; and the same in linen, silk, jute, lace and hosiery. Most of the smaller, and some of the largest, engineering firms, and nearly all the cutlery and pottery firms, were still private. Brewing was generally a family affair. So, with certain outstanding exceptions, were the Birmingham trades and a great, perhaps the major, part of the shipbuilding industry. In housebuilding and the associated trades there were very few limited companies; few in the clothing trades; few in the food trades. . . . Merchants of all kinds had rarely 'limited' their existing firms, and the flotation of a brand new mercantile company was not easy. Add the many scores of thousands of retail businesses, 'unlimited' almost to a shop.

Structural changes became more significant in the 1890s and after. Amalgamations and federations made an impact in iron and steel, brewing, cement, salt, wallpaper, tobacco, railways, shipping, oil, banking, chemicals, glass, sections of textiles, and areas of mining. Again the scale and implications need to be set in context. Consider the Fine Cotton Spinners' and Doublers' Association Ltd. Formed in 1898, from thirty-one firms, it embraced another sixteen by 1905. Ten of its incorporated firms were in Stockport but in that town alone there were still sixty-seven independent cotton mills, operating 2,644,600 spindles. It was not true that, with limited liability, merger or association, active management and ownership were suddenly divorced and the original family or partners decisively excluded. Resources were being added and the size of the average firm was growing; but proprietorial control was still exerted, largely by keeping most ordinary shares within the circle of family and friends. Preference shares and debentures were issued to a public without significant voting power at annual corporate meetings. Even in the case of a trust like the Calico Printers' Association Ltd. (1899), whose fifty-nine firms represented 85 per cent of the industry, the retention of so much independence by the separate companies demonstrably crippled the effectiveness of combination. Only gradually did a new order emerge in which salaried managing directors, who personally held tiny portions of company shares, were taking over the reins of business.

The late nineteenth and early twentieth centuries nevertheless are conspicuous in business history as times when vertical and horizontal integration was proceeding. Businessmen invoked 'rationalization' to achieve economies of organization, finance, administration, and marketing. The interpenetration of capital strengthened the chain of raw-material supply, production, and outlets. This was widely evident: in the food trades, where the Maypole Dairy Company established creameries and egg-packing plants in Denmark and Ireland, and Lipton's bought tea plantations in Ceylon and hog-packing plants in America; or in iron and steel, where John Brown's, Cammell's, Firth's, and Vickers' spread investment in coal and ore fields and in engineering, shipbuilding, and armaments companies. Collaboration to counter trade unionism was conspicuous on several fronts; but it was in securing the larger contracts and in marketing that business syndicates were most highly organized, fixing prices to restrict competition. The 'ring' of warship-building and armour-plating manufacturers was a classic case. Lord Rendel, a partner in Armstrong's, told the Liberal minister, Charles Hobhouse, in 1910: 'All profits on all contracts have to be divided amongst *all* members of the ring, who are scattered over the whole world.' The ring involved Armstrong's, the Coventry Co., Vickers-Maxim, Beardmore's, and Whitehead's. Hobhouse was indignant; but the companies had to carry high development costs as they introduced new lines of ships and weaponry and scrapped the old. Moreover, Rendel argued, though these firms were big, they were unable, 'like *Insurance* Companies, to take the whole of the risk of contracts running into millions'.

The size of operations evidently accounts for the different sort of combination in iron and shipbuilding compared with textiles. Still, the movement towards larger industrial concerns was general, to extend resources, and to finance the means by which economies of production or control of marketing were achieved. Towns acted as fulcra in the industrial system. Here were amassed the instruments of increased productivity – labour supply and market for consumption; banking and professional services; gas, electricity, and waterworks; component suppliers; transport – in sum, that miscellany which economists call social and economic overhead. Industry, however, incurred liabilities ('dysfunctions') as well as benefits in an urban setting. Vacant city sites for industrial purposes became scarcer. Land values rose through intensive use. The ability to make plant extensions was impaired by confined space and soaring costs. The social consequences of urban congestion frustrated industrial efficiency, too. Trade-union power might deter the introduction of new production methods; and urban living conditions might mean that labour was operating constantly with stress, therefore below capacity. The maturing industrial city seemed to ripen quickly, to the point of rottenness. Though there were forces at work apart from urban dilapidation, it is noticeable that in cotton, iron and steel, and building, the trend of increasing average output per head had practically terminated by 1900.

II

The prevalence of urban industrial living was such that many large towns overspread their core and coalesced with smaller towns in their region. Few observers, then and since, have had a good word to say for this development. J. B. Priestley saw the results at their worst, during the 1930s depression. South Lancashire was 'an Amazonian jungle of blackened bricks'. In the Midlands places had names, 'but these names were merely so much alliteration: Wolverhampton, Wednesbury, Wednesfield, Willenhall and Walsall. You could call them all wilderness, and have done with it. I never knew where one ended and another began.' He reserved his special scorn for Tyneside, Gateshead in particular: 'Insects can do better than this. . . .' He counselled: 'Every future historian of modern England should be compelled to take a good long slow walk round Gateshead. After that he can at his leisure fit it into his interpretation of our national growth and development.'

'Conurbation' describes this coupling of protuberant towns. It was a neologism of Patrick Geddes's invention, in *Cities in Evolution* (1915). He wanted some name for what he recognized as 'city-regions' or 'town aggregates'; but he defined 'conurbation' specifially as a cluster of contiguous urban administrative districts. This had too limited an application. Urban agglomerations, the geographer C. B. Fawcett noted in articles in 1922 and 1932, included 'enclaves of rural land . . . still in agricultural occupation' and marginal land, given to both rural and urban use. These rural–urban interludes within conurbations are epitomized by West Yorkshire, which contains the country's largest rhubarb-growing district. Seeking greater precision, R. E. Dickinson,

in *City Region and Regionalism* (1947), preferred different phrases –
'urban tract', 'city settlement area' and 'city circulation or trade area' –
to distinguish the built-up area strictly meant by 'conurbation' and the
peripheral rural–urban zones accessible to and served by the 'conurbation'. But Dickinson's terms have not ousted 'conurbation' in
ordinary vocabulary. Here 'conurbation' will be used, mindful of the
wider implications. The word has been blessed since 1951 by the
Census in regard to Greater London, South-East Lancashire and
North-East Cheshire, the West Midlands, West Yorkshire, Merseyside, and Tyneside; and the 1974 local government reform confirmed
their existence by the establishment of six Metropolitan Counties.

Adjusting figures to areas defined in 1951, the result is obtained that
about 39 per cent of England lived in conurbations in 1871. Before
1911 most conurbations experienced rates of population growth
greater than the country at large. Thereafter the pattern was reversed.
In 1951 the conurbations contained about 41 per cent of England's
population; but, considering that the nation in 1951 was nearly twice
the size of 1871, this signified that the population density within
conurbations had risen appreciably. The chief problems of the conurbations, then, related to housing and other amenities; and not only
were their problems of a larger order than confronted most towns but,
arguably, the conurbations were more poorly equipped to wrestle
with them. For, Fawcett observed in 1922, few conurbations
'developed a social consciousness at all proportionate to their
magnitude, or fully realized themselves as definite groupings of
people with many common interests, emotions and thoughts'.

Government fragmentation was blamed. Multiple jurisdictions
inspired little confidence that problems would be handled in an
effective and coherent manner; but political pettiness was as much a
consequence as a cause of the fact that, within conurbations, the iden-
tities of individual towns had not been effaced (see Fig. 2, for Manchester conurbation administrative units). Industrial linkages within
conurbations might be many, regular, and close, but social contacts
were few, irregular, and slight. The difficulties in the way of forging a
vital common consciousness within London have been noticed. The
point might be underlined by stepping outside the major conurbations to consider north Staffordshire. The Potteries had a distinct
economic base, more homogeneous than most conurbations. About
46,000 people, 21.4 per cent of the six Pottery towns in 1901, were
engaged in pottery work. The Potteries also had what J. B. Priestley

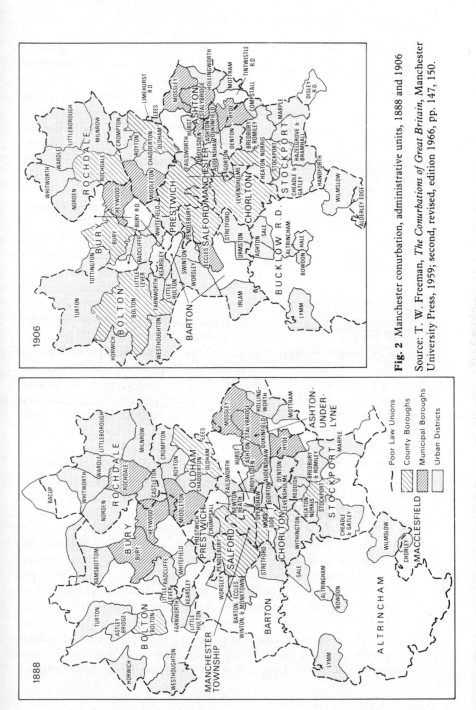

Fig. 2 Manchester conurbation, administrative units, 1888 and 1906

Source: T. W. Freeman, *The Conurbations of Great Britain*, Manchester University Press, 1959; second, revised, edition 1966, pp. 147, 150.

called a 'remote, self-contained provincialism', of an intensity perhaps unmatched within urban England. What accounts for this is difficult to say, but the special unhealthiness of pottery work, with its high mortality from respiratory ailments, may have produced a closeness in the community comparable to that found among miners and fishermen, who must reckon the chance of injury or violent death. But the Potteries' closeness infused the parts, not the whole. Regional consciousness, as a basis for effective administration, was in a lean condition. The Potteries was a congeries of separate communities (see Fig. 3). Stoke, the centre, had a municipal population of 30,458 in 1901. Another 184,500 people lived in the townships of Hanley, Longton, and Burslem, and in the urban districts of Fenton and Tunstall. These were formally united in 1910; later, in 1925, Stoke was advanced to the status of city. But an unreal quantity hung about these creations. T. W. Freeman observes that 'On the ground Tunstall, Burslem, Hanley, Fenton, Longton and Stoke are still recognizable as towns for each has its own shopping centre and even its own town hall.' In common opinion Stoke remains a non-city. Political federation alone could not animate regional-mindedness.

The Potteries was a region without a city. Sheffield was a city without a region, 'the capital of nowhere', unless 'Hallamshire' or the 'South Riding', Rotherham and the Don Valley, were counted as such. 'The population of Sheffield is, for so large a town, unique in its character,' observed the Medical Officer in 1889, when Sheffield contained 300,000 people; 'in fact it more closely resembles that of a village than of a town, for over wide areas each person appears to be acquainted with every other, and to be interested with that other's concerns.' The city was hemmed in physically, without a main railway line to London before 1870. The structure of industry further tended to concentration. Much of the edge-tool and cutlery industry in which Sheffield was pre-eminent from the fourteenth century was based in small workshops akin to village forges. There masters and men were separated by no great social distance and preference of admission was given to close relations and kin. Intimacy of this type could develop morbid conditions when many small men struggled in competition: witness the assaults on non-union cutlers in the 1850s and 1860s. Traditional patterns of recreation and work survived in Sheffield which were expelled from the factory routines of textile towns. In Sheffield 'Saint Monday' was commonly observed; in mill towns the workers' leisure was confined to the weekend. Soon,

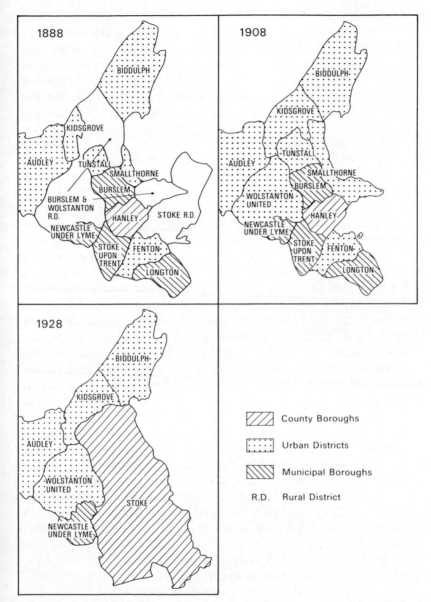

Fig. 3 The Potteries, administrative units, 1888, 1908, 1928

Source: T. W. Freeman, *The Conurbations of Great Britain*, Manchester University Press, 1959; second, revised, edition 1966, p. 255.

however, means of mass-producing steel, automatic stamping and cutting machinery, increased the larger plants in Sheffield. Sizeable silver and electroplating works were generated; and steel rails, guns, armour-plate, and other heavy goods were manufactured by giant companies. The system of interchangeable parts introduced a growing labour force of semi-skilled. But opportunities were not denied to the small workshop, which continued to have an influence upon the shape and character of the city.

Consciousness of place, then, is a peculiar phenomenon; but it is evident from the conurbations and other urban areas that, though physically and economically interlocked, a common mood was frequently elusive. The relationship was a bruising cohabitation not a harmonious marriage. Socially and politically the tendency to friction, localism, and sectionalism was strong. One cause, perhaps, was the discrete organization of work superimposed upon kinship alliances. This last remained a lively force, in country and urban parishes. Kilvert's diary for 4 February 1873 recounts a tradition of feuding between Chippenham, Langley Burrell, and Langley Fitzurse. Kilvert blamed the Chippenham roughs who taunted and assaulted villagers entering the town on market days. Raphael Samuel also notes the long-standing friction between Old Headington youths and Quarry roughs with their fierce dogs; and A. L. Rowse recalls that the 'principle of hating most your next-door neighbour held good all over Cornwall': hostilities between china-clay villages around St. Austell as well as ancient rivalries between Falmouth and Penryn, Fowey and Lostwithiel, Redruth and Camborne. They united only in mistrust of strangers. Great conurbations were equally riven: Manchester and Salford, Leeds and Bradford, Liverpool and Bootle, ritually tormented each other decade after decade. The progress of regionalism thereby flagged; but the account was not all on the debit side. Town improvements also stemmed from a spirit of emulation. Asa Briggs has given an exemplary digest of these mingled emotions in describing the building of Leeds town hall: pride and prejudice, generosity and pettiness, each had their ration.

The inconsequential should not be invested with unwarranted significance; but these emotions suggest a good deal of persistence in pre-class forms of social division. Customary bonds were vertical. One firm's workforce might feel its interest lay in serving its employer's purposes rather than in forging alliances with others in the trade against common masters. Gradually, the latter mood gained strength;

still, within industries, between towns, and between regions, disconnections were tenacious. During the seven-months' lock-out and strike in Preston, 1853–4, the cotton workers received sympathetic subscriptions from workers in other towns. But there was no joint industrial action. The 10-per-cent wage claim was pressed firm by firm or town by town. What advances were won, subsequently were lost in that way. The cotton industry was not a unit, nor perceived as such by masters or men. The same applied to other trades. We must recognize the obstacles in the way of trade unions negotiating national rates and uniform conditions or taking national strike action. Not only were separate working practices and customary differences in payment cherished, clannishness, too, supervened to prevent industrial communities adopting class lines of Marxist denomination. The spirit of highlanders and lowlanders held fast, and found fresh forms of excitement.

Attitudes depended greatly upon the particular issue and in what circumstances an appeal was made. The country was composed of a multiplicity of groups whose associated activities were very fluid, now joined, then disjoined. From one perspective it is possible to see a centre–periphery relationship, the metropolis versus the rest. Another angle of perception will reveal a polycentric world, a country of regional capitals. What was happening in Birmingham mattered more to the people of the West Midlands than what was happening in London. Above and below, across and between these levels were sundry layers of partisan consciousness, of class, religion, politics and more. When and with what intensity they surfaced differed according to context. When citizens celebrated the relief of Mafeking they behaved as fellow nationals. When Manchester United Football Club played Manchester City the organizing principle changed. The association was no longer with Britons all, Lancastrians or Mancunians even, so much as with the closed world of the vendetta.

III

Sport, George Orwell drolly observed, is an unfailing source of illwill. Towns were rivals not only in sport. Local patriotism was growing in diverse directions. According to G. M. Trevelyan (*English Social History*, 1944) it was all dispiritingly narrow: 'Urban and suburban life in modern England made no appeal through the eye to the imagination, as had the old village life of our island, or the city life of ancient and medieval Europe. Civic pride and civic rivalry among the industrial towns of the North were almost entirely materialistic and not at all aesthetic.' The past connection of commerce and culture in Greek, Italian, Dutch, and German cities was frequently invoked both to embarrass and to incite those in whom the power lay to make similar contributions to nineteenth-century English cities. Birmingham had more miles of canals than Venice. Aesthetically their impact was somewhat less.

Modern historians have documented extensive public and private patronage which enriched English urban centres with notable buildings. Still, Trevelyan's indictment is not answered by bricks and stones, however imposing their assembly. Beauty was booked to order like merchandise, and boasted of like credit in the bank. Ruskin upbraided members of the Bradford Exchange for seeking his advice, as an 'architectural man-milliner', on how best to spend £30,000 on a building which would reflect the 'leading fashion'. 'You cannot', he said, 'have good architecture merely by asking people's advice on occasion. All good architecture is the expression of national life and character; and it is produced by a prevalent and eager national taste, or desire for beauty.'

This was Ruskin's insistent message. In 'Modern Manufacture and Design' (1859) he contrasted the visual impact of medieval Pisa and modern Rochdale as brightness and blight. Ruskin's purpose was not to re-create in manufacturing England conditions which made thirteenth-century Pisa. The foundation of Pisa's beauty was 'the pride of the so-called superior classes; a pride which supported itself by violence and robbery, and led in the end to the destruction both of the arts themselves and the States in which they flourished'. A better priority was to feed, clothe, and house the population in a manner that made it healthy. The chances of achieving this were now higher than at any period in history. But there was a further responsibility: to elevate senses. Cities were a school of design. Herein lay the problem. Modern workmen were technically superior to their forebears but aesthetically impoverished. They suffered sub-standard levels of physical comfort and visual beauty. Solitary public buildings, however splendid, could not correct a general atmosphere that was sulphureous and insanitary. It was impossible, Ruskin concluded, for people 'to supply beautiful incident and action in their ornament unless they see beautiful incident and action in the world about them'.

Ruskin's preaching had moral force; but evidence did not entirely substantiate his case. Ceramic art flourished in the Potteries in spite of the routinization of industry and the appalling state of the six towns. Furthermore, it would be unjust to ignore the exertions made in amelioration. In 1882, at an Art and Industrial Exhibition in Manchester, even William Morris acknowledged a general improvement in industrial art. Another side was seen in the same city in the next year, at a banquet to celebrate the opening of the Manchester Art Gallery. The alderman seated next to Holman Hunt passed a note across the table enquiring, 'Who or what is Mr Holman Hunt?' Uncultivated town councillors were legendary, but philistinism was not their monopoly. Aristocrats, past and present, had summoned a stately home and stuffed it with treasures in the way members of Bradford Exchange or Manchester Corporation did now. Whether the result breathed sensibility or groaned with tastelessness was often fortuitous. Consider the epidemic of statuary which afflicted public squares and parks. Not only did no famous son escape, even the slightest reputations were commemorated. But the most controversial example, Gilbert Scott's Albert Memorial (1864), was not a local job. The mistake most councillors made, if it was a mistake, was to imitate their betters.

We may, therefore, criticize some results of civic patronage without disparaging the motives which inspired it. The professed 'main object' of the Fine Arts Committee of Liverpool Corporation, which held large autumn exhibitions annually from 1871, was to excite 'a widespread interest in Art among the masses'. From 1877 its exhibition was shown in the Art Gallery which the millionaire–brewer, A. B. Walker, donated in celebration of his mayoralty. The statues which surrounded the Gallery's porch symbolized the vision: Raphael on one side, Michelangelo on the other, Commerce on top. The Walker collection was subsequently built up from private gifts by councillors and businessmen and from the Fine Arts Committee's own purchase fund. The quality of that initial collection is now thought ponderous. That is explained by the limitations of the professional selectors – who dismissed Impressionist and post-Impressionist work as childish daubing – and by the naïve assumption that art could both educate the moral sense of the masses and rival commercial entertainment in occupation of their leisure. Attendances and purchases at the Liverpool autumn exhibitions declined from 1904. Perhaps this episode of civic patronage is best summarized by Augustus John's portrait (1908) of H. C. Dowdall, that risible rendering of an ermined lord mayor and his attentive footman, Smith, as a civic Don Quixote and Sancho Panza or Punch and Judy.

Patronage of art for its own sake, and artistic freedom, were luxuries not entertained overmuch in the chambers of nineteenth-century municipalities. Artists still served the caprices of the wealthy. The difference now was the changed composition of the rich: the individual industrialist and business or civic corporation had been added to the established aristocracy. Consider Manchester Corporation, which commissioned frescoes of the town's history for the town hall, that one-million-pound gothic pile of Alfred Waterhouse's design which was opened in 1877. Madox Brown found that the Committee would not accept a depiction of Peterloo. Peterloo had been banished from the official mind since 1856, when the Free Trade Hall was erected on the site in commemoration of the Anti-Corn Law League. Art and architecture were calibrated to serve civic self-esteem. Manchester's attitude to Madox Brown resembled Lever's use of W. P. Frith or Pear's use of Millais. He was there to advertise a city like the others sold soap.

A calculative quantity was evident too in the civic university movement. The founder of Birmingham's college, Mason, whose fortune was made from the steel-pen and electroplate industry, specifically excluded literary subjects from that institution. This scientific and technological emphasis was made with good cause. Pre-reform Oxbridge was obscurantist. It bristled with ignorant deference to the classics, ignorant reverence for theological authorities, ignorant hostility to philosophical freedom, ignorant opposition to research in the physical sciences. Post-reform Oxbridge was an improvement; but still the classics were regarded as essential equipment and compulsory Greek was not yet abolished. Even Jowett's Balliol was a factory to make politicians, lawyers, and public administrators, not scientists and industrialists; and those few graduates who avoided the professions gravitated to commerce rather than manufacturing industry. The provision of scholarships, fellowships, and professorships in the sciences was growing (more at Cambridge than Oxford) but was meagre compared with the arts. The crisis in some colleges' finances, with the late-nineteenth-century depression in agricultural rents, might account for some failure to expand; but it may reasonably be argued that the will was lacking anyhow. There were few signs of the ancient universities actively seeking endowments from, and ties with, industry; and their scientific work tended to be abstract rather than applied, fitting the students for academic rather than business careers. By contrast, the sciences were promoted at civic colleges and universities in the utilitarian spirit. Joseph Chamberlain, a drummer-up of endowments for Birmingham University, had no intention of competing with Oxbridge in the arts. He aimed to stimulate industry and commerce by giving a professional training comparable to that for aspirant doctors and lawyers in schools of medicine and Inns of Court. Vocational study was central to modern civic universities as it was in medieval Europe. Scottish, German, and American models sparked the recent movement in England; and commissions of inquiry into trade depression and the backward state of technical education gave urgency to the question. Scientists and industrialists, like Huxley, Playfair, Roscoe, Samuelson, and Brunner, naturally were busy in this cause but, with notable exceptions, politicians in London were without the same conviction. The vital advice of the Privy Council to the Government in 1903, to grant independent university status to Liverpool and Manchester, derived from a carefully orchestrated campaign. R. B. Haldane's *Autobiography* (1929) was scathing about his former cabinet and parliamentary colleagues' uninterest. There was not the quantity of votes to be swayed over the issue of science and industry in university or adult education as there was in the matter of religion and popular control in primary and secondary education. Most politicians were nonchalant unless their own city was keenly interested.

Civic pride joined with industrial enterprise to confute those who agreed with the *Saturday Review*'s prediction about Owen's College (1851), that 'Anyone educated in Manchester would certainly be dull and probably vicious.' In the pioneering days local businessmen provided financial backing, not always with the purpose of wanting city colleges to grow into independent universities; but, once this development occurred, both they and town and city councils, under permissive clauses of the 1902 Education Act, evinced an earnestness to see them prosper. In 1905 Liverpool Corporation gave the university a site, building, and grant of £10,000, to which neighbouring councils added £2,300; the LCC allocated to London University and colleges £15,000; Leeds and Sheffield Universities benefited by similar amounts from municipal sources, Birmingham University by £7,000, Manchester by £6,000. The connection between industry and the colleges was mutually reinforcing. Professor Ashworth in 1965 tabulated the growing and contracting industries between 1870 and 1914:

	Numbers of Employed	
	Plus	*Minus*
Metals, engineering, and shipbuilding	370,000	
Mines and quarries	202,000	
Public utilities	165,000	
Paper, printing, and allied trades	97,000	
Food, drink, and tobacco	93,000	
Chemical and allied trades	48,000	
Textiles		295,000
Clothing		114,000
Miscellaneous		31,000
Leather, canvas, indiarubber		3,000

Commenting upon this table in *The Universities and British Industry 1850–1970* (1972), Michael Sanderson observed that the civic universities contained faculties closely associated with the industrial growth sectors whose progress would have been 'jeopardized had this university linkage not been forthcoming' – a contrast to the take-off of the textiles industry before 1800. It was now 'increasingly difficult to pursue the career of inventor independent of university expertise'.

By investment in university education, museums, parks and the rest, provincial cities had evidence to contest the charge laid by mid-century visitors, such as Hippolyte Taine, that a place like Manchester was only 'a great jerry-built barracks, a workhouse for 400,000 people, a hard-labour penal establishment'. Some individuals, by their benefactions, expressed an assurance in civic improvement and, it may be, marked a contrast with selfish aristocracy. The superb Althorp library, collected by the Earls Spencer, was bought in 1892 by Mrs John Rylands, widow of a wealthy cotton-spinner, and given to the city of Manchester.

Still, no visitor in 1900 could mistake England's Manchesters. They remained foremost places of work. All improvement, whether humanitarian, educational or recreational, advanced the faster for serving that end. Sanitary reform was business sense as much as moral sense. Healthier workers would improve industrial output; and individuals and public authorities would be spared unproductive expenditure in hospital and funeral charges. Certainly a social conscience inspired civic improvements; but it is an error to neglect business needs. Consider the transformation of central Birmingham, using the Artisans and Labourers Dwellings Improvement Act of 1875. A ninety-acre area of 4,000 back-to-back houses was cleared, but the corporation selected for purchase only half this district. Rehousing the 18,000 dispossessed persons was left mainly to private enterprise. The resultant showpiece was not the new council housing but a thoroughfare, Corporation Street, fronted and bordered by commercial premises. Everywhere more slums were demolished by private enterprise to extend business facilities than were cleared by municipal authorities from a humanitarian commitment.

Cities age physically, not in entirety but in sections. The extremities are usually the freshest parts. The core is invariably in a state both of decay and renovation. As cities expanded, the occupation of central sites by slums was intolerable to businessmen – those, at any rate, who were not interested landlords – as well as to health officials. Land around the Liverpool Exchange multiplied four or five times in value between 1840 and 1870, in Water Street by that amount in half the time. Land prices in ten chief streets of Manchester rose an average of three times in 1862–71, in Market Street fetching the equivalent of £459,800 per acre. By 1900 prime sites not only in London, in provincial cities too, were valued around a million pounds per acre.

We may, therefore, corroborate Trevelyan's statement that city rivalry was often materialistic. But this statement should not be made disparagingly. It merely acknowledges the *raison d'être* of towns. Economic well-being was the ruling concern of their inhabitants.

IV

The changing positions of cities, how some grow and others stagnate, remains an abiding puzzle for urban historians. Linkages between capital formation and technological innovation, the spurt of new industry and the stunting of traditional industry, are screened from view. Statistical series are defective regarding the economic performance of individual towns. In an essay published in H. Schmal (ed.), *Patterns of European Urbanization since 1500* (1981), P. Kooij rightly complains that most statistics are 'available on a national, and not on a local level . . . it is impossible to determine the G.D.P. of a town for the 19th century, and also later. One is able to measure the contribution of individual towns to the increase in the national population, but it is impossible to subdivide the economic growth of a nation into urban growth.'

B. T. Robson ingeniously wrestles with this difficulty in *Urban Growth* (1973). Urban economic and population growth depend on the adoption of critical innovations. Three – gasworks and street-lighting, building societies, and telephone exchanges – are studied for their effects on the internal operations and external relations of towns. Electricity and tramway undertakings furnish additional tests. Robson correlates the sluggish growth of the large cities in the late nineteenth century with the shrinking rate of innovations. The climate created by indecision about the division of central and local government authority and about areas of private and municipal activity, was injurious to the development of large-scale utilities.

Some question remains about how fine an index population growth is for a city's economic vitality. Already industry was accounting disadvantages in certain large-city locations – congested space, high rents and rates, refractory or feckless labour. Modern governments induce industry to re-settle through programmes of financial incentives (loans, subsidies, and tax remissions) and land provision (industrial estates). We know less about the endeavours of nineteenth-century citizens to boost their cities and their effect upon the urban hierarchy. The promotion of railways and transport facilities is recognized, but not the work of chambers of commerce and other associations, diffusing market information about a city's enterprise and prospects, or the role of industrial exhibitions, prestige conventions and trade literature, publicizing the advantages of specific locations and technology.

Individual and collective effort to generate urban growth indirectly concerns Jane Jacobs, who argues in *The Economy of Cities* (1969) that diversification rather than specialization causes sustained economic growth. The mainspring is import-replacement, by utilizing surplus technical capacity, organizational expertise, and market accessibility to outbid the importer. Much nineteenth-century urban growth was at the expense of rural industries. Leicester and Northampton were two towns which finally subdued their regions after decades of struggling. The hosiery and boot and shoe trades became urban factory-organized and country work was curtailed. By 1900 this easy means of urban growth approached exhaustion. For Leicester and Northampton, however, the same process was repeated, this time against an urban competitor, East London, whose workshop and sweated out-work organization was progressively crushed. Generally, cities achieved continued expansion by generating novel goods and services or by stealing from other towns lines of activity whose production now, because of the city's differentiated skills, was economically feasible.

The tension between specialization and diversification, and

between efficiency and development, is illustrated by Manchester and Birmingham. Manchester was the early-nineteenth-century pundits' choice as the city with an inspiring future because of the remarkable productivity of its textiles manufacture. In fact its efficient specialization portended stagnation. Most local capital, skilled labour, even other trades, tied themselves to the leading industry. Their short-term advantage sacrificed long-term creativity in other directions. Manchester's work was so narrowed that it became in effect an inflated company town. By contrast Birmingham, though known as the metropolis of hardware and metals, contained heterogeneous trades. Many were small and inefficient; but, through flexibility of differential production, Birmingham continued to add new work and services. Ultimately it would surpass Manchester because its development rate was superior.

One weakness of this argument is that the issue of the respective fortunes of Manchester and Birmingham is presented in isolation. Cities operate within regional systems and are indivisible from them. This environment does much to dictate economic destinies. The distribution of resources and the types of activity that fall within regions set limits to opportunities for development in particular cities. Considering these constraints, late-nineteenth-century Manchester had an impressive record. If evaluation is made within the regional context, Birmingham had no relevance to Manchester. That they became in Edwardian England symbols of the conflict of free trade and tariff reform was political shorthand. Liverpool mattered more to Manchester. Their struggle in the north-west is one of the most pregnant episodes of late-nineteenth-century English urban history. It was a classic case of inter-city rivalry within a situation of inter-city dependency.

Manchester men, Liverpool gentlemen: this familiar tag represented the antagonism between the mercantile and manufacturing functions of the cities. Mancunians alleged that they suffered from a client condition. Liverpudlians controlled both the inward movement of raw materials for Manchester industries and the outward flow of finished goods. Liverpool battened upon Manchester enterprise and charged excessive tolls for menial services. The shipping of raw cotton constituted 40 per cent of the value of Liverpool's trade in 1820–50. In these decades began the first concerted agitation of Manchester interests against the dues levied by Liverpool. Liverpool Corporation, which then administered the docks, was accused of diverting proceeds to town purposes instead of improving or cheapening shipping facilities; but, though they were instrumental in persuading Parliament in 1857 to transfer control of the docks to an independent trust (the Mersey Docks and Harbour Board), Manchester interests were equally disenchanted with the Liverpool Corporation's successor. Furthermore, cartels ('Conference agreements') between freight carriers exacerbated the Mancunians' sense of frustration. Liverpool merchants countered that regular and efficient services were worth paying for, and that Liverpool and Manchester had a common enemy in the railway companies whose punitive rates for carriage of freight between the cities were the real trouble. Feelings against high railway charges were aired before the Royal Commission on the Depression of Trade and Industry, 1884–6, by several witnesses, in the coal and iron trades as well as in cotton and shipping, who complained that they suffered greatly compared with foreigners. Mancunians, however, were already fashioning their own solution: 'bringing the sea to Manchester'.

On 15 December 1882 the first Manchester Ship Canal Bill was placed before Parliament. Nearly three years later, when the Manchester promoters and Liverpool opponents had spent almost half a million pounds in parliamentary fees, a third Bill received royal assent. Navigation finally occurred along the thirty-five miles of canal in 1894. The cost was a terrible £14 million. The original £7m. subscribed capital, in preference and ordinary shares, was exhausted with engineering problems, which involved the diversion of railways and rivers. Manchester Corporation rescued the Canal Company with votes of £5m. in two instalments in 1891–2. This imposed a burden on ratepayers, and meant that the corporation was unable to spend as much as it needed on street improvements to relieve the traffic congestion in its commercial heart. The corporation exacted as its price majority representation on the Canal Company Board. Ordinary shareholders waited until 1915 for even a ¾-per-cent dividend; but the value of the canal must be measured differently.

The canal was designed for ships of up to 12,500 tons. In 1894 686,158 tons of sea-borne traffic and 239,510 tons of barge traffic brought receipts of £97,901; in 1913 5,457,218 tons of sea-borne traffic and 322,943 tons of barge traffic brought receipts of £654,937. At one end of the canal, Ellesmere Port became a boom town; at the other end Manchester became Britain's fourth-ranking port by value of trade. One major steamship company was founded as a result of the canal. For the rest, Liverpool firms still dominated shipping, but Manchester had made separate Conference agreements. The importation of raw cotton direct to Manchester, the *raison d'être* of the canal, required the agency of a specially formed pressure group, the Manchester Cotton Association, before satisfying results were achieved. High charges for use of the canal were complained of; and the railway monopoly remained. The canal's most important consequence, however, was the development of the world's first industrial estate, Trafford Park. This 1,200-acre estate of Sir Humphrey de Trafford, offered to Manchester Corporation as parkland in the early 1890s, had been secured by a business consortium while the corporation hesitated. In 1897 its rateable value was £2,869, in 1904 £52,098, in 1912 about £100,000. By 1920 130 firms were established there, giving employment for 30,000 persons; by 1938 200 firms employed 50,000 people. The trades embraced engineering, timber, iron, steel and wire, oil, granite and stone, chemicals, salt, provisions, soap, matches, candles, rubber, cement, pitch, creosote and tar, oilseed crushing, flour-milling, refrigeration, and miscellaneous warehousing.

Latterly, the shipping business has dwindled and heavy losses have been incurred by Manchester ratepayers, since canal dredging has to be maintained whatever the level of trade. By 1982 only one of eight docks in the port remained in use. The registered dock workforce, once 3,700, had shrunk to 66. Unable to receive the largest vessels or to compete with road haulage, the port was now 'a nonentity in the modern shipping world', according to one Manchester City Council representative on the Ship Canal Company Board. The recent collapse of the port of Manchester, nonetheless, should not cloud our picture of the late nineteenth century when, *pace* Mrs Jacobs, the city was diversifying its industrial and trading base. Indeed, it had begun to do so earlier in the century. Though about 24 per cent of the Manchester–Salford industrial workforce was engaged in textiles in 1861, engineering gradually burgeoned from a trade tailored to textile requirements into an independent force. Manchester by 1914 was one of the world's foremost engineering centres. The names of Roberts, Whitworth, and Fairbairn had resounded through the previous century; now, amid nearly 200 firms engaged in most branches of engineering in the Manchester district, there stood out the great companies of Armstrong-Whitworth, Metropolitan-Vickers, Mather and Platt's, and Crossley's. The chemical industry had grown too: the incorporated districts of Blackley and Crumpsall were engulfed in fumes almost as completely as Runcorn and Widnes. As a railway and banking centre Manchester had few rivals outside London; and its market facilities were elaborate. Manchester's Smithfield Market dated from 1854, the Water Street Abattoir and the Wholesale Fish Market from 1873. These were busy but small compared to the Coal Exchange, with 227 members in 1879 and over 1,000 by 1914; or the Corn and Produce Exchange, opened in 1837, enlarged in 1881 and 1890, and attracting a thousand dealers in each week of business. Of first importance was the Royal Exchange. The initial building was erected in 1729; the second, in 1809, was enlarged in 1841 and 1849; the third was built between 1867 and 1874; and a fourth was placed under construction in 1914, with double the floor space, to enable 11,000 subscribers to pursue business.

A great part of Manchester's work was thus commercial rather than manufacturing. The city serviced the textiles region, wherein the real one-industry towns lay, towns like Oldham, Rochdale, Bolton, Bury, Blackburn, Ashton, and Stockport. Each had a population of between 30,000 and 70,000 in 1861; and the textile part of their industrial workforce amounted to as much as 68 per cent (Blackburn) and nowhere less than 40 per cent (Rochdale). These towns had slender mercantile and professional sectors. It was Manchester where the lawyers, accountants, bankers, brokers, dealers, commercial clerks, salesmen and travellers mostly concentrated. Indirectly Manchester remained unusually dependent upon the cyclical fortunes of the textile trades: less as a primary producer, more as a servicing centre. The city had diversified its work during the nineteenth century; but no business community will readily or wholly drop an unprece-dentedly successful trade in order to cushion itself in a hypothetical future world. When cotton was king who would swear loyalty to a pretender?

An objection remains that, while not abandoning cotton, Man-chester and Lancashire men generally could have shown greater response to market changes and new technologies. Comparison might be made with the West Riding mixed-worsted industry. During the 1870s the French all-wool worsteds achieved superiority when femi-nine fashions turned against the hard cloths worn with crinolines. Changes were required in spinning, dyeing, and design; but, as Eric Sigsworth argued in *Black Dyke Mills* (1958), it is a hard decision to replace machinery and to retrain labour. Fashion is fickle. It once favoured West Riding manufacturers, it was now against. But it might swing back, and 'the spinner who had scrapped his "throstles" and "cap frames" for "mules" would then be as badly off as before. Hence, there was an obvious reluctance to make the change which was advocated.'

This is another argument against the capacity of cities to undertake dynamic economic self-renewal. Individual cities and industries had limited flexibility, and not only because of their regional circumstances. By the late nineteenth century cities were firmly tied into international economic systems; and their competitive positions were determined by conditions which the quality of management of their own resources might deflect in the long run only marginally. Worsted manufacture in the Bradford area again supplies an illustration. The late nineteenth century brought signs of renewal in the industry. There was greater appreciation of the vagaries of the dress-goods trade; and new lines of men's wear – overcoats, mackintoshes, and flannels – were developed. Company structure was altering too: on the one hand a tendency to increased individual specialization, with the decline of the combined spinning and weaving mill; on the other hand a growth of associations, like the Bradford Dyers' (1898). None of this could prevent the largest continental market for Bradford goods, Germany, falling steeply after Bismarck's adoption of tariffs in 1879; or Bradford's largest world market, America, tumbling to a third of its value after the McKinley and Dingley tariffs were imposed in the 1890s. One spokesman for the Bradford worsted industry phrased the question to the Tariff Commission in 1905: 'How can any degree of technical education or enterprise overcome such a tariff as we have to face in the United States, which varies from 104 to 140 per cent?'

In this context it is worth noting that Jane Jacobs's criticisms of urban specialization are not new. The charge was laid in the very period under study here, by tariff reformers who sought to indict the regime of free trade for the tendency towards metropolitan concentration of markets and centralization of finance. The founder of the school of geopolitics, H. J. Mackinder, taught in *Democratic Ideals and Reality* (1919) that 'Productive power . . . is a far more important element of reality in relation to modern civilization than is accumulated wealth.' More simply and grimly, 'All specialization contains the seeds of death . . .'

We can reconsider the rivalry of Manchester and Liverpool, and of Manchester and Birmingham, in the light of these observations. If

Liverpool had nothing more to fear than Manchester's rivalry as a port its future would have been serene. By 1914 Liverpool interests had been alerted to a greater menace, one ultimately impossible to fend off. This was a general turn away of trade following the growth of Southampton. Southampton had been relatively slow to develop because it was without a significant industrial hinterland. In the 1850s it was the fifth-ranked port of the country; but Liverpool, more or less equal first with London, entered and cleared more than nine times the shipping tonnage. Southampton, however, had natural advantages as a passenger and distributing centre, located in the busiest shipping lane in the world, to and from Europe, and a port of call in European services to America and elsewhere. Here was a spell whose attractions to shippers could not remain concealed for ever. This brute geographical fact, not exceptional enterprise, largely determined the fate of the two ports, for a comparison of their docks boards does not yield a convincing superiority to one or the other. Each had spasms of activity and inertia, since all ports were torn at different times over decisions on how to embark on expensive works to attract more and larger vessels without raising dues to an extent that would frighten away existing business.

Southampton doubled the tonnage of its shipping and doubled the value of its foreign trade in the decade after 1892 in spite of an unpropitious atmosphere created by warring commercial interests in its city council and docks board. Progress was not without price. The transfer from Liverpool of the White Star Line in 1907 required extra docks accommodation and deeper channels; and some speculated that, after all this effort, Southampton might sink like the White Star *Titanic* in 1912. But, as A. Temple Patterson observes, though for some time after the advent of the White Star Line no extraordinary improvement was felt at Southampton, 'the centre of gravity of transatlantic passenger traffic was now beginning to move from Liverpool into the English Channel'. This in due course suffered from air-passenger transport; but cross-Channel ferries grew, and in the movement of freight and fuel Southampton gradually established itself beyond Liverpool's capacity to interfere.

The question mark over a city's economic life, therefore, concerns the extent to which its business could establish a significant interest in one or several lines of work, then fight off external challenges or switch to other investments, with the least disturbance. The dependence of Manchester and the north-west on American supplies of raw cotton had been exposed during the Civil War in 1861-5; but alternative supplies were sought and investments made in new plant. Lancastrians were not foolishly sanguine, lazy, or defeatist. The European and American tariff-protected markets for Lancashire-finished articles contracted steeply, from 19 to 9.8 per cent of exported cotton piece-goods between 1860 and 1880, and to 7.1 per cent by 1900. There remained the British Empire and the rest of the world. Here competition from Asiatic textiles loomed; but Mancunians set about resolutely containing that menace, by structural reorganization and, in the 1890s, by agitating the Government to stem India's advance. Only with hindsight do we see the viability of the cotton textiles industry at risk before 1914. Ninety-five new cotton mills were built in Lancashire in the 1905-7 boom; the region was producing better-quality goods than any rival. The annual average export of cotton piece-goods rose from 3,446 million yards between 1870 and 1874 to 6,673 million yards between 1910 and 1913.

By contrast, Birmingham in this period hardly exuded confidence in the future. The metals trades were expected to collapse under American and continental tariff-nurtured competition. Algernon West, of the Inland Revenue Board, argued that, if England was taken as a whole, no depression existed in 1885; but the Birmingham Chamber of Commerce was unequivocal about its plight:

We are being ruined. We work as hard now as ever but without profit. . . . In the past we supplied the entire world with arms. Governments and private individuals always used to apply to us. . . . To-day the greater proportion of these governments manufacture for themselves, and America has popularized her arms from Springfield and Winchester; in fact, America obtained the orders for the Carlist and Turkish Wars. . . . We used to enjoy a monopoly for screws and nails. Protective tariffs have closed the civilized markets to us. . . . Under the shelter of tariffs, Germany and America have developed their factories, and making their profit out of home sales, the Germans throw the surplus on our markets at absurdly low prices. Time was when the Asiatic and Oceanic East purchased our nails. To-day German nails actually compete here on our own market of Birmingham. Buttons, which we used to sell to the whole of Europe, now come to us from Germany instead. German iron wire is now sold in our Birmingham shops.

Throughout the Birmingham region a tale of woe resounded. Black Country coal and iron production was in a terrible state. This was reflected in the population of Dudley, 45,000 in 1861 and still under 49,000 in 1901. Wolverhampton's population, too, was practically stationary from the mid-1890s to 1914, as the town's sheet-metal and galvanized-iron firms moved to coastal sites, Ellesmere Port and Newport (Mon.), in order to reduce their costs of raw-material supply and improve their overseas marketing. Bankruptcies were more common in Birmingham metals trades than in Manchester textiles. A ray of hope shone from Coventry in the south-east of the area, but that town had experienced so many past vicissitudes that its future success now was not guaranteed. Whatever share the rest of England enjoyed in the legendary mid-Victorian prosperity, it was certain that Coventry had taken little part in it. The silk ribbon trade was smashed following the Cobden–Chevalier commercial treaty with France. Coventry's population was declining or stagnant for nearly twenty years after 1860. It grew extraordinarily thereafter, from 45,000 to 106,000 between 1880 and 1911, surpassing 200,000 by 1939. First watches, sewing machines, and bicycles, then motor vehicles, machine tools, electrical goods, and rayon manufacture, inspired Coventry's phoenix-like resurrection.

As it happened, Coventry transformed the fortunes of Birmingham and the West Midlands too, but the renewal was neither uninterrupted nor infinitely sustainable, as the recipe of diversification and adaptability preached by Mrs Jacobs would imply. In the first place the bursting of the cycle boom, which followed the bankruptcy of the company-promoter, E. T. Hooley, in 1898, threatened to return Coventry and its collaborators to the toils of depression whence they had sprung. That crisis was survived by the shift into motor manufacture; but greater success here eventually visited upon the region those penalties of interdependent specializations and 'over-commitment' which allegedly caused the textile districts' previous downfall. When the Midlands' share in a shrinking world market for cars was eroded from the 1970s, its virtues of small independent production were exposed as fiction. The car industry's success had induced umpteen companies to tie themselves to it. Each car contained hundreds of parts, some manufactured by firms employing several thousands, others by small producers employing a couple of score. These component suppliers suffered from domino decline. Success in the Midlands motor and electrical industries thus eventually bred the same vices that the north-west's textile industry suffered from earlier. It is grotesque to applaud the Midlands' 'diversification' when it was unprofitable, and to condemn the north-west's 'specialization' when it was profitable, before 1914.

The perils of economic prophecy can be explored further by reference to Preston, which like Manchester became an inland port. Its history illustrates that, whether diversified or specialized, economic adventure was no guarantee of prosperity. In 1861 Preston contained 83,000 people. It was a seat of county administration for Lancashire and, although fully 60 per cent of the industrial workforce was occupied in textiles, Preston enjoyed some independence from the great conurbations to its south-east and south-west. Preston lay just outside their orbits, thirty miles from Liverpool and Manchester and sixteen miles from the sea along the Ribble estuary.

Quays had existed on the river before the corporation bought the Ribble Navigation Company (established in 1838) for £73,000 in 1883. In fact, the corporation as a body and councillors as individuals had been the Company's chief shareholders. They had sunk substantial capital into improvements, even alienating corporation lands to find the means to do so. Thus, as H. N. B. Morgan has argued, what underpinned the decision in 1883 was a narrow anxiety to recover money spent as well as a fantastic bid to emulate Belfast, Glasgow, or Liverpool. The main west-coast railway from London to Scotland passed through Preston yet, it was argued, for the town to expand, the river channel required widening, deepening, and proper dock facilities. The Albert Edward Dock, at forty acres the country's largest single dock, was opened in 1892. Ships drawing 19 feet could ascend to the town. In 1884 145 vessels of a total tonnage of 10,065 used the quays and carried 16,881 tons of imports, 14,082 tons of exports; in 1914 1,481 vessels of a total tonnage of 294,884 carried 530,251 tons of imports, 213,339 tons of exports. In the shipping business, however, Preston's mercantile community was at a disadvantage regarding capital and experience. Liverpool interests moved in, like Henry Tyrer's agency; and it was small consolation that by 1905 Tyrer's business at Preston was yielding greater receipts than at Liverpool. The most important new traffic was wood-pulp, which by 1914 constituted 30 per cent of import tonnage. Preston had become the leading supplier of Lancashire's paper mills. Timber, grain, foodstuffs, and assorted minerals comprised the other import cargoes. Coastal trading, to Ireland and Scandinavia, were the routine directions for Preston commerce.

Altogether the dock's potential for transforming Preston's economy was limited. The earlier textile revolution resulted in Preston achieving a decennial growth of above 30 per cent from 1801 to 1851.

Now, of the eight English towns of 75–100,000 population in 1861, Preston experienced the smallest growth, an average 8.2 per cent, over the five decades to 1911. There was minor shipbuilding activity, iron and brass works, electrical engineering and some machine-making. Altogether engineering employed over 10 per cent of Preston males around 1900, but much of it was geared to cotton-spinning which remained the staple industry (employing about 23 per cent). Equidistance from Liverpool and Manchester had given Preston some flexibility; but this was liberty on a leash. Both cities could choke off real advances. Moreover, maintaining the port of Preston proved costly for, unlike the Mersey, where the tides prevented silting, the Ribble required continuous dredging.

Preston was one of only three English towns whose docks were municipally managed. Boston and Bristol were the others. Preston incurred the largest rate-burden, about £36,000 p.a. by the early 1900s, over 20 per cent of the total rate. Bristolians contributed a similar sum for a much bigger operation and, in a city of 320,000, the individual ratepayer's burden was smaller. Boston docks were different again, tiny but profitable. They point up Preston's folly. A town of 16,000 in 1901, Boston was only four miles from the sea. Money was spent on deepening and widening the Witham channel, 1880–7; but the dock was inexpensive to run and well tailored to local and regional requirements. A deep-sea fishing fleet of some forty trawlers was the basis of prosperity. To this was added steamship traffic to Hull, London, and Hamburg, carrying a nice balance of goods: timber, pit-props, granite and ore as imports, coal, corn and agricultural implements (now made in Boston) as exports. Preston was incapable of more than lop-sided growth, trapped between Manchester and Liverpool. The want of return cargoes was serious. Apart from South Lancashire coal Preston could offer shippers few bulk exports. Hence the port's prosperity was always suspect and, though technical improvements were not shirked – Preston indeed was a pioneer of containerization in the 1960s – the docks were killed with startling suddenness by modern motorways. In the late 1970s Preston Corporation decided to close the docks, and with it terminate a meteoric episode of rise and fall in the town's history.

The Preston example may be judged a case of irrational speculation; but it is an inherent feature of capitalism that it corrodes the cities and businesses it has built, littering the landscape with dilapidated industrial fabric and squandered human skills. Sometimes a district's assets remain tangible, though rendered dormant. Later new enterprise revives them. Sometimes the assets become sterile and perish. Then the depression in a district is perpetuated, for the poorer an area the higher the per capita charges of its local government rates. Thus financially and socially the conditions deter new industry. Generally these problems, surfacing during twentieth-century recessions, are a legacy of unbalanced nineteenth-century growth; but that growth from the start was no respecter of persons or previous settlements. Dictated by the imperatives of the industrial, mercantile, and transport revolutions, the constructions of earlier times were progressively dismantled. By 1900, first suburban growth, then motor traffic, threatened to de-industrialize the core city only some sixty years after rail transport had encouraged more concentration and specialization.

In the eighteenth century the number of important ports had fallen. In the nineteenth century this process was accelerated as the growing volume of overseas trade and size of vessels advanced the position of the better harbours. By the early twentieth century twelve ports together moved over three-quarters of total foreign trade (apart from coal and iron); and much the greater part passed through the big six, London, Liverpool, Hull, Bristol, Southampton, and Manchester. What affected the import–export ports affected the coastal trading ports. As railway competition was felt in internal transport, of coal especially, only those with the financial and physical capacity to undertake harbour improvements were confident of a future. Thus, of the small harbours of Sussex in the late nineteenth century, Newhaven and Shoreham waxed while Rye, Arundel, and Chichester waned. Furthermore, the regional shift of industry, underpinned by the railway system, opened up new ports at the same time as it speeded the reduction of the historic ports. Thus Cardiff became a great coal port, Grimsby a great fishing port. The latter was one of several east-coast ports whose maritime economies were to an extent controlled by the railway companies which serviced them: the Manchester, Sheffield and Lincolnshire Railway Company invested over £1m. in facilities in Grimsby. Hull, Harwich, Hartlepool, and Goole were similarly placed. The last was originally, like Runcorn, Stourport, and Ellesmere Port, a canal-company creation; and the new coal port at Immingham in the early twentieth century was a reminder that the canals' successors, the railways, had not abdicated a talent for town-making.

The coal and iron economies released revolutionary energies in

urban growth. In 1865 the economist, W. S. Jevons, sounded a
warning about their insubstantiality because they depended upon
exhaustible mineral supplies. Jevons was unduly alarmist. The rate at
which new coal reserves were discovered outpaced the exhaustion of
seams, and the number of workers engaged in mining and quarrying
rose from 383,000 in 1851 to 1,202,000 in 1911. Coal was used to
generate a new form of energy, electricity; and, before the First World
War, the possibilities of the petroleum alternative were appreciated.
Still, mineral-working was a rough and heedless business. Places like
Barrow-in-Furness typified the crude exploitation, oblivious of past
and future. Before the discovery of pure haematite ore in the vicinity
in the late 1840s, Barrow was a huddle of fishermen's cottages
containing 325 people. Fifty years later it was a busy port of heavy
industry, with a population approaching 60,000. Dukes, of Devonshire and Buccleuch, were the principal property-owners; but real
power lay with James Ramsden and his fellow directors of the Furness
Railway Company. They reached this part of Lancashire in 1846.
Thereafter they constructed and controlled the docks and built four-
storey tenements, Scottish style, to accommodate the expanding workforce. Ramsden was the first mayor and, before a town hall and
council chamber were built, the corporation met in the railway
company's offices.

Unlike the port of Preston, over 75 per cent of the value of Barrow's
trade – which amounted to £2m. – was in exports by 1900: chiefly iron
ore, pig iron, and steel rails. In the import trade Barrow offered Liverpool some competition by lower charges for handling grain, flour, and
timber; and there was involvement in the Irish cattle trade, in Russian
petroleum, and in Isle of Man tourism. The dock capacity was never
fully used, because of the remoteness of Barrow from other centres of
population and manufacture. Still, it could be argued that the docks
were a subsidiary. Behind the port were huge iron, steel, and engineering works, jute factories, paper and pulp works. Along the Walney
channel rose great shipbuilding yards, led by Vickers, who absorbed
the Naval Construction and Armaments Company in 1897 and
doubled the labour force to 10,000 during the accelerating armaments
race before 1914. Furness Abbey shrank in the background, quizzical
witness to the revived worship of Vulcan. This juxtaposition enraged
Ruskin's sensibility in the 1870s. It was not just the drunken navvies
he met but the fact that 'the station itself is tastefully placed so that you
can see it, and nothing else but it, through the east window of the

Abbot's Chapel, over the ruined altar'. Barrow was a classic example
of a town whose existence was decided by the usefulness of its natural
resources at a particular phase of capitalist development, and by landowners and business entrepreneurs who seized this opportunity.
Barrow was also a monument of urban–industrial brutishness.

V

Unnatural landscapes stirred mighty emotions. In *Fors Clavigera*
Ruskin invited workmen to assess an achievement like the dynamiting
of the Derbyshire Peak District by railway companies, so that 'every
fool in Buxton can be in Bakewell in half an hour, and every fool in
Bakewell at Buxton; which you think a lucrative process of exchange –
you Fools Everywhere'. But ugly works could reach sublimity. Many
artists realized this, like Algernon Newton, 'the Regent's Canaletto',
or Atkinson Grimshaw, whose paintings of dampened gas-lit streets
and misty waterfronts conveyed an eerie warmth as well as alienation
in the urban scene. Camille Pissarro did not disdain the London
suburbs – witness his studies of Lower and Upper Norwood, Dulwich
College, Crystal Palace, Penge Station, and Sydenham Hill – or even
Bank Holiday crowds at Kew. Derain and Monet, too, were drawn to
London to paint. Monet pronounced the fog magnificent. The
vaporous quality of light gave a new dimension to the artist. Townscapes animated art and literature with fresh perspectives and, it may
be, threw them into moral confusion. The rent-collector who turned
out to be L. S. Lowry was a myope to see urban industrial folk as an
inferior race, stunted in imagination and physique.

Urban and industrial artefacts were both disturbing and inspiring.
When Arnold Bennett returned to his native Potteries, the mere sight
sometimes made him shudder; on other occasions he acclaimed the
'grim and original beauty . . . of the flame-lit expanses bearing witness
to the never-ceasing activity; the sky effects of fire and cloud; and the
huge dark ring of hills surrounding this tremendous arena'. True, this
was the Potteries by night, not daylight; but industry had not dimmed
the majesty of nature. Although the provision of employment usually
took precedence over the preservation of environment, industry was
more ruthless towards man's handiwork than towards nature. Many
manufacturing towns were actually very old towns. That past was
swept aside and built over. The surviving traces conjured a poor sense

of a heritage. Manufacturing industry deprived many towns of history.

How much ordinary people experienced elation and depression from their surroundings is difficult to judge. In *The Classic Slum* (1971) Robert Roberts reported only rare excursions from Salford's 'almost self-contained' working-class communities. Every area derived a character from the spill of its prevailing employment, be this the smoke unfurling from pot kilns and mill chimneys, the din of iron foundries, the fumes of chemical manufacture, the screeching and clanking of marshalling yards, the blankness of warehouse walls, or the deadness of slag heaps and polluted streams. But the human spirit is not predictably crushed by mean-looking towns any more than it is always elevated by paradisaical landscapes. The Middlesbrough iron-master's wife, Lady Bell, recorded, about a company settlement on the north bank of the Tees, that many inhabitants

have as deeply-rooted an attachment to it as though it were a beautiful village. There are people living in these hard-looking, shabby, ugly streets who have been there for many years, and more than one who has left it has actually pined to be back again. It is not, after all, every man or woman who is susceptible to scenery and to the outward aspect of the world around him; there are many who are nourished by human intercourse rather than by natural beauty.

The opportunities of life beyond work were very various, though the base was identified easily. In terms of amenities pit villages were the least urbane, encampments rather than towns proper. Rows of mean houses for miners, then, set apart, superior dwellings for over-seers and deputies, denoted the simplest social organization. A pub, chapel, and Co-op practically concluded the facilities. 'Dreary (O so dreary),' commented William Morris about a Northumberland colliery village, 'an endless back-yard.' Miners' houses, like agricultural labourers', were less likely than town labourers' houses to enjoy piped water, gas, and water-borne sewage disposal. Perhaps, placed on the edge of moorland, the release from dirt and dereliction was only a stride away; but miners did not invariably inhabit isolated, close-knit company colonies. In the affluent Derbyshire coalfield, according to a union official in 1914, 5,000 miners owned their own homes, some more than one; in the miserable Lancashire coalfield over one-third of miners lived in large towns, cheek by jowl with the workers in other industries, chiefly textiles; and in the Midlands mining came to established market towns, as George Eliot portrayed in *Felix Holt* (1866). Mineral exploitation in a traditional farming belt produced what

D. H. Lawrence described later in his novels, that 'queer jumble of the old England and the new'.

Everywhere exhibited a range of custom in individual and corporate leisure. Settling among Bacup mill-hands in the 1880s, Beatrice Webb felt as if she was 'living through a page of puritan history'. There the uncomplicated theology of the chapels ordered the tempo of the old folk and, though the younger generation conformed less and turned to the free Co-op library, it too was

spiritually still part of the 'old world'. It knows nothing of the complexities of modern life, and in the monotony of its daily existence likens the hand-loom village of a century ago. The restless ambition, the complicated motive and the far-stretching imagination of cosmopolitanism find no place in the gentle minds of Bacup folk. They are content with the doings of their little town – and say that even in Manchester they feel oppressed – and not 'homely like'.

Diversions other than the chapel could be found. All ten music-halls in Middlesbrough, the largest seating 2,000, the smallest 350, were projecting films on the cinematograph by Edwardian times. Six of these halls showed films on Sundays, 'an incalculable boon' to the leisure enjoyment of the working classes, thought Lady Bell. Altogether by 1914 there were over 3,500 cinemas in Britain. At the turn of the century there were also several touring theatrical companies. Most offered melodramas, but an account survives of Benson North, who brought Shakespeare to Lancashire and Yorkshire textile towns. A different play was staged every night, but always *Hamlet* on Saturdays, to packed houses.

Seeing *Hamlet* for the first time, many of the spectators had no idea how the play ended, so there was tense excitement when in the third act play-within-a-play Claudius starts guiltily and calls for lights. For dramatic effect Benson used to ring the curtain down at this point, leaving the audience buzzing with anticipation.

Music moved the provinces too. Manchester's Hallé Orchestra probably played to audiences above the common level. It grew from the presence of a sizeable middle class of German extraction. Music festivals likewise were patronized mostly by the middle classes. Those at Birmingham and Leeds had a high reputation, and there were several lesser ones, like the Potteries' which in 1893 induced Sir Arthur Sullivan to conduct one of his works and politely commend its rendering. Choral singing, however, attracted considerable lower-middle- and some working-class membership, vying particularly in productions of oratorio like Handel's *Messiah* or Mendelssohn's *Elijah*. The Huddersfield Choir, founded in 1836, was rated among the finest; so was many a Welsh choir. Welsh choirs raised funds which enabled the Penrhyn quarrymen to prolong their strike for almost a year in 1896-7. Brass bands - there were an estimated 4,000 by the late 1880s - occupied a similar place in the north. They were embedded in the general community, although nominally attached to work-places, like the Black Dyke Mills Band at Queensbury. The cup final of brass-band play was staged at Belle Vue, Manchester, annually from 1853.

As well as all kinds of concerts, there was a wealth of lectures and debates. Adult education was an emphasis of the age, from the rise of Mechanics' Institutes in the 1820s to the Workers' Educational Association in 1903; and diverse individuals delighted in expounding their intellectual hobbies. Travellers' tales were great draws. Roger Adelson notes the popularity of the amateur Orientalist, Mark Sykes, in the East Riding, 'especially after Sledmere's schoolmaster made slides for the magic-lantern show that accompanied Sykes's commentary. These he used to explain geography and architecture, gaining most attention when he used pictures to point up the different racial and moral characteristics of Turks, Arabs and Persians'.

Participating in and watching sport drew out more people. That most played and watched was football. This mass entertainment derived from quasi-tribal trials of strength. The raw original survived still in certain places as a Shrovetide spectacle, despite the authorities' warnings about civil disturbances and obstructions to traffic and trade; but the modern rules of football (and of rugby and cricket) were ordained and codified by public-school and university alumni, who acted as evangelists of the game in the provinces. Certain key stages in football's organization are plain: the foundation of the Football Association (1863), FA Challenge Cup (1871) and Football League (1888); the introduction of a Second Division (1892) and promotion and relegation (1898); the legalization of professionalism (1885); and the independence of the Rugby Football Union (1871) and amateur soccer (1907). A national fixture list was inconceivable before the railway age; likewise the systematization of rules, and miscellaneous apparatus - floodlights and fixed pitches in purpose-built stadiums - were consistent with an advancing urban-industrial society. None of this explains the patricians' motives as they trespassed beyond the public schools, or the provincial responses which made for football's success.

Historians have awkwardly framed the debate around concepts of 'rational recreation' and 'social control'. That these were contemporary concerns too does not rid the debate of contrivance. Those who encouraged the sport as a working-class counter-attraction to the pubs and music-halls, or simply as an alternative to loafing, soon encountered signs that football might be an additional vice, whose excitements generated more drinking, more gambling, more vandalism. Hopes that football would raise the physical and moral standards of working people were equally humbled. Players bent the rules in order to win; and always more people watched than played. Their health was hardly improved by, it may be, chain-smoking and standing in damp weather; their character not enhanced by submergence in a crowd, shouting themselves hoarse and provoking their favourites beyond the extremities of fair play. Those who backed the game as a means of promoting class reconciliation or of diverting the working classes from industrial and political militancy had disappointments too. Class co-operation did exist as well as class conflict; industrial and political conformity existed as well as dissent. The great symbolic contest of the late nineteenth century was Blackburn Olympics' defeat of the Old Etonians in the 1883 FA Cup Final. But historians exaggerate by suggesting that football made vast contributions either way. Perhaps the cynics had it: football, the working man's game, expressed above all the working man's imperviousness, deaf equally to appeals of Victorian respectability and Labour reformism, in his pursuit of a good time. Working men now had more leisure and money to spend in that search, and football satisfied them by its compendium of great drama, combining cunning skill and brutal effort, in an atmosphere which joined companionship and conflict.

Football as a movement grew spontaneously once the summons had been sent out because it encountered indigenous partisanship and pre-existing institutions in the provinces. Schools, churches, and YMCAs provided the beginnings of many a modern club, like Aston Villa, Birmingham City, Blackburn Rovers, Bolton Wanderers, and Everton. Works teams were the bases of others, like the Newton Heath railwaymen who grew into Manchester United or the Woolwich munitions workers who started the Arsenal FC. Given the need for the expression of strong attachments, some made an equation of popularity with power and profit. The sport became a business. Men like William Sudell, cotton manufacturer and founder of Preston North End, pioneered professionalism in the game. Great stadiums were erected: Chelsea FC's Stamford Bridge (1905), Manchester United's Old Trafford (1909–10), and Arsenal FC's Highbury (1913) were among the amphitheatres of the game, civic symbols as important as any church or town hall. With success on the field went money in the bank. The First Division's leaders in 1904–5, Newcastle United and Everton, took gate receipts of £17,065 and £14,054 respectively; and each turned a net profit of over £5,000.

More often football was not sound business. Losses were frequent. Even where a profit was made it was low and fitful compared to other forms of investment. The spin-off rewards make more interesting calculation. Oxo advertised that the 1904 FA Cup winners, Manchester City, drew strength from their product. Members of the food, drinks, and building trades swaggered in the boardrooms of football clubs. Expenditure on football may have roused their businesses. The football club subscription was also added to the politicians' list of causes, which bought popularity without incurring a penalty under legislation against electoral malpractices. Perhaps speculation is unjust, attributing sinister motive to innocent action. Businessmen and politicians are quite capable of paying for pleasure without wanting or expecting more in return.

Commercialization, nevertheless, was a blow to the gentlemen pioneers of the game; also to socialist observers concerned for the status of a new class of labour. By Edwardian times the transfer of players involved awesome sums. When Alfred Common moved from Sunderland to Middlesbrough in 1905 the fee was £1,000. Unionization among professional footballers was puny. Here was a new race of gladiators, performing, bought and sold, at their masters' bidding. But prizes were there too. A *Punch* cartoonist in 1911 caught the common opinion when he depicted a working man assessing the worth of an MP (now paid £400 p.a.): 'we could 'ave two first-class 'arf-backs for the same money.' The best players would be placed in that 5.5 per cent of the nation who in 1910 were income-tax payers (the threshold was £160 p.a.). They enjoyed national stardom and financial security while active in the game, and were cushioned in retirement. Pub management was a favourite occupation of retired footballers, like boxers. Even run-of-the-mill players experienced a life more eventful and wages a cut above the merest labourers'.

Football mania was most intense in the industrial north. League cricket and Rugby League flourished there too in the competitive atmosphere. The urban Midlands was not far behind. The commitment, even to poor performers, was remarkable. The Leicester team, called Leicester Fosse, made the First Division only once before the Great War – and suffered instantaneous relegation, in 1908–9 – but Mrs Creighton observed unwavering enthusiasm: 'The winter recreation of Leicester is football, and the Saturday half-holiday is spent by very many of the inhabitants either in playing or watching the game, whilst the great roar made by the cheers and shouts of the interested crowd penetrates to every part of the town.' Midlands and northern clubs dominated the FA Cup and Football League; 1901 was the only year before 1914 when the FA Cup went to a southern club, Tottenham Hotspur; but its team consisted of five Scots, three northerners, two Welshmen and one Irishman. Twelve teams comprised the original league in 1888; sixteen in the First Division, twelve in the new Second Division, in 1892; a total of thirty-six league clubs by 1898, forty by 1905. These were the leading lights: altogether 404 clubs entered the FA Cup competition in 1910–11. Crowds grew likewise. About 40,000 watched the 1893 FA Cup Final, but an average 80,000 watched the finals in the decade after 1895, including 113,000 at the north-versus-south clubs clash of 1901. The aggregate sum of spectators was around two million a season. Great passions were generated by club rivalry both between and within towns and cities. Football clubs issued a semblance of personality to places previously regarded only as work camps.

No other sport rivalled soccer in its comprehensive appeal, although cricket was reckoned its summer counterpart. Here the amateur, from the public schools, universities, and country houses, exercised a hold, both as player and administrator, more powerful than in soccer before 1914. The game's first expansion occurred in the eighteenth century, in the southern counties where matches were staged at the great hop-fairs; but, as with soccer, it was in the late nineteenth century that the real boost came, from facilities which only a network of well-developed urban centres could provide – the means to operate regular fixtures in stadiums with prepared pitches. Three-day county championship matches were played between nine counties from 1873, fourteen from 1895. The chief county grounds were all located in major towns, supplemented by numerous local leagues, staging one-day games between parishes, suburbs, factories, offices, big shops, and social institutions.

In football (both rugby and soccer) and in cricket individual players shone within the combined effort of teams; and spectators confirmed their popularity. Few other sporting activities were so well designed to attract a mass following, though several have enjoyed moments of fashion. Cycling became a craze with the velocipedomania of the 1860s and the popularity of Starley's Ordinary in the 1870s. In 1874 seven cycle clubs existed in London, twenty-two in the provinces. In 1882 there were 184 and nearly 350 respectively, with an average thirty or forty members. The Cyclists' Touring Club (1878) had 22,000 members by 1886. Its peak was 60,000 members in 1899, but thousands were outside club confines. Initially a middle-class fad, since machines cost between £12 and £25 in the 1870s, cycling captured the working classes when second-hand machines and instalment-payment schemes became available. J. Devey's 'The Working Man's Friend' was marketed at £4. 10s. in 1884; but the real boom followed the development of safety bicycles and pneumatic tyres from the late 1880s. Cycling to work, cycling for pleasure, cycling in competitions, each was rife.

The Molyneux Stadium, Wolverhampton, was attracting audiences of 15,000 for the cycle-championship races in 1876, and over 20,000 in the early 1880s. They did not congregate from enthusiasm alone. Bookmakers stimulated competitive cycling. Gambling habits were inveterate, a release from dullness, a flutter with fate, a controlled investment. The most popular proletarian pastimes were competitive and involved an element of gambling: pigeon-fancying, whippet-breeding and (from 1926) greyhound racing, bowling, and the pub-centred games of darts, dominoes, and skittles. None had the national reach of horse-racing. The suicide of Fred Archer, rider of 2,746 winners, in 1886, darkened many a working-class household. Respectable opinion was much charged by the expansion of gambling which followed the establishment of the starting price in 1889–90 and the distribution of cheap papers telegraphing the fixed odds. Periodic purges of street bookmakers hardly checked the punters. 'Respectability' conveyed no moral significance to the backers of the Prime Minister's Derby winner, Ladas, in 1894, or of the Prince of Wales's Derby winner, Persimmon, in 1896. The heroic 'man that broke the bank at Monte Carlo' in 1891, a Mr Wells, was extolled from a thousand barrel organs and music-halls.

The pub remained the greatest single forum of popular (but predominantly male) life. It provided amusement, distraction, oblivion; also politics and an informal labour exchange. Charles Booth estimated that 'public-houses play a larger part in the lives of the people than clubs or friendly societies, churches or missions, or perhaps all of them put together'. But historians who perceive an alternative, exclusively working-class culture operating through the pubs must reckon with the close official regulation of the trade and with the huge vested interests which fattened from its exercise. Estimates of consumer expenditure indicate a declining part played by drink, from a summit of perhaps 15 per cent in the mid-1870s to below 10 per cent in Edwardian times. If working-class incomes were increasing, however, this proportionate decline of expenditure on drink is expected. The total sales, averaging £171.4m. per annum in the Edwardian decade, remain awesome, and expenditure on tobacco (£27m. in 1900, £40m. in 1913) was beginning its fearful rise with the shift from pipe-smoking to cigarettes. A labourer might fritter away a quarter or a third of his income in this way, equal to his rent or more. Family hardship, ill-health, and industrial inefficiency were inevitable consequences. Still, the potency of liquor was gradually diminishing and evidence of alternative leisure expenditure is impressive, not to mention the influence of temperance crusading.

The surface spectacle of urban working-class life seemed a friendless environment of dirt, noise, and disease, an inferno of blighted homes, blasted characters, and banished hopes. Here it is countered that such impressions ignore the intricate social organization and instruments of pleasure and improvement. Ruskin was one who was usually misled in this but at least he acknowledged fortitude and toughness in the urban working classes. In a postscript to the fiftieth letter of his *Fors Clavigera* series, 27 January 1875, he wrote:

The two most frightful things I have ever seen in my life are the south-eastern suburb of Bradford (six miles long), and the scene from Wakefield bridge, by the chapel; yet I cannot but more and more reverence the fierce courage and industry, the gloomy endurance, and the infinite mechanical ingenuity of the great centres, as one reverences the fervid labours of a wasps' nest, though the end of all is only a noxious lump of clay.

VI

To style the march of manufacture a 'romance' affronted Ruskin; but Joseph Cowen, the Newcastle MP whose dialect speech made him unintelligible to Disraeli, was certain that there was 'a mighty poem of moving human interest in those bellowing blast-furnaces and grimy workshops'. He reminded the 'minister of civilization', Ruskin, that he 'preached from the railway-car and the telegraph'; and that 'towns of which Middlesbrough is a type are the indices of our advance: they record the rise of a nation'. Political overtones were evident in this assertion. Those with economic power claimed political freedoms. Among the intelligentsia reservations appeared. In equity the claims of these people should be admitted, but must they concede cultural leadership too? In the 1860s several Oxbridge dons combined with provincial manufacturers to press for the abolition of university tests against Dissenters. One, James Bryce, expressed demure discomfort: 'people sick of a southern squirearchy admire far off these Lancashire politicians; near at hand the roughness and the dirt are seen.'

City politicians gained a reputation as subversives of the aristocratic order and agricultural interest during the Anti-Corn Law League's agitation of the 1840s. They invested political and economic assertion with moral principle, caught in Carlyle's description of Cobden as 'an inspired bagman preaching a calico millennium'. Subsequent agitations maintained this tone – administrative and financial reform movements, radical land campaigns, the causes of education, parliamentary and church reform, and local government. 'There is no disorder, no confiscation, no revolution in all this,' John Morley wrote in the *Fortnightly Review*, January 1876, 'it is the line of passage from sentimental Radicalism to scientific Liberalism.' The urban reformers' demand was reasonable in both senses of that word: it appealed to the intellect and it was not excessive.

Peel had noticed this modesty and caution in Cobden's and Bright's sentiments, in spite of class rhetoric about aristocratic parasites and plunderers. Most urban men, big and small, new and established, were not beyond accommodation. The superstition of royalty and aristocracy, semi-feudal snobbery, and county society was positively attractive; and the prospect of stirring an upheaval of those below was positively repulsive. They boasted of upstart achievement while valuing the ascriptions of heredity. In this sense they were living testimony to the resilience of pre-urban and pre-industrial cultural and political traditions. Especially, most urban leaders were captivated by the myth of the balanced constitution, modified by succeeding generations of astute Englishmen to reflect current social and economic forces. Their object was to renew social and political equilibrium by implanting in it the dynamic properties which they associated with the management of urban industry and commerce. To reward urban enterprise by social prestige and political authority would maintain and perpetuate cohesion; to ignore it would destroy the entire system by defying the 'incorporationist' philosophy which allegedly was its informing spirit. The meliorist or progressive programme of urban radicals thus aimed to raise standards, not to release the unrestrained. John Bright was disgusted by aristocratic scurrility about the working classes but sensible that reservations were required. During the Reform Bill debates of 1867 Bright observed:

At this moment, in all or nearly all boroughs, as many of us know, sometimes to our sorrow, there is a small class which it would be much better for themselves if they were not enfranchised, because they have no independence whatever, and it would be much better for the constituency also that they should be excluded, and there is no class so much interested in having that small class excluded as the intelligent and honest working man. I call this class the residuum, which there is in almost every constituency, of almost hopeless poverty and dependence.

The residuum were ruinous to themselves and society, the pawns of publicans and, therefore, of unthinking Toryism. A liberal tendency in the rest of the working class was admitted, but hedged. At a meeting convened by the London Trades Council, 25 March 1868, Frederic Harrison recommended that their function 'is not to rule but to supply the motive to rule'. It was a matter of determining the best rulers and invigilating their work. Implicitly the enlightened were not working class. William Morris in 1883 cynically summarized the 'middle-class liberal ideal of reformed society':

There is to be a large class of industrious people not too much refined (or they could not do the rough work wanted of them) who are to live in comfort (not, however, meaning our middle-class comfort), and receive a kind of education (if they can) and not be overworked; that is, not overworked for a working man; his light day's work would be rather heavy for the refined classes. This class is to be the basis of society, and its existence will leave the consciences of the refined class quite free and at rest. From this refined class will come the directors or captains of labour (in other words the usurers), the directors of people's consciences religious and literary (clergy, philosophers, newspaper-writers) and lastly, if that be thought of at all, the directors of art; these two classes . . . will live together with the greatest goodwill; the upper helping the lower without sense of condescension on one side or humiliation on the other; the lower are to be perfectly content with their position, and there is to be no grain of antagonism between the classes: although (even Utopianism of this kind being unable to shake off the idea of the necessity of competition between individuals) the lower class, blessed and respected as it is, will have moreover the additional blessing of hope held out to it; the hope of each man rising into the upper class, and leaving the chrysalis of labour behind him; nor, if that matters, is the lower class to lack due political or parliamentary power; all men (or nearly all) being equal before the ballot-box, except so far as they may be bought like other things. . . . All the world turned bourgeois big and little, peace under the rule of competitive commerce, ease of mind and a good conscience to all and several under the rule of the devil take the hindmost.

The period between the Second and Third Reform Acts, 1867–84, was the heyday of middle-class political management in towns. The enfranchised working classes were outvoted anyway. Probably 80 per cent of voting power was possessed by their social superiors. But great importance was laid on the sentiment that the political system, though confined to men privileged to be property-owners, rested upon the consent of all classes. The most impressive organizations, therefore, were those caucuses boasting a large popular membership in good drill. Chamberlain claimed that three-quarters of 600 members of the Birmingham Liberal Association central committee in the mid-1870s were working men. Here was a plausible case for believing that politics could be purged of two ugly features – cliquish and self-elected wirepullers, and atomized and directionless mobs. Bad publicity was incurred after some MPs, like W. E. Forster at Bradford, refused to submit to examination by constituency committees. More thoughtful commentators were alarmed by the number prepared to undergo this ordeal.

Altogether the caucus movement promised more than it delivered. The transition from local to regional to national caucus organization was impeded by jealousy which the prominence of the Birmingham champion, Chamberlain, aggravated rather than allayed, as by his uninvited contest of Sheffield in 1874. Then the redistribution of seats in 1885, while it increased the sum of urban constituencies, arguably reduced the reputation of city members in national affairs. The MPs for Liverpool's nine separate constituencies after 1885 were thought of less consequence than their three predecessors who represented the undivided city before 1885. Constituency independence and parochialism thus fractured many a city caucus: the sense of total urban community was lost. Counterfeit organizations, however, had been exposed before then. Michael Barker, in his *Gladstone and Radicalism* (1975), identifies 'the stern economic realities of local politics' which everywhere undermined democratic sovereignty:

The democratic façade of the Liberal 'hundreds' was preserved intact, but in most cases the supremacy of the ordinary and uninfluential member was short-lived. The powerful and democratic Leeds association, which had been a founder member of the National Liberal Federation, demonstrated how rapidly the original ideal could be eroded. By 1883 the Leeds Liberals were obliged to rely upon the generosity of about twenty subscribers, even for the routine work undertaken between elections.

Most nominally popular organizations quickly returned to the self-appointed world of conclaves and conspiracies, exclusivity and intrigue, specialized pulse-taking and manipulation, whence they came. Others had never left it. In any case voters responded to influences other than formal party organization. Occupational and social connections involved manifold persuasions and pressures to conform to a particular political faith. George Brodrick, in articles in the *Fortnightly Review*, May 1878 and April 1879, observed, 'It is not perfection of organization in the mechanical sense, but rather the capacity of dispensing with organization in that sense, which is the most striking characteristic of narrow and selfish Toryism chiefly founded on anti-democratic jealousy of the working-classes.' This spirit animated 'the great body of clerks in public offices and private counting-houses, as well as that still more genteel *bourgeoisie* which resides in suburban villas' and 'the self-made men in our great cities of manufacture and commerce . . . clinging to the skirts of our landed aristocracy'.

Working men were not immune to the enticements of paternalism or to the exploitation of their fears and frustrations. Sectarian conflict characterized Liverpool, where Irish Catholic immigrants aroused a popular Protestant reaction. The Sunday School movement in the north was exceptionally strong. Stockport boasted the world's largest and, with a corresponding strength of denominational day-schools, dispensed with the need for a School Board. Localism was equally tenacious in work communities bounded by common dialects, as Patrick Joyce demonstrates from styles of Liberal and Tory mills in Lancashire. Politics were superficially rationalized and democratized with paid agents, printed propaganda, and organization to enrol and stimulate supporters; but decision-making and leadership over a wide range of subjects were vested in a handful of influential constituents or outsiders, who relied upon their native *nous* to pilot them over the course, here summoning talismen and heroes, there suppressing goblins and demons.

Democracy was dumbfounded, but not dispatched altogether. The editor of *The Observer*, J. L. Garvin, offered Lloyd George a prediction: 'The nineteenth century was the transfer of the vote. The twentieth century will be the transfer of profit.' Reviewing the political system in 1908, A. L. Lowell noted that parties did not cleave horizontally on class lines, between rich and poor, quarrelling over the division of property; but he identified 'the bidding for support of whole classes of voters by legislation for their benefit' as 'probably the most serious menace to which British institutions are exposed'. He observed, in contrast with early Victorian times, that 'political interest in England at the present day seems to be greater in the distribution than in the production of wealth, and this is in spite of the many business men in the House of Commons'. Cumulatively, franchise extensions made the masses felt. The ratio of adult males able to vote grew from 1 in 6 to 1 in 3 after the Second Reform Act (1867). It rose to 2 in 3 with the Third Reform Act (1884); but a significant number, perhaps 4½ million by 1910, remained disfranchised. Liberals championed further reform largely in respect of plural votes, the abolition of which, they presumed, would benefit their side. Neither Liberals nor Conservatives eagerly contemplated another leap in the dark to enfranchise the entire adult population.

To realize a more equable distribution of wealth, at the same time replenishing the power to produce wealth, was the priority for late Victorian and Edwardian progressives. The infirmity of Britain's imperial and trading positions was acknowledged. Milner, an architect of the Boer War, was convinced that 'Patriotism, like all the ideals of life can be choked, must be choked in the squalor and degradation of the slums of our great cities.' For him 'the attempt to raise the well-being and efficiency of the more backward of our people . . . is not philanthropy: it is business.' Actuarially, however, the arithmetic of social service provision, higher wages and reduced working hours across the board, constituted a political nightmare.

Some industries, usually those with low labour costs in proportion to invested capital, experimented in each of these directions. The TUC's case for an eight-hour day received a fillip in 1895 from the report of its successful introduction by Mather & Platt in engineering and Brunner, Mond & Co. in chemicals. Big companies too, like Elliott's copper and brass works at Selly Oak, Birmingham, provided medical and welfare services by the Edwardian period. The advice which E. E. Williams proffered in *Made In Germany* (1896), was being heeded, that, *ceteris paribus*, 'well paid workers . . . are the best workers, and a raising of wages or a shortening of hours is often a profitable investment. It is poor policy on the part of the masters to risk or throw away trade for the sake of a few pence.' However, in industries like coal mining, where wages amounted to between 50 and 70 per cent of the costs of production, employers made few concessions. Nor were all classes of miner convinced that a statutory eight-hour day, for instance, would be to their advantage, since this would necessitate a new shift system and curbs on customary absenteeism and rest periods. Regarding social security, the workers' self-financed systems, through Friendly Societies, were generally preferred by employers to company provision or government schemes, which might place financial demands upon industry that operated inequitably between trades. Profit-sharing and co-partnership arrangements had advocates too, particularly those concerned to inhibit trade-union growth. By 1912 133 schemes (embracing 106,000 workers) survived, being the residue from 296 schemes counted by the Board of Trade in 1894.

Quacks flock to the bedside of invalids. Eugenicists prescribed the severest medicine for an ailing nation: that the feeble be sterilized so as not to breed more congenital defectives, when the reproduction rate of the healthy and intelligent was becoming more modest. In contrast, the Webbs contemplated a Brains Trust of officials, trained to diagnose and administer a national minimum of civilized life. This meant, Beatrice Webb explained in *Our Partnership* (1948), 'sufficient nourishment and training when young, a living wage when able-bodied, treatment when sick, and a modest but secure livelihood when disabled or aged'. Then again, manpower for industry and war might be gingered by physical drill, the inculcation of yeoman codes and respect for authority. The National Service League, by advocating military conscription, outraged the liberalism of an island traditionally defended by its navy. This rendered the League politically hopeless, despite waverers in both Conservative and Liberal parties; in any case the trade unions were remorselessly against it. There were still alternatives. Delinquent youth might be discouraged from hooliganism and loafing, taught to inflate the chest and quick march, by joining uniformed and paramilitary organizations, the scouts, boys' brigades, and cadet corps. The cost of membership, however, tended to place these bands beyond the means of families of the unskilled: it might be reckoned also, *a priori*, that outlaws resist assimilation. We should not overvalue the nostrums of the compulsive improvers. Correspondingly we should not underestimate the socializing accomplished unsensationally day by day in schools. This could bear acceleration and expansion through the provision of school meals and medical treatment; but the schools' achievement in raising bodily and mental standards was acknowledged by an Inter-Departmental Committee in 1904. Allegations about persistent physical deterioration were unsound.

The *coup de grâce* to the launching of a new party of National Efficiency was administered by Joseph Chamberlain's preaching of Protection, his recipe of Imperialism and Social Reform, which quickened the New Liberal impulse among free-traders. Many were sceptical anyhow about the ability of the political system to accommodate a new party, for another existed already – Labour. This offered refreshment of a scope unrivalled by the various specialized staffs of Irish Nationalists, Liberal Unionists, Liberal Imperialists, or Unionist Free Fooders.

VII

Without the industrial towns there would have been no Labour party. In certain circumstances peasant communities experience revolutionary upheavals, of the *Jacquerie* kind, but not sustained social democratic organization. It has been argued in the foregoing section that the expectation that city interests would progressively command parlimentary affairs was facile. The internecine complexion of those interests, and the strength of established traditions, did much to neutralize their force. The weight of the great provincial cities and manufacturing towns in national affairs never matched their aggregate contribution to the country's economic wealth because they exhibited no common or consistent philosophical and political direction. Nevertheless, as midwife to the Labour party, urban England was instrumental in introducing a significant quantity to national political life.

The approximate origins of the Labour party lay in the class relations of the manufacturing towns and in the economic system which engendered them. A passage from Helen Corke's autobiography, *In Our Infancy* (1975), captures the mood. A woman uninterested in politics, who had lived entirely in rural or suburban Kent and Surrey, Helen Corke was well placed to mark the difference when she visited the mining and manufacturing Midlands in 1911. Introduced to members of the Nottingham Labour party, she understood how

poverty is not a vague, inescapable condition, but has a well-defined cause – the greed of capitalists and their exploitation of the labouring classes. The

Southerner still tends to see it as the state into which it has pleased God to call the majority, or as the outcome of individual misfortune or mismanagement. This has hitherto been my impression. But these Midlanders regard the capitalist as the common enemy, against whom the poor actively or passively unite.

It is a moot question how far the spatial organization of residence accelerated that process of class formation in towns which was begun in the industrial sphere. The portentous consequences of locked-up territorial quarters of rich and poor were considered in Manchester by W. Cooke Taylor's *Notes of a Tour in the Manufacturing Districts of Lancashire* (1842). Many Victorians accepted Taylor's premise that residential segregation first rationalized class separation, then raised class consciousness. Some caution is necessary before subscribing to this conclusion. Certainly the tendency was towards class and residential distinctiveness, but the chronology, pace, and intensity differed from place to place. Studies of particular urban neighbourhoods indicate rough, not sharp, definition by social class. Even the determined, like the Calthorpe estate at Edgbaston, which sought to prohibit industry and, with it, a working-class presence, suffered encroachments at the edges from lower-middle-class and artisan housing. The *reputation* of areas was known, exalted or unsavoury. Nevertheless, more areas were socially mixed than discrete. By taking clusters of streets rather than whole districts, this thesis of class separation holds up better. Streets notoriously had right sides and wrong sides to inhabit, their best ends and worst ends; yet it could be that class perceptions were heightened by intermixture and proximity as by segragation and distance.

No historian can be confident about the extent of class and community feeling. High levels of working-class residential mobility suggest that their communities were very unstable; on the other hand that mobility was most often short-distance and kinship and other ties countered the state of commotion. Use of the term 'community' involves real difficulties for the scholar. That word postulates common identity and reciprocity, a like-mindedness in pursuit of mutual benefits, with terms of incorporation that are available to some and closed to others. The moot questions are, how 'open' can a community be, how diverse the members' socio-economic status and social and political interests, without fatally weakening the coherence of the community? The answer may be that there coexist within broad communities many specialist communities or sub-cultures: workplace communities, residential communities, ethnic communities, religious communities and so forth, which may be alternatives to each other or strengthen each other.

Two other considerations should be weighed. Class co-operation cannot be disregarded in a variety of Victorian activity, religious and secular. The Victorians also understood that members of social classes rub against each other as well as against members of other social classes. Thus the heterogeneity of the working classes was stumbled upon. Tribal or national fissures were observed in regard to the substratum of Irish labourers by Engels's *Condition of the Working Classes in England in 1844*; and Henry Mayhew, for the *Morning Chronicle*, identified a chasm between those in casual and regular employment, the unskilled and skilled, the rough and respectable. Artisans, he declared in 1849, were Chartist-inclined and 'almost to a man red-hot politicians'; but the uneducated and unskilled were 'as unpolitical as footmen'. The differences were deeper than that, pluralized by the range of occupation, place, personal and family connections, by the respective standing of workers towards factors of production, and by varieties in the unit of production. In the late nineteenth century analysts of class were juggling with a multitude of tortuous weights and subtle quantities, factory and non-factory proletarian, craft, clerical, and service sectors, each with separate as well as shared experiences.

The concept of an unrestricted, mass tug-of-war between Capital and Labour was, therefore, a cartoon, as *Punch* portrayed in its title-page for 1912. Nevertheless, this was a simplicity in which more and more people found credence. *The Times*, never slow to perceive cosmic significance in outwardly ordinary affairs, argued as early as 18 September 1880, apropos strikes in the textiles industry, that the issue was not a wages question but 'a struggle for mastery'. On 21 March 1890 *The Times* was at it again, marvelling at the Midlands miners' successful four-day strike: 'Twenty or even ten years ago it would have been out of the question for 300,000 workmen to combine so perfectly as to stop work at one given moment and to resume it at another.' *The Times* seemed on the right track this time. By 1912 the miners were so organized that a national stoppage was executed in support of a claim for a minimum wage. Both groups, miners and textile workers, were among the first by virtue of their constituency concentration to employ parliamentary lobbying in pursuit of improved working conditions. But it was the miners who had it in their power to halt economic activity nationwide and to wreak such damage by a prolonged stoppage that government could not stand aside. Railwaymen and dockers began dimly to perceive their own latent power in the years before 1914. As industrial disputes forced political intercession, there was indeed substance in *The Times*'s fears.

The key was trade unionism. The Board of Trade's statistics of the embattled industrial world recorded that in 1890 62 per cent of strikes could be called wages disputes, in 1891 54 per cent. The rest it depicted as quarrels over working practices and conditions. Most ominous were those called in pursuit of union recognition or from sympathetic action by one trade in support of another, which portended a decline of narrow sectionalism. Trade-union membership was perhaps half a million in the 1860s. It may have doubled between 1872 and 1874, then retreated to about 600,000 by the late 1870s. From about 750,000 at the end of 1888 it grew to over 2 million in 1900. Spurts of growth occurred in different years, and setbacks too, according to economic climate, employer counter-aggression, and legal inhibition; but a membership of over 2½ million was reached in 1910 and over 4 million in 1913.

A perspective is required for these figures. This is supplied by H. A. Clegg, A. Fox, and A. F. Thompson in *A History of British Trade Unions since 1889*, volume 1, *1889–1910* (1964). Excluding domestic servants, the armed forces, the professions, and farmers and their families, the proportion of workers organized in trade unions was about 6 per cent in 1888, 15 per cent in 1901, 17 per cent in 1910, and over 20 per cent in 1913. Further refinement can exclude women – about 38 per cent of women, aged 15 to 70, were occupied outside their homes – youths and non-manual workers, upon whom trade unionism exercised a slender hold. This presents a degree of organization above 10 per cent in 1888, 25 per cent in 1901, 30 per cent in 1910, and about 35 per cent in 1913. We should contemplate too the density of unionization in particular trades, because of the strategic importance some occupied, as barometers of feeling in the labour world and for their effects on market activity and politics. In mining, metals, engineering, shipbuilding, sections of the textiles, printing and building trades, and latterly in government service and on the railways, trade-union recruitment was impressive. Regional concentration mattered too. This had advantages for solidarity (probably over half the members were in the north); also negative features.

Several trade unions (typically the miners) were loose federations, whose common policies and action were retarded by regional differences and competition.

Among casual and general workers trade unionism established few footholds. In *Stevedores and Dockers* (1969) John Lovell described the chronic insecurity of London port-workers, among whom 'the influence of unionism . . . was absolutely minimal'. The unions failed in the critical question of control over hiring arrangements and exertion of union preference. It was the same in other ports. Eventually the larger employers appreciated that their interests might lie in decasualization of the workforce, to secure efficient and regular services; but this negotiation placed the feeble authority of the unions in jeopardy as men apprehensive about redundancy accused the union executives of doing the bosses' job for them. The dockers' plight was not untypical of the general labourer whose unions remained inferior to the craft unions. It was not just a matter of numbers, although recruitment to the established unions outpaced that to 'new' general unions in the period after 1889. The general unions suffered from fundamental handicaps. Workers at any trade gained some premium from accumulated experience; still, general workers were more easily displaced. The interests of different types of labour within these general unions were less reconcilable. There was less acceptance of new technology, also less to bind men to union authority, since none could afford sizeable levies for benefit purposes. Finally, it should be remarked that craft unions were less prone to strike action, not because they were intrinsically less militant but because they might obtain objectives by means short of strike action.

Clegg, Fox, and Thompson argue that the 'development of collective bargaining was the outstanding feature' of the period 1889 to 1910; but reservations follow. A report for the Board of Trade, by D. F. Schloss, in 1910 reckoned that collective agreements covered some 2,400,000 workers, or less than one-quarter of the total workforce. Most workers, therefore, remained outside these formal arrangements; and, where collective bargaining was instituted, it did not guarantee industrial peace. Probably more disruption would have occurred without these procedures. Nevertheless, union negotiators were stretched to preserve craft rules as new technology and working arrangements were regularly introduced; and everywhere the rank-and-file demanded that unions maintain work and wage levels in bad years. The years before 1914 brought considerable unrest. Real wages had declined. This fall was not universal, just as the previous trend of rising real wages had not benefited every class of worker equally; and the judgement of how conscious workers were of these trends is ticklish. Probably it is right to observe that threatened or actual money-wage reductions produced instantaneous reactions from established trade unions, as in 1892–3 and 1908, whereas falling real wages from rising prices acted like a slow-burning fuse. This explosion could be devastating on occasion, as in 1911–14, during relatively full employment, when both organized and unorganized workers joined in strikes. Relatively full employment had occasioned strikes before, in 1889–91 and 1896–1901.

Stoppages were generally fewer in times of bad trade, though well-organized workers might moderate the scale of wage reductions. Our means of measuring unemployment are imprecise, being derived from trade-union returns; but, though these figures may mislead as to the true rate of unemployment, they are probably an accurate index of fluctuations in employment. Below 4 per cent unemployment can be counted a good year, above 7 per cent bad. In the 1860s the proportion of unemployed trade unionists exceeded 4 per cent in six years and 7 per cent in three years; in the 1870s three years and two respectively; in the 1880s six years and four, in the 1890s four and one. The years 1900–10, inclusive, saw unemployment exceed 4 per cent in six years and 7 per cent in two. These two years, 1908 and 1909, recorded an unemployment level higher than at any time since 1884–6; but the period 1911–14 was markedly easier, recalling the best years of the previous century. These are aggregate sums from 'all unions making returns'. Certain sectors, like the engineering, metal, and shipbuilding unions, displayed consistently higher rates of unemployment throughout the period. Underemployment is altogether more elusive. Dockers notoriously suffered from this. Three days a week was their average employment, which means little when neither docker nor dock work was average. Most outdoor employments pared work during bad weather; and seasonal factors upset numerous trades, like the hatting industry of Luton and Stockport.

The philosophy of trade unions broadly changed. Abstract ethics, like 'the right to work' and 'a fair wage', always jarred with classical economy, as did restrictive practices; but trade unionists in the 1860s and 1870s generally shared current assumptions that wages should dip during declining markets. Harmonious industrial relations were wanted so that all could prosper from a capitalist system to which all were wedded. In several industries sliding-scales of wages were tied to prices and profits, and codes of conciliation and arbitration followed these lines. According to Helen Lynd in *England in the Eighteen-Eighties* (1945), that decade brought changes in labour's attitude which afterwards were fulfilled in new organizations and parties. Previously, 'workers viewed their interests as a special problem within the going system, not as facts challenging that system. They were not class conscious.'

Mrs Lynd was over-emphatic but not without cause. There was little class-consciousness if by that is meant consciousness by a large proportion of the working classes of common interest, mutual dependence, and a preparedness both to make the interests and privileges of the middle and upper classes the focus of a struggle and to impose their authority on workers who failed to appreciate their purpose or who connived in the existing system. No single-mindedness existed. At the most basic level collective pressure was missing. To wield continuous political influence (if physical revolution is discounted) voting strength is required; yet, though the trade-union junta took some credit for the Reform Act in 1867, there was no marked demonstrativeness by working-class people and parties to press governments to introduce full adult suffrage. At best it betokens diffidence; at worst an élite satisfaction and a political uninterest beyond sectional trade-union concerns.

Politically active workers interpreted affairs in conventional party terms, mostly Conservative versus Liberal (or Labour) rather than Conservative–Liberal versus Labour or class versus class. Patriotic, national, and religious appeals, overriding class interests, did not go unheeded; and in Edwardian times the paramount question of free trade versus tariffs induced workers to respond to the narrow circumstances of their trades as much as to general class interest. If this division is apparent among politically minded workers, what of the rest, downtrodden or satisfied by the rate of progress? Yet it would be perverse to conclude that a pigeon-hole sameness obtained, all eternally trapped in sealed-off boxes. The rise of the Labour party cannot be passed over, despite its abiding modesty and initial reliance on electoral compacts with Liberals. Orthodox party supporters began to reconsider allegiances. Even the apolitical stirred in Edwardian times, reported Stephen Reynolds from one remote corner, a Devon fishing village. Its folk grumbled about grandmotherly legislation, meaning restrictions on children's employment without compenstaion, and compulsory health and insurance contributions. Here was an ambiguous distemper. It was partly a lumpish, conservative reaction, disturbed by bureaucratic prying and interference with customary ways. This was evident up and down the country: Lady Bell reported of Middlesbrough working people, 'Many among them have a quite insurmountable aversion towards embarking upon anything which would necessitate coming in contact with officials, filling up forms. . . .' There was also a sullen egalitarianism – a feeling that if state services and ordinances had to be extended, these should be financed principally, even wholly, by the better-off.

Industrially there was some closing of ranks too. The growth of trades councils augured city-wide and regional co-operation; the growth of centralized trade-union executives and the TUC portended nation-wide operations. The sympathetic strike was not common, unless sectional interests momentarily coincided. The craft unions' refusal to abdicate their élite status in the hierarchy of trades remained. But unorganized workers were encouraged to form trade unions; and experiments in municipal employment elicited enthusiasm. Calls for an extension of municipalization, and for the nationalization of mines and railways, became trade-union piety. Broadly, labour demonstrated increasing disinclination to abide by the precepts of classical economics. Trade-union resistance to wage-cuts during periods of slump was seen by employers as an attack on profits, which impeded investment and future growth in productivity (by which alone wage increases could be financed). Mischief followed equally from labour's indirect resistance, called 'ca' canny', that refusal to co-operate, systematic go-slow and shoddy work. This unwillingness to play according to the rules provoked an employer counter-offensive, since there were limits to which inflated costs through wage claims and inefficient working could be passed off into rising prices. This employers' reaction, perhaps, was the crucible from which a simulacrum of working-class consciousness emerged. It supplied definition in place of shapelessness, a target in place of aimlessness.

Change there was then, but always the historian is arrested by the abiding strength of forces conspiring to moderate the pace of change. It is different for the philosopher in prophetic, not analytic, mood. 'We live in a world of novelties', wrote J. S. Mill in 1867, drawing the conclusion that 'the despotism of custom is on the wane'. The wells of tradition were not drained that rapidly. In some cases they were replenished.

Consider the opportunities for, and attitudes to, female employment. Domestic service, textiles, and dressmaking occupied most working women in the nineteenth century; but the proportion of women in the total workforce (around 30 per cent in the late nineteenth century) was not greater than in pre-industrial times. Textiles and domestic service had expanded; later, nursing, typing, teaching, shop assistance, post-office work, some consumer industries which were factory-based, like confectionery, jams, cigarettes, footwear, even light engineering, like cycle manufacture – all provided 'new' opportunities of female employment. But for as many prospects as industrialization and urbanization opened, others were closed. Women's work in agriculture diminished and the decline of cottage by-employments was drastic. Less work – other than purely domestic tasks – was now done in homes than ever before. Women in paid employment were chiefly young and single. By 1911 about 90 per cent of married women were housewives and mothers only.

We can draw several inferences. It indicates something about the labour market: rising male wages allowed their families to dispense with secondary contributions. It also suggests something about social attitudes: the ideal was 'separate spheres' for male and female. Custom, both general and local, prescribed a great deal of women's work. Domestic service was acceptable because it trained women in wifely duties. Factory work was suspect – initially, at least – because the woman's supervision of home and family must deteriorate. The improvement in infant care registered in Lancashire during the cotton famine, when unemployment forced working wives back into the home, did not pass unnoticed. Occupation, region, and birth-rates were correlated. Low birth-rates characterized the textile districts; high birth-rates the agricultural and mining areas. There the men's earning capacity was maximized early in adulthood; they tended to marry young; and fewer opportunities of women's work were available.

The most striking feature of the labour history which focuses on ordinary women in the fifty years before 1914 is how marginally their lot improved and how reluctantly attitudes changed. The suffrage question scarcely touched them; and family limitation had barely begun its emancipating course. From 1877 the crude average annual birth-rate plunged from 36 per 1,000 population to below 24 per

1,000 by 1914; but, when occupational and class differences in fertility were so marked, the overall impact is difficult to read. The skilled
working class was starting to share with the middle classes some
benefits from family reduction; but labourers both in town and
country still saddled themselves with too numerous dependants, and
condemned their wives to some ten to fifteen years of continuous pregnancy or nursing. Widowed or abandoned women constituted the
most helpless paupers; but wives were often victims of the working
man's self-indulgent spending. It was commonplace for a wife to be
ignorant of her husband's wages, and to 'go without' so that the man
might maintain his physical power. Women in work suffered a
second-class status too. Factory codes of protection, which by 1914
included the sweated trades, reflected the traditionally defenceless
state of working women. Under 10 per cent were incorporated into
trade unions. Most of these were in unions which maintained customary views about unequal pay and the proper taks for men and
women. Hence when historians allude to a growing labour consciousness in the late nineteenth century they implicitly exclude about half
the members, the subdued undermass of women. Only part of the
impulse towards different attitudes might be assigned to abstract intellectual conversion, a release from prejudice. More men were compelled to review the position by force of circumstances. New technology and, with it, new methods of using labour, gradually eroded
traditional lines of demarcation between men's and women's work, as
between skilled and unskilled. Thus trade unionists were induced to
modify their conventional outlook on sex discrimination and
exclusion.

Here was one trend in the labour market which deserves notice. The
wage differential between skilled and unskilled showed signs of contraction; and the number of intermediate wage levels was growing
owing to expanding opportunities for the semi-skilled. Universal education, wider trade-union organization, and minimum-wage tribunals
were upsetting traditional distinctions. It would be facile to suppose
homogeneity inexorably followed. E. H. Hunt emphasizes that 'wage
differentials at any one time were as great as the overall improvement
in wages between 1850 and 1914', although the proportion of the
national average wage by which the maximum regional wage surpassed the minimum, 44 per cent in 1867–70, was down to 28 per cent
in 1907. The mensuration of class distinctions, a fashionable science,
marked signal differences in height and weight *within* the urban

working classes, between children of skilled and casual workers as well as between them and the comfortable classes. A working-class hierarchy was very real still, and convention exercised an influence on pay relativities which was practically independent of market conditions. Regional wage variations for the same job in different places were officially acknowledged by most trade unions; and assaults on the differentials of craft and unskilled work excited antagonisms more than they promoted fraternity.

It can be suggested, cautiously, that the late Victorian and Edwardian years saw the maturing of the working classes of the first industrial revolution. As E. H. Phelps Brown argued, by 1900 'the application of steam to power and transport, and of steel to equipment, had been largely worked through. New techniques, in electricity, chemicals, the man-made fibres, and the internal combustion engine . . . were being developed, but . . . their impact would not be massive until after the First World War.' The rate of increasing productivity slackened and the mood of industrial relations was soured. Though more employers accepted collective bargaining as a regular part of industrial management, negotiations were made more difficult against a background of well-publicized assaults on trade unionism by judges and employers' federations. The lock-out and defeat of the proud engineers' union, July 1897–January 1898, and the fine imposed on railwaymen in the Taff Vale dispute, 1901, bred bitter reproachfulness. Again, though both sides of industry and, when called upon, arbitrators too, broadly subscribed to notions of equity and convention in determining wage relativities between different classes of labour, there was inflammable conflict at the margins. Unions were accused of holding a surly, antediluvian attitude, of wanting to maintain inefficient practices, of seeking to ossify the settled structure of trades, in the face of employers who were espousing a new science of management, involving time-study, complex piece-rates and continuous reallocation of jobs. According to management, men would be compensated for the regrading and subdivision of tasks. Productivity and earnings would rise by job individuation and selective bonuses. According to the unions, management aimed to dilute skill, break corporate solidarity, thrust greater pressure and responsibility on the worker, and force some unemployment.

At the same time perceptions of social-class distance became more acute, between those who owned things and gave orders and those who supplied and obeyed. Though the family firm remained the typical business organization, employers were less personally evident in the workplace. Boards of directors delegated to middle management and foremen who, being employees themselves, were under compulsion to get results, if need be by driving the workforce and by overriding customs. And how did employers enjoy their positions? In swagger and ostentation, in expensive sport and travel, in emulation of the aristocracy, according to the popular press or in the view of all who noticed the proliferation of motor cars, yachts, golf courses, and private schools.

Political education was growing. Working people accepted the concept of unequal pay and status to reward superior skill, special risk, and manifest ingenuity; but they had a developing sense of injustice about profit and position divorced from meritorious function and capacity. Knowledge about wealth distribution was disseminated by Fabian pamphleteers and others – that wage-earners comprised about 80 per cent of the occupied population and received about 35 per cent of national income. Always the working classes knew a great deal about the circumstances of middle- and upper-class life through contact in domestic service. Now their accredited representatives in the Labour party, not to mention a quantity of New Liberals and Protectionist Tories, were ready both to question the fairness of the distributive system and to suggest means to alter it.

It was in the established industrial regions that support for the Labour party was accumulating. Recent tendencies of urban morphology abetted this. Migrations from agricultural districts had tailed off. Relative stability ensued in the older industrial towns of the north as growth was transferred to service occupations and to new light industrial centres, chiefly in the south Midlands and Home Counties. Halifax reached its maximum population in 1901, Blackburn, Bolton, Bradford, Burnley, Bury, and Oldham in 1911. Others, like Carlisle, Dewsbury, Preston, Rochdale, Salford, Stockport, Wakefield, and Wigan were approaching their peak. A network of class loyalties had arisen in the older manufacturing, commercial, and mining communities; and a taste for social change and more justly distributed wealth was developed. By framing policies to register these concerns the Labour party gradually enlisted many urban working-class communities on its side.

It might appear from this that relatively settled, even stagnant or recessionary, industrial conditions conduce to labour class-consciousness more than do circumstances of rapid industrial change and urban growth. The position is complex. It can be argued, as it is *a priori* by Marxists, that class-consciousness will grow in proportion as once discrete parts of the capitalist economy interlock and interact, as each industry and each town loses more of its independence within the regional, national, or international systems which both connect them and force them into conflict. We have seen, however, that towns contained significant structures of social cohesion other than economic class. The very multiplicity of urban systems and varieties of internal urban organization ultimately safeguarded capitalism by scattering rather than exposing it as a target. Moreover, we should remember that the urban–industrial influence was not unambiguously paramount in the nation. There was strength still in rural–landed and intermediate quarters. Hence government apparatus, in individual towns and in the state, was far from being a mirror of bourgeois-capitalist power.

4 New growths

A prevailing feeling among late Victorian and Edwardian social theorists was summarized by Richard Remington, protagonist of H. G. Wells's *The New Machiavelli* (1911): 'Muddle is the enemy.' Muddle was another way of saying laissez-faire individualism. This meant 'a crowd of separated, undisciplined little people all obstinately and ignorantly doing things jarringly, each one in his own way'. Muddle by 1900 seemed ubiquitous and quintessentially English. Abroad, muddle was embodied in the Boer War; at home there was the 'muddle that gives us the visibly sprawling disorder of our cities and industrial country-side, muddle that gives us the waste of life, the limitations, wretchedness and unemployment of the poor'.

Kipling, too, apostrophized muddle in *The 'Eathen*:

> All along o' dirtiness, all along o' mess,
> All along o' doin' things rather-more-or-less.

Kipling's raw recruit was shaken out of sloppiness by the crack of the NCO, 'the backbone of the Army'. Wells looked to a civic idealism and social service to combat his muddle. These ethics were not new, though their secularization and harnessing to science were relatively recent. A profounder knowledge of medicine, technology, and social organization encouraged the thought that society might be re-ordered and the obstructions to collective happiness removed. Wells's Remington directed some of his ambition towards the Local Government Board: 'I had great ideas about town-planning, about revisions of municipal areas and reorganized internal transit.' The professoriate in this new school of Human Ecology was confident and benign. No nightmares anticipated Stalinist planning in this urgent desire to banish 'infinite higgledy-piggledy discomfort and ugliness' from Britain's towns and cities. The transition from muddle to order would come serenely, by consent and co-operative endeavour, for the masses would be guided by comprehensive, unselfish minds which would systematize all social services, having once established 'the reciprocal relationship between facilities of locomotion and community size'. Opulent optimism suffused these projections. Respect for private ownership of property alone was a formidable obstacle, although the subsequent failures of Soviet town planning illustrate that, even in a society which is ostensibly stripped of private property rights, the task of co-ordinating the multitudinous diversity which makes up a living city is close to insuperable. Wells's futurology, however, was chiefly inspired by carping frustration that the ameliorative instruments lay to hand and hitherto had not been taken up or had been adopted crudely, partially, and ignorantly. Individualism, in other words, had assumed the garb of collectivism to free itself of muddle, and in the process compounded chaos. This was the indictment directed against most new urban growths – that as solutions to urban problems they were impostures. The same capitalism which made congested cities now sought to relieve them; but the old spirit contaminated the new. Every outlet tried would be found wanting. The pent-up pressure in the machine was too high for safety valves to regulate.

Wells was jeering at Fabian Efficiency. There was a Morrisian component too. William Morris's idealism was as fashionable as his fabrics. In *How I Became a Socialist*, Morris described capitalism as a defilement: 'Apart from the desire to produce beautiful things, the leading passion of my life has been and is hatred of modern civilisation. . . . What shall I say concerning its mastery of and its waste of mechanical power, its commonwealth so poor, its enemies so rich, its stupendous organisation – for the misery of life!' Pleasure and pride in work were strangled by 'blind, competitive commerce'. In a letter to William Allingham, 14 April 1883, he nominated Victorian England the 'age of shoddy'. Reform was hopeless. Revolution was required. Only by transforming the economic and class system would they restore self-respect to the workman and genuineness to his work. The socialist future was envisaged as a federalization of communities. Government would emanate from discussion in provincial assemblies, then dwindle to leave voluntary association as a habit. All this begged a question: 'Come the revolution', as the Marquess of Salisbury used to say. This was brought no nearer by the Morrises, Hyndmans, and Champions selling their heavily subsidized newspapers on street corners, dressed in well-cut suits, frock coats, tall hats and gloves; by yearly pilgrimages to Highgate Cemetery after Marx's interment in 1883; by junketings at Kelmscott House, Hammersmith, on Boat Race day; or even by experiments in craftwork and community living like C. R. Ashbee's Guild of Handicraft at Chipping Campden (1902–8). Every political party has its innocents and tyrants, its self-advertising adventurers, its morbidly mistrustful, its silly and conceited, its pedants and humbugs, popular and unpopular. Socialist parties seemed to have more than most. They did not. Their heterogeneity was magnified by their minuteness.

Neither Morris, personally, nor his conception was ridiculous and futile. The trade slump of the 1880s stimulated disenchantment with orthodox liberal economics in trade-union circles; and not a few politicians, though averse to socialist prescriptions, contemplated departures from both free trade and laissez-faire. But there were flaws. The low wages, irregular and sweated conditions of labour which made for poverty, the ignorance and viciousness which made for brutal living, the overcrowded back-to-back housing, cellar dwellings, slum courts and all the squalid warrens of human habitation which made for insanitary cities, these were pre-industrial as well as industrial problems. The Industrial Revolution might bring cruel deprivation to certain workers and deepen environmental pollution; it also brought hope that conditions could be alleviated by economic growth. If there was certainty it was that population increase *without* industrialization meant distress, even disaster. Witness those rural counties of England in the early nineteenth century, with their low wages and underemployment; witness, too, miserable Ireland. Many circumstances which Victorian critics (and historians subsequently) indignantly charged to industrialization and urbanization had stemmed from mere population pressure.

Mechanized work in towns was relied upon, not to nullify human values but to generalize satisfactions above the bare necessities. Factory work was improvable, by regulation and inspection. The standard working week in mid-century was various but probably between 60 and 72 hours. Those in the vanguard to secure a reduction were cotton workers and engineers. By the early 1870s their claim to a working week of between 54 and 56½ hours was accepted. Subsequently, others received the same concession. Most of the organized industrial classes had done so by 1880. Government decreed limits to working hours by miners, railwaymen, and shop-workers in the late nineteenth and early twentieth centuries. Most urban public authorities established an eight-hour day norm at the same time. English workers generally, factory workers especially, enjoyed this advantage over their European counterparts. We may debate the exact measure of relief. Perhaps pressure at the factory increased from 'speed-up' now that the working day was shortened. But work was not so fatiguing that overtime, at higher wages, was avoided; and the expansion of leisure facilities is impressive. Late-nineteenth-century factories were brighter, safer, better ventilated than before; and they employed fewer children. No comparably thorough system of regulation and inspection could have been devised to cover domestic work. The extension of domestic work, as an alternative to factory work, portended only the multiplication of misery.

It is false, however, to label socialist intellectuals as 'anti-machine'. They appreciated the machine's labour-saving attributes and its productivity, which enabled the many to enjoy material comforts undreamt of by previous ages. The socialists' objection was summarized by Sidney Webb in 1891: machines had been utilized 'in the wrong way for the wrong ends'. Their contemporary machine culture represented 'the apotheosis, not of social service, but of successful financial speculation'. This demoralized both producers and consumers. Commercial considerations involved all in the ruin of taste, for the handicraft worker, striving to compete with the machine, had lowered his traditional standards and lessened his individuality. The socialists' indictment of the machine, therefore, was phrased carefully. Morrisian ideals seemed to exist in contradiction of the Industrial Revolution. Actually they flourished only because of it. Only because of the Industrial Revolution could men argue realistically about social responsibility, redistribution of wealth, equality of opportunity, and quality of life. Economic progress was assumed. Higher incomes, enlarged resources, were taken for granted by the majority who were not perversely insistent on an imminent immiseration. Thus the lively debates concerned the division of spoils; how rates of progress could be accelerated in relation to Germany and America; and how to eliminate the extravagant mistakes and preventible social distress that ensued from unregulated industrialization. These were arguments about controlling a force which had a demonstrable capacity to do both good and harm. Capitalism was a good servant but a bad master.

It was natural that new urban developments, resulting from expansive capitalism, should excite polemicists. The interrogatives were inevitable. Did this favour some social groups more than others; was this simply more 'eyeless vulgarity' doomed to end, in Morris's words, 'in a counting-house on the top of a cinder-heap'? These questions can be considered against the background of new urban growths in the late Victorian period: the resort and pleasure towns, suburban and satellite towns, and planned communities of both businessmen and utopians.

I

'I do like to be beside the seaside', John Glover-Kinde's song, was issued in 1909. No previous society gave so many people the chance to be beside the seaside. The most copied artist of mid-nineteenth-century England was W. P. Frith. He found drama in the commonplace of crowds. Appropriately, among his most popular paintings were *Ramsgate Sands or Life at the Seaside* (1853-4) and *The Railway Station* (1862). By 1911 55 per cent of English people were visiting the seaside on day excursions and 20 per cent were taking holidays which required accommodation. A rise in real incomes, social emulation, the parliamentary institutionalization (1871) of Easter, Whitsun, and August Bank Holidays, the negotiation of general vacations in industry, together with cheaper consumer services and travel, all contributed to the growth of a seasonal holiday trade. By 1911, following John Myerscough's reckoning, the holiday industry involved about 1.25 per cent of the occupied population and 1.5 per cent of consumer expenditure.

A typology of towns might classify resorts as parasites, towns not of production but of conspicuous consumption, places where people waste time and money. This generalization contains as many pitfalls as *Alice's Adventures in Wonderland* (1865): 'Alice had been to the seaside once in her life, and had come to the general conclusion, that wherever you go to on the English coast you find a number of bathing machines in the sea, some children digging in the sand with wooden spades, then a row of lodging houses, and behind them a railway station.' There were, indeed, such sparse resorts. They would now be called unspoilt. Molly Hughes visited Clacton-on-Sea in 1884: 'The look of the place appalled us when we walked out of the station. Bare!' Her memory was of a few village shops, lodging-houses practically on the shore, a tea room which served gargantuan farmers' fare, and half-made streets which quickly melted into the countryside. A circulating library completed the town's amenities. A pier, pavilion, and promenade were not constructed until the 1890s. Clacton still had fewer than 7,500 inhabitants in 1901; but, positioned seventy miles from London, it was a favourite resort of day excursionists and holiday-makers. Some came by the Great Eastern Railway, others by steamboat.

Transport permitted the expansion of coastal resorts and presented to each a problem of how to define and preserve its character. The Thanet resorts, Broadstairs, Ramsgate, and Margate, had a popularity before the railway reached them, owing to the cheap fares available on the hoys and, after 1815, on the Thames steam-packets. These were responsible for introducing the concessionary rates of travel, for daily, weekend, and period excursions, and for children and family parties, which are generally assumed to have been started by railway companies. They conveyed an annual average of 85,446 passengers to Margate throughout the 1830s, compared with 53,225 throughout the 1820s. In peak years, 1835–6 and 1842–3, they carried above 100,000.

Margate was the first resort to win a reputation for vulgarity, though not so long before it had had a Master of Ceremonies modelled upon Bath. Ruskin speculated that the vulgarization of Margate was why the painter J. M. W. Turner lived there, attracted and repelled as he was by this national characteristic. But, despite gibes that it was Cheapside or Wapping by the sea, Margate at that time was vulgar only in so far as it was unaristocratic, therefore unfashionable. The historian of pre-railway Margate, John Whyman, places most visitors in the shopkeeper–tradesman middle class. Later it perhaps deteriorated further. The town had to fight harder for clients with the coming of the railway, as other resorts became competitors. A pier was built in 1842, another added in 1856, and a pavilion in 1871. 'Lord' George Sanger's circus had a seasonal fixture there, until pushed out by a skating rink. Margate had 10,099 residents in 1851, 23,057 in 1901; and a middle-class air lingered in the eastern quarter, Cliftonville, where we can find in 1907 holiday-makers such as William Nicholson and William Orpen, two painters who, like Turner before, were amused by the tawdriness of the popular part of the resort.

The steamboat services which accelerated the growth of the Thanet resorts had had an impact in other areas. Steam-packets from Liverpool after the Napoleonic Wars awakened a response from places along the Lancashire, Cheshire, and North Wales coastline, as well as from the Isle of Man. There was a comparable stirring at Minehead, Lynton, and Ilfracombe from Bristol Channel steam-packets, and on the east coast at Cleethorpes from services along the Trent and Humber. Turnpikes and other road improvements, chiefly to move goods, had indirectly benefited several resorts, in Sussex particularly; but altogether the pre-railway coastal resorts are quickly described. Court connections had been influential. George III visited Weymouth in 1784, then almost every August and September from 1789 to 1805. Weymouth, however, remained chiefly a market town and port, for coastal trading and Channel Isles traffic. Among seaside resorts *tout court*, Worthing and Southend were briefly favoured by royal princesses, but Brighton indisputably led, distinguished by the Prince Regent's patronage from the 1780s. This was gay and lively where his father's association with Weymouth was domestic and discreet. Doctors also stimulated the seaside-holiday trend, none more than the Lewes doctor, Russell. His treatise on the tonic properties of sea-water exercised great influence, which he capitalized by establishing a practice in Brighton. Nevertheless, in the eighteenth century the seaside largely took second place to the spa. The north's only prestigious seaside resort, Scarborough, was also a spa. This, combined with picturesque gothic, ruined castle and ravines, was irresistible to its merchant, gentry, and aristocratic clientele. The spas' hydropathic appeal persisted. Dr A. B. Granville's map of 1841 showed seventy spas, but the 1830s depression had taken its toll of their prosperity. Those that were towns with a spa, rather than spas with attendant villages, were better placed to survive. They always offered pleasure and fashion as well as an elixir: witness the Bath of Beau Nash and the Woods. Still, this largest of eighteenth-century spas had attracted no more than 12,000 visitors annually, and J. A. R. Pimlott's verdict seems sensible:

As long as visits to the spas were confined to the leisured it is difficult to regard them as holidays – they were rather phases in the social routine like Ascot and Goodwood in the life of London Society to-day [1947] – but when they were made by City merchants and professional men as breaks in the routine of counting house and office they at last began to assume the character of holidays properly so-called.

In the nineteenth century railway links, and individual initiative, brought renewed spa development. Thus Tenbury Wells and Droitwich (Worcestershire) grew as offshoots of John Corbett's salt-extraction industry; and the Derbyshire spas, Matlock and Buxton, experienced some revival with the coming of the railway in 1863 and with the stimulation of the seventh Duke of Devonshire's purse. More novel altogether was the enlistment of municipal enterprise. An

Improvement Committee took over the failing pump rooms at Leamington in mid-century and Bath Corporation made extensive renovations in the late 1880s. The most vigorous municipal investment was at Harrogate, England's only rival by the late nineteenth century to Marienbad, Homburg, and Karlsbad as an aristocratic and upper-middle-class centre. By 1913 some 75,000 visitors a year trudged through the pump rooms; but the pulmonic, rheumatic, gouty, dyspeptic, and diabetic classes were not the most reliable bases for an urban economy. Though the practice of immersion persisted, that of drinking the waters diminished in reaction to adverse medical opinion. Hydropathy gave way to more general medical treatment at the spas.

An outbreak of typhoid destroyed the reputation of Malvern's hydropathic establishment in 1905. Already, however, Malvern had mimicked Cheltenham and become a school town: Malvern College was opened in 1865. Tunbridge Wells had done likewise; indeed, soon no spa or resort was complete without preparatory schools or private academies. Equally, the spa towns grew as select residential centres. Here were the embarrassed peers whose fortunes had stumbled too often short of the winning post; here were the old-fashioned urban gentry, younger sons with modest competences, well-connected bankers, solicitors, doctors, and clergy; and here were the spinsters and widows who practised elegant economy in reduced households, tremendously knowledgeable about 'county families', excessively huffy about 'vulgar trade', and hugely frightened by 'wicked cities'. Here too were the retired military and naval officers and imperial servants, who dyspeptically lived out their days in homes heaving with memories and plunder of far-off places, stuffed beasts, pelts and ivories, and assorted native pots, jewellery, and weapons.

The spas also developed as locations for fashionable sport – horse-racing, golf, and tennis – or as general tourist centres. Epsom established this pattern in the eighteenth century when the quackery of its water-cures was exposed. Now Harrogate invited inspection of the Yorkshire Dales, Fountains and Bolton Abbeys; Cheltenham promoted general tourism in the Cotswolds; Leamington exploited Shakespeare country. This last was provisional, until Stratford awoke to its fortune as the Bard's birthplace. The Stratford-upon-Avon Shakespeare Festival began modestly in 1879. By 1904 its devotees numbered 14,000. Late-developing spas, like tiny Llandrindod Wells, exhibited comparable features. The railway having reached

Llandrindod in 1866, visitors were drawn to the scenery as to the springs. Llandrindod became a conference centre for Welsh associations.

For recreation and bodily restoration the hydropathic spas lagged in popularity behind the inland tourist centres, and inland tourist centres ran second to seaside resorts. The aggregate population of forty-eight places classified as seaside resorts by the 1871 census was 522,444. They had grown 21.5 per cent in the previous decade. In 1901 their population surpassed 900,000, a further growth of around 75 per cent. By then another score of towns had been formally designated 'seaside resorts'. Altogether their resident population reached 1,200,000. Tourist guides and handbooks categorized over two hundred places in this way; but J. A. R. Pimlott, in *The Englishman's Holiday* (1947), reckoned that residents of seaside resorts, properly styled, constituted about 4 per cent of the nation in 1901. Each played host to several times their size in seasonal visitors, the most popular attracting perhaps fifteen or twenty times the number of their inhabitants during a year.

Seaside towns were not homogeneous types. Not only did they cater for different classes of visitor, they often combined holiday facilities with other pursuits, usually shipping and fishing, but not exclusively so. Moreover, this puzzle exists: why some places boomed and others barely stirred; and why, of those which did flourish, they assumed one character and not another? The variables relate to communications, patterns of landholding, local politics, alternative economic development, and trends in personal incomes and cultural preferences.

Whole regions which were superficially ripe for development remained comparatively unexploited. The railway reached Cornwall in 1859; but, leaving aside the yachtsmen, novelists, and artists' colonies such as the 'Newlyn School' of Henry Tuke, no great numbers of ordinary visitors appeared. Cornwall lost population in every decade from 1861 to 1901, and grew only 1.86 per cent in Edwardian times. Failing mines, unproductive agriculture, and the absence of large towns inhibited trade through the seaports. Falmouth received some calls from London and Southampton steamers; but the mail-packet days were gone. Fisheries and a little shipbuilding, with granite-dressing in neighbouring Penryn, mostly occupied the population of under 15,000 in 1901. Penzance served the Scilly Isles, was a rail-head for West Cornwall broccoli-growers, and retained some coasting trade; Looe and Padstow clutched on to meagre livings as small ports. St. Ives' business was pilchard fishing: indeed, there, so Kilvert was told in 1870, 'the smell of fish . . . is sometimes so terrific as to stop the church clock'. Each of these places engaged in petty holiday custom, but the only Cornish town to specialize in this business, Newquay, had fewer than 3,500 inhabitants by 1901. The county was beyond the reach of the masses.

A pall hung over most old western seaports. Plymouth remained important; on the other hand Seaton, Sidmouth, and Budleigh were sand-locked. The scale in between mostly tipped to the unenterprising end. Teignmouth, with a once flourishing Newfoundland trade, engaged in yachtbuilding and shipping china clay; Bridport dealt in Canadian and Norwegian timber; Poole exported pinewood and clays; and Swanage, with over a hundred quarries in the neighbourhood, shipped Purbeck marble. Each maintained a level of coasting trade, also minor reputations as watering places for the south-west gentry; but neither Dorset nor Devon was much transformed by a holiday traffic. Indeed their fugitive visitors cherished these counties' peace. The moody middle classes could contemplate dramatic coastal scenery, solemnly finger fossilized fauna, or gravely gather seaweed and shells, without disturbance. The Darwinian vogue had consecrated the holiday by permitting idleness to be called improvement.

Only one resort in the south-west enticed visitors in any quantity. This was Torquay, whose population of 33,625 in 1901 had quadrupled since 1841. Torquay retained some port traffic, of coal, timber, slates and stone, as well as minor industry (marble-polishing and pottery works); but its position as a social centre, first claimed by naval officers during the Napoleonic Wars, determined its growth. Further development had been inspired by one large landowner, Sir Lawrence Palk, who was active in the 1820s; thenceforward the creation of modern Torquay was in the hands of a miscellany of individuals and companies to whom the Palks let land for building, and under the direction of public authorities who supervised street improvements, laid out promenades and gardens, and equipped the town with sanitary services. The railway's arrival in 1848 had been greeted with a town holiday; but the burgesses' eye was towards Society, not whelk-or fried-fish-devouring trippers. A *rentier* class settled there, as Agatha Christie described in her *Autobiography* (1977). Most property was villadom of good quality; grand hotels were built; and a regatta in late August emphasized that this was an expensive playground. Especially, Torquay was distinguished by being 'a *winter* resort . . .

the Riviera of England, and people paid large rents for furnished villas there, during quite a gay winter season with concerts in the after-noons, lectures, occasional dances, and a great deal of other social activity'. Typical of the permanent residents were 'fat old ladies with obese landaus', occupying ample villas with 'clipped hedges and shaved lawns'. So observed Rudyard Kipling, who lived at nearby Maidencombe in 1896–7. Such ponderous gentility provoked in him coarse urges, including a desire to dance through Torquay 'with nothing on but my spectacles'. Torquay's domination of this market in the south-west was unrivalled. Some crumbs spilled over to benefit Teignmouth, with a population of 5,149 in 1851 and 8,636 in 1901, and Dawlish, half that size. These had fewer pretensions as retreats for the wealthy and began to tap a lower-middle-class custom. In north Devon where Ilfracombe (8,557 population in 1901) was a lonely standard-bearer, the Bristol Channel steamships remained important, since the late-coming railways did not compete with excursion rates.

The promotion of autumn and winter seasons was deliberately designed to offset the spasmodic conditions of the holiday trade. But late-season holidays were largely a middle- and upper-class preroga-tive, and to attract this clientele resorts needed to offer both creature comforts and the right tone. Hence, though most resorts boasted exclusive enclaves – the north shore at Blackpool, or Westcliff at Southend – the working-class resorts were disadvantaged in this bid. The new middle-class resorts, like Bournemouth and Eastbourne, or established Brighton, were better placed to lengthen their seasons. Bournemouth and Eastbourne grew remarkably from a population base of 695 and 3,433 respectively in 1851. Rail links were forged but exclusivity was cultivated by both places. A branch did not reach Bournemouth until 1870; and there were no Sunday trains before 1914. As for Eastbourne, its London connection was laborious before 1880 and between 1868 and 1888 the price of third-class tickets rose while first- and second-class fell. Both towns consciously appealed to the upper end of the social scale, with centrally-heated hotels, private hospitals and rest-homes, golf courses, broad parades and formal gardens. Each contained a residential *rentier* class, investors in limited liability companies, municipal stocks, or foreign and colonial bonds; people who, as G. M. Trevelyan wrote with unusual asperity, 'had retired on their incomes, and who had no relation to the rest of the community except that of drawing dividends and occasionally attend-ing a shareholders' meeting to bully the management'. This is not the whole story. The Bishop of Stepney, afterwards of London, Winnington-Ingram, always found in Bournemouth, Eastbourne, Brighton, and Torquay a precious source of charity to boost his metropolitan diocesan funds. Nevertheless, their reputation for being stuck-up was not undeserved. The cacophony of itinerant musicians and beach performers was displaced at Bournemouth by the disciplined movements of Dan Godfrey's municipal orchestra. Bournemouth also banned donkeys from its beaches; and Eastbourne in 1891–2 banned Sunday marches of the Salvation Army. Their 'corybantic Christianity' was bad form, as upsetting as insurrections of socialists. The Revd C. L. Dodgson (Lewis Carroll), who habitually holidayed at Eastbourne, stated the case: 'These musical processions are not only a great nuisance in themselves but are a means of bringing together a mob of all the worst and noisiest of the roughs and of producing . . . an awful amount of profane fun.'

The Eastbourne authorities were unable to maintain their ban when the Home Office decreed it *ultra vires*; but the incident was suggestive. Victor Bailey has noted anti-Salvation Army feeling widely throughout southern small towns and resorts. Their civic leaders opposed a presence that threatened to disturb not merely trade but also traditional social and sectarian authorities. These communities were structured on older, almost pre-class lines. Intitially Eastbourne was a kept community of the Dukes of Devonshire, as Catherine Walters was a kept woman. Compton Place was their seat, and the development of Eastbourne was determined by their investment and controlled by their agents, in particular George Ambrose Wallis who levered himself into a position of strategic authority. As the population grew to 43,337 in 1901, the ducal will was inevitably circumscribed by market forces which their initiatives had set in motion, and in strict business terms the dukes profited much less than their factors. Following the town's incorporation in 1883 the Duke, his representatives, and leading townfolk began to jostle for the greater say in public utilities and estate development, as David Cannadine details in *Lords and Landlords: the Aristocracy and the Towns, 1774–1967* (1980). Still, principal landowners at one time were not easily thwarted. Many burgeoning seaside resorts were shaped to their designs, before civic authorities began to assume a larger role.

At Bournemouth the trustees of the estate of Sir George Tapps Gervis (who had begun to develop his property before his death in 1842) commissioned the landscaper and architect, Decimus Burton;

but after 1856 first the local Improvement Commissioners, then the corporation, acquired the greater influence. At Folkestone the resident Earls of Radnor were responsible for the new town which emerged on the cliffs, with ample hotels and houses, promenades and lawns, to attract a genteel society. At Skegness the prime mover was H. V. Tippet, bustling agent of the Earl of Scarborough. Fleetwood even commemorated its developer by name. From 1836 Sir Peter Hesketh Fleetwood determined to forge a port and resort out of what was once a rabbit warren. He gambled upon the failure of locomotives to climb the northern hills and enlisted Burton to build the Grecian-style North Euston Hotel to encourage passengers to break their journey at Fleetwood before proceeding by sea to Scotland. This venture misfired; and speculation in resort-building remained a hit-and-miss affair, as the activity of Henry Pease at Saltburn or Colonel Tomline at Felixstowe underlines.

The history of pleasure resorts, then, is more complicated than a story of property tycoons or corporations sniffing ozone and cashing in on an inevitable boom. One factor is evidently the potential for alternative business. A certain level of port traffic would not upset the holiday trade, especially if it was shipment of people rather than goods, as at Dover or Folkestone. More than that, as at Bootle, Swansea, or Southampton, was a death-blow. Industries of considerable size or stench were a liability. Yarmouth's holiday and herring-fishing seasons happily fell into different parts of the year; but the chemical and soap works around Runcorn (styled 'the Montpellier of England' in 1834) made tourism impossible. Deterrents are rarely unilateral, however, and thousands of tourists were no small menace. Their accumulated sewage killed Cleethorpes' oyster beds in 1903. Such struggles between different interest groups and market forces in seaside towns are now beginning to be studied. Together with external movements – real wages and cultural trends – these were the decisive factors in resort development. Railway companies made fewer contributions, so J. K. Walton argues in respect of the north-west. Most lines were laid for other purposes, and railway companies responded poorly to the seasonal holiday traffic, providing inadequate rolling-stock and services. Only after resorts had grown, and when sustained growth could be assumed, in the late nineteenth century, did railway companies generally take an active part in holiday promotion.

The outstanding new resort, Blackpool, and the miscellaneous classes who competed within its economy and politics, have been sharply observed by Walton (*The Blackpool Landlady*, 1978). Land-ownership was parcellated. Local government was important, too, in attracting investment capital, or actually furnishing amenities. Black-pool Corporation had unique powers to levy a rate to advertise, which it did extensively from 1881 by posters and publicity stunts. Even by neglect local government was influential, winking at Sunday trading or at the infringement of building by-laws. Blackpool's host of small speculative builders were largely unconstrained by landowners' cove-nants but pressurized by high land prices and by their own and their potential tenants' and visitors' scant resources. The result, in central Blackpool especially, was high-density housing, sub-letting and over-crowding. Working-class holiday-makers were undeterred, already accustomed to such conditions. Landladies who huddled visitors together like hamsters cultivated a homely image of value for money, cheap and cheerful. Indeed landladies commonly hailed from the same towns as their visitors. Bishop Knox, who in 1905 inaugurated mission services on the beach, noticed how they all 'loved to meet one another, to continue the gossip of the mill or the street from which they came'.

It was the customs of the textile trades that made modern Blackpool. The turning-point was the late 1860s and 1870s. The cotton famine was ended, and the working week was reduced to five-and-a-half days (about 54 hours). The *Manchester Guardian*'s editor, C. P. Scott, a regular weekend visitor to Blackpool at this time, observed the bustle and understood its origins. 'The high wages', he wrote in July 1873, 'are producing a wonderful development of popular amusements.' As prices of many essential commodities fell from the 1870s, these wages were stretching further; and in the friendly societies and holiday clubs a habit of saving was encouraged. The organization of holidays in the textile regions was peculiar. Traditional celebrations of the dedication of a parish church – the wakes – were secularized as general holidays. Tight-knit mill communities were unbroken in leisure as at work. There was an employer interest in this, to reduce absenteeism at other times and to quench the unruliness of pre-industrial festivals; but improvement was a diffused ethic, and the amount of working-class self-regulation generated through churches, temperance societies, and trade unions should not be underestimated. The very fact that numerous textile workers took out-of-town holidays betokens uncommon self-discipline, for holidays were without pay, a luxury painstakingly saved for. One or two northern employers, like Lever's and Brunner, Mond's, granted holidays with pay from the 1880s; so did several railway companies (an obvious perk) and the odd progressive local authority. But these groups of manual workers were altogether unusual: by and large only white-collar workers in commerce and industry enjoyed paid holidays before 1914.

Textile workers, therefore, insisted on spending money to its best advantage. Fairs were a traditional entertainment. Every textile town supported three or four fairs annually between 1830 and 1870. These now sought to add to their attractions through the application of steam traction in the 1860s and electricity in the 1880s. On the other hand their trading function disappeared, overtaken by local retail facilities; and professional circuses and showmen could be seen in hippodromes at other times of the year. The fairs' circuits by the late nineteenth century were thus tending to avoid the textile towns, visiting instead agricultural villages like Hollins Green, where most folk spent their holidays at home, or agricultural capitals like Oxford, where a large concentration would gather at the St. Giles' Fair. In the north's industrial centres Wakes Weeks were ghostly times. 'In the place of the fair,' a Rawtenstall man reminisced, 'we see hundreds of workpeople carrying boxes and bags on their way to the railway station for a few days at the seaside.' By 1900 holidays in the textile areas were longer than in most industries, running to a full week in July or August; afterwards a long weekend in September was added by many firms.

The organization of holidays also varied broadly by region. Although block bookings and bargain rates became widespread, as railway companies competed for custom, in the north the organization was generally handled by the workers' own clubs and associations, in the south by railway companies themselves, by travel agents, or by some independent national society. The relative sobriety of the northerners' excursions was contrasted with the Londoners'. There too traditional fairs were in retreat, from the march of bricks and mortar and local authority curbs; but the concentration into one or two days of the working-class Londoners' holidays made them conspicuously more hectic than those of the north. Arthur Morrison's short story, 'Lizerunt,' in *Tales of Mean Streets* (1894), pictures a rowdy Whit Monday fair on Wanstead Flats. Bank Holidays were famed as days when 'you may be drunk and disorderly without being locked up – for the [police] stations won't hold everybody'.

Blackpool did not discourage middle-class visitors. As Walton notes, some posh parts were sustained in spite of an overspill of down-market lodging-houses. Lytham St. Anne's offered sanctuary for those whose sensibilities were affronted by Blackpool's common side; but the working-class season was too narrow for Blackpool to risk specialization. Without scenic attractions other than sands, it was prudent to provide diversions for both tripper and superior clienteles. Ultimately, by drawing upon capital which was broadly Lancastrian in source, Blackpool was established as the mecca for amusements. Of course, Blackpool was not the only municipality to engage in 'booster-ism' to satisfy, even to create, wants. One curious shift in fashion was from sea-bathing to sun-bathing. Initially, the curative properties of this ritual were stressed; but a minor aesthetic revolution was under way too. To sport a tan previously offended ideals of gentle beauty: toasted skin denoted coarse, outdoor labour. Now it was beginning to indicate healthfulness; also to carry status – it was the visible symbol of the privileged holiday-maker, who loafed while the rest of the world laboured. Blackpool on the north-west coast was not a predestined sun-trap. Though its boosters gamely entered the propaganda war of publishing sunshine hours, they countered suspicions of natural coolness by exuberant amenities.

The country's first electric tramway was started in Blackpool, in 1885. Southend sported the country's largest pier, Brighton the grandest; but when the Victoria (later South) pier was opened in 1893, with its thirty-six shops and bandstand, Blackpool had three. There were winter gardens, pleasure pavilions, aquaria, music-halls, ball-rooms, and theatres up and down the English coastline; there were towers, too, at New Brighton, Morecambe and elsewhere. But Blackpool's 500-foot imitation Eiffel Tower (1891–4) was astonish-ing. Nowhere was everything gathered together, and in such propor-tions, as at Blackpool. It was there that the theatre-architect, Frank Matcham, created his masterpiece, the Grand Theatre (1894); there that fantasy illuminations were begun (1912). Much of this invest-ment was classless, to make Blackpool the premier, not just a plebeian, resort.

Blackpool gained this reputation, though Brighton (including Hove) vastly exceeded it in size, having a population of 153,000 in 1901. As an older community, Brighton contained deeper pockets of resistance to the new tourist trends. Blackpool had three times more lodging-houses than Brighton, Brighton three times more hotels than Blackpool. The town's flirtation with royalty and aristocracy, however, evoked misgivings. George IV, as Prince Regent and monarch, placed Brighton on the map; Queen Victoria nearly took it off. Preferring the Isle of Wight, in the 1840s she demoted the Pavilion from the ranks of royal residences. In 1855 the post of Master of Ceremonies was abandoned. An aristocratic autumn and pre-Christmas winter season lingered up to about 1870; thereafter Brighton's mantle of fashion seemed shaky. Only summer middle-class holiday-makers and all-weather adulterers were left.

The alternative, swarms of revelling low-born Londoners, was distasteful. Fearing the reactions of their richer clientele, certain residents and hoteliers lobbied the railway company to stem the sale of cheap return tickets from London: 117,000 persons travelled to Brighton by coaches during 1835; 132,000 arrived by trains on one day, Easter Monday, in 1862. The racecourse drew the gamblers along with the trippers at points in the year; but Brighton was not without investment in amenities. The corporation built a three-mile-long protected sea front, and the aquarium in 1901 was converted into a concert-hall and winter gardens. There were also two substantial piers, one erected in 1866 and another to replace the old Chain Pier (1823) washed away in 1896. But the principal investment in late-nineteenth-century Brighton was in baroque hotels, to seduce the aristocracy from the French Riviera or, more realistically, to pander to the aristocracy's successors, plutocrats, *les nouveaux riches* of America and South Africa, Midlands and northern industrial magnates, quick-killers in the City. In 1908 R. D. Blumenfeld recorded in his diary: 'Brighton is regaining its place as the most fashionable resort in England. I met Admiral Lord Charles Beresford today after his return from Brighton, where he has been taking the air. He says the King and Queen Alexandra are going there next week'. As Prince of Wales, Edward had visited Brighton before, savouring the luxury of the Sassoons' mansions. Royal crotchets remained influential in the volatile holiday business. Twice the usual number of first-class railway passengers travelled between London and Brighton in the year following the King's visit.

A jaundiced estimate of Brighton's Edwardian success can be found in Arnold Bennett's diary. Bennett stayed at the Royal York Hotel in 1910, sketching the chapters of *Clayhanger*. It was during the January General Election, when 'all wealth and all snobbery is leagued against the poor'. Brighton, he noted, was 'full of wealthy imperative persons dashing about in furs and cars'. The town was solid symbol of a 'system that is built on the grinding of the faces of the poor', in which the poor were compelled to act as accomplices, like the hotel door-keeper whom Bennett overheard 'politely expostulating with a guest: "Surely, Mr. ——, you don't mean to say you're anything but a conservative!" Miserable parrot.'

There was more to Brighton than grand hotels like beached Cunarders. In the 1870s Samuel Smiles observed that both Brighton and Hastings were 'but the marine suburbs of London'. Certainly, Brighton was literally in part a suburban annexe, for the retired and also for active City businessmen. Even in 1823 Cobbett noticed stockjobbers commuting by coach. More were to use the railway's service. Galsworthy, in *The Man of Property* (1906), has Soames Forsyte live in Brighton, journeying up and down to London, after the separation from his wife. The big increase in this traffic, as from Southend, came after the 1890s, and even more in the inter-war years. Already, however, this trend was established, particularly in seaside places which were closer than Brighton or Southend to expanding urban centres.

Hence, the classification of 'resorts' is problematic. Several qualify as satellites or suburbs too. Roker, on the north side of the river Wear from Sunderland, or Southsea, formally included within the borough of Portsmouth, exemplified this mixed status of resort and suburb; likewise Cleethorpes, three miles south-east of the country's largest fishing port, Grimsby, and connected by trams and trains. By 1901 Grimsby contained 63,138 people and Cleethorpes was a fifth of this size. More striking as a satellite was Southport, twenty miles north of Liverpool and connected by rail from 1848. This had a borough population of some 5,000 in 1851, 18,000 in 1871, and 48,000 in 1901. Probably the true total was about 62,000, for Southport's boundaries only matched the residential pale when Birkdale was included in 1911. Southport had all the trappings of a middle-class holiday centre – handsome esplanade, botanical gardens, zoo – but it also represented Liverpool wealth by the sea. The second-home phenomenon, too, was evident at resorts both inland and coastal. Leeds and Bradford businessmen colonized Scarborough as well as Ilkley and Harrogate, wealthy Mancunians and Liverpudlians settled in the Lake District and at the seaside as well as in Cheshire; prosperous Bristolians at Weston-super-Mare as well as at Clifton; and rich men from Hull at Withernsea and the Holderness peninsula. It was part of a general movement of evacuation, temporary and permanent, from big cities.

II

Suburban growth is one great feature of the nineteenth century. The subject has not been neglected by historians. In his classic miniature, *Victorian Suburb: A Study of the Growth of Camberwell* (1961), H. J. Dyos supplied an unobjectionable definition: 'In essence, a suburb is a decentralized part of a city with which it is inseparably linked by certain economic and social ties.' He also gave a warning: Camberwell cannot be considered typical of even London suburbs. The suburb is a versatile form.

The suburb was not a nineteenth-century discovery. It was as old as the city itself, but time brought metamorphoses. Suburban development around medieval and early-modern English towns was of the 'faubourg' type, industrial suburbs of small tradesmen, craftsmen, and foreigners free from guild or city company restrictions; or slum-like, a reception tank for migrant workers, a focus of crime, disorder and disease, with low alehouses and insanitary dwellings congested in unpoliced streets. Improved road communications, by public coach or personal carriage, facilitated the first suburban extensions in the modern sense, that is, primarily for residential use. City merchants built grand villas, dispersed in what would now be termed ribbon development, in the most picturesque settings proximate to the highways which radiated from the capital. From the mid-nineteenth century a new wave emerged, which threatened to engulf exclusive villadom with an unfashionable petty villadom of the lower- and middle-middle classes. In the late nineteenth century the status of suburbia was menaced again, by working-class dormitories. In both processes there was detected the debasement of a dream.

That dream itself was widely deplored. There seemed retributive justice in this 'spoiling of suburbia', for had not suburbia first spoiled the city? The suburban dream equalled selfishness, a rejection of obligation and commitment to the city where the suburbanite earned his living. A suburban house, whether detached or semi-detached, bred utter detachment from public responsibility. It imperilled community spirit by highlighting class distinctions residentially; moreover, the city core was devitalized and the municipalities' fiscal resources were depleted as a consequence of suburban development. Suburb and slum thus remained intimately connected, though no longer as in earlier ages the same thing. The suburbanites' callousness was epitomized by one who abetted suburban movement still more, the car manufacturer Henry Ford: 'We shall solve the City Problem by leaving the city.'

These judgements are useless without historical perspective. What prompted suburban development? First there was the demographic upsurge. Then there was the ability of people to extend their journey to work. The combination of rising real wages and reduced hours of work (allowing more travelling time) were necessary preconditions for the growth of mass suburbs. The presence of an agile building industry, ready capital, and compliant landowners was essential to organize and effect the transfer. Finally, there was the matter of taste. Visions of family privacy and class exclusiveness gave a special tone to the constructions.

These were positively reinforcing conditions. Negative corroboration existed too, in prejudices against apartment-building, which ensured that English cities expanded mostly outwards and not upwards. Luxury apartments were built in several parts of central London, but purpose-built flats for the poor only emerged after it was clear that all could not take advantage of decentralized housing. These people were the lowliest sorts, those roughly cleared by railway companies and commerce hungry for central-city sites, or by municipal authorities intolerant of slums. 'A slum,' declared the LCC Progressive, B. F. C. Costelloe, 'in a word, represents the presence of a market for local, casual labour.' The need for cheap, central accommodation was undeniable to this class of labour, to be close to possible work. It was in such as the dockside areas of London and Liverpool that housing-companies and public authorities built most of the multi-storey flats which appeared in England before 1914. The chief exception was the industrial north-east, where two-storey flats were commonplace. Anthony Sutcliffe, introducing *Multi-Storey Living* (1974), speculated that 'the emergence of this type in the Newcastle area is the product of that city's relatively late fortification and certain natural obstacles to its outward expansion, combined perhaps with the proximity of the Scottish example. . . .' The fixed location of industry in riverside yards, and the small space it left for houses, were mutually affirming. So was an accumulated tradition of building. As industrial Tyneside increased tenfold in population during the nineteenth century, builders simply repeated the existing standard. The Tyneside case reflects the persistence of vernacular traditions of building which distinguished the layout of different places: back-to-back housing in Leeds and Manchester, or courtyard styles in Liverpool and Nottingham, are others. The use of local materials also gave a distinctive colour to different areas: brown brick in the south-east, white brick in the east, bright red brick in the West Midlands, yellow stone in the Cotswolds, grey stone in Yorkshire and flint in Norfolk and the Sussex Downs. The repeal of the brick tax in 1850 and the railway network, however, spread the distribution of mass-produced bricks and slates. It was mostly in country areas that local traditions survived – thatch-roofing, earth or stone floors, and wattle and daub walls – although even here, Enid Gauldie notes, the 'vernacular threshold' was crossed and, by 1900, 'the most noticeable variation in cottage accommodation was caused not so much by regional as by social differences.'

Generally, relatively low-density housing spilling out of open towns was the norm. City centres were vacated for residential purposes, left to the bankers by day and prostitutes by night. G. K. Chesterton thought that the urban exodus expressed the Englishman's spirit: 'Every man, though he were born in the very belfry of Bow and spent his infancy climbing among chimneys, has waiting for him somewhere a country house which he has never seen but which was built for him in the very shape of his soul.'

The strength of this emotion needs to be emphasized. It is mostly taken for granted as having natural, general appeal, whereas there are many social types – childless couples, the aged, the unmarried – for whom the individual dwelling with garden is inconvenient, a less rational form of habitation than an apartment. In fact, well-appointed blocks of flats, which offered personal amenities and communal facilities, privacy without social isolation, were never built in quantity in England. The Chestertonian ideal was never realized either. Most folk fell short of the countryside and made do with suburbia instead. There was romance here too, of the trivial, anxious, self-deceiving kind, thought Lewis Mumford, who called the suburb 'an asylum for the preservation of illusion'. Building habits seemed to confirm this. There was an escapist quality about the picturesque in the most prestigious suburbs. Even in humdrum suburbs, where houses were superficially the same, differences were measurable in street names, the quality of greenery, size of bay windows, in porch and door ornamentation, coloured tiles, bricks and glass. That Karl Marx, according to Bernstein, frequently mistook his home in Kentish Town upon returning from his daily brooding in the British Museum and tried to enter the wrong house, may be attributed to that grim philosopher's disregard for petty-bourgeois vanities as well as to his myopia. For, inside houses as well as outside, embellishments in the woodwork or about the fireplaces, and personal decorations and fittings, betokened a proud demonstration. The pride seemed of the insecure, not insolent, kind. Max Beerbohm captured it in an essay of the 1890s:

Not long ago, in the high-street of a small suburb, I saw a symbol that was even more tragic than the symbolic young man at the stage-door. I saw a bow-window through which a bust of Minerva gazed down at me. Minerva's back had been turned upon the inmates of the room, not in Divine discourtesy, but by the very inmates. Imagine the back view of a bust!

Most adverse comments about suburbia were directed against the lower-middle-class sort. The archetypal representative was the clerk. The clerk was the butt of snob jokes, immortalized in the Grossmiths' *Diary of a Nobody* (1892). Their liveliest topics involved minute distinctions separating grades of respectability. C. F. G. Masterman knew a play in which the *dramatis personae* debate the respective social advantages of Clapham and Herne Hill. This indicates an important feature of suburbs. They were characteristically in flux, for ever changing composition and tone. Clapham, once among the most affluent Georgian suburbs, remained in the 1860s a citadel of stock-brokers and merchants, within easy walking reach of countryside. By Edwardian times Clapham was closed in and had deteriorated socially, a clerkly capital. Herne Hill, likewise, was cheapened after the 1860s when it became a railway junction for lines to Victoria, Blackfriars, and Holborn Viaduct. Around provincial cities similar processes were observable. Acock's Green, a village four miles south-east of Birmingham, became unbearable to wealthy suburbans as the expanding city engulfed it. Thus they decamped, joining the prescient who had settled already, five, six, and ten miles out, in Olton, Solihull, and Knowle. Acock's Green was abandoned, as the *Birmingham Daily Mail* observed in 1903, to 'the smaller house – the house adapted to the means of the family man of limited income who likes to live just outside the artisan belt encircling the city'.

Clerks were part of a white-collar or black-coated workforce which expanded hugely, from 2.5 per cent of all occupied males in 1851 to over 7 per cent in 1911. This meant a rise from fewer than 150,000 individuals to over 900,000. They comprised local government facto-tums and schoolteachers, shop workers and commercial travellers, as well as clerks. While evident in all urban centres, commercial clerks were more numerous in trading cities like Liverpool than in primary industrial cities like Sheffield. Students of the clerkly class emphasize that the single category conceals a range of character, responsibility, and income. There was a higher professional element with assured position; there was, too, the racy, profane, good-for-nothing bachelor clerk, represented by 'Arry in Gissing's *Demos*, who lived in lodgings and was heedless of social pressures to conformity. But the most enduring impression is of a drab class, the Pooters with uncertain status and pretensions. Their timorousness and puniness were aggravated by market conditions. Those capable of doing routine tasks about an office multiplied with the spread of elementary education and mechanical typing. Furthermore, conformity to the employers' codes inhibited clerks from organizing in trade unions, unlike artisans whose wages were hardly inferior.

This opinion which sees clerks and their colleagues in a dejected condition should not obscure one striking fact about the 'near-middle classes', as Ethel Mannin once called them. Indeterminate though their status often was, collectively they represent evidence that industrialization and urbanization provided more opportunities of social ascent and occupational mobility than ever before. This was not meteoric rising in melodramatic pauper-to-millionaire style. That remained a special category. Some historians aver that the growing capitalization and complexity of industrial organization precluded the self-made advancement of ambitious and gifted working men, though the late nineteenth and early twentieth centuries probably afforded no fewer examples of this catapult careerism: witness (Sir) John Craig, born in 1874, a puddler's son, who rose from office-boy to managing director of Colville's huge steel business. Still, the small firm was not displaced, even in the established textile and engineering trades. The maturing economy opened up new possibilities of entrepreneurship as it closed down old – witness Barney Barnato, one of the richest Randlords, born a poor Cockney; or, at home, that fast-expanding consumerism which elevated grocer Lipton or car-maker Morris. However, we can agree that these were mavericks. The substantial case for upward group mobility rests on those (perhaps between 5 and 10 per cent of the working classes) who reached more modest positions, that lower-middle class of the new service sectors and the petty officialdom of industry and government. Within the working classes occupational mobility was considerable.

From field-hand to urban-domestic was elevation of a kind for the country girl. So was the wage promotion and prospects which urban employment held out to her country brothers. More sophisticated factory organization engendered numerous positions of minor authority, foremen and various supervisory grades, not to mention opportunities through trade union, friendly society and co-operative society bureaucracies, and through working-class politics. The first working-class factory inspector was appointed in 1882, the first working-class magistrates in 1885; there were numbers of working-class guardians and members of school boards and town councils, too, in the late nineteenth century. Such openings propelled thousands to a higher station, if not entirely out of the working class and altogether into another.

Most sorts of workers participated in this occupational and social mobility, but there was a downward as well as upward propensity in the spiral, most notably in the convergence within the ranks of the semi-skilled of former craftsmen with former labourers as jobs were regraded through technical advances. Insecurity dogged the working classes, in the shape of cyclical depressions or that seasonality of demand which afflicted whole trades. The force with which these pressures might bear down was augmented by personal circumstances. Age was the commonest enemy. Labour which was past the peak of physical fitness was most likely to be discharged or relegated to inferior tasks. The risks attached to bad habits and temperament – heavy drinking, unpunctuality, a shuffling or rebellious nature – are impalpable since these might result from rather than cause vulnerability in an unpropitious economic climate.

Among non-English groups, the Irish may have contributed proportionately fewer upwardly mobile than the Welsh or Scots. The Catholic Irish suffered from religious prejudice and anti-alien feeling; but so did the Jews, whose upward social mobility was perhaps greatest of all. Jews constituted the smallest immigrant group, always less than one per cent of the occupied population, mostly used to towns, and possessing some education and craft skills. Moreover, the Anglo-Jewish establishment supported the poor Jewish immigrant better than the English Catholic establishment did the Irish immigrant. For the rest, leaving aside the immigrants, the identification of the upwardly mobile is obscure. What historian would notice Enoch Bennett had not his son, Arnold, become a professional writer? Here was one example of pertinacious effort to rise, in spite of vicissitudes.

Born in 1843 and descended from a line of potters, he quit school at twelve to learn the potter's craft; went back to school as a pupil teacher; rejoined the pottery industry and became a partner in a business which collapsed; and took to small shopkeeping, in drapery and pawnbroking. Then, taking advantage of a small legacy left by his father, he became an articled clerk and in the late 1870s entered the ranks of solicitor. The climb of many another may not have been so slippery, or in the end so high; but the historian is ill placed to detect them. Charles Booth explained upward mobility by Darwinian imagery, a matter of selecting the most fit. He also noticed the ascent of generations, imbued with fresh tastes and expectations:

. . . it is common for the children to aim at a higher position than their parents held; and for the young people when they marry to move to a new house in a better district. A new middle class is thus forming, which will, perhaps, hold the future in its grasp. Its advent seems to me the greatest social fact of to-day. Those who constitute this class are the especial product of the push of industry; within their circle religion and education find the greatest response; amongst them all popular movements take their rise, and from them draw their leaders. To them, in proportion as they have ideas, political power will pass.

Booth, peering into the future, consciously painted his picture with strong colours. The contemporary scene was not so clear. The subjects of his prediction were not confident. Typically, for instance, clerkly suburbs were those with shifting frontiers, as well-paid manual workers continually seeped into their neighbourhoods. By 1901 clerks were inconspicuous in London's old working-class districts, comprising fewer than 3 per cent of Shoreditch or Bethnal Green. In burgeoning suburbs north and south, like Stoke Newington and Lewisham, they comprised 13 per cent. Sieving was evident, too, in Aston, part of Birmingham. This area grew rapidly from mid-century when Aston Hall came on to the market. By 1901 the population totalled 77,000. The Hall itself, which had harboured Charles I before the battle of Edgehill, was turned into a museum and aquarium; and the district was built over, with streets half or three-quarters of a mile long. The development was not planned as such but informal segregation arose, as E. A. Knox, vicar of Aston 1891–4, related: 'The houses were built to accommodate commercial travellers, foremen of large businesses, school-teachers, in fact, all the "black-coated" industry created by the development of Birmingham. In courts behind these streets survived what had been country cottages, but had now degenerated into slums'. These suburbs were not homogeneous as a whole, but within them particular zones and even individual streets might have a decided class character.

It was in the suburban regions, H. J. Dyos remarked, that the mentality of flight and pursuit seemed most pronounced. The use of psychological labels by historians, however, can dim more than it illuminates the social process. Charles Booth noticed the very real element of choice. All above a certain income were not persuaded to move to a suburb. Suburbs might offer 'the certainty of lower rents and the hope of better hygienic conditions'; but this was not decisive. Booth elaborated:

many other influences, besides mere flight, are effective in proportion as the mechanical means of communication are perfected and made convenient for all classes and for transit at all hours. Many may still move out to as great a distance as their purse permits; but others will pause, hesitating to lose central advantages in education or amusement, in pleasure or in profit of one kind or another; ready to set off accessibility to suburbs and country combined with a home nearer the heart of things, against the reverse of these. The decision depends not so much on class or on the amount of income (over a certain minimum), as on the constitution of the family. The father of young children finds it best to establish their home as far from the crowded parts of London as he can afford to travel to and from his work.

Thus historians should attend to the age composition and style of life of families, as well as to income and occupation, in studying suburbanites.

This follows an observation of A. F. Weber, in *The Growth of Cities in the Nineteenth Century* (1899): 'The city is the spectroscope of society; it analyses and sifts the population, separating and classifying the diverse elements.' The price of this systematic subdivision of people and things was paid in the suburbs which, many alleged, were unsociable. Here were the stuffy troglodytes in separate caves, the lonely crowd of shrivelled personalities and sham gentility, not knowing neighbours, yet regimented by neighbours. Self-repression followed after that dreadful doubt, what will the neighbours *think*? Suburbia was dedicated to privacy; and this engendered unadventurous, seemingly uniform, petty individuals, because their relationship to the community was wary. Suburbanites, wrote Masterman, had 'incorrect standards of value' and a

noticeable absence of vision. Suburban life has often little conception of social service, no tradition of disinterested public duty, but a limited outlook beyond a personal ambition. Here the individualism of the national character exercises its full influence: unchecked by the horizontal links of the industrial peoples, organizing themselves into unions, or by the vertical links of the older aristocracy with a conception of family service which once passed from parent to child.

Hence, suburbia tended to Conservatism in politics, a counterweight to urban radicalism and socialistic collectivism, which were hated for their high-spending, egalitarian philosophies. Central city–suburban conflict fast replaced the town–country conflict which agitated politics in previous ages. Lord George Hamilton's election for Middlesex in 1868 is commonly noted as having inaugurated the Conservative trend in suburban south-east England; but controversy over poor-law expenditure had brought tensions to the surface earlier in several northern cities. Perspicacious Tory politicians took account of these tendencies in the redistribution of constituency boundaries in 1885. By 1900 the mould was set. One party organizer told Rosebery that as the middle and artisan classes had 'prospered or acquired their houses they have inclined to the Conservative party because they dread the doctrines which Sidney Webb thinks would be so popular'.

The suburban movement represented the gradual turn away from a society in which most people rented accommodation to one in which many envisaged owning their homes. Tenancies remained the condition for 90 per cent of people, since the building and freehold-land societies which were active from the late eighteenth century invariably limited loans to 75–80 per cent of the purchase price before 1930. About 1,500 building societies existed by mid-Victorian times, with a membership of perhaps 300,000. By 1895 there were some 2,600 societies with 600,000 members. They were placed on a statutory basis in 1874 and again in 1894, following the crash of the Liberator Building Society in 1892. In some East Lancashire and West Yorkshire textile and mining communities building societies were well entrenched. Several proclaimed as their object 'to help working men become home owners'. The way for artisans to achieve this was to take a pair of cottages, paying off the mortgage by letting one house, or to sub-let within a single dwelling. Ironically the political potential of this development – for the vote was tied to property – was first exploited by Anti-Corn Law League radicals in the 1840s. Later, home-ownership reinforced popular Conservatism.

Together with insurance companies, friendly societies and banks, the building societies acted as tributaries of capital for the speculative builders in whose hands suburbia was fashioned. Still, H. J. Dyos emphasized, most capital reached builders via solicitors acting for private investors. Capital was generally abundant: there is 'more evidence of over-building in periods of easy money than of under-building when money was tight'. Most builders operated on a small scale. Dyos's figures, concerning the peak of speculative building in Camberwell, 1878–80, may be cited. Some 416 builders were at work on 5,670 houses; but over half built no more than six houses in these three years and nearly three-quarters built twelve or fewer. By contrast 1,800 houses were built by fifteen firms, the largest building 230 houses.

Few historians have imitated Dyos's patient work. The structure of the provincial building industry is particularly obscure, though it is presumed that larger firms steadily engrossed more of the market. Dyos himself reckoned that, whereas in the 1870s 80 per cent of London builders achieved fewer than six houses a year, in the 1890s only about 60 per cent operated on this small scale. Still, the question remains why the bigger firms did not dominate the scene more? Two explanations arise. One is that the building industry remained, compared with manufacturing, technologically backward and too labour-intensive to achieve very great economies of scale and productivity. Second, small builders had the flexibility to bend with market movements, shifting easily from repairing or jobbing to construction whenever the mood, dictated so often by petty capital, changed.

What sort of job did the builders do? On a quantitative scale their achievement ranks fairly high. Activity in the building industry ebbed and flowed according to trends in personal incomes and interest rates and the counter-attractions of other investment both external and internal to the trade. As for the last, the building of commercial premises was to some extent competitive; but so far as the metropolis was concerned, the evacuation of the residential City, the continuous expansion of Greater London, and actual and expected extensions of the transport network, all ensured that house-building was a popular speculation. So strong was this confidence at times that it created its own counterweight in over-building. During the last quarter of the nineteenth century empty houses constituted usually no less than 4 per cent of the total across London. In the suburbs, particularly in the late 1870s and early 1880s, the proportion of unoccupied houses was greater, since building was not synchronized with cheap and efficient retail and transport facilities, without which people would not move in large numbers. Over-building, however, was chiefly in evidence at the middle-class end of the market, where it was assumed profits lay. The working classes were dealt more meagre rations. The poor especially suffered famine in the midst of plenty, a circumstance which induced municipal authorities to intervene in the house-building market. Finally, we should acknowledge the contribution of Avner Offer's *Property and Politics, 1870–1914* (1981) to this topic. Building activity, he argues, was conditioned by political factors as well as by purely economic phenomena. Thus fiscal controversy, meaning both a rise and a reapportionment of taxes, local and national, played a significant part in depressing property values, land transfers and building, by fuelling the atmosphere of uncertainty and insecurity which existed from the late 1890s.

Qualitatively the speculative builders' work is difficult to assess. Piecemeal development militated against synoptic design. Architecture was derived from pattern-books and technical manuals. This should not lead us instantly to condemn suburban architecture. Architectural canons are notoriously fickle. The services of a professional architect do not guarantee a building's quality. In the disjointed building of a suburb, inevitably a medley of styles ensued, some contemptible, others pleasing. Always the setting and extent of the site were controlling forces. Inescapable too was the fact that builders were tailoring their wares for customers whose purchasing power was significant only as part of a mass market serviced cheaply with ready-made goods. Carlyle's strictures about the London environs having become 'a congeries of plastered bandboxes' by the 1860s, lose their force when read in a market context.

The suburban house should be lumped with the canned foods and machine-made clothes and shoes, that host of utilities and accessories, from sewing machines and typewriters to cooking-ranges and flush-water closets, which gave increasing value for money and benefit to growing numbers in the late nineteenth century. The shabby and shoddy were sometimes issued in quantity; but the credit side was plain. Thousands gained a precious privacy in a home of their own in quiet and healthful suburbs, within reach of countryside. This last virtue needs underlining, for many twentieth-century developments have exterminated the open fields spared by Victorians. Richard Jefferies, when resident in Surbiton, was delighted to find undisturbed countryside a few paces beyond the tramway terminus. Nowadays, too, cars, lorries, and motor-bikes regularly break the silence of suburbia. In *A London Child of the Seventies* (1934) Molly Hughes – brought up in Islington – made the point that 'No London child today can realize the quiet of the road on which my window looked. A tradesman's cart, a hawker or a hurdy-gurdy, were the sum total of the usual traffic. Sometimes everything had been so quiet for so long that the sound of a passer-by or of a butcher's pony would take on a distant, unreal tone. . . .'

Walter Besant drew up a balance sheet about suburbia in 1909. Initially, indeed for long, suburbs were 'without any society; no social gatherings or institutions; as dull a life as mankind ever tolerated'. He elaborated:

The men went into town every morning and returned every evening; they had dinner; they talked a little; they went to bed. . . . The case of the women was worse; they lost all the London life – the shops, the animation of the streets, their old circle of friends; in its place they found all the exclusiveness and class feeling of London with none of the advantages of a country town.

Lately, according to Besant's notice, 'the suburbs have developed a social life of their own; they have theatres, they have lawn tennis clubs, they have bicycle clubs, they have dances, dinners, subscription balls, concerts, and receptions.' It was in the suburbs, especially, that the physical fads took hold – not just football and cricket, tennis and cycling, but archery, badminton, golf, hockey, ping-pong, and skating. Moreover, shopping facilities – for extravagances as well as everyday needs – had improved considerably. 'A resident of Westbourne', wrote Besant,

finds in its principal streets all the shops which he desires. The ladies are not obliged to go to Regent Street and Bond Street for the newest fashions and the most costly materials, for they can find these things on the spot. In the same way there are centres, High Streets, at Islington, at Hackney, at Clapham, at Brixton, where everything can be procured. These places are quite independent of the City and of the West End.

In Camberwell the sophistication of suburban retailing can be plotted in two phases. In the 1850s and 1860s came the first displacement of the stall-holder, itinerant trader, general dealer, and local craftsman by the lock-up shop providing specialized retail services. From the 1880s came the shopping centres, occupied by multiple groceries such as Lipton's, Maypole, Home and Colonial, branches of clothing and footwear chains, such as Dunn's, and Freeman, Hardy and Willis, a Lyons restaurant, a Boot's chemist's and so on.

Multiples and department stores both aspired to economies of scale, the former by trade in standardized goods, the latter by 'universal provision' (to cite William Whiteley's famous slogan), the sheer aggregation of goods on one site. Altogether by 1914 department stores, multiple shops, and Co-ops accounted for 16–20 per cent of all retail sales. This proportion would be greater in vital urban and suburban areas.

Whether these giants and multiples grew at the expense of smaller shops is a nice question. It may be that the market was expanding fast enough to accommodate both; also that the giants stimulated consumerism, and were not the only retailers to benefit. Small shops happily coexisted in streets with a big store: their business was animated by the casual custom of clients drawn to the great emporia.

As well as multiples with a regional or national spread there were smaller chains, usually groceries of high reputation in specific localities. One was Williams of Manchester, which established five branches between 1865 and 1895, all in middle-class suburbs, and thirty shops by the time of the founder's death. Williams's growth was in a lower gear than the likes of Lipton, limited to what family management could encompass; and, wishing to own the freehold of their shops, they expanded from profits only. Conscious of middle-class tastes, they fitted out their shops expensively; and they scorned to imitate the fastest-growing chains which relied upon quick turnovers of popular, commercially processed commodities such as tea, sugar, bacon, butter, margarine and jams. Williams's stocked over 2,000 items. In strict business economics Williams's methods may be pronounced 'inefficient'; but the quality of service which they rendered make up part of the impression we have of middle-class suburbs with increasingly abundant amenities.

How much better or, rather, how differently supplied with shopping facilities were these suburbs, compared with other urban neighbourhoods? Attempts to quantify the question, by relating the number of shops to population, founder upon the impossibility of measuring shop floor-space and stocks. Then there is the need to consider alternative outlets – the producer–dealer; street markets; and that rabble of hawkers, hucksters and costers, whose composition was ever in flux from intermittent incursions by casual workers discharged from seasonal work and by those seeking a supplementary income. Two trends are suggested by the available evidence, statistical and impressionistic. One is that production and distribution were gradually divorced, although the compilers of the 1891 census cautioned that 'the maker and retail seller being very frequently one and the same person', it was a flaw in their enumerations that the 'man . . . who makes bread, and the man who only sells bread, are alike called "baker" and the man who sells shoes calls himself a shoemaker, as much as the man who actually does the cutting and sewing'. Second, the relative proportion, perhaps even the absolute number, of informal retailers was diminishing in the late nineteenth century. Their sites were built over, like Hungerford Market which became Charing Cross Station. Public control tightened too. Local authority clearances and improvements, and by-laws against obstruction, nuisance and Sunday trading, led to the closure of street markets and to the building of fixed covered markets. Probably the 'shopocracy' influenced police and magistrates to harass and suppress itinerant vendors. For a long time street traders and shopkeepers may have been complementary, the former dispensing mostly perishables. Gradually they became antagonistic. In sheer number of trading outlets working-class areas probably remained better equipped than middle-class suburbs. The rich could always afford to travel for purchases, or induce a domestic or the shop to fetch and carry. The poor had need of a more informal system – where evening trading was available, where 'tick' was negotiable, above all, where convenience, cheapness, and quantity reigned before quality. The corner-shop economics and psychology which Robert Roberts describes in *The Classic Slum* was altogether a different world from the middle-class experience.

Shopping facilities constituted only one aspect of the changing infrastructure of suburbs. Churches, schools, pubs, theatres, doctors' surgeries, solicitors' offices, naturally settled there. Evident, too, was an incipient decentralization of industrial and business activity. Some businesses catered entirely for suburban needs: building and repair trades, coal and timber merchants, gas and electricity works, laundries, bakeries and breweries. But constricted space and high rents and rates in city centres were driving other businesses to suburban sites. There they could expand on freehold land, and reach regional and national markets with little inconvenience, given adequate rail links, telephone lines, and electric power. This extension of industry into suburbs, however, was an unregulated development, which aroused the consternation of the emergent planning movement.

These developments need to be carefully weighed by historians for another reason: places gradually so changed in structure as to defy consistent categorization. Camberwell, for instance, began as a detached village outside London, became a satellite community, then was fully absorbed as a suburb. By 1900 it is far from certain whether the historian is dealing with a suburb or a veiled new town because many, perhaps a majority, of the occupied part of the population of 259,000 both lived and worked in Camberwell itself. Suburbs, then, vary not only in the circumstances of their estate development and class composition, but also in their structural complexity, particularly in the degree of dependence upon the metropolitan area which they initially sprang up to serve. This dependence may be of shorter duration and lesser substance than first appears, for many residential suburbs developed their own social and economic matrix. Certainly the amount of commuting to work outside the suburb by public transport, rather than proceeding independently to work within the suburb by foot or bicycle, can be exaggerated. J. R. Kellett has estimated, about south London, that in 1890 only one person in twelve used train, tram or omnibus to reach his work. Still, this commuting population was of strategic importance for, as D. J. Olsen remarks, had not that one person maintained that habit the other eleven would hardly live where they did. The rest were mostly dependants – family, domestic servants, and purveyors of services. These client categories were smaller in working-class than in middle-class suburbs.

III

Emphatically this was the railway age. Except for the Great Central (built in the 1890s), the main network was established before 1870; but between 1870 and 1912 the track mileage increased by 50 per cent, from 13,562 to 20,038 miles. Much of this extension was in rural branch or suburban services; and third-class travellers, attracted by falling prices, preponderated in the expanding traffic. Seventeen per cent of railway passengers travelled third-class in 1845; 77.5 per cent did so in 1875, 95 per cent by 1905. During the 1870s the annual number of passengers other than season-ticket holders rose from 322.2 to 596.6 million. By 1912 there were 1,295.5 million. But the historian of suburbs should not be a railway maniac. Many railways followed rather than anticipated suburban building. The extent of London suburbs before the 1880s was determined mostly by the reach of horse-drawn omnibuses; thereafter trams were important. The number of journeys made by individual Londoners on local railways, trams, and omnibuses was 52.7 in 1878, 133 in 1902, and 271 in 1913; but by far the greater proportion of these journeys was by road, not rail – 96 out of 133 journeys in 1902 and 210 out of 271 in 1913. The railways' contribution to working-class suburbia was uneven. The Great Western, London and North Western, and Midland Railway Companies provided very few workmen's trains, while the Great Eastern supplied extensive services. This confirmed as much as caused the direction of suburban growth, although railway and suburban-building could proceed in close conjunction, as in the Hither Green district of Lewisham. Lower-middle-class estates were developed there in the 1890s, to which tenants were enticed by free season tickets. Correspondingly, meagre public transport would limit suburban frontiers.

About 6,000 people daily travelled into central London by trains in 1854. By 1900 the Great Eastern alone brought 19,000 into Liverpool Street by early-morning workmen's trains; another 35,000 pursued them on trains which offered reduced fares; and quantities of season-ticket holders arrived around 9 o'clock. This staggered arrangement reflected an order of manual and clerical workers and managers; also length of journey, because the affluent had moved deeper into Essex and Hertfordshire. By 1900, when 4,697 trains daily arrived at the twenty-two London stations which could be called termini, 4,252 represented suburban traffic. A system of underground railways had been developed meanwhile, from 1863, linking these termini; and electrification was pursued from the 1890s. London's underground and surface railways carried about 600 million passengers per annum by 1900.

Outside London the railways were underused by commuters. Nottingham's civic authorities obliged the railway companies to provide suburban stations, and thirty-two were established within a six-mile arc of the city centre; but the Nottingham Suburban Railway, opened in 1889, could not withstand the competition of the trams and was to close in 1916. Around Manchester some wealthy commuters came into the city from Alderley Edge and Wilmslow along the main line from Crewe; and Altrincham had been linked by the Manchester South Junction line from the 1840s. But working-class railway commuting was inconsiderable in the absence of a cheap-fares policy. In Birmingham suburban lines were constructed from the 1870s. By Edwardian times falling receipts from many stations indicated the supremacy of alternative travel as well as the decline of the central city as a place of work. There were trams and there were bicycles; still, most people went to work under their own steam, as always. Provincial cities could be crossed on foot in an hour or less. The majority of people either contrived to live close to their work or were not deterred, as the post-1960 generation, by a walk of a couple of miles.

To estimate the influence of railways on suburbia only by the number of their passengers is to minimize unduly. Though short haulage was mostly by road, railways furnished suburban economies with significant goods and services. Their appetite for land for stations, engine depots, and carriage and wagon yards meant, too, that railways aggravated the housing crisis in city centres and hastened the movement outwards. By 1900, according to J. R. Kellett, railways occupied between 5 and 9 per cent of land in central London, Liverpool, Manchester, Birmingham, and Glasgow. Railways thus considerably influenced urban morphology. Many thousand persons – perhaps four million – required re-housing as railway stations and yards displaced them in the half-century from 1850. Furthermore, railway cuttings, embankments, and viaducts stimulated variable land use, here sequestering urban and agricultural land, there distinguishing one type of built-up area from another. Slums and wasteland, allotments and marginal usage, were defined by railway lines.

Few Victorians of sensibility failed to execrate the railway as a vandal of noise, ugliness, and destruction. The price of convenience appeared too high to A. J. Munby, contemplating in 1864 the railway extension from Charing Cross to London Bridge: 'Who are we, that we should decimate the population and defile our children's minds with the sight of these monstrous and horrible forms, for the sake of gaining half an hour on the way to our work or our dinner?' And when railway companies sought to curry favour by embellishing their stations, a critic like Ruskin was moved to greater wrath, pronouncing this tendency 'strange and evil'. Strange because a station 'is the very temple of discomfort, and the only charity that the builder can extend to us is to show us, plainly as may be, how soonest to escape from it'. Evil because it consumed moneys which might be better used to raise railwaymen's wages or to reduce fares; and because the traveller's sense of beauty would be so corrupted by 'old English-looking spandrels to the roof of the station at Crewe . . . [that] he will only have less pleasure in their prototypes at Crewe House'.

Some proposterous shams were erected, but more generous (or deteriorated) tastes now appreciate the architecture of several railway stations and hotels. British Rail in 1980 had 300 protected properties, listed for historical interest. There is quality in the work of architects like John Dobson (Newcastle), Thomas Prosser (York), William Barlow (St. Pancras), Lewis Cubitt (King's Cross), Sir John Fowler (Manchester Central), and Sir William Tite (Carlisle and Edinburgh) who were without Ruskin's defeatist functionalism. Dobson contended that, as 'structures seen by thousands', stations might contribute 'towards improving the taste of the public'. At least they stirred argument about dignity in public buildings and harmony in setting. Waterhouse, Gilbert Scott, Hardwick, and many less known, produced buildings of force and imagination; and John O'Connor's painting, *St. Pancras Hotel and Station from Pentonville Road: Sunset* (1881), was one artist's acknowledgement of the exciting townscapes which could result.

The railway's impact, then, was felt in most cities but, outside London, its share of suburban transport was small. For those not content with pedestrianism, the horse-omnibus and tramways provided greater flexibility. By 1900 sixty-one tramway systems were managed by local authorities, another eighty-nine by private companies. They were not innocent contributors to the urban scene, any more than the railways. Horse-trams, like hackney carriages – 'crawlers' and 'growlers' – were abominated by many compelled to use them; dirty, smelly, slow and not infrequently accident-prone, 'only fit for firewood', said *The Observer* of 13 April 1873. In Cambridge, according to Gwen Raverat, the horse-tram was so ponderous 'a running child could beat it easily'. Together with increasing numbers of private carriages and business carts, the horse-buses and tramcars brought traffic jams to many cities.

London was the chief sufferer and a Royal Commission was appointed under Sir David Barbour in 1903. It well understood that traffic delays represented both a hidden cost to industry and a scourge to individuals. Its report, in 1905, advocated a £24-million investment in two 140-feet-wide avenues, east–west and north–south, carrying four lanes of electric trams above the surface and four lines of electric railways below. Generally, it recommended broader streets, more extensive, frequent, and cheaper suburban transit, and a traffic board to co-ordinate systems and to overrule local authorities which presently impeded through-running. Apart from the Kingsway–Strand improvement, however, nothing was executed on any great scale. At this date 500 million passengers were carried annually by

London's 4,000 horse-omnibuses, and only 165 million (10 million at workmen's or reduced fares) on the LCC's tramways. The LCC supplied only one mile of single tramway for every 21,200 of population, compared with one mile for 6,781 persons in hilly Liverpool or 3,942 in flatter Manchester. Only 30 of the 107 miles of the LCC's system were electrified. Worse, north and south were disconnected, because the House of Lords prohibited tram lines along the Thames bridges and embankment, a ban it maintained until 1906.

At a time when heavy investment was incurred in extending this network, some objected that the tramcar was doomed like the horse-omnibus. The latter indeed had disappeared from London streets by 1914; but the majority of the Barbour Commission seriously underestimated the importance of motor omnibuses, thinking them unlikely to supersede trams to any degree, their function being rather to supplement them. Of course, the whole subject of traffic mobility drew visionaries and practical men in debate – about slow and fast lanes, suspended railways, pedestrian subways, fly-overs and double-decked streets – but in motor vehicles visionariness and practicality already seemed joined.

In 1904 there were 8,465 private cars, about 4,000 goods vans, and 5,345 public transport vehicles (buses, coaches, taxis); in 1914 132,015 cars, 82,010 lorries, and 51,167 public transport vehicles. Mostly the buses' substantial impact was deferred beyond 1918, owing to the expense and unreliability of the first products and to local authority investment in alternative transport. London was the exception: motor-bus traffic increased hugely after its appearance on London streets in 1905. The Webbs explained why, in *The Story of the King's Highway* (1920): first, motor-bus working costs, even after Lloyd George's taxes (1909), were 7½*d*. per mile compared with 11*d*. or 12*d*. for trams; second, the LCC, unlike most municipalities, was not both tramway authority and omnibus-licensing authority. It could not guard its tramway investment by restraining motor-bus services. By 1913 investment in London motor-buses was about £4m. compared with £20m. in trams; but the buses carried almost the same number of passengers and yielded vastly greater profits. Motor-bus services extended as far as Windsor, Barnet, and Epping.

In the provinces, Liverpool introduced motor-buses in 1911, Birmingham in 1913; altogether eighteen local authorities ran a bus service by 1914. However, the recent heavy investment in electrification meant that most protected their tramways, and these survived into the 1940s and 1950s. Elsewhere a progressive middle-class resort, Eastbourne, ostentatiously introduced buses in 1903; and the bigger railway companies, like the Great Western, North Eastern, and London and North Western, employed them to stimulate their rural stations. Still, outside London, buses were mostly auxiliaries before 1914, and their appearance only aggravated long-standing complaints: more congestion, noise, danger, and breakdowns, more expensive road administration, more disturbance to country as well as town. Later, motorized transport accelerated that de-industrialization and residential disintegration of the city which the railways began.

IV

As suburban–city transport redoubled the traffic congestion, some thought to encourage satellite towns to restore advantages of scale that big cities and their suburbs were losing. Industry might benefit by reduced costs, employees benefit from housing, ease of movement, and as part of a more intimate community. Furthermore, it would counter that tendency of small towns to become drained by the migration of their more enterprising inhabitants to metropolitan centres. There was danger, however, in approaching questions functionally, because not every small town could sustain the shock to its organic system which industries would bring. Increased rates, to support expenditure on new streets, sewers, main water and power services, were likely to be borne grudgingly by established inhabitants. They must reckon, too, the social costs of industrialization – environmental disruption – and the prospect that it might come to dominate local affairs. The result would be that the indigenous life would perish as surely as if the metropolitan centres continued to aggregate industry.

Already these tensions were suspected in 1876 when the antiquary, James Thorne, published *The Environs of London.* In Hertfordshire New Barnet, a railway suburb growing around the market town of High Barnet, scene of Warwick's final stand in the Wars of the Roses, attracted Thorne's disapproval. The newcomers were probably not unlike Molly Hughes and her lawyer husband, who, with a growing family in the 1890s, wanted to quit their Ladbroke Grove flat – 'we felt that more space was wanted, and a bit of garden. We consulted Bradshaw [the railway timetable] to find some spot that was "country" and yet provided with a few fast trains to town.' Barnet was not exceptionally strained by this suburban growth. As yet this was residential not industrial, and the town comprised under 8,000 people in 1901. Thorne's prognostication about Redhill in Surrey was more accurate. Though this railway suburb of Reigate was chiefly a transit camp of the well-to-do, its transforming potential was considerable and Reigate's population topped 25,000 by 1901. South of London, Bromley, Chislehurst and, archetypally, Croydon, were other market towns which moved uneasily between the categories of suburban subjection and satellitic independence.

In the 1890s Croydon was among the eight fastest growing places in England. The other seven were all suburbs or satellites to the north and east of London. A coaching station on the London–Brighton road, Croydon already had over 5,000 citizens in 1801. The town was a rendezvous for City hunt followers, like the ineffable Jorrocks; otherwise it supplied market facilities for rustics who, according to Jorrocks's creator, R. S. Surtees, retained 'much of their pristine barbarity'. Croydon contained 20,000 people in 1851, 134,000 by 1901. This dramatic upsurge brought equally dramatic social conflict, between established Liberal Nonconformist tradesmen and predominantly Conservative Anglican commuters, as R. C. W. Cox has traced. Incorporated in 1883, Croydon was kicked from one age to another within twenty years. The medieval market place and central slums were displaced by a modern shopping centre and panoply of public buildings, including a new town hall and police station. Industrial establishments grew apace: breweries naturally, also boot and shoe factories, a large clock factory, and, around the First World War, a typewriter factory. Croydon was 'improved' from an independent market town to substantial satellite town by a familiar combination, according to Dr Cox, 'of indifference and apathy, of greed and selfishness, of benevolence and faith'.

The satellite model of town planning was very ambitious, even visionary. It amounted to the regional city. The advantages which a metropolis could provide, such as university education, quality theatres and superior services, would be retained in the central city; the disadvantages of megalopolis, such as traffic turmoil, diminished civic consciousness and distance from the countryside, would be avoided in the satellite cities. Thomas Sharp summarized the case for satellite planning in 1940: the remedy for over-centralization was 'not *de*centralization, for that would involve the loss of the attractions which can only be centrally provided: but *sub*-centralization for certain purposes, round a lessened centre maintained for other purposes'. In practice the distinction between a satellite town and large suburb has been hard to define, because developments have been unplanned and because of circumstances of economic flux and social and political friction. Nor has this been an academic question. It had material significance after 1888 when county councils met applications from suburban townships which wanted to secede from county administrative control and assume the status of county boroughs. Surrey County Council acknowledged several principles, which are worthy of consideration by urban historians. The County Council's vice-chairman, Alderman E. J. Holland, accepted Croydon's application on two grounds: 'there was an industrial community in Croydon, and . . . [a]lthough Croydon might have attained its present size because of its connexion with London, it would have existed independently of London. . . .' The Royal Commission on Local Government in 1925 summarized the position:

[Most] County Boroughs constituted by or under the Act of 1888 had been complete communities, not only industrially, but because they had their own residential population, and in many instances a traditional form of government. They were, therefore, correctly described as complete civic organisms covering a variety of interests, and could not be compared with the Non-County Boroughs in Surrey, Richmond, Kingston, and Wimbledon, . . . although both Kingston and Richmond had a good deal of local interests and civic pride, and Kingston was one of the oldest Boroughs in the country. The Surrey County Council, in opposing [in 1913] the proposal to constitute Wimbledon into a County Borough, had put forward the view that Wimbledon was in fact a suburb of London, and was not a place which had an independent existence in the sense already indicated.

Croydon was a market town whose independence, though of a different character from what it once was, survived the pressures of suburban growth. Before 1914 it retained a genuine personality as a satellite town in a way that the Kentish small market town, Bromley, subjected to similar strains, did not. In his novels and *Experiment in Autobiography* (1934) H. G. Wells described the swamping of his home town under 'the deluge of suburbanism'. The core grouping of shops, school, and church of the old market town distended into 'a morbid sprawl'. Meadows were built over, hedges became iron railings, and the little river Ravensbourne was engulfed by a new drainage system and general rubbish. Bromley in 1901 contained over 27,000 souls. The result of their undisciplined efforts was a mess, but an unexceptional mess: the usual villas and slums, railway, unsightly hoardings, misplaced and poorly designed business premises, made-over gardens, unfinished and aimless roads, intense enterprise resulting in a community without coherence. Wells's requiem for Bromley was not finally without hope, however:

It was a sort of progress that had bolted; it was change out of hand, and going at an unprecedented pace nowhere in particular . . . ; it was a hasty, trial experiment, a gigantic experiment of the most slovenly and wasteful kind. I suppose it was necessary; I suppose all things are necessary. . . . Well, we have to do better. Failure is not failure nor waste wasted if it sweeps away illusion and lights the road to a plan.

V

Planning was the thing. It is difficult now to empathize with this mood. Few still imagine planners as public champions, riding out to slay the dragons of selfish vested interests and to release the captive maidens of beauty, justice, and order. Modern disenchantment with planning is well advanced. The planners seem an even worse risk than the planless, equally insensitive but more deadly because more ambitious. In fact this suspicion is not new. Historians have revered planners unduly. A distance always separated the planners and the public, and not only in proportion to that distance between the planners' professions and performances. The Town and Country Planning Advisory Committee to the Ministry of Health, in 1938, summarized the problem:

A planning scheme for a large area is necessarily both complicated and technical. Members of the public frequently complain that it is unintelligible. There has been a tendency to regard planning as a combination of faddism and technical jargon, and its main impact upon the lay mind lies in what appears to be a series of irritating restrictions on the individual. To this extent planning has lacked the popular interest and the sense of achievement associated with services where results can be seen in a short period of time.

Sir John Maude's Committee included two notable planners, Patrick Abercrombie and Raymond Unwin, whose formative years lay within the period encompassed by this book. From the Government they sought wider prescriptive powers for controlled land development. The Committee also berated past governments for their failure to encourage planners or to educate the public in the need for planning. Governments had given some consideration to planning suburbs or to renovating run-down districts; but governments gave very little consideration to planning whole towns and almost no consideration to planning between towns and on a regional or national scale.

The very first Town Planning Act (1909) was infirm, although the President of the Local Government Board, John Burns, presented it to Parliament in ringing tones. This would secure 'the home healthy, the house beautiful, the town pleasant, the city dignified, and the suburb salubrious'. Instead, its ideas were narrowly conceived, within existing housing-of-the-working-classes legislation. The most significant step was to enforce on local authorities the previously permissive section (part III) of the 1890 Housing Act. The specific town-planning clauses were designed to regulate *suburban* development; but local authorities remained without power to acquire land compulsorily outside their boundaries in order to plan expansion. Facilities were hedged with a customary regard for private interests, whose agreement and compensation were preconditions for any scheme winning the Local Government Board's approval. Altogether the Government's impetus to planning was, Herman Finer caustically observed, as effective as 'talking in their sleep'. Later, the Ministry of Health's first annual report, 1919–20, identified the issue.

The town itself has become too small a unit for regulating development. The administrative boundaries of Local Authorities frequently do not coincide with the boundaries of a geographical, industrial or economic unit, which may include the areas of a number of districts, urban and rural. In order to provide for the proper development of such a unit, a regional survey and regional planning are required. . . .

Moreover, financial incentives to town planning were absent. The Manchester Liberal, Ernest Simon, observed:

Town planning, if well done, tends to increase the value of property as a whole, but where individual owners are benefited the local authority generally fails in practice to secure any betterment. Where individual authorities [*sic*] are damaged the local authority has to pay compensation. This weighting of the scales in favour of private interests and against the community is probably the greatest bar to effective and extensive town planning.

Thus, though several enterprising corporations were spurred further by the town-planning clauses of the 1909 Act, planners before 1914 worked mostly on their own and within a legal framework devised for other purposes. Burns was uncomprehending. He complained in

1912, 'I get more letters about my town planning and housing scheme from the United States than I do from England.' The egotistical Burns faulted the local authorities rather than doubted his legislation. Nineteenth-century planners had no shortage of precepts and illustrations. *Reliquiae* of past planners survived in several towns with Roman, medieval, or renaissance centres. The lay-out of Salisbury, a cathedral city of 20,000 people in 1901, still exhibited the thirteenth-century chequers pattern; and there were many more examples from nearer their own times, such as the planned estates of Edinburgh, Newcastle, or London. Indeed, it is important to stress, as did Thomas Sharp in *Town Planning* (1940), that a specifically English tradition of town planning may be identified up to Victorian times. The values it reflected, compared with most foreign traditions, were decent and domestic rather than spectacular and monumental. Quite early on, needs of defence – battlemented walls – ceased to be a major consideration in English town development; nor did English towns much suffer from a compulsion to glorify by physical symbols the power of absolute monarchs. What architectural orderliness obtained in English towns was unpretentious, the result of a striving after comfortableness more than vanity. The problem facing the Victorians, therefore, was not an absence of sound theories and examples but how to fit them together, to preserve the best of the planned and random beauty of the past while coping with modern social and industrial needs. Rapid economic growth especially taxed the imagination of nineteenth-century planners and confounded them with its appetites. Industrial towns commonly burst out of their projected limits, to spoil an original design. At Middlesbrough some symmetry from the gridiron pattern of the planned settlement (1829) persisted in the expanding town; otherwise the conceptions of Joseph Pease and his co-founders were dashed, for, as Briggs has written, 'once the town spilt out of the original rectangle there was no inducement to retain homogeneity of style or architecture. There was no inducement either to relate working-class housing to any other criterion than nearness to work.'

The distinctive English tradition of town planning was not extinguished by nineteenth-century industrialization. It was, however, repressed. Hence, when the term 'town planning' gained currency in England in the early twentieth century, it emerged partly as an anglicization of debates in Germany and Austria between theorists and practitioners such as Reinhard Baumeister, Joseph Stübben, and Camillo Sitte. The American, Albert Shaw, introduced English readers to some of their work in *Municipal Government in Continental Europe* (1895); and the Ruskinian industrialist, T. C. Horsfall, made much of German examples in his housing survey on behalf of the Manchester and Salford Citizens' Association in 1904. When Raymond Unwin issued *Town Planning in Practice* (1909) the leading German ideas were widely diffused. Unwin, however, conceded that he and Barry Parker might have organized Letchworth (1903) differently had they properly known Sitte's writings. Sitte's informing spirit was humanistic: city buildings, streets and squares should be so scaled and diversified as to be congenial, intimate. Sitte's antagonist was the architect-as-engineer or 'geometer', the Haussmanns of the nineteenth century and the Le Corbusiers of the twentieth century, who transformed living cities into road–towns and thought of houses as machines. Wells's novel, *When the Sleeper Wakes* (1899), was not so much science fiction as a projection of existing trends. Technocracy already obsessed the imagination of municipal authorities. Only economists could hold engineers in check. Aesthetes were overwhelmed by both, because their conceptions seemed less relevant to problems of public health, traffic congestion, and land use. Straight streets, subways, ring roads, elevated monorails, automobiles, aircraft, machine-built houses, skyscrapers, electric lifts, central heating, these were the artefacts of future cities.

The constructions of Baron Haussmann and his disciples upset the aesthetes, who felt summoned to defend individuality from what Henry James called their 'huge, blank, pompous, featureless sameness'. Socialists struck a different note: Haussmannesque planning was a capitalist deceit. Engels stated the indictment:

In reality the bourgeoisie has only one method of solving the housing question after *its* fashion – that is to say, of solving it in such a way that the solution continually reproduces itself anew. This method is called 'Haussmann'. . . . By 'Haussmann' I mean the practice which has now become general of making breaches in the working-class quarters of our big towns, and particularly in areas which are centrally situated, quite apart from whether this is done from considerations of public health and for beautifying the town, or owing to the demand for big centrally situated business premises, or owing to traffic requirements, such as the laying down of railways, streets (which sometimes appear to have the strategic aim of making barricade fighting more difficult). . . . No matter how different the reasons may be, the result is everywhere the same; the scandalous alleys disappear to the accompaniment of lavish self-praise from the bourgeoisie on account of the tremendous success, but they appear again immediately somewhere else and often in the immediate neighbourhood! . . . As long as the capitalist mode of production continues to exist, it is folly to hope for an isolated solution to the housing question or of any other social question affecting the face of the workers.

The indispensability of the communist alternative was reached by means of false syllogism. There *was* a political component to planning, architectural, aesthetic, technological, legal, and sociological aspects, also. The fault with too many planners was that their thought was one-dimensional. Architects concentrated on house-building, engineers on roads, and so forth. Few thought in terms of communities except in the haziest way, that a better physical environment would raise the level of social harmony and economic efficiency. The need was to co-ordinate people and functions, to complement social and industrial organization, and to produce models which would permit growth and change. There was some excuse for their modest endeavours, however, for every element of comprehensive planning was plagued with controversy. Take the aesthetic qualities of individual buildings, for instance. Whose senses were blessed? William Morris founded the Society for the Protection of Ancient Buildings in 1877, on the occasion of Sir George Gilbert Scott's plans for the 'restoration' of Tewkesbury Minster. This was a major trophy to be contested; but the 'craze for indiscriminate church-restoration' already affected humble parishes, as Thomas Hardy, architect-turned-novelist, registered in *A Pair of Blue Eyes* (1873). Hardy and Morris held views as strong as Sitte about genuine art having its roots in local or national cultures, which should be snapped only at peril. In fact the late nineteenth century was more active, not more sinful, in this respect. The Gilbert Scotts only followed such as James Wyatt, whose restorations in several cathedrals, particularly Salisbury and Durham, earned him the reputation of 'the Destroyer'. Now wholesale demolitions occurred as well as clumsy restorations – several City churches, by Wren and others, were 'sacrificed to the Mammon-worship' in the 1860s and 1870s; ancient schools, like High Wycombe Grammar and Eton College, were recast in the 1880s; famous old streets, like the Broad and Holywell in Oxford, were brutally invaded at the same time. Morris in 1881 was devoid of hope: 'we have begun too late and our foes are too many; videlicet, almost all people, educated and uneducated. No, as to the buildings themselves, 'tis a lost cause; in fact the destruction is not far from being complete already.'

The case for reserving a place for the past in any future scheme was strong and, *pace* Morris's tantrums, did not go unheeded. G. J. Shaw-Lefevre, as first commissioner of public works, was Morris's *bête noire* after Gilbert Scott's death in 1878; nonetheless, he piloted through Parliament the Ancient Monuments Act, 1882. This was insufficiently forceful, a permissive act enabling owners to place ancient monuments under State protection. Vehement campaigns were required to spare the Avebury stones and Vale of the White Horse from development in the late nineteenth century. Still, Parliament had not made an empty gesture, and educated opinion was awakened in the cause. A register has been maintained ever since the Royal Commission on Historical Monuments was appointed in 1908.

The prime concerns of physical planners, however, revolved around the functional bases of all civilization, homes and workplaces. Charles Kingsley's Bristol lecture, 'Great Cities and their Influence for Good and Evil' (1857) imparted an axiom for progressives: 'if you cannot bring the country into the city, the city must go into the country.' Cities should be reserved for work, country for dwelling. But proper decentralization was unattainable without a greater degree of public action. Planning was thus a totem of collectivist ideologues: individuals left to themselves would not act to the community's benefit. Moreover, a managed economy seemed an inescapable corollary of political democracy, with its quest for social justice.

In progressive opinion none of the planned communities of the nineteenth century fulfilled these conditions, since they were tainted with industrial feudalism as surely as Whitehaven in the seventeenth and Maryport in the eighteenth century, those West Cumberland ports born of the prosperous Irish coal trade and the Lowthers' and Senhouses' greed and imagination. Similar examples now were impersonal company dormitories, like the railway centres, New Swindon or Crewe, where captive workers were caged in regulation housing. The locomotive workshops in these towns employed 14,000 and 7,000 persons respectively by 1914. Their housing was model compared with many a colliery village; still, private enterprise could show a better face than either railway or mining towns, as J. E. B. Meakin emphasized in *Model Factories and Villages* (1905): 'In standards of housing and in imaginative town planning it was business that gave the lead to local government.'

The enlightened employer was a curious type, so singular perhaps as not to be a type at all, for his humanitarianism and desire to experiment derived from many springs. Robert Owen's phalanstery at New Lanark in the early nineteenth century queerly blended utilitarian capitalism and paternalism with millenarian communism. According to Sidney Pollard, 'managerial necessity' drove a variety of employers in the early industrial revolution to provide houses, truck and other shops, schools and churches. They were supplied by employers either because no other agency was forthcoming, or from a desire to fasten workers to them. This may be too severe a verdict on the Oldknows, Ashworths, and Gregs; but clearly historians should resist a tendency to confuse this provision of basic services with heroic and original philosophies of improvement or communitarian living.

Some model factory villages did involve ideas beyond the utilitarian or disciplinarian. The factory estates outside Bradford and Halifax, planned by Titus Salt, Edward Akroyd, and Francis Crossley between 1850 and 1870, were essays in urban regeneration. The alpaca manufacturer, Salt, had pronounced ethical views. He banned public houses from his estate, which comprised 820 houses and 4,400 people when he died in 1876. Saltaire was equipped with school, Congregational and Wesleyan chapels, institute, hospital, laundry, public baths, park, and almshouses for the aged. Moreover, the three-bedroomed houses were built to better specifications than utilitarian considerations strictly warranted, although the density of persons per acre was higher than thought desirable by later town-planners.

Factory villages were inspired by compact aristocratic rural communities, real or imagined. This vision imbued Akroydon and Crossley West Hill Park Estate, where allotments or gardens were supplied with workers' cottages. Akroyd, unusually, permitted workers to buy their homes; but this was a new means to an old end, to close 'the breach in feeling between the ancient village and the new industrial age', and to curb the residential mobility of the lower classes. All these establishments – and others of the same period, like James Wilson's estate at Bromborough (1853) for Price's Patent Candle factory – were based on the premiss that personal supervision, contact, or example would transmit bourgeois values of thrift, family life, sobriety, smartness, regularity, sexual morality, rational recreation, and spiritual comfort. But these persuasions were strained by the unequal relationship of master and men, and weakened as the suburbs of neighbouring towns encroached upon the self-containment of the factory estates. Stanley Pierson concludes that 'cohesion nowhere long survived the passing of the men from whose will and vision it derived'.

Industrialists were not finished with the idea of the factory estate. In Somerset the Quaker family of shoemakers, C. & J. Clark Ltd., built model housing for their workers in the industrial village of Street, an annexe of Glastonbury, after production was mechanized from the 1850s. It was in the industrial Midlands and north, however, that the most significant extensions of the tradition were made: in Lever's Port Sunlight (1888), Cadbury's Bournville (1895), Rowntree's New Earswick (1902) and Reckitt's Garden Village at Hull (1907). These owed more to contemporary notions of urban and suburban planning than to lingering perceptions of archaic rural forms. Not that it is easy to separate these visions. One stylistic influence upon Lever, for example, was R. Norman Shaw's *Sketches for Cottages and Other Buildings* (1878); even more, Shaw's practical expression of these ideas, his buildings on the upper-middle-class garden estate, Bedford Park, London (1877–82). Unashamedly, the Lever, Cadbury, Rowntree, and Reckitt estates were ventures in business efficiency. These employers were convinced that it paid to secure healthful, methodical workforces; and, since their products were mostly for personal consumption – soap, cocoa, chocolate, and starch – the advertising advantages of a sparkling environment were unmistakable. But they were also employers who were concerned for the welfare of their workers in a manner which cannot be passed off as cynical or specious. A conjunction of religious and secular service was apparent. Reckitt, Rowntree, and Cadbury were Quakers; Lever was also a Free Churchman. All four men were Liberals. Their chief conviction was simple: it was good business sense, also moral sense, to disperse manufacture from town to country.

Lever was a proponent of profit-sharing; and at Port Sunlight he wanted more than a tied village or rich man's toy. Rather he sought to establish a vital community, superior to existing towns not only in its housing and sanitary facilities but also in its public interest in common concerns. Lever argued that the slum landlord's habit of compounding rents and rates bred popular indifference to local government. In Port Sunlight rates and rents were itemized separately and, so Lever alleged, this raised popular consciousness about civic expenditure on education and other amenities. Twenty years on, Lever proudly pointed to the physical specimens reared by his model housing and schools. Port Sunlight children were generally taller and heavier than their social-class counterparts in Liverpool Council schools, approximating instead to those in Higher Grade schools in the wealthier parts of Liverpool.

Bournville was different again. Here Cadbury founded a self-governing community with an independent Trust, rather than a charitable and dependent works village. Houses were leased at economic rents, to defray interest charges on invested capital. They were not subsidized at below cost price. The whole thing paid its way. Without relatively high wages this was impossible. Facilities existed to convert leasehold to freehold; and all revenues were reinvested by the Trust, in more model housing or amenities. Cadbury set an example to public authorities in estate allocation. No house occupied more than a quarter of its own site; factories occupied no more than a fifteenth of the developed area; parks and gardens occupied a tenth of the land. By 1901 Bournville covered 500 acres, upon which 370 houses had been built. In 143 the occupants paid ground rent; the rest were let on weekly tenancies. Twenty years later the estate had grown to 720 houses, and 1,000 houses were achieved within thirty years.

Cadbury's detractors used Bellocian imagery from *The Servile State* (1912), arguing that Bournville workers sold their liberty in exchange for security. Thus J. B. Priestley in 1934 thought that Cadbury's workers were in danger of believing that the

factory is the most urgent and grandest of human activities, that cocoa is not made for man, but man for cocoa. Pensions and bonuses, works councils, factory publications, entertainments and dinners and garden parties and outings organised by the firm, these . . . can easily create an atmosphere that is injurious to the growth of men as intellectual and spiritual beings, for they can give what is . . . a trading concern for private profit a falsely mystical aura, can drape its secular form with sacramental cloths, and completely wreck the proper scale of values.

Again, A. G. Gardiner, in *The Life of George Cadbury* (1923), observed that though Cadbury recognized trade unions 'the conditions at Bournville tended to weaken the sentiment of trade unionism'. But humbug resounds in these charges. Where was the perfect state of liberty for Cradley Heath chain-makers, working at domestic forges for sweated rates of pay? Just as Cadbury, a rich man, coped with the temptations of being miserly or profligate, so his employees had to cope with the temptations of welfare. Social democracy was not inevitably imperilled. In any case the Bournville estate was not built exclusively to house Cadbury's workers. It had been designed more broadly, a new venture in urban living. The Cadbury model influenced Sir James Reckitt's village at Hull and Rowntree's New Earswick estate at York. Again, these estates were not reserved for employees of the founders' business: by 1930 only half the Earswick families worked at Rowntree's. The New Earswick architects were Raymond Unwin and Barry Parker, co-planners of Letchworth. The Garden City was the ideal. Its prophet was Ebenezer Howard, author of *Tomorrow: A Peaceful Path to Real Reform* (1898), revised and reissued as *Garden Cities of To-morrow* (1902). A one-time stenographer, Howard is sometimes upheld as an exception among the generally unenterprising clerkly class. Others see in his simplicity and quixotism an exception that proved the rule. Howard was a physical planner. Town and country must be married in garden cities, to enjoy the best of both, with low-density housing, green belts, and separate industrial and agricultural zones (see Fig. 4). He also possessed a sociological imagination. To develop into complete communities, garden cities required representatives of various classes. That this organic vision suffused the modern town-planning movement was largely due to the popularization of the concept of 'Civics' by the Scottish biologist, Patrick Geddes. The so-called 'father' of town planning, Geddes never planned anything in practice apart from extravagant and largely abortive schemes for Dunfermline, India, and Jerusalem; but his lectures strengthened the conviction that a mixed community was essential for balanced growth. Port Sunlight and the rest were stricken as largely one-class artisan settlements.

The derivative nature of Howard's writing was clear. 'The same old vision' was George Bernard Shaw's reaction upon reading Howard's book in 1899. He reckoned that a similar project had come to his attention at least once every seven years, and he privately advised friends not to contribute a farthing more to Howard's scheme than they were anxious to lose. Buckingham, Paxton, Pemberton, and Richardson among other utopian town-planners; Carlyle, Ruskin, Morris, Bellamy, Kropotkin, and Henry George among other critics of capitalist uglification: the list of influences upon Howard can be extended to a length that becomes pointless. What needs underlining is the conjunction of co-operativism and progressivism in late-nineteenth-century thought. 'Associated individualism' was how

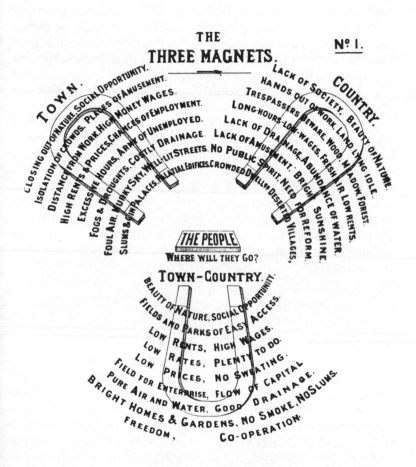

Fig. 4 The three magnets: town, country, and town–country

Source: E. Howard, *Garden Cities of To-morrow* (1902).

Howard defined his social philosophy. Others, like the university settlement movement, had idealized the small mixed community or 'neighbourhood'. The gentrification of working-class districts might restore the political and moral influence of the educated and obviate the trend to impersonality, conflict, and tyranny inherent in overgrown cities where commercialism and bureaucracy were unfettered. Capitalism could be sanitized without surrender to state socialism. Rich and poor might be diverted from a collision course. The lion would lie down with the lamb.

Howard's programme was altogether grander – a constellation of medium-sized and balanced townships. Believing that the evils of overcrowded cities and depopulated countryside were related and should be tackled together, the aim was, as near as possible, self-contained towns. Independent of other cities for essential services, the garden cities would retain community control of the freeholds for factories as well as for housing. Howard's ideal town size was 32,000 people, of whom 2,000 followed agricultural pursuits. The first instalment was laid out at Letchworth in 1903–4. In *John Bull's Other Island* (1904) Shaw included this dialogue:

> BROADBENT. Have you ever heard of Garden City?
> TIM (*doubtfully*). D'ye mane Heav'n?
> BROADBENT. Heaven! No: it's near Hitchin.

The playwright's scepticism subsequently faded, replaced by an admiration for the man whom he once dubbed the Garden City Geyser. When Howard was knighted in 1927 Shaw wrote: 'He deserved a knighthood for his book, a baronetcy for Letchworth, and an earldom for Welwyn.' Howard was astonishingly direct. He proposed no new legislation. He simply got on with the job , although it must be stressed that he would have got nowhere without influential contacts from the Garden City Association, like Lever, Cadbury, and a Liberal lawyer, Ralph Neville. By 1910 the First Garden City Company (1903) comprised 2,300 shareholders. Shortage of capital remained a problem. No dividend was paid before 1913, when one per cent was given; but the promoters did have their site of six square miles, purchased from fifteen different owners for £155,587, that is, about £40.15s. per acre. On it by 1910 had settled 6,500 people and 1,300 houses and other buildings, at a cost of £365,000. By the First World War the population was about 9,000 and £600,000 had been spent on buildings.

The intention was to confine the city-space to a third of the acreage, and to divide the rest into small farms and allotments, supplying fruit, vegetable and dairy products. In practice the agricultural scheme was curtailed: most land was leased to those farmers in occupation when the estate was bought. Industry was relegated to a 135-acre site to the north-east, screened by trees and a hill, and close to the railway. Nineteen factories were established by 1910, with another two taking shape. The Garden City Company offered cheap water and power as incentives. Most was clean, light industry, typified by the printing and book-binding businesses of Messrs. J. M. Dent & Co. and W. H. Smith & Co.

The Great War introduced an uncomfortable presence, a munitions factory; and housing controls were waived to accommodate Belgian refugee workmen. Still, as Zeppelin bombs fell harmlessly in nearby fields, there was satisfaction that a garden city was a more elusive target than a densely crowded, unplanned industrial centre. Thus Letchworth, though not consciously constructed for an air-transport or even motor age, was remarkably adaptable to new technologies. The complaints about planning deficiencies mostly did not concern the industrial structure.

The biggest nuisance was the citizenry: 60,000 trees could be planted without difficulty, 6,000 people could not. They required nine miles of roads, seventeen miles of water mains, twelve miles of gas mains, eleven miles of sewers. They had six churches, three banks, shops, comprehensive sports facilities, debating, theatrical and musical societies, horticultural clubs, camping and scouts associations. They also inherited two pubs with the original site. These were administered by a trust. A proposal to open another, near the station, was defeated in a parish poll three times in the first seven years. A non-alcoholic pub, furnished with games, was opened meantime. This armistice was temporary, thought C. S. Bremner, writing in the *Fortnightly Review*, September 1910: 'The brewers do a brisk trade in selling small barrels of ale to the working classes; so much is this the case, that probably the way is being slowly paved for the licensing of a house in the centre of the city.' The two existing pubs were 'remote from the working-class quarter'.

This last phrase told a familiar story. Letchworth comprised a mixture of classes who did not mix. The middle classes distributed themselves around Norton Way and in the south-west, popularly known as Snobs' Hill. Among them were faddists, cranks, and crackpots. A new town predictably attracted them. But where did practicable and impracticable idealism divide? Now that Howard had realized the Garden City, who was sure that the Letchworth Esperanto Society would not enthrone a language of universal understanding? The idealists numbered about seventy, distinguished by their hatless condition, aesthetic dress, sandals (the export of Edward Carpenter's homosexual soviet at Millthorpe), consumption of vegetables, and refusal to rail their front lawns. The socialist section tended to quarrel. Each one was his own committee and they failed to gain representation on the first Parish Council. The working classes congregated around Bird's Hill, near the factory area. Their housing was supplied mostly by two companies, the Garden City Tenants Ltd. and Letchworth Cottages and Buildings Ltd. Building societies advanced other money. Weekly rents and rates were usually 5s. 3d. (26p) for two-bedroomed cottages, 6s. 3d. (31p) for three-bedroomed. These were comparable to charges in artisan suburbs elsewhere; but some tenants fell into arrears, and a branch of the Guild of Help was organized to bail them out. What they got for their money was not prodigious. The largest room was 12 feet square, the kitchen poorly positioned, the stairs narrow, the bedrooms poky. From this general shortage of space, old complaints about the working-classes' bad habits resurfaced – fowl-keeping; unkempt gardens; bicycles and whatnot stored in the lavatory or living-room.

The social side of the Garden City worked out less well than the physical plan. This was unsurprising. Social disharmonies, economic inequalities, and personal pathologies would not disappear by offering the working classes scaled-down middle-class amenities. Letchworth, moreover, was not the nation in microcosm. Only about 40 per cent of the population by 1930 was reckoned working-class. Financially, lower-middle-class groups were better placed to take advantage of garden-city concepts. In Parliament Henry Vivian trumpeted their virtues; and some sixty estates, espousing tenant co-partnership, were founded before 1914. Their aim, said Bishop Gore of Birmingham in reference to the Harborne Tenants Ltd.'s Moor Pool estate (1907–12), was 'to make an Edgbaston for the less wealthy'. In fact these were modifications of the suburb under garden-city influences, not fulfilments of garden-city philosophy. Embraced by out-growing cities, these estates never possessed the 'unity, symmetry, completeness' of the town–country combination which Howard prescribed. Still, it would be wrong to slight Howard's impetus. Another comprehensive experiment was undertaken after 1919, at Welwyn; and governments belatedly acknowledged his work by the new towns policy after 1945.

Individuals and groups thus pointed the way to government, whose commitment alone could ensure widespread town planning. For too long government only dimly appreciated the lessons. Low-density housing without a dose of Geddes's civics was no salvation. Quite the reverse: it produced deathly settlements bereft of social organization; sprawling, monotonous suburbs in which motor travel was forced on people if they were to find work or amenities. And certain happy hits of Howard and the rest turned sour when cast into legislation. The green-belt and zoning policies were two examples. Designed to protect the countryside, inhibit conurbations and preserve the character of separate towns, the green-belt policy fuelled the price-inflation of urban land; and zoning strengthened the division of middle-class owner occupancy and working-class council housing. Hence public interference with the land market tended to maintain middle-class property values. There was nothing new in this, as the history of public parks shows. From the start – the Birkenhead park landscaped by Paxton in the 1840s – two motives combined in their promotion: to provide a regulated place of recuperation, and to protect property values in the neighbourhood. The irony is that a more complete segregation of classes has resulted in the twentieth century from ostensibly philanthropic town planning by democratic governments.

One other planning drive of the late nineteenth century might be mentioned. This was the City Beautiful movement, chiefly associated with the American, F. L. Olmsted. Its English devotees derived inspiration from native sources too, among them the Arts and Crafts movement. City beautifiers were already active before the publicity of the Chicago Trade Fair in 1893 aroused greater individual initiative as well as corporate commitment. Liverpool was one centre of activity. There the Kyrle Society was founded in 1876. It spawned eight or nine branches in other towns by 1888, aiming 'to bring beauty home to the people' by equipping hospitals, schools, workmen's clubs and other assembly rooms, with works of art. At the same time Liverpool Corporation embarked on formal programmes, art purchases for the Walker Gallery and the laying-out of radial roads and public gardens. It also added a personal touch in 1897–8, distributing over 2,000 window-boxes among working-class districts, where the rentals ranged from 1s. 6d. to 5s. per week, and presenting prizes for the best displays. A City Beautiful Conference was held in Liverpool in 1907. The city's prominence in the movement was sustained by its university. A department of Civic Design was added to its School of Architecture, after an endowment from Lever; and in 1910 the *Town Planning Review* issued from the university, where S. D. Adshead and Patrick Abercrombie were luminaries.

Most of this theoretical and practical town planning occurred with little participation or aid from the Government. The *Daily Chronicle* of 20 August 1912 lamented: 'What is painfully lacking . . . is that alliance between the expert innovator and the public administrator which alone enables a high standard to be attained on any really large scale.' Municipal by-laws prescribed minima with regard to width of street, houses per acre, sanitation and structural solidity; but by-laws were negative constraints. They could not engender or even safeguard constructive schemes. They could not reserve a reasonable proportion of a building site for park-land, trees, gardens, or public buildings; they could not zone industry and housing; and they could not protect a model scheme from jerry-building on a neighbouring plot.

Part of the trouble lay with the Local Government Board, which remained in large part a disciplinary body, invigilating the Poor Law. Its traditions were keener in correcting error than in stimulating initiative. But public property rights generally were inferior to private. Only when the legal and fiscal conditions were right was public town planning feasible. Historians mostly explain the 1909 Town Planning Act as a grudging recognition of the experiments that have been detailed above, and as a belated response to ever more frequent requests from municipal corporations to control the development of suburbs. This influence and pressure was certainly strong; but the evolution of the Government's fiscal programme enforced the case. The 1909 Budget taxed undeveloped urban sites, to induce owners to release land for house-building. Town planning was required, therefore, to prevent the ensuing expansion from being marred by over-building and under-provision of greenery and public amenities. The budget and town-planning legislation, however, were not well co-ordinated. The building trade was depressed, not exhilarated, by the land duties; and fewer new houses were constructed in 1911–14 than at any point in the previous half-century.

Birmingham Corporation was one public authority that responded to the 1909 Act. Its City Council had been the first, in 1906, to resolve in favour of town planning and local authority land purchase; now it was one of 74 local authorities whose 105 schemes, covering 167,571 acres, were approved by the Local Government Board by 1915. As a proportion of the total area covered by these local authorities, the planned areas were small; and, since the landowners' consent was obligatory, it was likely, as Anthony Sutcliffe notes, that 'most of the districts chosen would in any case have been laid out for low-density housing'. In Birmingham a constructive cousinhood may be noticed. The chairman of the Housing Committee, J. S. Nettlefold, was a cousin of George Cadbury; and the chairman of the newly formed Town-Planning Committee, Neville Chamberlain, was a cousin of Nettlefold. In 1911 Greater Birmingham was created; and in 1913 authority was given to develop 2,300 acres at Edgbaston, Harborne, and Quinton in the south-west, and 1,500 acres in East Birmingham. Further schemes, for Yardley, Stechford, and South Birmingham, taking in parts of Warwickshire county, followed in 1914. The members of the Town-Planning Committee, as Sir Keith Feiling noted in *The Life of Neville Chamberlain* (1946), also passed a resolution 'far beyond their present legal powers' in authorizing the city surveyor to plan for the entire Greater Birmingham area, defining new ring and radial roads, and allocating open spaces and residential and industrial zones.

The Great War forced more central government intervention. Thus the Ministry of Munitions intervened to supply housing in the engineering districts, now swollen by an expanded labour force of dilutees. The Ministry defrayed part of the costs of houses built by the local authority in Coventry and Sheffield and by the arms manufacturers in Barrow and Weybridge. From 1916 the Ministry began to provide housing directly. It founded the first 'new town', at Gretna, for efficient munitions production. The garden-city architect, Unwin, was involved in its design; and Gretna may be seen as the bridge connecting the factory-estates and garden-city conceptions of the pre-1914 era and the council-estates and new towns policies of post-1918 and post-1945. The state was thus roused to action finally by the detonations of foreign war rather than by the rumbling discontents of its urban heartland; and, given the circumstances of the Government's shotgun marriage with the planners, no fairy-tale ending emerged. William Ashworth reached this sombre conclusion about inter-war urban developments: '. . . there was usually little recognizable difference between the outcome of development under town-planning schemes and development outside them.'

VI

The new urban forms sketched in this chapter are not easily reviewed. Muddle was the legacy which late Victorians inherited. Their efforts in extrication were muddled too. Caliban's rough works were as conspicuous as the sensitive arts and sharp wits of Prospero and Ariel. William Morris had issued his advice in *The Earthly Paradise* (1868):

> Forget six counties overhung with smoke,
> Forget the snorting steam and piston stroke,
> Forget the spreading of the hideous town;
> Think rather of the pack-horse on the down,
> And dream of London, small, and white and clean,
> The clear Thames bordered by its gardens green . . .

Oblivion and reverie hardly constituted a practical course of public action. A sanitized medievalism was unattainable. Later, Morris, in common with many, latched on to the electric and transport revolutions as the means to effect urban and political decentralization. The detractors of the Victorian city thought of it as a prison wherein most inmates endured physical and spiritual privation and became standardized parts drawn to the specifications of Mammon. Town life, nonetheless, remained the most alluring condition for most people. Here were the greatest opportunities for employment, comfort, and amusement, though some never won any of these things and others did not secure them without penalties. Progress was partial and halting, so ambiguous that there was endless disagreement whether the lurch was two steps forward and one backwards or one step forward and two backwards. Progress in urban structure was clearer. In the decanting of inner-city populations to the suburbs and elsewhere, the trend was towards deformation of the traditional shape of urban life. Elements of instability were thus pronounced. On the other hand this diffusion of the city via the urbanization of the countryside was designed to distribute the satisfactions of life among more people. Mere urban 'improvement' was being dismissed in favour of a controlled reallocation of resources.

5 Country and town, and country towns

Few students of English history will argue that the late nineteenth century can be understood without reference to the Empire. In the second line of *The English Flag* (1891) Kipling posed his famous question, 'And what should they know of England who only England know?' To those urban historians who are content to remain within walls, an analogous question may be put, And what should they know of towns and cities who only towns and cities know? Unless the rural scene is surveyed, the measure of what was special about the urban condition will be misconceived. Already, in the introductory chapter and in that which dealt with suburbia and new towns, some consideration has been given to the mixture of town and country. This chapter will develop the theme of the urban–rural continuum, to indicate links which joined town and country and stresses which shook them. In the market town rural and urban society met together; but it was not in that one area alone that exchanges occurred. Though the urban invasion of the countryside seriously disturbed the balance, the relationship was far from one-sided. Country still influenced town in direct as well as subtle ways.

I

Before journeying into the country it may be useful to be reminded of the city's distractions and distortions. In 1918, when the Thames was flooding, Virginia Woolf mused, 'They say it's been raining heavily; I daresay it has, but such is the civilisation of life in London that I really don't know. What with fires, electric light, underground railways, and umbrellas, how can one take notice of the weather?' Not all townsfolk could discount the weather so cheerfully. Employment in many outdoor trades – building, characteristically – was subject to favourable weather; so was public health, as exceptionally hot spells tended to raise the level of infant mortality and exceptionally cold spells struck at the old. Nevertheless, the conceit could be maintained that city life carried on regardless of the weather. In the country was fuller exposure. The weather had direct importance for agricultural productivity and thus for market towns. Indirectly the effects of the weather reverberated throughout the entire economy. Activity, first in the footwear, clothing, and drinks industries, then in one trade after another, registered harvest fluctuations. So Bagehot observed in *Lombard Street* (1873). In later years, as food imports grew hugely, domestic harvests exercised a much slighter impact on the industrial cycle, although a series of terrible harvests through heavy rain, like those of 1878–82, or drought, as in 1892–5, might deepen business gloom. In 1801 agriculture contributed about one-third of gross national income. This fell to 20.3 per cent in 1851, to 10.4 per cent in 1881, to 6.1 per cent in 1901, to around 4 per cent from the 1920s. The breaking of this agrarian grip upon the economy had wide implications: for labour migration and wealth distribution; for the social and political influence of landowners and craftsmen; for the pattern of country life generally.

The weather remained important for the conceptualization of town and country. Foggy cities, sunny villages: these were common images. In the greetings card industry and in children's literature, especially, the dainty view of the countryside was projected. The vast sales of Kate Greenaway's *Under the Window* (1879) testified to the popularity of this style. Beatrix Potter perpetuated the tradition. In *The Tale of Johnny Town-Mouse* (1918) she proposed that town and country had definite marks of distinction. Timmy Willie, the country mouse, has an unaffected appearance, passes days serenely among flowers, birds, insects, and grazing animals, enjoys a natural diet of herbs, milk, and corn, and slumbers on grass clippings under an earth bank. These ways are contrasted with Johnny Town-Mouse's elegant apparel, suave habits, rich diet, and life amid feather pillows and ferocious cats. The town is mannered and alarming to Timmy, the country dull and dirty to Johnny. The story concludes: 'One place suits one person, another place suits another person. For my part I prefer to live in the country, like Timmy Willie.' Beatrix Potter was a city-dweller who translated her yearning for the countryside into nursery tales, until in middle life she quit South Kensington for the Lake District.

Some townsfolk maintained a profound ignorance of the country. The urbane even boasted of it, like A. P. Herbert whose election address for Oxford University proclaimed, 'Agriculture: I know nothing about agriculture.' Perhaps this candour was excusable, for agricultural issues were increasingly technical. A failure to identify ordinary flowers seemed another matter, so R. C. K. Ensor implied. In 1902 he escorted four crippled workmen about fields outside Manchester. The men were recently handicapped and three had once enjoyed high wages; but 'none of them knew or could name forget-me-nots, daisies, dandelions, clover, pansies or lilies of the valley, three of them were baffled by a poppy, and the fourth felt confident that it was a rose'. An anecdote is not conclusive evidence. The existence of urban working-class naturalist clubs is known; and it may be that Ensor's story only reveals the closed worlds of class. How well, asks Derek Fraser, would Ensor have performed if he had had to identify the common tools and machines in a workshop? But that intimacy with nature which Hardy depicted in *Under the Greenwood Tree* (1872) – 'To dwellers in a wood almost every species of tree has its voice as well as its feature' – was plainly incomprehensible to people who could not distinguish one tree from another.

Provincial geography was also perplexing, and not only to low-born city men. G. M. Young mischievously noted Winston Churchill's defective education: 'Churchill, hammering out a speech for Worcester, was surprised to learn that the Malverns were in that county and that the Severn flowed through it. "I was brought up in London," he explained.' The metropolitans' ignorance of the country had its counterpart in the rustics' bewilderment at the city. Contrast Molly Hughes in the 1870s, a London child whose eyes were opened to farm life by Cornish holidays; and her domestic servant in the 1890s who, fresh from Norfolk, was 'dreadfully afraid, as the train rushed through several stations, that it wouldn't stop at London'.

A romantic view of both town and country was born of this mutual ignorance. Of course, a townsman's single expedition to the wilds might snuff out this mood, just as a rustic might falter when faced with Coketown. Visiting Skye in 1908, Lytton Strachey cried out in disillusionment to J. M. Keynes: 'We're nine miles from Portree, the nearest centre of civilization (and beauty), and we're surrounded by deserts of green vagueness, multitudes of imbecile mountains and eternal rain.' Others did not require a drenching to conclude that the idealization of nature was make-believe and rot. Arnold Bennett was so infuriated by Cowper's oft-quoted sentiment, 'God made the Country, and Man made the Town', that in 1907 he forsook prose and perpetrated a poem, a modern *Town and Country*:

God made the country and man made the town
And so man made the doctor, God the down.
God made the mountain, and the ants their hill,
Where grinding servitudes each day fulfil.
God doubtless made the flowers, while in the hive
Unnatural bees against their passions strive.
God made the jackass and the bounding flea;
I render thanks to God that man made me.
Let those who recognise God's shaping power
Here but not there, in tree but not in tower,
In lane and field, but not in street and square,
And in man's work see nothing that is fair,
Bestir their feeble fancy to the odd
Conception of a 'country' ruled by God;
Where birds perceive the wickedness of strife
Against the winds, and lead the simple life
Nestless on God's own twigs; and squirrels, free
From carking care, exist through February
On nuts that God has stored. Pray let them give
The fields to God's kind hand for just a year,
And then of God's own harvest make good cheer.

This cant of God and man would turn me sick,
Did I not deeply know the age was quick
With large conception of a prouder creed
Whereon we shall not feel the craven need
To count ourselves less noble than a weed.

For me a rural pond is not more pure
Nor more spontaneous than my city sewer.

II

The sober witnesses testify that even if God originally made the country, man busily re-made it and now was busier still. In a preface to a new edition of *Far from the Madding Crowd* (1874), written in the 1890s, Hardy recognized that a new Wessex had arisen, 'a modern Wessex of railways, the penny post, mowing and reaping machines, union workhouses, lucifer matches, labourers who could read and write, and National school children'. New kinds of farming had been developed by cities for cities. Draft animals and manual labour still had a large part in agriculture, but they were daily being supplemented, sometimes subordinated, by the instruments of urban industry: artificial fertilizers; ploughing, sowing, mowing, threshing and reaper-binding machines; scientific research into plant and animal diseases, soil fertility, and stock breeding; modern methods of fencing (barbed-wire and wire-netting), drainage and irrigation; new means of preserving produce by refrigeration and canning; efficient systems of transport and marketing. The most advanced and profitable farming was found closest to cities, the most backward and impoverished farming furthest from cities. This was observed by Adam Smith in 1776, and by James Caird in 1851. Afterwards it was less the rule. Urban growth was no longer limited by the surplus of the nation's agriculture. Now international transport of meat and cereals both enabled more people to live in towns and compelled more people to leave the land. The agriculture that survived was ordered by town rules. England was far in advance of most countries, where much agricultural production persisted at near-subsistence level and for purely local consumption. One measure of the extent of market organization in nineteenth-century England is the rapidity with which the practice of trade through shops was established even in villages.

The chief change in agriculture was the transfer from tillage to pasture under the impact of foreign competition. In 1880, when about a quarter of Britain's food supplies were imported, 17,674,950 acres were arable land, 14,426,959 acres permanent grass. By 1910, when about 60 per cent of the country's food was imported, these figures were reversed. Vegetable and fruit production was extended; otherwise the decline of arable farming was general. By the 1890s the fall in rents and prices had bottomed out. Nonetheless, for arable landowners especially, buoyancy of income was increasingly sought from commercial, mineral, industrial, and urban sources. Economies were enforced elsewhere, by adopting time- and labour-saving machinery, by selling property, or by curtailing customary expenditure on personal luxury and on political, social, and charitable activity.

Agriculture is no more homogeneous than industry. Different types experience different fortunes in different places. Essex corn-growers suffered nightmare conditions; but Essex was viable for Scottish cattle-farmers who migrated there and supplied London with milk, and for soft-fruit producers whose preserves made famous jams, like Wilkin of Tiptree. England's population rose by 10 million from 1871 to 1901, and, as starch products fell in price, there was expanded demand for the protein produce of livestock husbandry – milk, butter and margarine, eggs, cheese and meat – and for market-garden produce. These farmers, far from suffering from the collapse of cereal prices, benefited both from cheaper animal feedstuffs and fertilizers and from enlarged urban demand. From 1901 to 1911 the male agricultural workforce increased by 7.2 per cent, although proportionately the agricultural sector continued to decline. From 1851 to 1901 it had declined both relatively and absolutely. Some 27 per cent of occupied males worked in agriculture in 1851, 17 per cent in 1881, under 12 per cent in 1901. In individuals the fall was from 1,788,000 to 1,339,000. Those that remained were possibly of inferior quality, having, in Richard Jefferies's famous phrase, an 'Oriental absence of aspiration'. Certainly the age structure of the workforce was unusual, being mostly aged under 20 or over 55. In 1901 over 20 per cent of male agricultural workers were aged above 55 years, the highest of any occupational group. It is a rough token of the additional power given to agriculture by the instruments of urban industry that the product of this adolescent and senescent workforce was improved. At 1913 prices, the output per head in 1867 was £74.3; forty years later it was £85.2, an increase of 14.7 per cent. Generally, their wages were improved by scarcity, and their overall standard of living by falling prices. In 1851 the average agricultural wage was about 49 per cent of the average industrial wage; in the 1880s and 1890s about 55 per cent. Everywhere differences due to trade-union organization, age, skill and region, and sundry supplements – female and child earnings; overtime; free cottages and fuel; and opportunities of independent food production, by a vegetable plot or pig- and poultry-keeping – brought infinite deflexions from the average wage. Still, it should be borne in mind when considering the plight of the urban working classes that probably the proportion of farm labourers whose wages placed them below the poverty line was greater. This must have exercised a drag on labour efficiency.

Allotments and smallholdings were advocated by agriculturalists concerned about levels of rural emigration and poverty; also by urban politicians alarmed about housing and employment shortages. Allotments and smallholdings might restore the attractions of rural work, reduce the number of poaching and other offences, encourage personal thrift and enterprise, and maintain the national character and physique. Sections of both radical and conservative opinion could find encouragement in this programme. It might lead to the break-up of great estates and the decay of landlordism; or it might safeguard social stability by multiplying the number of proprietors. As it happened, the amount of land released by legislation was insufficient to test either hypothesis, owing to the obstructions of interested parties in both national and local government; and for as many smallholdings and allotments as were created, others were lost to urban building. Probably the imagined social benefits of the policy account for its attractiveness to the professional classes. Land-cultivation conjured up pictures of contented peasants dancing round maypoles. Certainly, the economic credentials of the policy were dubious. Even given public credit or marketing facilities, the ability of peasant proprietors to exceed the productivity of large tenant farmers was questionable. By Edwardian times the enthusiasm of urban progressives was directed more to the establishment of farm colonies for the urban unemployed and work-camps for the urban degenerates.

The allotments and smallholdings policy was based on misunderstanding about what caused the rural exodus. There was simply insufficient employment on the land to absorb the rising population; nor were the attractions of living and working in the country obvious. Rural housing, generally, was inferior to urban housing – there was the same overall shortage and overcrowding but country cottages were even more badly built and ill-equipped with sanitary and other services. Where model housing existed, as in Lord Wantage's village, East Lockinge, the labourer felt irksome restraints on his freedom of behaviour. The Liberals' Land Inquiry in 1913, at any rate, argued that dissatisfaction with housing was 'a potent cause of migration to the towns'. As for rural work, this was notoriously demanding – hard physical labour for long hours. Furthermore, urban wages were a positive inducement. A Norfolk farm-worker reported home from Sheffield in 1873: 'Instead of working for 13*s.* a week we get 22*s.* 6*d.*; and instead of working with bread and cheese, and sometimes with bread and nothing with it, we get a thumping bit of beef with it. . . .' Progressive opinion gradually moved in the direction of a minimum wage for agriculture (achieved in 1917); but wages were not the only incentive to migration. As the *Westminster Review* commented in August 1901: 'Young men are not so much influenced by long hours, hard work, and the small opportunity of getting on that the country affords, as by the desire to . . . better themselves, that is, not necessarily to get higher wages, but to get more into the thick of life.' The social advantages of towns were paramount. To remain in a village, wrote Rowland Prothero, was to pass through life without really living.

England's rural areas suffered a net loss of 4.06 million people, and England's cities, towns, and mining districts received a net increase of 2.56 million people, from migration, between 1851 and 1911. These movements cannot be correlated easily because of cross-currents, emigration from both urban and rural England to the Empire and America, immigration from the Celtic regions and from continental Europe to urban England, and the backward flow represented by the suburbanization of the countryside. The movement is uneven, too, in direction and in time. London attracted as many migrants as all other towns combined; and both 1881–91 and 1901–11 saw an exceptionally strong exodus overseas, from urban as well as from rural England.

The migrants' destinations were frequently determined by connections forged by kinsmen or neighbours. Cornish miners, for instance, colonized parts of Scotland, America, and South Africa, places which became more familiar to those left behind than London and 'up country'. The migratory networks of Warwickshire villagers, described by M. K. Ashby, were different in direction but observed the same principle. Hard times also drove men to America or the colonies; and other connections were built up nearer home. 'From one small area the migrants flowed to Birmingham and its neighbourhood, from another chiefly to Coventry [a boom town of bicycle, later car, manufacture], and again to the railway works at Crewe and the breweries of Burton-on-Trent. A certain number of young men, encouraged by the clergy, were joining the Metropolitan Police Force'. By the late nineteenth century, according to Charles Booth, about 70 per cent of London constables were country-born. Booth also reckoned that 'one of the most powerful and efficient migration agencies is . . . the letters written home by the country girl settled in domestic service in the great town'. Country labour was far from being disadvantaged in towns. Country skills were valued, especially in work involving animals. Horse-dealers, blacksmiths, saddlers, carters, and dairymen led in this respect. According to F. M. L. Thompson, the number of working horses more than doubled during the Victorian period, peaking at 3½ million in 1902. In the commercial sector their use more than quadrupled between 1851 and 1901. Railways had curtailed long-distance horse-drawn traffic but expanded the local demand. A small army of attendants, in town as well as country, was required to supply, feed, stable, groom, and drive animals, and to clear their dung from the streets. Country craftsmen

were also men with marketable skills, particularly in the urban building industry. Finally, country labour was attractive to urban
employers because it was thought physically fit and mentally compliant. The anti-trade-union preference of businesses which required
more muscle than skill – typically, in the routine ranks of the gas and
brewery industries and in transport – was upheld by their taking on
country labour.

III

The evacuation of the countryside did not set town and country
dwellers apart. The links were intricate. George Ewart Evans and the
school of oral history, and Raphael Samuel and the History
Workshop, have emphasized how much rural and urban economies
were interwoven by studying both itinerant craftsmen and casual
workers who habitually transferred environments. Thus several
hundred East Anglian farm labourers customarily sought winter work
among the herring fleets of Lowestoft and Yarmouth or in the
breweries of Burton-upon-Trent. In the other direction numerous
urban labourers (with their families) joined in cereal, vegetable, fruit,
and hop harvests. *The Times* in the 1880s reckoned 20–30,000
Londoners worked as hop-pickers in Sussex and Kent. They slept
rough in huts 'in rather worse than a state of nature', and created
havoc in places like Maidstone which they invaded on drunken sprees.
The cider and beer industries of Herefordshire and Worcestershire
similarly needed the harvest labour of West Midlands townsfolk.

Industry survived in country districts but was placed under increasing pressure from urban manufacture. The disfavour of urban-based
trade unionists should not be underestimated. They held the country
workers (alike with the urban sweat-shops) responsible for the
depressed wages of certain trades, and were determined to end cottage
industry if they could. In 1901 a sixth of the 30,000 male and 12,000
female boot- and shoe-makers of Northamptonshire were village-
based; but the National Union of Boot and Shoe Operatives from
about 1890 had been pursuing a policy of driving workers into factories and by 1914 had for the most part achieved its goal. Glove-
making, similarly, was an established industry in parts of Devon,
Dorset, Somerset, Herefordshire, Worcestershire, and Oxfordshire.
The stitching was traditionally done by domestic out-workers, the
skilled cutting by craftsmen in a central workshop. The trend in

demand, however, was towards cheap leather gloves. The workshop system gave way before factory mechanization. Chair-making in Oxfordshire and Buckinghamshire villages followed the same trend, subdued by factory-made furniture at High Wycombe, while lace-making (mostly a female and child employment) perished under the competition of machine-production and changes in fashion. The number of lace-workers in Oxfordshire, Buckinghamshire, and Bedfordshire fell from over 20,000 in 1851 to under 2,000 in 1901. Straw-plaiting was in precipitate decline too, though the numbers in the trade had been expanding between 1851 and 1871. This affected a broad band of counties, east Buckinghamshire, Bedfordshire, Hertfordshire, north Essex, and parts of Suffolk and Cambridgeshire. The straw-plaiting capital was Luton, where the Plait Hall was the greatest single emporium; but this town of 36,400 people also harboured rivals to the trade, manufacturers of felt hats.

The co-operation of town and country in industrial activity was gradually severed from the town side. The trend was towards more rigid polarization of industrial and agricultural work between town and country; still, the amount of occupational mobility was remarkable. The harvest contract especially remained a magnet for all comers. From knowledge of south Gloucestershire and north Wiltshire in the early 1870s Richard Jefferies asserted that farmers, faced with a rural labour force which was declining in number and deteriorating in quality, had 'a growing reliance upon floating labour'. Hardy noticed the same in Wessex and, by the 1890s, concluded that the 'supplanting of the class of stationary cottagers, who carried on the local traditions and humours, by a population of more or less migratory labourers . . . led to a break of continuity in local history, more fatal than any other thing to the preservation of legend, folk-lore, close inter-social relations, and eccentric individualities'.

Who constituted these scratch-packs, and how long did the demand for their services persist? Some were Irish, but Irish harvesters mostly worked Scotland and the English north and Midlands. Their ranks declined from 50,000 in the 1840s, 20,000 in the 1880s, to 8,000 by 1914. Similar native troupes have been noticed leaving their Oxfordshire and Buckinghamshire villages to mow the London parks. Then they worked around Middlesex, haymaking, or hoeing for market-gardeners, before returning for their local harvest. Lincolnshire men, too, regularly participated in Suffolk harvests and Suffolk men in Essex harvests or in grass-cutting in the London parks. Such practices were encouraged by the staggered times of harvesting in different counties; on the other hand, all the signs are that by 1914 the demand was less. The main challenge to this enterprise and to opportunities of women's and children's field-work was presented by mechanization and decasualization. More farmers used regular labour, and more urban authorities employed their own parks and gardens staff. Country craftsmen showed as much versatility as country labourers. In *A Pair of Blue Eyes* (1873) Hardy emphasizes this about the rural stonemason, John Smith: 'There was not that speciality in his labour which distinguishes the handicraftsmen of towns.' At different times he might be bricklayer, slater, or tiler; in unkind winter weeks a feller of trees, in very slack periods a gardener. This flexibility in work was very characteristic of villagers living close to towns. Here were found the free-lancers of the plebeian world, scraping a living ambiguously from both rural and urban economies. One example is Headington Quarry, outside Oxford, which contained 1,437 inhabitants in 1901. Here the womenfolk took in laundry from the colleges and hotels. The men worked variously in brick-works and stone quarries; in building the new suburbs, waterworks, and schools; in miscellaneous rural and urban by-employments. Here, typically, lived the men with horses and carts, the carriers between towns and villages of people and goods. Life in these open villages, without resident gentlemen, was also known for its freedom with the law of trespass. Cows and horses were grazed on land without the owner's permission, woodland was pillaged for fuel, and poaching was rife.

Poaching constituted a thriving rural–urban occupation, as James Hawker's journal, *A Victorian Poacher* (1961), indicates. Hawker was at times cobbler, groom, farm worker and factory worker, but always a poacher, wherever he happened to be living in town or village in Northamptonshire, Leicestershire, or Lincolnshire. His journal advocated poaching from economic necessity, also as a form of republicanism; but his chief contention was that most sections of society practised poaching – magistrates, policemen, keepers and farmers, as well as town and country labourers. The town connection is the aspect which needs emphasis here. Charles Kingsley gave a melodramatic account of poaching expeditions by London gangs in *Yeast* (1848); more down-to-earth were Hawker's statements about the urban retailers who received goods, directly or through intermediaries. Townsmen were not only receivers but active poachers. In the urban districts there is some synchronization between figures of day poaching offences and high food (especially meat) prices in mid-Victorian times. Many townsmen, being of recent origin, possessed the prerequisites of skilled poachers: pond and field lore, cheek, coolness, and a good hand and eye in the use of gun, trap, and net. Everywhere were opportunities, not just near small country towns but near big cities too. Lord Derby's Knowsley estate was vulnerable to raids by Liverpudlians.

Poaching was a joint rural–urban enterprise; so was robbing birds' nests and snaring birds. The fashion of having a caged song-bird was still current. Coventry Patmore was one who kept an aviary of sixty birds, including a raven to shred newspapers whose Liberal opinions he detested. Birds were considered pests by farmers. At Berrick Salome (Oxfordshire) they paid threepence per dozen caught by villagers' nets. Some were killed as vermin, some were eaten, others were transported to towns. The rural economy was thus tied into town economies in a hundred ways, small and great. Many practices were not peculiar to one but common to both.

IV

The subject of crime and vice underlines this connection. This is not immediately obvious because much contemporary opinion emphasized urban problems rather than investigated social processes. It dwelt not only on the problems of the metropolitan centres and overblown industrial cities (rather than on those of small market towns or resorts), but on particular areas within these major cities, twilight zones rather than respectable working-class districts or middle-class suburbs. Sociologists, subsequently, have stressed broad distinctions between town and country criminal or unsocial activity, the former being largely directed against property, the latter against persons; but few generalizations are tenable. An economic motive may be extrapolated from the criminal statistics which were published from 1857. The number of crimes often fluctuated inversely with commercial prosperity and distress but the 1880s, according to some, marks the incipient change from poverty- to prosperity-based crime. Again, we may assume, about the amount and gravity of crime, that there was less in country areas than in large cities. The alleged communal surveillance of villages and small towns explains this difference. Theft is minimal because stolen articles cannot be used without risk; likewise morality is maintained by gossip and other sanctions. There was no serious crime in the country, wrote Jefferies in the late 1870s. The vast majority of cases brought before the sessions concerned 'drunkenness, quarrelling, neglect or absenteeism from work, affiliation, petty theft, and so on'.

Historians accept that the 1860s and 1870s mark a turning-point, a reduction in the number of serious crimes; but Jefferies's statement about rural crime is unusually reticent. It implies that the countryside was rid of the tensions which socio-economic transformations brought to towns. From the 1840s right through the 1860s a major worry in the countryside was malicious damage to property, especially arson. Some areas were more affected than others – East Anglia notoriously – and in this there was a substantial element of social protest, reflecting grievances about inferior wages, machinery and unemployment, and ill-feeling about the Poor Law or curtailment of customary rights. Here, far from suppressing crime, the strength of rural community feeling plainly conspired to conceal the criminal. At particular times the crime rates of these districts surpassed those of certain manufacturing towns, in respect of violent assaults and destruction of property. The last remained a regular part of the rural scene until the 1870s when migrations to towns, gradually rising wages and, perhaps, allotments and trade-union organization combined towards an acceptance of new working practices and brought a more settled state of affairs to the countryside. Thenceforward, it seems plausible to argue, towns gave greater opportunities and incentives to criminal and unsocial practices. It may also be that politico-legal authorities operated different standards in an urban environment and outlawed more infractions of more rules. The corollary of the sociological premiss that societies get the criminals they deserve is that the social authorities determine what is categorized as crime.

From the 1860s to the second quarter of the twentieth century, statistics indicate a decline in the number of serious offences against persons and property and involving a grave threat of public disorder. Most crime was petty. The single most common appearance in the courts by 1900 was the person charged with drunkenness; but new social codes and more zealous policing had engendered a bumper crop of offences previously unknown – for technical breaches of education, highway, and health acts, and for defying restrictions placed on vagrancy, gambling, and promiscuity. Certainly, newspapers exaggerated the amount and the violent and organized character of urban crime and disguised its often localized features. In 1855–6, 1862–3, 1868–9, and 1874–5, press scares reached exceptional levels but were clearly fuelled by exogenous factors. Stedman Jones notes a background of unemployment, with bread riots in the East End, in the mid-1850s and early and late 1860s. In addition the growth of middle-class suburbia raised two concerns: one psychological, about what might follow from class separation; the other physical, about the vulnerability of ill-lit and thinly policed residential areas. Altogether it is necessary to focus these press panics within the context of current debates, about the expansion, distribution, and efficiency of police forces (*vide* the 1856 Police Act), about penology (the end of transportation; introduction of tickets-of-leave; deterrent or clement sentencing), about criminology (the concept of a hereditary criminal class and identification of criminal types by physiognomical and other features), about pauperism (whether public relief funds and indiscriminate private charity demoralized the poor), and about licensing control (the propaganda of the temperance movement). None of this encourages the historian to reach firm conclusions about the incidence of urban crime; but there may be a case for arguing that towns were the means of *raising* standards of behaviour by furnishing recreational facilities and by introducing new regulatory systems to protect the general body of working people (as well as the middle classes), whose incomes and 'respectability' were growing, from anti-social elements. What matters is the perspective. In the mind of the suburban spinster London was one vast Alsatia. In the appraisal of the Director of Criminal Investigation (in 1883) London was 'the safest capital for life and property in the world'.

The respective place of town and country in the nurturing of crime and vice is no easier to determine. Town and country connections in respect of 'the social evil' were frequently ignored. Prostitution was mostly a city profession; but the female underemployment and underpayment which was a significant cause had country as well as town origins. The initial corruption might well have occurred in the country; and, as Frances Finnegan notes in her study of Victorian York, *Poverty and Prostitution* (1979), farmers and country hobbledehoys were commonly numbered among their clients.

It is not difficult to find disgruntlement about personal behaviour in the countryside. An article in the *Gentleman's Magazine*, September 1907, argued that a moral tonic was urgently required in country districts as well as in urban slums. The author was partisan. He advised the Liberal Government, instead of meddling with the rights of property, to raise standards of decency. Still, he based his protest on twenty years' knowledge of a country district containing some fifteen villages. Such complaints attracted little notice by comparison with city problems. Many villages had their rookery, wrote Jefferies, originally a squatters' settlement upon waste ground, now packed with 'low pitched, dirty, narrow, and contracted [cottages], without proper conveniences, or even a yard or court'. Village rookeries he distinguished from city rookeries in that they did not issue quantities of 'burglars and accomplished pickpockets . . . but they do send out a gang of lazy, scamping fellows and coarse women, who are almost useless'. It was easy to defame this population as loafers in alehouses, the natural denizens of workhouses, immoral, shady, vicious and unreliable; but their existence indicated that a submerged population, suffering irregular employment and mean housing, and bereft of education and opportunity, was at large in the countryside as well as in cities.

Open villages which blended agricultural and other work were commonly assumed disreputable. The ecclesiastical living of Embleton in Northumberland was such a place. The leading occupations were agricultural work and the quarrying of basalt. The parish incorporated five villages, with 1,700 people in the mid-1870s. There was no resident squire. The employers 'were on much the same level of cultivation as those they employed, and in some cases owned the public houses and paid the wages there'. So wrote Mandell Creighton, the vicar from 1874 to 1884. He added: 'The unchastity of Embleton was terrible – low, animal.' Creighton was probably alluding to the numbers of illegitimate births; but his observation needs focusing. Unmarried mothers were a disappointment to their kin (because of the hardships of maintenance) rather than a social disgrace. Working-class people dealt with such circumstances in a matter-of-fact manner. Recent research, by Peter Laslett and others, rejects the hypothesis that the incidence of illegitimate births can be correlated with the action of urbanization, industrialization, and 'modernization' upon traditional communities. In many districts, town and country, prenuptial pregnancy and bastardy were common. One of the few certainties about this subject is that mortality rates among illegitimates were higher than for legitimates.

Some changes in village life were firmly blamed upon the towns, particularly the passing of rural craftsmen. This was interpreted as an intellectual impoverishment as well as economic tragedy, for traditionally craftsmen provided independence of thought and action to redeem the abasement of agricultural labourers. Culturally, this signified a break: many local customs were due to craft variations, and dialect speech had been sustained by continuity of pre-industrial work habits. For those who suspected an intimate connection between humble crafts and high artistry this was an aesthetic catastrophe too. Countless churches memorialized the art and personality of generaations of village craftsmen.

Village craftsmen suffered as a consequence of the general rural exodus, since there was a smaller population to support their work. But the proportion of craftsmen per thousand population was falling in most counties from 1861–71 and in many from 1851. The reason was competition from cheaper factory-made goods and town trades. Shoemakers, tailors, hedgers, thatchers, sawyers, saddlers, blacksmiths, wheelwrights, stonemasons, millers, bakers, even mole- and rat-catchers, all faced supersession from the growing reach of town services. Shopkeepers, too, felt the pinch, especially in villages less than seven miles from a market town. The result was a mortal blow to village self-sufficiency, and it fell within a generation. Craftsmen retained their names for the census enumerators to register, but the jobs were losing their specificity. Wainwrights and coopers, for instance, increasingly practised general carpentry and joinery as factory-made wagons and carts, barrels and buckets, dominated the market. Some crafts withstood extinction by turning more to the repairing than producing side of their trade; others cannily sought to join the new forces. Blacksmiths, for example, still had a custom in making and repairing iron tools and in shoeing horses, since more horses were employed in agriculture, hauling the new machinery. But the most enterprising blacksmiths turned to agricultural engineering, establishing famous firms like Hornsby of Grantham. Others became their commission agents, supplying or repairing factory-made machines and spare parts. The resourceful also moved into bicycle and motor repairs, eventually opening a garage perhaps. Hence, in several remoter counties such as Devon and Norfolk the number of blacksmiths fell between 1871 and 1901, but the total increased overall in England and Wales from 112,000 to 137,000.

The typical village existed no more than the typical town. Thomas Hardy wrote in *Tess of the D'Urbervilles* (1891): 'Every village has its idiosyncrasy, its constitution, often its own code of morality.' Nevertheless, one common trend can be identified with confidence, that country villages were increasingly exposed to urban attentions. Take two areas as different as the Hartland peninsula in Devon and Hollins Green, a rural enclave of south Lancashire. Hartland has been chosen for its remoteness, although the majority of counties contained 'remote' spots. Lancashire and Yorkshire, by-words for manufacture, had vast tracts of wilderness. Some whole counties were 'remote'. The Westmorland dalesman's contact with townsfolk might be no more than a brush with a Kendal tradesman or a Lake District votary; and in the heart of England pastoral counties like Huntingdonshire could offer no greater urban bustle than what Huntingdon, St. Ives, or St. Neots provided. As for Hartland, a study published in 1891 advertised its anachronistic queerness. There was surviving belief in sorcery, the practice still of ancient civic ritual and of communal sanctions against unsocial activity, and evidence that cruel sports were only lately extinct. But many places could claim as much or more. The significant point is that to be held remote in late-nineteenth-century England meant in the case of Hartland being merely thirteen miles from Bideford and sixteen miles from Holsworthy, the nearest market towns and railway connections. Neither town had much pretension as an industrial centre – the larger, Bideford, had a population of eight to nine thousand employed in various maritime activities and in a minor way in potteries, tanneries, and collar manufacture – but both towns funnelled market services to the rural hinterlands.

Those links, which were already forged and which would multiply in future between the Hartlands and urban England, can be itemized from an account of Hollins Green in the early twentieth century. This South Lancashire village was thinly veiled under the name 'Moss Ferry' in Margaret Penn's memoir, *Fourteen Miles from Manchester* (1947). It boasted a butcher and cobbler, and a general storekeeper who at Christmas supplied home-made treacle toffee. Otherwise, villagers now relished manufactured sweets: aniseed balls, Fry's Chocolate Creams, or American gums. They also had a taste for fish-and-chips sold at weekends from the village's parlour-shops, or for bottled Kola and cakes obtained from nearby Cadishead. Cadishead ('Daneshead' in Margaret Penn's account) contained a 'big, bright Co-op'; also several shoe shops which, selling fashionable manufactured footwear, were enticing custom from the Hollins Green bootmaker. Co-op Library books circulated in Hollins Green; and a dentist visited Cadishead once a month for those prepared to abandon traditional for professional pain. Tallymen from Manchester or Cadishead drapers' shops mostly supplied Hollins Green with hats, frocks, blouses, and underwear; but the attractions of department stores were now known. Some villagers regularly made trips to Lewis's at Manchester.

The village's occupational structure was changing, too, as the non-agricultural sector gained. A railway clerk lived there, and Margaret Penn's foster-father quit being an agricultural labourer, though he was friendly with the farmer, in order to work with the council road gang. This gave him a higher wage and status; and one of his sons worked at a Cadishead iron-foundry. Other villagers' families had enlarged ambitions too: no farm work for the sons any more or domestic service for the daughters, if they could avoid it; clerical or industrial work in Warrington or Manchester for the enterprising boy perhaps; the post office, pupil-teaching, or an apprenticeship with a fashionable dressmaker or shopkeeper for the capable girl – these vistas were opened by elementary education and city journals. Of course, some older folk warned against it. 'Book learning' was inferior to common sense derived from real experience and oral tradition. Dangerous dissatisfactions might be generated; anyway, Manchester life was too quick-moving and immoral. Others, however, knew that there lay excitement and riches. By now some villagers had even been to London, on day trips for 't' Cup tie'. And so youths left the village to see for themselves. What they found was that all their elders' opinions were true. There were dismaying revelations about their gawkiness and the city folk's dishonesty; but adventure and improvement were begun. The scales tipped against the village. The new city worker 'began to find continual fault with their simple rough way of living at home. Although she loved her mother and father, their illiterate ways made her feel ashamed.'

The social revolution in villages was most conspicuous in diet, dress, and speech. Villagers were becoming more like their town counterparts. The agricultural labourer's larder by 1900 might contain bakers' rather than home-made bread, tinned corned beef and sardines, cans of condensed milk, jars of manufactured jam and pickles, packets of currants, rice and porridge oats, coffee, drinking chocolate and cocoa. Hardy, with his habit of poignant detail, observes that the flower vase which Tess places on the grave of her bastard infant is a converted brand jar of 'Keelwell's Marmalade'. Some longstanding north/south differences remained; still, many regional and local recipes were under pressure to survive.

The change in country apparel is equally documented. T. H. S. Escott ascribed this to intensive marketing, writing in 1885 that 'the last new mode finds its way to the neighbourhood market town very nearly at the same time that it does to the capital of the empire; and cheap bonnets of the latest shape, or ribbons of the approved tint, are displayed in the window of the village shop a very little while after they have first been exposed to the view of the buyers of Regent Street.' Marketing did not explain this trend entirely. The peasant smock and gaiters were cast off by younger agricultural labourers as a mark of servility and backwardness. There was an expanding revolt against traditional sumptuary codes, still enforced in some closed villages by squires who frowned upon those who sought to dress beyond their station.

All this was upsetting to a fetishist like A. J. Munby. In Surrey in July 1860 he noticed 'a grey old peasant in his Sunday smock with his strong hearty wife beside him, in her high cap and old-fashioned russet gown, whilst a couple of pert flimsy girls, in worthless garments of a pseudo-fashionable kind, stood talking to them, gaudy with ribbons and crinoline'. It was the same in the north where grandmothers in the hill, dale, and pit villages would sit by their cottage doors enjoying a smoke from a black cutty-pipe. The next generation of women in their old age would not imitate them. For all the abiding roughness of life in these parts, womanhood had been dowered with aesthetic distinction. Munby blamed the railways. These would 'ultimately destroy all the refreshing ruggedness, all the valuable folk lore, of our rural dialects, and all the charming differentia – or what little is still left – of our rural dress and manners. God forbid that one should live to such a time, when all England shall be one dead level of Americanized half-educated vulgarity!'

This distress was unnecessary. Standardization was not round the corner. Nevertheless, many organizations sought to preserve rural traditions from urban influences. A sense of irretrievable pending loss drove the glossarists and philologists of the English Dialect Society (1873) to expand the record of rural dialect vocabularies before they were extinguished by town speech. It stirred the Society for the Protection of Ancient Buildings (1877) to mount a campaign in 1902 to preserve Celtic, Roman, and medieval bridges from replacement by modern iron and brick constructions capable of bearing steam-waggons, traction-engines, and motor vehicles. It stimulated the antiquarians, anthropologists, and ethnologists of the Folk-Lore Society (1878) to collect and classify the tales, traditions, and superstitions of past and departing cultures. And it compelled the Revd S. Baring-Gould, Cecil Sharp, and the English Folk-Song Society (1898) to register customary songs and dances before they passed with the failure of oral memory, and the onslaught of commercial songs from the music-halls.

What hampered the efforts of these societies was not so much want of allies in the towns as the defeatism, even opposition, of people in the countryside. They did not wish to remain as they had been, or else social pressures in favour of change were too compelling. William Morris in 1896 was driven to the grave in a harvest waggon by the architect, Detmar Blow, who wore a smock. Most common labourers, given the means, would have ordered a shining hearse, pulled by plumed horses and managed by professional undertakers in formal mourning rig-out.

What was true of dress was true of speech. Another way of speaking was manufactured, from the metropolises and independent private schools. Dialect already was a matter of residual accents, idioms, and syntax rather than fully fledged languages; still, dialect-speaking areas were daily more circumscribed, reported a Surrey glossarist in 1893. The rustics' growing self-consciousness was indicated in imitative styles of speech but bilingualism was more general, like the maintenance of two sets of costume, work clothes and Sunday best. It was reported of Worcestershire in 1882 that young people, now subject to the authority of both the printed word and an improving-minded pedagogue, would talk among themselves in broad Worcestershire but address 'their pastors, masters, and betters in the nearest approach to Queen's English to which they have been able to attain'. Hardy, in *Tess of the D'Urbervilles* (1891), noticed this too, giving emphasis to the generational aspect: 'Mrs Durbeyfield habitually spoke the dialect; her daughter, who had passed the Sixth Standard in the National School under a London-trained mistress, spoke two languages: the dialect at home, more or less; ordinary English abroad and to persons of quality.'

The persons of quality in the countryside were also changing in composition, counting more townsmen among them. 'Where are the great families', it was asked of Buckinghamshire in 1885; 'where are the Lees of Quarrendon, the Dashwoods of Halton, the Chesterfields and Stanhopes of Eythorpe, the Whartons of Upper Winchenden, the Lakes of Aston Clinton, the Dormers of Wing? All their once noble residences have been swept away by the ruthless hand of time, and their lands have become alienated. The members of the Rothschild families are now the owners of the principal of these estates.' The significance of this change was debated in 1902, following an article in the January edition of the *Nineteenth Century* which lamented that the traditional gentry was near extinction. This seemed the final act in an age-old drama. That squires were forced to sell to city parvenus was a cry heard during any agricultural recession; and urban wealth was customarily ambitious to purchase country property and status. The *Spectator* now umpired the argument in terms not discreditable to the newcomers. Admittedly their connection with the farmers was less intimate, since they were generally landlords on a small scale. But they were employers of labour and in some cases took an active part on vestry, council, and board of guardians, to which they brought fresh ideas.

The countryside was being settled permanently by some townsmen; it also saw more seasonal visitors. The lure of rugged scenery was well developed from the Romantic period; but the late Victorians organized these emotions, through the National Trust (1895) and a miscellany of ramblers' associations. Baden-Powell's Boy Scouts (1907) practised wood-craft and field manoeuvres, while a genteel gipsydom was cultivated by the Camping Club (1901) and Caravan Club (1907). Literary and artistic celebrities unwittingly acted as mascots of specific locales: Wordsworth for the Lakes, the Brontës for the Yorkshire moors, Landseer for the Scottish Highlands, Tennyson for the Lincolnshire wolds, Hardy for Wessex. The most regular visitors were those in pursuit of game. The number of gamekeepers increased from 9,000 to 23,000 between 1851 and 1911 (twice the quantity of rural police), when the total male agricultural workforce fell by 352,000. By Edwardian times, proclaimed Lord Granby, shooting for sport was 'as democratic as the omnibus'. He reckoned that £3,000 was spent in the country each week from London alone by shooting parties, during the six months from September. It was not the democratic omnibus but the plutocratic automobile that brought them; and in the *Fortnightly Review*, February 1908, Basil Tozer indicated how the country was profiting from new business. He had allegedly been the first to attempt to motor across Dartmoor, some years before; but that expedition ended in mechanical failure, and the vehicle was towed to the nearest village, Two Bridges, by a horse taken from a plough.

In Two Bridges, at that time [Tozer recollected], the accommodation was severe in the extreme, while the food – to speak with self-restraint – was of the simplest. To-day there is a well-appointed inn there, and I speak quite without exaggeration when I say that the catering at that inn is, in the summer, almost upon a par with the catering at some of our popular London restaurants. The automobile is almost wholly responsible for this change.

The dust clouds raised by unconscionable motorists were evidently thought a small price for rustics to pay; but C. F. G. Masterman was not alone in believing that these motorists, by their exhibition of 'wealth's intolerable arrogances', were in part responsible for the exacerbation of class enmity in Edwardian England. Only the country doctor, whose ability to visit patients was enhanced, offset the road-hogs by demonstrating the socially beneficial uses which motorized transport might bring to the countryside.

The commingling of the wealthy of town and country in sport was one manifestation of a broader intercourse. T. H. S. Escott in 1885 extolled the fusion of the landed, merchant, and industrial aristocracy as both a sign and guarantee of 'the diverse sources of our national power'. More landlords administered their estates on professional lines, employing agents to weigh profit maximization and non-monetary considerations in a more detached manner. Rural landlords were also 'commercial potentates' – owners of mines and urban rents, stockholders and bondholders, active or passive company directors. By 1897 over a quarter of the peerage held company directorships, many more than one. Here may be a case for considering a thesis of *embourgeoisement*, in connection with the aristocracy not the working classes. The evidence for this, however, is less impressive than that which argues for the gentrification of the businessman. Certainly, the more successful urban middle classes became country gentlemen, although, if the newly ennobled are a guide, their investment in land was less than might be supposed, considering the jeremiads about falling property values which resounded in country districts. The commonest course was to take a token dip into property and resist full immersion. As F. M. L. Thompson puts it, they 'contented themselves with a country house without surrounding it with property extensive enough to be called an estate'.

Nevertheless, it was Escott's contention in 1885 that everything pointed to a union of agricultural and business establishments. The public schools were cumulatively integrating and standardizing manners, as the 'bottle-merchant's son and the Plantagenet' were set side by side. Here the ideal of the gentleman was cultivated. By Edwardian times about 70 per cent of Conservative MPs had come through the public schools; about 58 per cent were university-educated, chiefly at Oxbridge. In the county magistracy there was further cross-fertilization, as J. M. Lee details in *Social Leaders and Public Persons* (1963). On the Cheshire bench of magistrates traditional county names mingled with Liverpool and Manchester bankers, shipowners, manufacturers, solicitors, and accountants.

This quiet recruitment was proceeding before county government was placed on an elective basis in 1888. Generally, commercial men found favour more readily than industrialists, Anglicans and Tories more easily than Dissenters and Liberals. This last feature characterized town benches as well as county. In 1892, when Gladstone's fourth ministry entered office, only 22 per cent of borough magistrates were thought Liberal. Herschell, the Lord Chancellor, responded to party pressure to redress this balance. The proportion of Liberal borough magistrates quickly rose to 36 per cent. Ostensibly, fitness in dispensing justice, not party service, remained the prime consideration. Loreburn, a later Liberal Lord Chancellor (1905–12), tried to tackle the problem at source, establishing advisory committees to act with the Lord-Lieutenants in forwarding recommendations. Generally, for working people in town and country, political party concerns were immaterial. What mattered was judicial bias, particularly in labour questions; that the law was made and interpreted by the employing classes. In the Black Country, which David Philips examined in *Crime and Authority in Victorian England* (1977), the iron-masters and mine-owners flagrantly discriminated in their own interests when they occupied the bench. The nation's first trio of working-men magistrates, all trade-union officials, was appointed in May 1885; but the situation which Keir Hardie deprecated at Hull in 1893, during the dock strike, remained common – there, out of thirty-nine JPs, four were shipowners and nineteen were shareholders in shipping companies. In the counties class favour was unabashed.

The history of the county councils, first elected in 1889, displays similar features. In 1885 Leonard Courtney had articulated the Liberal expectation that an elective system of county government would 'sweep away the last refuge of clan supremacy'; but the nobility and gentry were not displaced in a revolution. Instead they became, David Spring remarks, 'constitutional rulers'. Tenant-farmers disturbed the establishments in Wales and in some English counties, like Leicestershire and Lincolnshire. Even trade unionists appeared in industrial and mining counties like Durham. But most county councils were cast in the image of the old quarter sessions, composed of the same individuals, class, or outlook. In twenty -two counties the council chairman had presided over the quarter sessions; in another six the chairman was the Lord-Lieutenant. Altogether 87 MPs and 131 peers were elected to the new county councils. Public interest was slight. Even at the first election 1,491 of the 3,240 seats in England and Wales went uncontested. In 1901 2,916 of the 3,349 seats were uncontested. The assimilation of a few new men was more easily accomplished than the adoption of new responsibilities. The chief discomfort to the country élites was the expansion of public business and bureaucracy as central government obliged them to undertake more duties. Spending by county administrations rose from £2.5m. in 1871 to £15.3m. in 1905, from 8 to 14 per cent of expenditure by local authorities.

V

Continuity was equally apparent at Westminster. Those MPs who were heirs to peerages fell from 108 in 1860 to 51 in 1897; but forty out of sixty-nine cabinet ministers between 1885 and 1905, and twenty-five out of fifty-one between 1906 and 1916, were sons of nobility. The representation of the traditional landed classes (nobility, gentry, and squirearchy) remained powerful in the Commons. Their connections, relative youth at first election, and relative security of seats, explain this. Before the 1867 franchise revision large towns were grossly under-represented compared both to counties and to small boroughs within county folds. Thus Knaresborough, with under 5,000 people, returned two MPs, the same as nearby Leeds with 250,000 people. Some correction was then made but between 1867 and 1885 small market towns of fewer than 16,000 population returned over one-fifth of the Commons's representation. After 1885 the complaint was different, that a vote cast in a medium-sized borough of 15–50,000 population was weightier than one cast in a large town or suburban district. The extremities were glaring by Edwardian times. The smallest English borough seat was Durham, with a population of 15,000 and an electorate of 2,600. The largest constituency was the Romford division of Essex, with a population of 220,000 and an electorate of 53,000. Still, the Romford division, when created in 1885, had a not exceptionally large electorate of 12,600. Its subsequent suburban growth was unpredictably massive. Altogether the 1885 redistribution should not be underestimated. London's representation increased from 22 to 59 seats, the five largest provincial cities from 15 to 32. The number of other borough seats was reduced from 244 to 135 by submerging most boroughs of fewer than 15,000 inhabitants within subdivided county constituencies.

It was commonly alleged that political power in small boroughs and counties was too susceptible to territorial influences or money. These factors should be separated. Proprietary borough and county seats remained, though fewer after 1868 than before. H. J. Hanham, *Elections and Party Management* (1959), reckons that thirty-nine borough seats (four uncertainly) were controlled by patrons between 1868 and 1885. Among these were the truly abject like Calne, whose MP, Robert Lowe, was stung by John Bright's assertion in 1866 that the Marquess of Lansdowne might have returned his butler or groom. The majority of these seats had no independent political life. What influence was possessed by local worthies was invested in brokerage on behalf of outside interests. Any difficulty over Hertford's representation was the result not of Hertfordians' political ardour but of arrangements made for the Whigs by the Cowpers at Panshanger and for the Tories by the Cecils at Hatfield. By the 1870s the standing of the former waned and the latter waxed. Patronage, then, was not constantly in the same hands; nor was it exercised exclusively by traditional landowning families. Millowners wrestled over Westbury; elsewhere railway companies, the Great Western at Cricklade and the Great Eastern at Harwich, exerted authority too.

Few possessed an absolute or stable interest. Hence the venality which accompanied elections in these seats; but the most corrupt, like Barnstaple, Bridgwater, and Beverley, were not counted among the proprietary seats since the ruling interest was cash alone. That an election might be declared void or a seat disfranchised were traditional checks. Subsequently, the secret ballot was introduced in 1872, and stricter legislation against malpractices in 1883. Neither made the system watertight against corruption. The inviolability of the secret ballot was mistrusted by working people. Several places maintained unsavoury reputations, even quite sizeable towns, like Cheltenham, Gloucester, and Worcester. Gathering information for *The Government of England* (1908), A. L. Lowell was reliably told that about 'a score or two dozen' grossly corrupt constituencies existed. These were 'mostly boroughs in the South of England containing a considerable number of ancient freemen . . . but even in these boroughs the increase in the number of voters has lowered the price paid for votes, and in some of them the practice is slowly dying out.' Election petitions were mounted sometimes; but the courts were an expensive and uncertain resort. Generally, private knowledge and party interest conspired to keep the lid on disclosure. Following the 1897 by-election in Salisbury, the wife of the defeated Liberal, John Fuller, remarked that 'to wallow in the mire was bad enough, but to wallow unsuccessfully was worst possible'. But Fuller did not petition, for, his brother-in-law Charles Hobhouse admitted, the 'corruption on *both* sides [was] deliberate and great'. Wiser candidates simply avoided places where bribability ruled.

In the counties traditional influences obtained. Hanham distinguishes sixteen county constituencies controlled by patrons between 1868 and 1885, another five where a large interest was persuasive. After the 1885 redistribution perhaps a dozen seats remained under a single, though less absolute, influence. Landlordism was ubiquitous – only 10 or 12 per cent of farmland was independent, farmed by owner-occupiers – but counties were not alike in patterns of landownership or aristocratic residence. F. M. L. Thompson calculates that 24 per cent of the country was occupied by great estates, those which in aggregate exceeded 10,000 acres. At one end were Rutland and Northumberland with over 50 per cent, at the other end Essex and Middlesex with 9 and 4 per cent of their area in the grip of great estates. Warwickshire was among three counties which conformed to the norm exactly. There county society, wrote Willoughby de Broke, was plainly ranked:

Lord Lieutenant	Member of Parliament
Master of Foxhounds	Dean
Agricultural Landlords	Archdeacons
Bishop	Justices of the Peace
Chairman of Quarter Sessions	Lesser Clergy
Colonel of Yeomanry	Larger Farmers

Politically the hermetic seal of the counties was breached by 1885. Gladstone's practice registers the changing mood. In 1868 he accepted the traditional view that politicians did not, uninvited, speak in a foreign constituency. In by-elections in Buckinghamshire in 1876 and in Middlesex in 1880 he stayed out, acknowledging that 'the appearance of a stranger in a County Election would raise the cry of intrusion and dictation'. Following the Midlothian campaign, however, Gladstone began to claim almost the freedom of the country, which stirred the Queen to peevish comment about his 'royal progress'. In the 1885 and 1886 general elections he criticized candidates with safe seats, and Liberal peers, who were inactive in speaking round the country. Of course, certain courtesies were observed still; and before the mobility of the motor car outsiders were unable to make great impact. Thus Willoughby de Broke needed relays of horses to canvass the Rugby division of Warwickshire, 'a straggling rural constituency, about thirty miles long and fifteen miles broad, consisting of about ninety villages and the town of Rugby'.

Willoughby de Broke's memoirs, *The Passing Years* (1924), are rightly valued for the picture they present of county society. They colour for historians an otherwise empty abstraction, the deferential community, and divest it of unnecessarily scornful associations of the hubristic and menial kind. The outstanding feature is class assurance almost as solid as phenomenal objects. M. K. Ashby observes that 'in the whole volume of *The Passing Years* there is not one metaphor which is not drawn from sport or game or weather or the table'. Here is the clue to the influence of the landed families which persisted apart from that autocratic capacity to insist on their way anyhow. It reflects that shared outlook among countrymen which reinforced the landed families' claims as *natural* leaders of county interests. The points of reference were local, personal, customary.

From a modern perspective Willoughby de Broke's record is appalling: an indulgent, unproductive, thick-headed bigot, resisting all change, whether technological or for social and political justice. On the other hand it is a fond tribute to a privileged caste who were forthright about their title to live as their forebears lived – and as their tenants and servants expected them to live. The maintenance of this style was expensive, time-consuming, and physically exacting. Hunting four times a week for seven months of the year demanded intimate knowledge of country people and country ways. When Willoughby de Broke wrote about his estate employees – that 'there was a mutual bond of affection that had existed for many generations between their families and the family of their employer, a bond that cannot be valued in terms of money' – he was underlining the strength of the patriarchal system. Within the circumscription of a rigidly defined hierarchy a rough democracy thrived. Willoughby de

Broke's 'first and best friend' was Jesse Eales, gamekeeper during four generations of the Verney family, and Eales's qualities occupy over six pages of the memoirs.

It is proper to ask how typical or how enduring was this scene. The foremost historian of county society, F. M. L. Thompson, is sceptical about the degree and effectiveness of aristocratic and gentry paternalism, since landlord provision and support of churches, schools, cottages, allotments, village charities and social clubs, even in closed parishes, was patchy and unsystematic. Nevertheless, before the Great War, many of these traditional bonds of county society survived. Special occasions emphasized this mode of life, none more so than the coming of age or marriage of heirs to the estates.

For all this, the counties were not stagnant politically. Several Conservative county candidates met defeat in the 1885 General Election. The automatic assumption was that franchise extension generated an agricultural labourers' revolt, for allotments and the restoration of customary rights; or that a Liberal interest had grown among small tenant-farmers, grateful for the repeal of the Game Laws and greedy for compulsory tenant-right. Some evidence from East Anglia, Devon, and Wiltshire corroborates this; otherwise it is unconvincing. The explanation may lie in the Liberal traditions of those small boroughs of under 15,000 inhabitants which in 1885 were merged into county constituencies. In 1880 they had returned fifty Liberals out of a total of eighty-seven MPs. After 1885 the traditional equation, that a county constituency signified chiefly agricultural interests, cannot be made. Many county divisions contained a suburban overspill, several small towns or industrial villages. Miners in numerous counties, textile workers in Pennine villages, potters in Staffordshire, all gained by the 1884 enfranchisement and swelled the Liberal vote in county constituencies after 1885.

Aristocratic scalps were thus taken more regularly. This made tremendous news but may signify less. In 1906 South Lancashire resounded when the heir to the earldom of Derby was beaten in Westhoughton – a mixed agricultural, mining, and industrial seat – by a Labour representative, a carpenter from nearby Bolton. But Stanley influence in the north-west was not dismissed. The owners of 70,000 acres, whose rents totalled £300,000 p.a., were automatically invited to supply or recommend candidates for numerous Conservative Associations in Lancashire and Cheshire. This customary influence lingered in a political system where a candidate's ability mattered less than his connections, that priceless, ill-defined quality of having 'a stake in the country'.

VI

An understanding of this structure of country life is essential to explain why so many of the professional middle classes, of both conservative and radical persuasions, found in the countryside models for ideal urbanization. Large cities were disorderly, denatured, dehumanizing: hence the fear inspired by the propensity towards larger urbanization. Consider George Eliot's reaction to H. T. Buckle's *History of Civilization in England* (1861): 'I am very far behind Mr Buckle's millennial prospect, which is, that men will be more and more congregated in cities and occupied with human affairs, so as to be less and less under the influence of Nature – i.e., the sky, the hills and the plains; whereby superstition will vanish, and statistics will reign for ever and ever'. Then there are Gissing's desultory speculations in *The Private Papers of Henry Ryecroft* (1903): 'London is the antithesis of the domestic ideal; a social reformer would not even glance in that direction but would turn all his zeal upon small towns and country districts, where blight may perhaps be arrested, and whence, some day, a reconstituted national life may act upon the great centre of corruption'. The foreigner who would understand England's greatness must avoid the manufacturing centres and visit instead 'those old villages, in the midlands or the west, which lie at some distance from a railway station and in aspect are still untouched by the baser tendencies of the time'. Order, stability, comfort, lay in the small organic community, in harmony with natural surroundings.

What G. K. Chesterton called a 'fancy for having things on a smaller and smaller scale' seemed widespread, a reaction to two great movements, Imperialism and Socialism, which 'believed in unification and centralisation on a large scale'. Actually the polarization was not that extreme. Many an imperialist dreamed of the Empire as an extension of the English country town, wherein the essence of national life was captured. The Countess of Warwick pictured the future Socialist State in similar terms (*Fortnightly Review*, March 1912): few great cities, more small to medium-sized towns, linked by free public transport. Future communist agriculturalists would live in towns, benefiting from urban culture, fellowship, and scientific skills; but the morbidity of monster city growth would be checked by expert state direction, exploiting electricity to disperse industry. It was now understood that megalopolis, to use Patrick Geddes's jargon, evolved from rural decay. To avert further stages of 'parasitopolis', 'patholopolis' and 'necropolis', a revival of the regions was obligatory. Hence the advocacy of city devolution and village reconstruction, by public transport, land redistribution, industrial dispersal, education and so forth. Sociologically the vital requirement was the restoration of neighbourliness. This was why so many resolved their abhorrence of rural backwardness and city discomfort by apostrophizing the country town. Here the best of what was traditional and modern might be blended. Freedom and enterprise would obtain still, but viciousness would be neutralized by a stability and civic-mindedness fed from deep wells of continuity and convention. The reason was that most families would be native to the community. Social and religious teaching would be heeded; personal and class co-operation would be a habit. Political overtones in this picture are apparent. In an age of incipient democracy the urban middle classes were sceptical of their ability to control the industrial working classes as the aristocracy traditionally controlled the rural community. Moreover, they disliked both equally. Working-class politics were crude and class-jealous, run by unpractical agitators or unprincipled 'bosses'. Aristocratic politics were illegitimate and degrading, a mixture of bribery, coercion, and flunkeyism. The vision was a democracy led by the responsible, liberal-minded professional middle classes, enjoying popular trust.

How closely did country-town society approach this idealization? Authors of travelogues agreed: it was hard to discover 'unspoilt' country towns. Ludlow, however, with 6,000 people, struck Henry James in the 1870s as an excellent example of a town not disfigured by industry: 'it exhibits no tall chimneys and smoke-streamers, no attendant purlieus and slums.' A dignified relic of pre-Victorian carriage society, Ludlow was where the provincial aristocracy once 'entertained itself in decent emulation of that more majestic capital which a choice of railway lines had not as yet placed within its immediate reach'. James's vignette of the grass-grown ruin was overdrawn. Ludlow contained a malt trade, glove-making, and a paper mill. This was not very intense industry; still, it illustrates an important point of Professor Everitt, that small market towns altogether retained considerable industrial capacity. Typically workshop and small-factory industry, located in courts and yards proximate to the market places and high streets, this was found in towns 'as unlike and as far apart as Faversham in Kent, Market Harborough in Leicestershire, Yarm in Yorkshire, Kendal in Westmorland, Louth in Lincolnshire and Newark in Nottinghamshire'.

It is difficult to generalize about the collateral social relations of country-town industries. The reason is that the economic activities were so diverse. A selection from Worcestershire adumbrates the problem. Consider Redditch and Bromsgrove, two centres of small metal manufacture. Redditch (population 13,493 in 1901) specialized chiefly in needles, pins, and fishing tackle; Bromsgrove (8,416 population) chiefly in nails, though there was also button and cloth manufacture and a railway works. Both towns had grown recently from villages. Originally their small metal trades were organized around domestic out-work. Factory concentration came later, sited on the outskirts; but small workshops remained in the courts and rows behind the high streets. The conditions of employment were generally of the scraping and sweated sort, exploiting in-migrants from the countryside. This hardly substantiated a thesis that country towns embarked upon industrial enterprise in a more wholesome way than larger towns and cities.

Baldwin's iron works at Bewdley exhibited a different character, but again not a condition unknown in big-city manufacturing. Bewdley was certainly a small country town, smaller than Bromsgrove, though comb-making, tanning, rope-making, and brick works were located there as well as ironware. In 1925 Stanley Baldwin fondly recalled the quality of corporate life at Bewdley in late Victorian times.

It was a place where I knew and had known from childhood [Baldwin was born in 1867], every man on the ground; a place where I was able to talk with the men not only about the troubles in the works, but troubles at home and their wives. It was a place where strikes and lock-outs were unknown. It was a place where the fathers and grandfathers of the men then working there had worked, and where their sons went automatically to the business. It was also a place where nobody ever 'got the sack', and where we had a natural sympathy for those who were less concerned in efficiency than is this generation, and where a large number of old gentlemen used to spend their days sitting on the handles of wheel barrows, smoking their pipes.

G. M. Young commented about industrial paternalism that it was a 'curious blend of discipline and good nature, fairmindedness and competition, sound workmanship and indifference to science'. The last was the enemy. Technological advances and structural reorganization would blast this halo of industrial peace and transform the relationships, with formal collective bargaining between employers and workmen to wrestle for the greater say in the conduct of industry. After 1918, following the changing balance of trade and extension of state pensions and insurance, once paternal employers displayed a more dispassionate attitude to redundancy in pursuit of company efficiency and survival.

VII

The corporate life of the countryside had other sources of sustenance apart from paternal landlords and industrialists. Traditionally the most substantial support was the Church. Its embodiment was the cathedral city. Wells in Somerset, with barely 5,000 inhabitants in 1901, seemed the perfect expression of this type, a snug peculiar. Its atmosphere was redolent of a permanent Sunday afternoon. There was a little general trade, some surviving stocking knitters and lace makers, and no factories. The completeness of this ecclesiastical presence in a town was already rare before Trollope whetted the public's appetite with his Barchester novels, begun with *The Warden* (1855). Except for the three years, 1827–30, which he spent at Winchester College, Trollope never lived in a cathedral city. A midsummer evening stroll about Salisbury sparked the inspiration of his fiction.

Perhaps there was something singular about a cathedral city. Kilvert was informed by a canon of Worcester in 1870 that lunatics were attracted to cathedrals and created a nuisance by raving during services. Otherwise, it is questionable whether by late Victorian times the cathedral city was sociologically a distinctive type, even if the new sees are excluded from the survey. The new themselves were a motley lot. Most were industrial sees – like Manchester, Liverpool, Newcastle, Southwell, and Wakefield – but others were country-suburban sees like St. Alban's (1877) or Chelmsford (1914), which relieved the diocese of London of its straggling Hertfordshire and Essex parts. Established cathedral cities were allegedly conspicuous for their stability and conservatism. The intellectual and social authority of the ecclesiastical garrisons was bolstered by the deference which they received from the governing classes in the surrounding agricultural districts and from dependent urban tradesmen. Some semblance of this survived. Mrs Creighton's view of Worcester in the mid-1880s was roseate, that of a well-ordered, integrated community, obeying traditional patterns of practice. 'With all the varied life around it the Cathedral stood in close connection. The chapter and city were on the best of terms, and in all matters of educational and philanthropic concern the help of the chapter was freely claimed and liberally given'. Worcester was mocked as the Dead See by the citizens of Birmingham, who lay uncomfortably within this diocese until the bishopric of Birmingham was cut out in 1905. Worcester, however, was not a museum like Wells. Though its politics were charged with old-fashioned bribery and treating, it was a sizeable place of above 40,000 people, with a thriving hop market and various manufactures, led by the porcelain works, glove factories, sauce and vinegar makers, and metal and engineering firms.

By the late Victorian period the established cathedral cities spanned a wide scale of magnitude. Out on its own for size was Norwich, but Norwich was a long-standing provincial capital like Bristol, rather than a cathedral city *tout court*. This past lustre was retained; indeed, it may be, rural depopulation was actually enhancing the dominance of the city over the county. Between 1851 and 1911 Norwich prac-tically doubled in size, from 68,000 to 121,000, but the numbers left in rural Norfolk (that is, the county minus the aggregate populations of Norwich, Yarmouth, and King's Lynn) fell by 7.4 per cent, from 325,000 to 301,000. Norwich was now a significant railway and manufacturing centre but J. B. Priestley, in *English Journey* (1934), understood whence its reputation derived:

In a very large slice of England, to thousands and thousands of good sensible folk who live and work there, Norwich is the big city, the centre, and has been these hundreds of years. My own native town [Bradford] is more than twice the size of Norwich, but somehow it does not seem half the size. This is not merely because Norwich has its cathedral and castle and the rest, but also because it has flourished as the big city in the minds of men for generations. It is no mere jumped-up conglomeration of factories, warehouses and dormi-tories. It may be minute compared with London, Paris, Rome, but neverthe-less it lives its life as a city on the same level of dignity.

In like manner most county towns – these may or may not have been cathedral cities as well – maintained a pride of position. This was not correlated with population. The demographic weight of the county towns on the total urban scale was slight. The county town's position was upheld by the pomp and circumstance of local government. None was more impressive than that which attended the assize circuits, with a history of seven hundred years behind them, though now that system was beginning to decay. The trend in legal as in other business was towards concentration in the big cities, as a Royal Commission which investigated delays in the King's Bench Division noted in 1912–13. There had been a marked decrease in the number of causes tried in the smaller assize towns and increase in those tried in London, Liverpool, Manchester, Leeds, Birmingham, and Cardiff, where a local Bar was centred. Mr Justice Hawkins, accompanied by pet terrier, was one who made the most of the dwindling circuit. His favourite spots were old rural assize towns like Warwick, Bedford, and Oakham, where he could retreat in the evening to a nearby nobleman's castle; or bustling county capitals like Lincoln, where he was received at the station by 'the Sheriff . . . in full robes, his chaplain in full canonicals . . . a great many other worthy dignitaries, . . . [and] a goodly crowd outside and in, some well dressed and some slatternly, some bareheaded out of respect to the Judge, and others of necessity, but all with the look of profoundest awe'. The assize sermon preached at the parish church or cathedral solemnized these towns' contract with tradition.

The Established Church thus acted as one of several custodians of customary authority; but this common presence evoked variable respect. E. W. Benson reckoned that by 1850 'the cathedral bodies were in the very depth of unpopularity'. Thereafter there was a substantial revival of the cathedral ideal (to which Benson contributed by building Truro between 1877 and 1882), owing to the pastoral exertions of the episcopacy and cathedral chapters. Still, there were limits to their influence. At Chester and Lincoln, for instance, the ecclesiastical authorities were regularly overwhelmed by the saturnalia of race-weeks, which no amount of homilies about betting and bad company could deter. Viewing the ancient cathedral cities, we find many remained much as before, mere market towns whose economic base showed little diversification or capacity for growth in the half-century from 1851. Chichester grew from 8,662 to only 12,241. Malt and timber trades remained its staple, with sundry woollen and copper wares. Its harbour was without a commercial future, accessible only to very small vessels, in an age when the railway increasingly compelled a rationalization of the port system. Elsewhere Durham remained penned within a mining county; Winchester lived off its school and barracks; and Hereford relied still on the cider and leather trades, though the manufacture of encaustic tiles had grown in response to Victorian fashion. Canterbury was engaged in the hop trade and as a military station; Salisbury served its region as before; and Exeter, having suffered the extinction of its manufacture of coarse cloth, was more dependent than ever on alternative railway work, paper mills, tanneries, breweries, iron and brass foundries, and coastal shipping. All this activity was circumscribed by geographical disadvantages.

By contrast, some ancient cathedral cities expanded significantly in size. Mass-produced foods manufacture had raised up Carr's biscuits in Carlisle and Rowntree's cocoa and confectionery in York. Railway locomotive, carriage, or wagon workshops, and marshalling yards were other important sources of employment there, and at Gloucester and Peterborough. There was an adventitious element about the progress of the last two places as railway centres. An inland port, Gloucester profited from the break in traffic as the point where the broad-gauge Great Western and the standard-gauge Midland lines met; and Peterborough received the Great Northern main line when the Marquis of Exeter prevented its passage through his pocket borough of Stamford. Peterborough, along with Lincoln and Rochester, became a centre for agricultural machinery. This enterprise was in urgent response to the crisis in the corn counties. Instead of remaining distribution centres and markets for agricultural produce, they developed a manufacturing base and also ventured into extractive industry – brick works at Peterborough, cement works at Rochester. In Rochester's case, though, it would be absurd to pretend that it was ever in danger of being forced into a rural backwoods. The city's economy had ties with an agricultural region but not to the extent to which it was joined to the fortunes of Chatham and Gillingham. Together these three municipalities embraced 110,000 people in a Medway conurbation by 1901.

Whether there was continuity or discontinuity in the economic structures of the older cathedral cities, it was evident that the Church's position in 1900 was not that of 1800. The Ecclesiastical Commissioners reduced considerably the size and wealth of cathedral chapters in order to assist poor parishes. Broadly, Anglican authority and privilege were retreating, as evidenced in the abandonment of compulsory church rates, reduction of clerical magistrates, and removal of educational restrictions. An account of the cathedral and university city of Oxford will epitomize what flowed from these last changes.

Oxford doubled in size between 1801 and 1841, and doubled again from 1841 to 1901, when the population reached 49,000. The city gained two railway stations but no great manufactories. Speculation that the Great Western Railway might establish a works in Oxford in 1865 was dashed by university hostility. Most town corporations in the region did not trouble themselves about industrial disfigurement. Swindon was eventually chosen as the GWR's site, but Abingdon, Banbury, Reading, and Warwick each made offers of suitable land. Oxford was deprived of this contract and so Hyde's clothing and Lucy's light-engineering factories, Morrell's and other breweries, and the Clarendon Press, were significant employers in Oxford mostly by virtue of their isolation. An artisan district was growing eastwards but only after 1914 did Oxford become the 'Latin Quarter' of Cowley. Servicing the rural economy of the region and the needs of the university was the city's chief employment. The colleges owned about 25 per cent of the land within the municipal boundary and more near by. Still the city grew, and not only because the university grew but also because the university signally changed. In 1850 the university was an Anglican blockhouse. By 1880 it was effectively disestablished – de-Christianized, the parsonical contingent maintained. Religious tests had been abolished and endowments transferred to lay purposes. Some *odium theologicum* survived and was given brick-and-mortar expression in the Puseyites' foundation of Keble College in 1870. This grand demonstration against secularization was as futile as that individual protest against modern conveniences made by W. P. Ker, who refused to admit the electric light into his room or use the newly installed bathroom, in All Souls College. Vestiges of historic importance survived in the university's separate representation in Parliament, and its studies remained concentrated in the classical mould. But the admission of the sciences, the expansion in the numbers matriculated, the relaxation of the ban on married dons, the formation of women's colleges, the involvement in city settlements, university extension and adult education services, all were signs of adaptation to a new order. One token of change was land use. In the High Street the contrast of ancient and modern was symbolized by the demolition of the old coaching inn in whose kitchens Mrs Frank Cooper perfected her 'Oxford Marmalade'. In its place in 1882 stood the Examination

Schools, a temple dedicated to the new pedagogy of lectures and examinations. When Max Beerbohm wrote *Diminuendo* (1895) he drew attention to the Manchester in modern Oxford. Amid 'remnants of beauty' was 'a riot of vulgarity': 'hideous trams and brand-new bricks', electric street-lighting and newsboys screaming the headlines as in any other city. The once dramatic contrasts of town and gown were fading – 'the townspeople now looked just like undergraduates and the dons just like townspeople'.

More profoundly, Seebohm Rowntree underlined this theme of similarity in *Poverty: a Study in Town Life* (1901). This anatomy of York was modelled after Charles Booth's investigation of London. The same 'mass of stunted human life' was discovered: 'nearly 30 per cent of the population are living in poverty and are ill-housed, ill-clothed and under-fed'. Rowntree's technical definitions, his distinction between 'primary' and 'secondary' poverty, his emphasis upon the 'poverty cycle' of a family, his criteria of 'physical efficiency', are not important here. Rowntree viewed York not as an exceptional entity, a cathedral city, but as 'a typical provincial town'. His own works employed 2,000, and the railway was another big employer; but neither distorted the wages series overmuch. Rowntree's contention that York was 'fairly representative' was subsequently disputed by Arthur Bowley's and A. R. Burnett-Hurst's sample survey of Stanley (Co. Durham), Northampton, Reading, and Warrington in 1912–13. They indicated variable levels of primary poverty according to local labour market conditions. Still, they would not quarrel with Rowntree's conclusion that the social questions of England's towns must be understood to have certain common features, 'dealing with land tenure, with the relative duties and powers of the State and of the individual, and with legislation affecting the aggregation or the distribution of wealth'.

Historically, every church had undertaken to relieve poverty as a Christian duty. The State, too, provided poor relief as an obligation of property; but the Victorian period saw a steady drain of confidence in customary procedures. Indiscriminate charity was held to be counterproductive by the influential Charity Organization Society (1869), which enshrined the conventional wisdom (and ignorance) of the professional middle classes. The vicar of St. Jude's, Whitechapel, Samuel Barnett, put the belief of the COS in strongest fashion in 1874: 'the poor starve because of the alms they receive.' Personal service and painstaking investigation by the urban gentry were the

COS's conditions to distinguish between those whom charity would encourage to be self-supporting and those for whom charity would be ruinous of character. By the 1890s Canon Barnett was not alone in being sceptical of the COS's ability to reform the poor as the COS was sceptical of traditional methods a quarter of a century earlier. Already the churches' role as educators was rivalled by state provision. The conviction grew that for relief of poverty, too, additional state services were required, in housing, health, employment, and old age. From Booth's and Rowntree's studies it was plain that neither the poor-law system nor private charity was capable of effecting adequate short-term relief or real long-term improvement. By Edwardian times the emphasis had shifted, from the manner in which boards of guardians and ecclesiastical and other charities dispensed alms and administered correction, to the provision of minimum standards guaranteed by selective state intervention.

Broadly, then, all churches were finding it more difficult to maintain touch with, let alone directoral control over, the social collectivism of the times. As for the Anglican Church, a traditional conspectus was that it united the nation in the service of God and King; but comprehensiveness through religious monopoly never approached realization. By the 1880s this ambition seemed particularly remote. Then John Morley asked, 'what in the name of common sense is to be made of the talk about a national Church?', because only 14,000 Anglican churches existed as against 21,000 Catholic and Protestant Dissenting rivals. The prestige of the church was always thought more secure in rural areas. As Bishop of Peterborough, Mandell Creighton in 1891 declared, 'our villages are but a collection of houses gathering around their church'. In fact, those who placed their hopes on the church repeating in towns the corporate stability of the countryside, seriously overestimated its strength in rural areas. Perhaps also they were too pessimistic about the failures of the church in towns and too readily equated urbanization and secularization.

Serious defects beset the Anglican Church's organization. In country areas they were compounded by the depression in agricultural prices and rents, because the average tithe-rent charge fell too. Although the capitalized value of all church property was probably increasing owing to urban and mineral holdings, by 1900 some 1,500 livings were worth under £100, and 4,700 under £200 (a minimum acceptable standard), per annum. The plight of church schools was worrying too. About 9,000 existed in 1870. Furious competition ensued, as the Church strove to match the School Boards' rate of building 5,700 in the next thirty years. Ultimately, in the 1902 Education Act, the Conservative Government conceived of rescue by rate aid. An income was thus secured, but at the price of political controversy. Offsetting these disturbing trends was a palpable increase in activity, and improvement in conduct, of the clergy. Even those ructions caused by diverse modes of worship, where fine points of orthodoxy and heterodoxy were disputed, reflected their raised dedication. Fewer pluralistic and non-resident clergy existed; and Communion, at one time rarely administered except at Christmas and Easter, was now regularly taken. Clergy of all persuasions, Low, Broad, and High, were more devoted in their sacramental functions and more professional in their parochial organization – mission work, pastoral visiting, fund-raising, and recreation. The contribution of the theological colleges, especially from the 1860s, in the preparation and examination of ordinands, was important here. The Ecclesiastical Commissioners, too, for all their inhibitions, were a significant force of regeneration, transferring endowments to areas of need and creating new benefices in pursuit of a maximum parochial population of 3–4,000 souls. Socially, both ordinary clergy and bishops were being drawn from a less privileged and exclusive class. Compared with the civil service, law, medicine, and business, clerical stipends were unacceptably low to ambitious public-school men.

By the late nineteenth century there were many signs of an Anglican revival outpacing Nonconformist growth. Some were negative conditions, problems which afflicted dissenting congregations, such as the changing economic structure of the countryside. Declining village craft-work undermined a conventional source of Nonconformist recruitment. Nonconformity also suffered the penalty of success: a reduced emphasis on 'saving' religion and flagging combativeness as the status of Dissent improved. Regular ministers and pompous chapels betokened the 'establishment' of Nonconformity. This transition was incomplete, indeed spasmodically arrested by evangelical revivals (1859–60, 1874–6, 1881–3, 1905) and by political–sectarian controversy; still, it was well observed by the Congregationalist theologian, A. M. Fairbairn, in 1897 that 'the very decay of the disabilities from which our fathers suffered had made it harder for us than it was for them to dissent'.

Nonconformists were as aware as Anglicans that a crisis of faith affected all religion. In the 1850s the atheist, Charles Bradlaugh, was sure of an audience only in London. In the provinces meetings were difficult to arrange. Bradlaugh's sympathizers risked ostracism and economic loss by public avowal. The 1880s marked a change. As MP for Northampton, Bradlaugh won his conflict with parliamentary procedure, in affirming rather than taking the biblical oath, though his success did not incline the newsagents, W. H. Smith, to remove their ban on his newspapers. When Bradlaugh died in 1891 his official biographers reported triumphantly that almost every town of any size had its own Freethought speakers. Instead, secularism was undone. George Bernard Shaw explained the position paradoxically: 'When . . . "God is dead", Atheism dies also.' The true victor was indifferentism.

The ranks of unbelievers were swelling, but reason never destroyed, just as it never made, a faith. Darwinism insensibly modified religious beliefs, and theologians began to revise fundamentalist concepts of the Creation and the miraculous life of Christ. The first springs of ecumenism grew out of this, to find common points of security amid the general erosion of confidence and strengthening of secularization. The Anglican Church was well placed to lead and rally the retreating religions. Ironically, what in large part had prompted the Anglican Church's decline in the recent past now propelled its resurgence: that is, the parochial system and identity with the governing classes and State. That these had damaged the Church is indisputable. Hatred of clerical magistrates – 'squarsons' – was enduring. Certain Anglican dignitaries, like the Bishop of Manchester, James Fraser, had welcomed the agricultural labourers' trade unionism in the 1870s; but this was less general than the Bishop of Gloucester's opinion that it was 'iniquitous'. In his autobiography Joseph Arch – champion hedgecutter, trade-union organizer and Methodist lay preacher – observed that the agricultural labourers' agitation throve on sectarian animosity, a link with the 'old Civil Wars, when the Puritan preacher was the soul of the army of the Commonwealth'. Arch never forgot the order of service in his native parish in the 1830s. 'First, up walked the squire to the communion rails; the farmers went up next; then up went the tradesmen, the shopkeepers, the wheelwright, and the blacksmith; and then, the very last of all, went the poor agricultural labourers in their smock frocks. They walked up by themselves; nobody else knelt with them; it was as if they were unclean. . . .'

The distribution of Anglican support long reflected what has been called the 'dependency system' in agriculture, strongest in compact arable villages with resident squire and parson. At Helmingham (Suffolk), a village remodelled by John Tollemache, whose family had owned the place since the sixteenth century, it was even written into the cottage agreement that the labourer must attend church. The Church was weakest in large or scattered 'open' villages, where land-ownership was divided and where country industries and independent crafts were prevalent.

The urbanization which accompanied the industrial revolution had caught the Church unprepared, with an ossified parochial system and insouciant clergy. Nonetheless, from the 1830s, the machine was re-equipped and resources were redirected in ways that cast doubt on the postulate that urban life and Anglicanism were inimical. The church-manship of W. F. Hook at Leeds (1837–59) was celebrated and, though mostly unsung, there were downright contributions from many others, like G. D. Grundy, who ministered to a mill parish near Oldham from 1840 to 1902. The ecclesiastical parish maintained a prominence as a theatre of communal operations, although increas-ingly its use for local government purposes was abandoned. Between 1818 and 1895 over 3,600 ecclesiastical parishes were formed, without regard for civil organization. By 1895 13,822 ecclesiastical parishes and 14,896 civil parishes existed; but in only one-third of cases did boundaries coincide. The correspondence of civil and ecclesiastical rule ended formally in 1868 when compulsory church rates were abolished. *De facto* this had been conceded in many places long before. Thereafter the parish performed a civil function only as one of several statistical units, for the registration of births, marriages and deaths, and (when coincident with poor-law divisions) for the tabulation of rating and voting qualifications. Just as the politicians found the parish unsuitable for modern services and engineered supra-parochial or alternative spheres of action, so the Church increasingly supplemented the parish in its arrangements – by mis-sionary settlements, for instance, or by new urban bishoprics with suffragans.

Despite this revitalization, the feeling persisted that the Church was both too fat and too thin, overstocked in favourable localities and starved in unpropitious environments. Stewart Headlam, of the socialistic Guild of St. Matthew, complained in 1905 that the Church was still 'run in the interest of the idle monopolizing classes'. Never-theless, in so far as the Church was allied in the public mind with traditional authorities in society and government, it could be rejoindered that this was what the Church did best and, on balance, it now stood to profit rather than suffer from the association. The Church's late-nineteenth-century revival was essentially a middle-class rally, not a recruitment of previously unchurched working classes. That some did make an effort in the other direction is clear; but lighted candles in a slum parish or the back-slapping matiness and hearty theology of such as Winnington Ingram, Bishop of London, could not seriously redress the scales. There was an unmistakable snobbery and class defensiveness about this Anglican resurgence, summarized by Henry James thus: 'Conservatism has the cathedrals, the colleges, the castles, the gardens, the traditions, the associations, the fine names, the better manners, the poetry; Dissent has the dusky brick chapels in provincial by-streets, the names out of Dickens, the uncertain tenure of the *h*, and the poor *mens sibi conscia recti*.'

The Church had few qualifications or opportunities to act as an instrument of social progress as Headlam wanted. It was well placed to address to middle-class congregations sermons about character and service, chivvying these comfortable citizens to recognize familial and civic responsibilities, spiritual as well as material properties. These ministrations were part ablutionary, part exhortatory. Sir Lawrence Jones's memories of Eton capture the vein. Religion was practically synonymous with ethics. The boys were trained as gentlemen rather than Anglicans or even Christians, for little was made of the sacramental or salvationist sides of religion. Not to be confirmed was as unthinkable as 'breaking ranks'.

The caste system bolstered Anglicanism. An agnostic, Frederic Harrison nevertheless attended church from social form. Similarly Lady Strachey, wife of a retired Anglo-Indian official and mother of Lytton, was a convinced free-thinker; yet she had all her children christened. Her example suggests that a sense of propriety was keener in country than city. She attended church when in the country, never when at her London home. Probably, though, the pull of conformity was felt generally. In the solemnization of customary rites – christening, confirmation, marriage, and death – the Established Church maintained an unrivalled position. Not only the personally devout, but careless and ignorant members of the middle and upper classes – those incapable, like Lord Palmerston, of theologically differentiating Moses from Sydney Smith – all could respect the Church as an institution. Churchmen were not slow to respond on this level. A. P. Stanley, as Dean of Westminster from 1864 to 1881, converted the

Abbey into a Valhalla for heroes of all types. On numerous occasions, in jubilee and imperial demonstrations, the Anglican Church functioned as a symbol of national identity.

Overall, the picture that obtains is not clear-cut between docile, religiously observant villages and obstreperous, irreligious townships. The position was regionally variable, a pluralistic order in which, from historic ties, modern developments, and individual contributions, different denominations were capable of exercising significant persuasions on particular classes in particular places. Differences between town and country church attendances were less notable than extremes of observance or indifference found in both urban and rural parts. Where sectarian adherence did exist it had an important bearing upon social–political systems. Loyalty to one creed was not a matter of conscience alone but of social position and expectation too.

Sectarian divisions were social divisions, sectarian strife was civil strife. The persistent clashes of Protestant and Catholic communities in the north are well known, although it would be a travesty to suggest that only sectarian dogmatism provoked these disturbances. The most frequent public battlegrounds for religious groups were education and politics, but many a silent social war was waged on other fronts. The main street of a small East Anglian market town pictured in *The Auto-biography of Mark Rutherford* (1881) contained 'two shops of each trade; one which was patronized by the Church and Tories, and another by the Dissenters and Whigs. The inhabitants were divided into two distinct camps – of the Church and Tory camp the other knew nothing. On the other hand, the knowledge which each member of the Dissenting camp had of every other member was most intimate.'

These networks had two notable features. They were valuable instruments of mutual support, masonic and guild-like; they were also oppressive agencies of mutual surveillance, prone to moral and social terrorism. Neither characteristic was peculiar to small country towns. In *Confessions of an Economic Heretic* (1938) J. A. Hobson described Derby in the 1860s, approaching 50,000 population, with a mixed ruling class drawn from county families, professional men and respectable trade, textile and porcelain manufacturers, and leading officials of the Midland Railway Company. Their political divisions conveyed no great economic or class meaning in a modern sense; instead, sectarian sensibility was sharp, and 'the social cleavage between Church people and Dissenters was clear and strong'.

The degree to which the rural and urban working classes were moved by sectarian commitment was highly variable. A beleaguered minority, like the Irish Catholics, had cause to maintain their religion as a form of communal support and cultural nationalism, although the areas of priestly and political influence were fluid and controversial. At the other extreme were the 'unconscious secularists' observed by the official census of religious attendance in mid-century – people who were 'engrossed by the demands, the trials, and the pleasures of the passing hour, and ignorant or careless of a future'. Examples of strong religious attachments were not uncommon but more usually an impartial pragmatism or dull resignation prevailed. The same person might attend church and chapel at different times or go long spells without attending either. One might be drawn by festivals, charities and treats, and use the Sunday School as a means of getting children out of the home; another might be repelled by the social discrimination of pew rents and 'Sunday suits' and by the contradictions of Christian preaching and performance.

It is not clear how far the surroundings determined the response. 'Hell has no terrors for me. I have lived there', declared Jim Larkin, scion of a Liverpool slum, in 1913. In privation and suffering slum dwellers might turn to the churches for consolation or turn against the churches from bitterness. Missionaries, salvationists, and revivalists made a spasmodic stir; and omnipresent death gave the churches awful inspiration and authority. Ordinary funerals brought out the working classes, especially women, in scores. Extraordinary occasions released ghastly emotions. The burial of a twelve-year-old girl, murdered after sexual assault on the Smithdown Road, Liverpool, attracted a crowd of 20,000. The officiating clergyman did not neglect his opportunity, and comprehensively damned the Sabbath breakers, brawlers, fornicators, and drunkards.

Generally, what seemed to matter was whether regular and pious attendance at church or chapel separated an individual from his class, his neighbours or workmates; and whether this behaviour brought credit from employers. The former calculation was probably more persuasive. As the engineer, Thomas Wright, observed in *The Great Unwashed* (1868), 'if a working man does not attend a place of worship from an active feeling of religion, he need not do so from reasons of caste. It is not essential to his maintenance of a character of respectability.' Employers generally welcomed sober, punctual, and dextrous workmen whatever their religious scruples, though

Country and town, and country towns 229

religious attendance might be reckoned allied to these qualities. This consideration of religion in late Victorian society may now be summarized. The countryside was not characterized by a commonalty based upon religious conformity. This was insufficiently general to serve as a useful criterion of distinction; and several industrial towns contained thriving religious communities, with fully as many features of cultural integration as the most close-knit rural parish. In *Far from the Madding Crowd* (1874) Hardy observes about Gabriel Oak that he inhabited 'that vast middle space of Laodicean neutrality which lay between the Communion people of the parish and the drunken section – that is, he went to church, but yawned privately by the time the congregation reached the Nicene creed, and thought of what there would be for dinner when he meant to be listening to the sermon'. England's Oaks were uncomfortable in Sunday clothes; anyway they 'lived six times as many working days as Sundays'. The Bible was familiar, if the scraps of scripture which flavoured the common speech was an indication; but so was pagan superstition, Shakespearian humour, and Anglo-Saxon forms. The conversation of many labourers, thought Richard Jefferies, sounded 'like a dialogue of the Heptarchy.' Religion touched their lives occasionally but was mostly kept within limits. Altogether the religious vein did not amount to much.

VIII

Religious devotion was as marginal to the life of the countryside as industrial activity. The central business, as always, was agricultural work; and the main purpose of the country town was to provide market and retail services. Railways now multiplied the number of outside contacts; but G. M. Trevelyan exaggerated their invasion in *The Heart of the Empire* (1901). He argued that 'Titan forces' from great cities – science, machinery, and vulgar culture – destroyed 'the old natural school of craftsmanship and art', 'the traditional piety and the honest customs of the countryside'. In fact the historic ties of the provincial town to the agricultural region which it served were not severed. There were still lively traces of that individuality which Trevelyan extolled, when 'each shire, each town, each village, had its own local piety, its customs, its anniversaries, its songs, its ethics, the indefinable but peculiar tone that marked it off from its neighbour'.

The extent of a town's influence in its region has been traced by geographers using a variety of indices. The most commonly drawn radii are local government and school districts, and areas of newspaper and retail distribution and banking and medical services. Other measurements are very imprecise, like the circles of family and social class or the orbits of rumour and gossip. Tess travels forty miles to outrun the reputation of her seduction, and Hardy comments: 'To persons of limited spheres, miles are as geographical degrees, parishes as counties, counties as provinces and kingdoms.' No exact coincidence of lines can result from such indices, therefore. Only broad regions are discernible. In the twentieth century motorized transport has unsettled boundaries still more. Earlier, the overhanging canopy of market-town influence was more tightly fastened. Here the nineteenth century still bore traces of medieval times when small market towns stood at intervals of six or seven miles, a reasonable pedestrian task, while larger markets and shire capitals were approximately a day's horse ride at their catchment perimeter.

The boundaries of market-town influence were marked not on the map but in minds, generation upon generation. Consider Richard Jefferies's account of Marlborough, which he calls Fleeceborough, in *Hodge and his Masters* (1880). The population had peaked around mid-century at just over 5,000 people. In 1901 the population was counted at 3,887. The chief nineteenth-century development was the establishment of the College in 1843, a public school which first attracted the sons of clergymen and had a roll of 600 boys by Edwardian times. But Marlborough had an influence not measurable by groaning numbers or by new industries, for it remained as it had been, the capital of an agricultural kingdom. This was imperceptible to the ordinary traveller, being without tangible legal boundaries; but its limits were understood by the farming community who talked of other districts as 'a separate country, as distinct as France'. The distinctiveness lay in 'little peculiarities in the fields, the crops, the stock, or customs'. There were special characteristics in local patterns of rotation, in agreements of tenure, in the construction of gates, hedges, walls, farm-houses and barns; and the people behaved as a 'nation amongst themselves', with their own dialect, 'their own folklore, their own household habits, particular dainties, and way of life'. Each farm, hamlet, village, and minor town of this kingdom acknowledged the principal market town as the capital. Its authority was historic and familiar. Everyone knew somebody there – where girls had gone into service and boys to find employment; where labourers drove their masters' stock and their wives went to shop; and where the farmers regarded it as 'a religious duty to be seen there on market days', staying at the same inn as their forebears, occupying the same parlour seat and washing down the customary food with the local ale. The gossip was naturally marked by local themes; but even talk of wider things bore the local imagination from those Marlborough papers which supplied the news and arguments.

Studies of Victorian market towns are not plentiful but their importance is emphasized by Alan Everitt. He estimates that 'a third or a half of English people . . . either lived in or were dependent upon provincial market towns'. Our means of reckoning the number of market towns are rough. One guide is the number of poor-law unions. The Commissioners who remodelled the administration under the 1834 Act operated on the principle of taking a market town as a unit, combining those parishes whose inhabitants resorted to its market. Nearly 650 poor-law unions existed in Victorian times, a total which includes large cities with more than one union. Everitt's estimate seems plausible, therefore: there were over 400 Victorian market towns 'with an average population of perhaps some 10,000 each, and two or three times that number in their rural hinterland'.

Everitt stresses the importance of village carriers –reckoning some 30–40,000 throughout the country – as servants of market-town influence. Undoubtedly this traffic was great. It was a feature which struck foreign observers. The English landscape, wrote Henry James, was always a 'landscape with figures'. Everywhere carriers' networks can be traced, threading webs around market towns, and defining their sway. The first issue of the *Banbury Guardian* in 1843 declared of its town: 'To the 140 places within a circuit of ten miles it may be said to be a metropolis.' The influence of a larger place, like Cambridge, stretched further, according to Gwen Raverat's *Period Piece* (1952): 'As late as 1914 I knew the carrier of Croydon-cum-Clopton, twelve miles from Cambridge; his cart started at 6.30 in the morning and got back about ten at night. Though he was not old, he could neither read nor write; but he took commissions all along the road – a packet of needles for Mrs This, and new teapot for Mrs That – and delivered them all correctly on the way back.'

During the nineteenth century the hierarchy of market towns became more pronounced. Larger markets demonstrated an imperial tendency to annex the trade of the smaller, by virtue of railway connections and superior shopping facilities. Leicestershire contained above thirty significant markets in the early fourteenth century. By the late seventeenth century they were reduced to thirteen; by the 1880s to seven – Leicester, Melton Mowbray, Hinckley, Loughborough, Lutterworth, Market Harborough, and Ashby de la Zouch. The geographical centrality of the shire capital, common to most Midlands counties, abetted the dominance of Leicester in Leicestershire. The county's other six market towns were all fringe locations. By the 1880s Leicester contained 40 per cent of the county population. Its carriers reached directly to 220 of the county's 350 villages, on average supplying five services a week. Leicester thus dominated the market traffic of the county; but it did so because it was a fully-fledged urban economy, a producer and service city in its own right. Everitt reckons that perhaps two-thirds of Leicester's vast 'shopping population' lived in Leicester itself, unlike Melton Mowbray, where over three-quarters of its smaller 'shopping population' lived in the country. The picture that needs to be constructed, therefore, is the proportion of town–country populations within each county, plotting too the rank order of town size in order to determine the scale of market-town influence and dependency on the rural economy.

In shopping the increasing sway of the larger centres characterizes the nineteenth century. In other respects, too, the intimacy of the small market town suffered invasions, and the local provision of services was encroached upon. The press, the labour market, brewing and banking, supply further indices of this trend. Jefferies thought it remarkable how 'the old-fashioned local newspaper' retained its position. Parochial activity and family curiosity sustained it. The local newspaper was an institution of agriculture, with its business advertisements placed by farmers, solicitors, auctioneers and land agents, and its calendar of country events and markets. Nevertheless the big-city press was reaching into country areas and finding a welcome, like the *Daily News* whose reporting encouraged the agricultural labourers' trade unionism at a time when country newspapers mostly reflected the hostility of farmers and landowners.

The declining respect for traditional authority was identified as a city disease carried by city journalists and agitators. The London Trades Council gave Arch material help; and the Radicals' charter of action, on labour and land questions, housing, education and the Church, was seen everywhere as proof that the rural labourer was no longer sealed off from outside influences. The allegiance of place was, therefore, surrendering something to the allegiance of class; but it would be a misjudgement to suppose that the shift was great or irreversible. The agricultural labourers' trade union membership of 100,000 in 1872–4 was freakish, and even in the most unionized counties no more than one in three or four men was embraced. Barely half that total was reached again during the animated years of general union formation, 1888–92, and less than a quarter in the similar season, 1909–13. Arch, who represented North-West Norfolk in Parliament, 1885–6 and 1892–1900, believed that emigration, combined with the vote and land reform, was the surest way to improve the farm workers' lot. Certainly trade unionism had less influence on agricultural labourers' wages than market conditions; and union capacity depended vitally on regional easement – for instance, the circumstances of the East Anglian corn counties, where the present-day agricultural workers' union had its origins in 1906. It must also be emphasized how much economic self-interest, rather than fraternal sympathy, inspired the big-city efforts to stimulate trade unionism among agricultural labourers. Thus the London dockers' encouragement of agricultural labour unions in Oxfordshire, Gloucestershire, Wiltshire, and Lincolnshire in the 1890s aimed to strangle a source of blackleg or 'free' labour in the docks.

The labour unions made a less successful penetration into the rural and market-town economies than did the business and professional classes of the big cities and manufacturing centres. Increasingly the country town acted as agent or client of the big city. Developments in milling, brewing, and banking underline this. In 1851 37,268 people were classifed as millers but two trends conspired to drive many out of business in the next fifty years. One was the increasing amount of imported grain which stimulated the port-based milling industry at the expense of inland country millers; the other was the adoption of roller-grinding techniques by big companies from the 1870s, together with the diversification of the trade into seed-crushing and animal-feed-compounding. By 1900 the market was effectively dominated by actual or emerging giants, Joseph Rank, Spillers, Bibby, Thorley, Silcock, the CWS, and BOCM (British Oil and Cake Mills Ltd.). Bibby's alone, for instance, employed 600 people in Liverpool by 1899, 3,000 in 1913.

The rationalization of the brewing industry proceeded apace too. The ales of Burton and the big cities, with their standardized quality, were increasingly evident. In 1880 about 22,000 breweries and 110,000 private brewers existed; in 1900 about 7,000 and 13,000 respectively. The 'tied' system of public houses, owned by a brewery company and run by a salaried manager, was spreading. This made an impact first in the large towns; then a general movement was revealed, as many small breweries and individual publicans who brewed their own beers were squeezed out.

In banking, concentration was even more conspicuous. According to Joseph Sykes, in *The Amalgamation Movement in English Banking* (1926) in 1825 554 private banks (with 681 branches) supplied on average one office per 18,739 population. In 1900 303 private and joint-stock banks provided one branch per 6,900 persons. By 1924, when only two private banks survived, a mere thirteen joint-stock banks with 8,081 branches provided on average one office per 4,777 persons. The service was more dense, the competition more intense. Joint-stock banks, authorized by the 1826 Act and accelerated by the 1862 Act, were the better placed to spread risks and exploit narrower profit margins. Between 1862 and 1900 the joint-stock banks absorbed 130 private banks. Each had cannibalistic appetites too, the former eating up ninety-one of their own species in the same period, the latter sixty-eight. The merger of private banks was usually defensive, to build a bulwark against the joint-stocks by geographical concentration; but take-over by a joint-stock concern was merely delayed, not defeated.

Audrey Taylor's *Gilletts, Bankers at Banbury and Oxford* (1964) epitomizes the operations of a private bank. Gilletts had moved into banking in 1823, from sheep farming, wool trading, and plush weaving. Local reputation was their talisman in business. Farmers in the Banbury region, even in the late nineteenth century, preferred Gilletts's notes to Bank of England notes. This, however, was a fast diminishing resource. The country banks' note circulation had been halved by the mid-1860s, from a peak of over £11m. in 1836. It was halved again by the late 1880s; and by 1910 it amounted to less than £200,000, loose change compared with the Bank of England's £28m. Gilletts survived, despite the agricultural depression, through their connections with the Witney blanket industry and in the university and city of Oxford. By their personal credit assessment, and by not moving too closely to the Bank Rate, Gilletts had a flexibility which local entrepreneurs appreciated. It was Gilletts's Oxford branch which advanced W. R. Morris £4,000, to match what he had borrowed from Lord Macclesfield; and this enabled Morris to commence motor manufacture. Nonetheless, merger was contemplated from the 1890s. As their profits slowed down Gilletts found the offers of joint-stock companies irresistibly tempting. No private concern could rely infinitely on hereditary ability, or persistently flout the standardization of rates. They could not compete with the joint-stocks' facility to manage the accounts of customers who moved from one district to another. Furthermore, the joint-stock banks impressed by their large reserves and publication of accounts. Before 1883 no private bank published its financial position. Even in 1891 when 36 out of 149 private banks issued annual statements, these rarely disclosed the separate state of capital and reserves. By then, two more influences were hastening the inclination towards joint-stock banking into a precipitate slide. One was the feeling that banking combinations were necessary to keep abreast of the rationalization and integration movements in industry. Another was the growing size and financial weight of government. In the 1840s Gilletts had managed the accounts of forty-eight public bodies – poor-law unions, schools, friendly societies, and public utilities such as gas companies and turnpike trusts. By the late 1880s municipal corporations and other public bodies noticeably preferred to entrust their accounts to joint-stock banks which followed standard practices. In 1919 Gilletts surrendered to Barclay's. It was almost the last of a line.

Finally, we should consider physical organization in order to assess just how like cities the market towns were becoming. The evidence suggests that spatial redistribution was taking place according to social class and special function. Business and residence were separated. The solicitor's office in the high street of Jefferies's market town was once the home of an independent gentleman, who now lived in a substantial villa outside the town. Jefferies enlarged this instance into a general observation: 'Like large cities, country towns are now almost given over to offices, shops, workshops, and hotels. Those who have made money get away from the streets as quickly as possible.'

It is difficult to summarize what such development might signify. In *Change in the Village* (1912) 'George Bourne' (George Sturt) argued from knowledge of the Farnham region of west Surrey and Hampshire that modern class distinctions had gained as market towns 'passed far beyond the primitive stage of dependence on local resources and local skill'. Suburban and commuting classes settled there; town property values had risen, and so had the wealth and refinement of the town's employing classes who, whether professional men or tradesmen, were increasingly wrapped up in urban and inter-urban business and services. They were less intimately concerned with what happened in neighbouring agricultural districts. They were less watchful of local harvests, less grateful for the farmers' and labourers' pounds and pennies which passed across their counters, less familiar in social intercourse. The townsmen were ceasing to be countrified, discarding their provincialism, and tending to visit upon the village folk a hundred small slights, without sympathy for their habits of speech and thought, as urbanity callously accelerated its course. Sturt recorded this as a change over the previous fifty years: what may have been a subtle flavour of superiority, a natural complacency in the 1870s, amounted to a great social gulf by Edwardian times.

The building and rebuilding of physical and social shapes were, then, features of late-nineteenth-century market towns as they were elsewhere. Geoffrey Martin, in *The Story of Colchester* (1959), has described the transformation in that town of the High Street and Head Street in Victorian times. Cattle and stall-holders' markets were removed from the main streets; old houses and even a church were demolished; and purpose-built shops, commercial premises, and civic buildings took their place. Colchester was more than a simple market town or small rural port. Its population, 38,373 in 1901, was larger than most, having doubled in the previous half-century. There was a military barracks there, the Essex county hospital, a technical college and sundry industries, as well as customary corn and cattle markets; but what was occurring there was liable to happen to many market towns sooner or later. Thus nearby Chelmsford, the county town, with a population only one-third that of Colchester, became the home of new electrical factories (Marconi's in 1899) and of an expanding middle-class commuter traffic to London. Building and rebuilding, however, were not always marks of expansion. It was sometimes involuntary, caused by fires in old timber buildings or paltry new dwellings. Still, opportunities were seized to embark upon area redevelopments or particular modernizations.

Fire was a universal hazard. Its depredations were severe when fire-fighting services were restricted in mobility and proficiency. The index of Joseph Irving's *Diurnal of Events . . . from February 24, 1871 to the Jubilee, June 20, 1887* (1889) devotes three columns to fires, and these referred only to blazes which involved loss of life or destruction of well-known properties. There was nothing in England comparable to the devastation of Chicago in 1871; nevertheless, widespread damage occurred. Commercial premises, mills, warehouses, theatres, inns and hotels, were the commonest victims. Major conflagrations occurred, in big cities down to ordinary market towns of under 7,000 population, like Market Harborough, where a fire in 1874 resulted in the destruction of a tan yard and nine other buildings. At this time even towns of over 20,000 population did not always possess a full-time fire brigade; and where one did exist, it might not be run by the local authority. The London Fire Brigade was managed by insurance companies before 1865 when it was transferred to the Metropolitan Board of Works. By 1900, the London brigade comprised 911 men, commanded by an ex-navy officer. Telephone lines connected police and fire stations, and 600 alarm call-points had been set up throughout the London county. Excluding false alarms, the London brigade attended on average 3,014 fires annually between 1889 and 1899, of which 156 were classified 'serious' and 2,858 'slight'. Progressively, therefore, central and local government made a concerted effort to combat fire hazard – the former to lay down codes appertaining to building construction, storage of combustible materials, and safety in workshops, tall buildings, and public places; the latter to underpin these guidelines by local by-laws and inspection, to improve water supplies, and to establish professional fire-fighting services. Leyland motor fire-engines were beginning to appear in the more advanced municipal brigades in the years before 1914; but most small market towns and rural areas remained seriously at risk.

IX

Continuity and change, the eternal themes of historians, are etched in any account of late Victorian and Edwardian country towns. Cambridge, glimpsed through the diaries of Josiah Chater, which Enid Porter edited in 1975, will furnish us with some summary illustrations. Cambridge contained 20,000 people when Chater was born in 1828 and (including suburbs) over 50,000 when he died in 1908. His diary records the conventional middle-class concerns of family and friends, business, chapel, and party political connections. Through it we can chart the progress of one business community, as Chater's drapery firm expanded and moved to more advantageous sites, from Sidney Street to Bridge Street to Market Hill. Josiah left the business in 1876 and afterwards set up as one of the first chartered accountants in Cambridge. The growth of such professions, with certificated standards, is a feature of nineteenth-century urban economies. Cambridge was now sufficiently large and complex to support and require these services. The university was an important customer and its terms produced unusual fluctuations in the town's trade. Otherwise Cambridge was a not untypical market town, in which a miscellany of new light industry was emerging: a jam factory in 1873, a scientific instruments works in 1881.

Markets and fairs still constituted the busy times for Cambridge tradesmen. Old ways lingered. In mid-January Plough Monday was celebrated, when village labourers congregated and morris dancers performed in the market square. Likewise, the traditional Stourbridge Horse Fair struggled into the new century. But the economic infrastructure of Cambridge changed in conformity with national developments, especially after the railway's arrival in 1845. Furthermore, the preoccupations of local politics were those that affected all Victorian towns sooner or later. In the 1860s they concerned the privileges of rival gas companies; in the 1870s and 1880s the rising death-rates owing to inadequate water supply and sewerage systems; in the 1880s and 1890s the functioning of rival tram companies, with the usual disputes over the level of fares, state of the roads, and type of traction. Chater's involvement in institutional work mirrors a public life little different from that of most places. He was secretary of the Cambridge Improved Industrial Dwellings Company, of the Reform Club Building Society, of the Steam Laundry Company, and of the Street Tramways Company; he was involved, too, in a branch of the YMCA, and in the administration of borough charities, the penny savings' bank, and the working men's college. This list reads like a roll-call of official and voluntary service throughout Victorian England. The Cambridge versions were not without singular features; but these were only variations on a theme.

Increasingly the nation was drawn together and the pull was felt in country towns as anywhere else. The business life of the Cambridges of England was still regulated in a measure by the surrounding shire; but they were more regularly in communication with the wider world. In 1892 the National Telephone Company established an exchange in Cambridge. There were 128 Cambridge subscribers after four years and, nationally, 122,000 by 1910. Local employers maintained particular habits, but it was ever more difficult to disregard the prescriptions of Bank Holiday, factory and workshops, and Shop Hours, legislation. Government, central and local, was a growing presence. This tipped the scales against the self-sufficiency and individuality of country-town life. One last example from Chater's diaries will underline this. His family belonged to a book club whose members – about twenty – met monthly in each other's homes over supper. They bought books from subscriptions, circulated them, and sold them when their interests were satisfied. Such clubs had been common in towns for the past hundred years. They represented a culture of serious improvement and mere amusement, both reflecting and generating group *esprit de corps*. Two or three book clubs survived among Cambridge townsfolk into the 1870s; but a free public library had opened in 1858, and their disbandment was only a matter of time. Local life was not conspicuously the poorer for their passing. The public library amplified the service, but one more element of local distinctiveness had slipped away.

The historian's review of town and country in this period exercises his skill at equilibration. For though the balance was tilted more to the side of the town, there remained some weighty and durable elements on the side of the country. Evidence is plentiful, on the one hand of the delocalization of country life, on the other hand that the locality remained the focus of interest and satisfaction. This is not paradoxical. It indicates that moods and expressions vary according to context and according to what aspect of personality is addressed. Localism was dominant still, but less exclusive. Village life, country-town life, and city life intermingled more than before. Though fanciful, it is not fantastic to write about the emergence of a national life at this time. The rural–urban continuum was unbroken from metropolis to hamlet.

6 Central and local government

Self-government was both the foundation and coping of the Victorians' political edifice. It was an ability prized above all, for it was held to mark the superiority of free Englishmen over foreigners with their systems of absolute rule. But the Victorians' pride in self-government was not primarily pride in local government. The imperial Parliament remained the focus of this sentiment. It was upon decisions at Westminster that depended the right balance between individual liberty, local government, and central authority.

Historical continuity, the organic nature of development, was often cited as one virtue of England's local government system. This can mesmerize its students, as it did the Webbs, who in 1898 set out to explore contemporary local government. The past diverted them to such a degree that, except for the poor-law and road administration, their *English Local Government* series was concentrated in the 'formative' period, 1688 to 1835. But antiquities did not explain the local government of the Webbs' day. The reason might be discovered in a paradox of W. B. Odgers, a lawyer who published a popular manual about local government in 1899: 'Local government is at once the oldest and the youngest branch of our political system.' The system was substantially recast during the nineteenth century.

Historians at the time commented upon this. Spencer, studying municipal origins before 1835, concluded, 'The modern system of English local government owes little to historical development. It is not a growth: it is a creation.' The foremost constitutional historian, F. W. Maitland, endorsed this. 'The new movement set in with the Reform Bill of 1832: it has gone far already and assuredly it will go further. We are becoming a much governed nation, governed by all manner of councils and boards and officers, central and local, high and low, exercising the powers which have been committed to them by modern statutes.'

Still, Maitland was not so struck by the modern accessions that he ignored the persistence of historic features. It was impossible to deny the significance of 'immemorial liberties' in local government. Localism was not a nineteenth-century liberal bourgeois discovery. This ideology, mistrust of a tyrannical executive, infused county politics in the eighteenth century and earlier. Hence the principle of locality, of independent, self-nurturing communities, was respected by nineteenth-century politicians not out of mawkishness but because this was a living force. 'There hardly can be a history of the English borough,' Maitland proclaimed, 'for each borough has its own history.' The past diversity was not crushed by the new tendency to administrative uniformity. This was George Brodrick's argument in *Local Government in England* (1875):

in spite of the levelling policy embodied in the Municipal Corporation Act, differences of local history, of local situation, and of other local circumstances make themselves sensibly felt. . . . No anatomical resemblance of outward structure can assimilate the inner municipal life of quaint old cathedral cities with the new and fashionable watering places, that of seaports with that of inland towns, that of manufacturing or mining settlements with that of market towns in the midst of agricultural neighbourhoods.

The nineteenth-century transformation of government allegedly originated in Bentham's Constitutional Code. This, as Josef Redlich interpreted it in 1903, taught that 'the territorial bases and divisions of government should be the product, not of history and accident, but of the actual needs of existing society – in short, that the country should be planned out into administrative districts by the rule of utility and convenience'. This interpretation can only begin, not resolve, debate. What puzzles historians is whether the mainspring of government reform was the Benthamites' perception and organization of needs, or those needs forcing themselves on government and eliciting *ad hoc* or systematic responses. The definition of local and national interests remained contentious. No broad appeal to principles of economy, efficiency, and representative democracy plainly disclosed a formula to fit all cases. Very often the leading question was not whether 'the State' ought to intervene but how far and by what agency. In respect of poor relief and public health, for instance, the combination of central supervision and local executive action was differently decided. The nineteenth-century reformation of government was both a deliberate and a dodging process, a sequence of considered changes of position interspersed with impromptu shuffling and evasion.

I

The structure of borough government should be presented. Three pieces of legislation, the Municipal Corporation Acts of 1835 and 1882, and the Local Government Act of 1888, determined that the responsibilities of borough governments were defined more by parliamentary statute than by historic convention, common law, or singular chartered privilege. The Commissioners of 1835 inquired into 246 boroughs but only 178 were incorporated by the 1835 Act. London's significance called for separate treatment; the other exclusions were places considered too petty to warrant modern facilities of government. Still, those 178 municipal boroughs were 'so various, ranging from the smallest market town to the largest new industrial centres, that it was difficult to frame general provisions about the powers which each should have' (K. B. Smellie). Accordingly the chief prescriptive clauses of the 1835 Act referred to the constitution, not the purposes, of borough government. The administration of justice generally, and of the Poor Law particularly, was formally placed outside the purview of municipal councils. The Government wanted to sharpen local responsibility in each of these areas, public order and poor relief. Hence, it separated their work from local council politics. Otherwise, responsibility for the good government of the locality was firmly laid upon the municipal corporation, but the ability to act upon that responsibility was equally firmly controlled by Parliament. Parliamentary authority determined whether a local authority must or could act in a certain fashion, through general legislation giving facilities to all boroughs or by special acts allowing local initiatives. There was no freedom to tackle problems opportunistically. Local government was always legally encumbered.

By 1860 over twenty places had been added to the original 178 towns which enjoyed municipal incorporation. With four exceptions these new incorporations were Midlands and northern industrial centres. The four were Brighton, Devonport, Honiton, Yeovil. Brighton and Devonport were defensible inclusions on the principle that these were places of economic significance and growth potential. No such claim could be advanced about Honiton and Yeovil. These were small market towns with, in Honiton's case, a withering manufacturing sector in lace-making. Far from growing, Honiton fractionally declined in population between 1835 and the year of its municipal charter, 1846. It remained stagnant, with under 4,000 population, until after 1945. Honiton, however, was politically significant. It returned two MPs at intervals from 1300, continuously from 1640. Here was a concession to past prestige and to pulsating, political interests. Honiton was not a singular anomaly. Seventy-four of 178 boroughs in the 1835 Act contained under 5,000 citizens, places like Chippenham, Marlborough, Shaftesbury, Tewkesbury, and Wells. Fifty years later, though these had mostly lost their separate parliamentary representation, small boroughs remained a conspicuous part of the English municipal landscape (Table VI).

Table VI Number and size of municipal boroughs, 1835–88

Population	Number of Boroughs	
	1835	*1888*
under 5,000	74	70
5–10,000	52	42
10–20,000	26	44
20–50,000	18	69
50–100,000	5	32
over 100,000	3	23
Totals	178	280

The incorporation movement was accelerated after an Act of 1877 permitted the costs of a petition to fall on the rates rather than on the individual promoters. There were 313 municipal boroughs by 1901. Every application did not meet acceptance. Between 1888 and 1902 thirty charters were granted, a score rejected. The Government had to weigh the interest of the counties and other municipalities against that which moved the petitioners. The dictates of efficiency and equity rarely pointed in one direction. This is evidenced by petitions from suburban areas. For example, the Wallasey petition in 1901 may have originated in defensive motives of a selfish kind, a desire to resist absorption in the borough of Birkenhead and to escape the rate rise which would follow union with a poorer area. But the Wallasey application was not without force. As an urban district of 54,000 people (half the size of Birkenhead) it already ran remunerative services, ferries, trams, water, gas and electricity works. It had established free libraries, a fire brigade, hospital, technical schools, and cemetery. Wallasey was evidently a growth area. The charter of incorporation was conceded in 1910 when the population approached 79,000.

Another comment should be made about this incorporation movement. One borough was not amalgamated with another borough
without its consent, even where residentially the distance between
towns was invisible and economically interests were indivisible. Manchester and Salford were permitted to become and to remain separate
boroughs, though joined physically. So were Liverpool and Bootle,
Newcastle and Gateshead, Brighton and Hove, Penryn and
Falmouth, and Rochester, Chatham and Gillingham. The disappointed party in these abortive mergers was inclined to suspect mal-
feasance in high places. This suspicion prevailed in Liverpool when
Bootle became a municipality in 1868. A substantial property-owner
in Bootle, Lord Derby, was Prime Minister at the time. Subsequent
proposals by Liverpool to absorb Bootle, in 1890 and 1903, were
annulled. From the point of view of efficient administration this decision appeared irrational. Economically Liverpool and Bootle were as
one, their docks administration united under the Mersey Docks and
Harbour Board. Bootle already depended upon Liverpool for its water
supply; but the development of other services, transport and secondary education, was impeded by the division of authority. The whole
saga seemed to bear out Sidney Webb's complaint in the *Nineteenth
Century*, September 1901, that the trouble with the liberal tradition
was that it ' "thinks in individuals". . . . When the "higher freedom"
of corporate life is in question, they become angrily reactionary, and
denounce and obstruct every new development of common action.'
Thus the private interest generally prevailed over the public interest,
the small municipality over the large municipality.

The issue was not clear-cut. The civic consciousness of Bootle, even
if it resulted from rather than caused the original incorporation,
should not be ignored. The 1903 rejection of Liverpool's annexation
was celebrated as 'Independence Day' in Bootle. The policy of permitting the growth of separate municipalities, contiguous to others, was
not a failure if the generation of a stubborn civic consciousness and
lively local administration was the test applied. It may be that small
local government units were advanced by nineteenth-century politicians out of a kind of occult conservatism, hoping that their multiplication would insure the stability of the State. Infinite delegation of
powers from the central government was the advice which Sir Charles
Wood, Chancellor of the Exchequer, gave to the Prime Minister,
Lord John Russell, in 1850: 'It is evidently wise to put as little on the
Government whose overthrow causes a revolution as you can, and to

have as much as you can on local bodies which may be overthrown a dozen times and nobody be the worse.' This prejudice persisted in government circles; but it found favour in the Bootles of England too. Perhaps, therefore, as B. D. White suggests, the fault was the Liverpool proposal not the Bootle resistance. Annexation might have weakened the civic consciousness of *both* Liverpool and Bootle, diluting the one and draining the other.

Federation, a two-tiered structure or, at the least, co-partnership in specific regional schemes through joint boards of transport, energy and town planning, were alternatives to absorption in a unified authority. These possibilities were insufficiently explored before 1914, because governments remained phlegmatic about the precise determination of the public advantage. Broadly, they subscribed to the maxim enunciated in the Liverpool–Bootle case, that governments were not justified in transferring a self-governing population unwillingly to another authority. This rule had the merit of being easily applied, whereas arguments relating to the improvement of services and pursuit of economy were uncertain and involved projection and hypothesis. Only with pressing cause did governments depart from this simple practice. Local opposition to the amalgamation of Plymouth and Devonport (with Stonehouse) in 1914 was overruled for reasons of national security, to which putative benefits in local government were secondary. By the same token the Secretary of State for War enjoyed, from 1857, the power to appoint three town councillors in Aldershot, as invigilators of the military interest. This was the only instance in which a government minister imposed nominations upon a municipal council, and his placemen there were far from constituting a majority. Another exception to the otherwise perfect freedom of qualified citizens to choose their borough councils might be noted, though this was not, as in Aldershot, a ministerial privilege. In Oxford and Cambridge the universities withstood the jurisdiction of the borough councils within their precincts until 1889, when college dons made up separate constituencies which returned in Oxford nine, in Cambridge six, town councillors.

Otherwise the great principle of the 1835 Act was the establishment of representative councils, elected by resident ratepayers of above two-and-a-half years' standing, in the corporate towns. The Whigs' difficulty in piloting their Bill through Parliament resulted in certain checks on the democratic principle. One-third of the councils was composed of aldermen, who would enjoy double the term of office (i.e. six years) and be chosen by the councillors, not directly by the electorate. Furthermore, boroughs of over 6,000 inhabitants were divided into wards, determined by reference to aggregate rateable value as well as to numbers of ratepayers. Their councils' abilities were subsequently defined and expanded by general and local Acts, adoptive legislation and provisional orders. These were collated in the 1882 Municipal Corporations Act. Technically this was a feat. M. D. Chalmers, himself a parliamentary draftsman, considered it 'probably the best drafted Act on the statute-books'. It gave short shrift to old corporations which, though excluded from the 1835 Act, still survived, like New Romney where the burgesses pocketed the revenue of municipal lands. Some 106 charters were rescinded; henceforth a borough was defined, with brisk uniformity, as 'any place for the time being subject to the Municipal Corporations Act, 1882'. The powers of corporations – originally to hold property, to regulate markets and harbours, to establish policing and lighting systems, and to make by-laws – had grown since 1835, especially in public health matters, albeit in a permissive rather than mandatory way. The franchise had been enlarged, too, to include all ratepayers of one year's standing, and not excluding women. All these changes were consolidated in the 1882 Act. Certain new corporations were added but no new powers.

The system was overhauled by the Local Government Act, 1888. Principally, this placed county administration on a representative basis; but the Act was pregnant with significance for urban England too, for it reclassified corporate status. A new category resulted, the County Borough, whose powers were mostly equal to and independent of the County Council. The rest – ordinary municipal boroughs and urban sanitary districts – in various aspects of their administration, such as highways, hospitals, and (if under 10,000 population in 1881) police, were subject to the jurisdiction of the County Council and liable for assessment in county rates.

This bald description simplifies the late-nineteenth-century local government structure. There is no harm in that; but two points call for special emphasis. One is that it embodied a doctrine of concentric, not exclusive, units. This was not peculiar to local government. In the distribution of parliamentary representation boroughs might be sunk into counties or, where borough seats remained separate, voters enjoy plural qualifications, able to vote in borough, suburban, and county constituencies if their property was so scattered. The second emphasis concerns the politics of the scheme. The great issue in 1888 was the survival of municipal autonomy, given the understanding that rural government could be improved only by the involvement of the towns through shared administrative costs. A combined rural and urban service was aimed at, with the administrative county the unifying instrument of authority.

The Local Government Board intended to except only ten cities – Liverpool, Birmingham, Manchester, Leeds, Sheffield, Bristol, Bradford, Nottingham, Hull, and Newcastle – from this scheme and to concede to them practical autonomy, independent of county government. Each had contained above 145,000 population in the last census. Hence, 150,000 population was proposed as the basis for other boroughs in future to apply for county borough status. Borough MPs, however, conspired to reduce the qualification to 50,000. The desolation of the Parliamentary Secretary to the Local Government Board, Walter Long, was still apparent in the 1920s when he recalled what happened: 'We came to the 50,000 line for a reason which very often obtains in the House of Commons – because we could not help ourselves.' He alleged that local sentiment prevailed over local needs. Parliament failed to exercise foresight about urban expansion and rural depopulation. As more towns qualified as county boroughs, they would impair county government by narrowing its fiscal base. Ten holes in the carpet were evidently tolerable to Long; sixty-one holes, being the number of county boroughs actually approved in 1888, or eighty-one holes, as the number had become by 1914, made a mockery of the scheme (see Fig. 5).

Long's verdict seems plausible. Sixty-one towns designated county boroughs in 1888 quickly became sixty-four. They were a queer lot. At the 1891 census two contained over 500,000 population; three between 250,000 and 500,000; eighteen between 100,000 and 250,000; thirty-one between 50,000 and 100,000; and ten between 20,000 and 50,000. The last group were mostly shire capitals or cathedral cities, like Canterbury, Chester, Exeter, Lincoln, and Worcester; but Long dissembled when he gave the impression that the wreckers of the Bill were blinkered sentimentalists or that he and his cabinet colleagues were prescient champions of efficiency.

The Government made no attempt to ascertain an optimum size of urban unit which returned the best value for money spent on public services. One study by C. A. Baker (*Journal of the Royal Statistical Society*, 1910) argued that a town of about 90,000 inhabitants represented the lowest cost per capita for most public services.

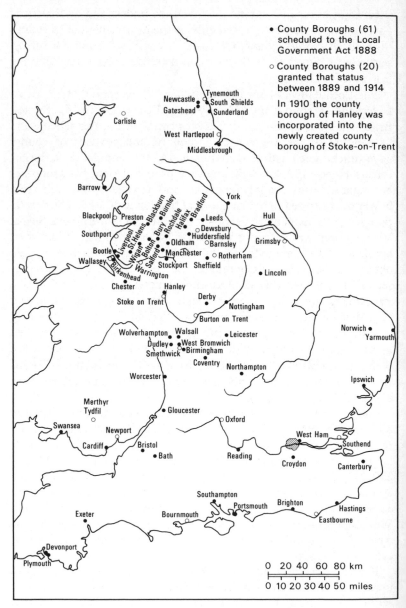

Fig. 5 County boroughs, 1888–1914

Source: R. C. K. Ensor, *England 1870–1914*, Oxford, 1936, map 7.

Subsequently, the Barnett House *Survey of the Social Services in the Oxford District* (edited by A. F. C. Bourdillon, 1938) suggested that 'towns of moderate size – between 100,000 and 200,000 – are the cheapest to govern; at both extremes – in the mammoth cities and in the "dwarfs" of 70,000 or less – local government is disproportionately costly.' This was a technically complex exercise, involving many variables of public needs, not least the quality and density of property, character of industry and occupation, age structure of population and proportions of high- and low-income groups; and it is evident that if governments were to fashion policies by reference to such data, they would saddle themselves with a regular revision of local government areas in the event of new public services being authorized and in the light of changing technological and economic circumstances. In fact these criteria never impinged upon the consciousness of government in determining county borough size. Similarly no attempt was made to equalize the fitness of the new administrative counties. Instead the Government surrendered to historic interests. Lilliputian Rutland was ordained an administrative county the same as the huge shires. Altogether the Government sped the country into the twentieth century with virtually unaltered medieval administrative units. Indeed it resurrected, or perpetuated, some preposterous subdivisions of ancient shires – the Soke of Peterborough became an administrative county separate from Northamptonshire, as did the Isle of Ely from Cambridgeshire, the Ridings in Yorkshire, the Holland, Kesteven, and Lindsey divisions in Lincolnshire, and East and West Suffolk and Sussex. It was as if the Government had slept through the industrial and transport revolutions.

The heart of the controversy in 1888 was not a maudlin contest over antiquarian form and nomenclature: it was the disposition of power and resources between town and country. The 1888 readjustment prescribed two things: a formal separation of town and country in the case of most towns of above 50,000 population, and a formal combination of town and county for the rest. The incongruity of these decisions was calamitous. As for the first, the Redcliffe-Maud Report (1969) justly observed, 'The division between counties and county boroughs has prolonged an artificial separation of big towns from their surrounding hinterlands for functions whose planning and administration need to embrace both town and country.' London and the provincial conurbations were notably hampered in this respect; so too were county boroughs bordering upon two administrative counties, like Brighton and Plymouth. As for the second, the historic struggle of borough and county was not resolved in 1888 by the establishment of a clumsy two-tiered structure. Local government became a battleground between municipal and county authorities, over the principles of county borough creation or boundary extensions, over the management of rural–urban services, and over the political representation and fiscal burden apportioned between town and county.

Between 1889 and 1921 county boroughs increased in number from sixty-one to eighty-two. Twenty-three were actually created but two (Hanley and Devonport) were merged in other county boroughs (Stoke and Plymouth respectively). These changes involved a loss by county councils of about 100,000 acres, 1,300,000 people, and £6½m. rateable value. In addition 109 extensions of county borough boundaries occurred (70 of these before 1910) which involved further losses by county councils of 250,000 acres, 1,700,000 people, and nearly £8m. rateable value. The problem was exacerbated by the regional concentration of these activities. The northern counties, Lancashire, Yorkshire (West Riding) and Durham, and Midlands counties, Warwickshire, Worcestershire and Staffordshire, suffered the most, losing above a fifth of their population and rateable value. At the same time there were 107 boundary extensions of non-county boroughs which, though they involved no permanent displacement of people and land from county jurisdiction, required painful fiscal adjustments. The counties endeavoured to resist the urban vivisectors by parliamentary representations. In fifty-four cases they successfully trimmed or won the rejection of municipal demands on their territory. But their complaints were substantially unredressed until a Royal Commission, under the Earl of Onslow's chairmanship, was appointed in 1923.

The gist of the county case was that loss of areas entailed a loss of revenues at a time when more costly duties were being imposed by legislation or by raised expectations. The range of public health, education, and social welfare provision supplied by local government by 1910 was much broader than what had been conceived in 1888. But the average rateable value per head was half as much again in county boroughs as in county areas, because urban property commanded higher rents and assessments. The counties were faced with a choice between overburdening their ratepayers, furnishing them with inferior services, or supplicating more central government grants and suffering more central government dictation. Far from being embarrassed by their claims on urban funds, the counties asserted as a just principle that the richer should assist the poorer parts in a community. The urban liability in respect of main roads was transparent. The counties demanded indemnity for the wear of their roads caused by through traffic and heavy vehicles plying between urban centres. Finally, the counties argued that economy and efficiency of services went hand in hand and that, for both country and town, the sensible solution was joint participation in the larger authority – the county.

The county boroughs fastened upon the weak points of the counties' case. They questioned whether the county was technically the best or appropriate area for all or any services: why should an administrative unit of William I suffice for the realm of George V? The county boroughs argued that, under the 1888 Act, the counties had the same power as they did to apply to alter their boundaries. If a county was too indigent to provide services or too small to achieve economical administration, it should merge wholly or partly with another county. There was no instance of this. The county boroughs also impugned the character of county government. County services were inferior because their administration was unimaginative and obedient to conservative agricultural interests. County borough government was progressive because it enlisted more vigorous and socially varied politicians and attracted better staff. They were stimulated by public interest in elections, by a vigilant press and by corporate pride. As for boundary extensions, the county boroughs asserted a right to incorporate not only suburbs which had sprung up from their towns' enterprise but also unbuilt land which would allow them to improve their amenities, especially housing.

The modern town and its environs, in short, was a natural unit of local government, both compact and comprehensive, in a way that the ancient county was not. The county boroughs vehemently resisted the counties' suggestion that the qualifying population for a county borough should be 250,000. They were content that it should remain at around 50,000, and the town clerks of Exeter, Lincoln, Blackpool, and Southport testified to their capacity to provide efficient services. Where difficulties arose, with regard to secondary, technical, and adult education or mental asylums and hospitals, it was always possible to come to a reasonable financial arrangement with a county or another borough authority.

The county boroughs thus contemplated joint services with the counties – this was imperative in some circumstances – but argued that collaboration was best arranged as a partnership of equals. Their case was strengthened by reference to the complaints of some non-county boroughs which bridled under county dominance. They had resisted a proposal of the Local Government Board in 1898 to confer greater authority on the county councils, for instance certain duties of sanitary inspection and the authorization of loans up to £5,000. The non-county boroughs appreciated that the Local Government Board was clogged with work, but preferred that it take on more staff or transfer powers directly to them, rather than enhance the ability of unsympathetic county councils to order their affairs. The counties, they argued, were unwilling to entertain new or improved services, or else inclined to saddle the boroughs with disproportionate costs. There was plentiful evidence of friction between rural and urban representatives on county councils, for instance over policing strengths and, most of all, over the maintenance of main roads. As the Town Clerk of Luton put it, 'the only question worth talking about is main roads, and the rest does not matter'.

The roads question highlights an important aspect of local government which is concealed in the documentation of the poisoned relations between counties and boroughs. This is the central government's failure to establish its proper role and to apportion burdens equitably between taxpayer and ratepayer. From Tudor times it was the parish's duty to maintain roads. For 400 years parochial incompetence was tolerated, although the Highways Acts of 1835 and 1862 encouraged the combination of parishes and appointment of salaried surveyors. From the late seventeenth century parochial responsibility existed side by side with turnpike trusts, which levied tolls on stage-coach routes; but their management was never unimpeachable even before the railways ruined their business. In 1864 a Select Committee concluded that turnpike tolls were 'unequal in pressure, costly in collection, inconvenient to the public, and injurious as causing a serious impediment to intercourse and traffic'. It recommended their abolition. Parliament responded, and the turnpike trusts were steadily dissolved as they applied for renewal of contracts. Their roads, mostly in serious disrepair, were transferred to the parishes or highway districts, whose financial plight was acknowledged when the Government conceded a £200,000 grant-in-aid for maintaining disturnpiked roads. London was freed of tolls in 1871; the remaining 854 trusts were reduced to 71 by 1883, and eliminated by 1895. From 1888 county councils were made responsible for main roads – to which a grant-in-aid contributed – and allowed to make discretionary payments towards the upkeep of secondary roads by their non-county boroughs and urban and rural district councils. Thus the parish was ousted from control, but the system which supplanted it was the source of endless wrangles over costs, and stricken by the absence of a national strategy for transport. Between 1890 and 1902 expenditure on main roads in rural districts was nearly doubled, in urban districts more than quadrupled, burdening ratepayers without significantly raising the efficiency of the road network. The fault was primarily that of the central government and its responsible ministry, the Local Government Board, which failed to co-ordinate or direct local authority work, to establish clear maxims about road classification, or to remedy the inadequate fiscal basis upon which administration rested. Representations from the Road Improvements Association led to a Departmental Inquiry in 1904, under the chairmanship of J. G. Lawson, Parliamentary Secretary to the Local Government Board and a county MP. This exposed the incoherence of a system which relied upon 1,900 different authorities, many without the technical capacity to fulfil their duties; but the Committee lamely recommended the establishment of a new central department in respect of highway administration, equipped with advisory powers only. The ever-growing consequences of motor traffic were examined by a Royal Commission, under Lord Selby, in 1905–6. This reported on new types of road surface and recommended certain motor taxes whose proceeds should be devoted to road improvements. These subsidies were forthcoming after the 1909 budget introduced vehicle licences and a petrol duty. But the Road Board which administered these funds was not empowered to support ordinary road maintenance, only road improvements; and its assistance was directed towards county councils, not county boroughs and other local authorities. Lobbies of road-users, particularly motorists – the RAC was founded in 1897, the AA in 1905 – achieved what advances there were, all the time constrained by ratepayers. Ultimately, it was the standing Select Committee, to which all private Bills promoted by local authorities were referred, that recommended in 1912–13 a new central authority to decide which roads should be main roads and whether taxes and not rates should maintain them. In 1919 a Ministry of Transport was founded and the beginnings of a national strategy were laid.

II

This depressing tale of inaction and ineptitude prefaces a major debate of our period, how to define local and national services so as to determine what was properly a local or national charge, divided between ratepayer and taxpayer. The classic exposition of spheres was by J. S. Mill in *On Liberty* (1859) and *Considerations on Representative Government* (1861). Local government was valued for its promotion of public education in efficiency and economy only in so far as central government prescribed and supervised its work. Otherwise, local government would resemble 'a school in which there is no school-master but only pupil teachers who have never themselves been taught'. Purely local business, as classified by Mill, was street paving, lighting, and cleansing: this could be left to local imagination and execution. Then there were matters in which the national interest was paramount: prisons, police, and justice. While local management might be convenient, it must follow a set standard. A third category was indeterminate – both local and national: poor relief, for example. Mill asserted, however, that 'no locality has a moral right to make itself by mismanagement a nest of pauperism, necessarily overflowing into other localities, and impairing the moral and physical condition of the whole labouring community'. The same might be true of public health administration. The result of these cogitations was a maxim:

The authority which is most conversant with principles should be supreme over principles, while that which is most competent in details should have the details left to it. The principal business of the central authority should be to give instructions, of the local authority to apply them. Power may be localised, but knowledge to be most useful must be centralised.

Mill may have satisfied political theorists but, since money was at stake, the practical application gave rise to bitter debate. Two major public investigations were mounted, a Royal Commission on Local and Imperial Taxation (1896–1901), led by Lord Balfour of Burleigh, and a Treasury Departmental Committee on Local Taxation (1911–14) under the chairmanship of the Comptroller and Auditor-General, Sir John A. Kempe. Neither made any theoretical advance from Mill in distinguishing local and national services. Both complained of the impossibility of determining the issue precisely. But the applications were different. To poor relief, police, and justice the Balfour Commission added education and, prospectively, main roads as preponderantly national services. Likewise, an Inter-departmental

Committee in 1904 argued the case for public health: 'public health is obviously a question of the highest general concern, and, to the extent that local independence militates against its security, the principle of local self-government must be subordinated to more important interests.' The Kempe Committee pursued this reasoning further. It argued that the semi-nationalization or full nationalization of services was accelerating and localism fading. This it ascribed to the permeating power of scientific knowledge and modern communications, and to a growing sense that the community was the nation as well as the immediate neighbourhood. What was once only a vague admission – that actually most useful local expenditure benefited the whole nation – was now given prominence. This organic emphasis, however, threatened the very theory from which the division of costs between local and national government was derived. Not the seclusion but the affinity of the nation's localities was affirmed.

This conclusion was reached at a time when the entire structure of government finance was exposed as inadequate for modern purposes. Politicians sought both to broaden and to vary the tax base. Nationally the controversy concerned the merits of tariffs and graduated and differentiated income tax; locally the controversy concerned rating assessments, and the assignment of grants-in-aid for local purposes. It is in a context of expanding functions and straitened resources that debates about centralism versus localism should be focused, because this in many respects decided the distribution of authority.

III

The fires of the debate were enkindled in the 1840s by an antiquary and lawyer, J. Toulmin Smith, who formed the Anti-Centralization Society to resist Edwin Chadwick's Health of Towns legislation. With a romantic conception of constitutional history, which countered statute law by common law, Toulmin Smith reminded the Government that parliamentary liberties derived from free local institutions, not vice versa. He lamented the present feebleness of local government and the cocksureness of central government: 'the two mutually re-act to increase and spread each other'. He sensed a predisposition in central government towards 'bureaucracy and functionarism'. It employed to this end factious and factitious commissions of inquiry whose reports were sycophantically extolled by a press which failed to stimulate a 'real and healthy formation of *opinion*'.

Toulmin Smith was answered by Tom Taylor. This versatile figure, a dramatist and sometime editor of *Punch*, was secretary of the Board of Health, 1854–71. Taylor observed that the fault of central departments in dealing with local authorities was rather 'over-timidity than . . . excessive dictation'. In so far as central power and officialdom had expanded, this was caused by, not the cause of, local neglect. In turn this local neglect was 'the result of excessive addiction to money-making . . . of a forgetfulness of the claims of all classes of society upon each other . . . mainly due to the vast operations of the new industrial economy created by steam power. . . .' Not power-hungry officials, cramping local initiative by 'vicious and shortsighted uniformity', but 'the rule of unmitigated selfishness and penny wisdom under the specious mask of local liberty' was to blame for the parlous condition of local government.

Toulmin Smith and Tom Taylor argued about motivation. We should consider capacity and cost-effectiveness too – the best means of financing services and the best unit for administering services. In these murky regions Josef Redlich's apophthegm is a useful lantern: 'Rate collectors far more than any central Boards of Control are the real schoolmasters of municipal policy.'

The fundamental source of local government ability was its revenue from rates, a tax which fell exclusively on the occupier of land and buildings. Most borough corporations had some additional finance – profits from municipally-run utilities, and moneys from tolls, fines, and licences due to their supervision of markets and harbours. Manchester Corporation, for instance, was receiving £15,000 per annum from markets alone around 1900; and Birkenhead Corporation profited by £9,545 from the Mersey ferries. Certain towns even luxuriated in corporate property so extensive that its revenue eliminated the need to levy rates. Aldeburgh in Suffolk, Doncaster in Yorkshire, and Penryn in Cornwall were three such fortunate rate-free towns; and some cities, like Bristol, Hull, and Liverpool, profited from their property to achieve rate-reductions or exceptional civic expenditure. Among the more unusual possessions were oyster beds owned by Colchester Corporation; but its receipts were mostly squandered on an annual feast. These exceptions apart, then, the rate was the spring of local government activity. By Edwardian times, this was determined in most towns at from 10 to 20 per cent of gross rent.

A steep rise in rates was commented upon and widely deplored throughout the Victorian period. Goschen's 1870 report disclosed that revenue from rates in England and Wales had doubled, from £8m. in the early 1840s to £16m., with an especially high rise from the mid-1850s. Of this increase, £6½m. fell on urban districts. Poor relief accounted for about £2m., though this was not a municipal expenditure properly so-called, because the poor rate was separately collected and administered by Boards of Guardians, not by town councils. The police establishment accounted for about an eighth of the rate increases, and town improvements for the major part, about five-eighths. The rise continued. In crude figures the average combined (municipal and poor) rate levied in 1885 was 3s. 6d. in the pound; in 1895 4s. 2d., in 1905 6s., in 1914 6s. 9d. In the largest towns rates were generally between 25 and 45 per cent higher than the national average.

In isolation these figures have little significance. They should be related to the index of financial capacity, that is, rateable value. The nation's rateable value increased thus: about £60m. in the early 1840s, £110m. in the early 1870s, £150m. in the early 1890s, £180m. in the early 1900s, about £215m. in 1910. In the towns individual wealth and the rateable value of property rose faster than in the countryside, but people still felt that the burden of local taxation was growing. Broad comparisons confirmed their supposition. In the quarter-century from 1875 the population of England and Wales grew by 37 per cent, the rateable value by 61 per cent, the revenue from rates by 141 per cent.

Why did ratepayers protest? Rate expenditure was not begrudged entirely. That rates were spent partly in socially beneficial ways or in reproductive undertakings (which increased the value of land) was transparent. Public works, the Goschen Report argued in 1870, were 'not so much a burden as an investment'; but rising rates, whether for municipal enterprise or for any other social good, were onerous in periods when property values were stagnant or falling, as from the late 1890s to 1914. The complaints concerned chiefly four features: the nature of rate assessment; the apportionment of rate liabilities between different classes of ratepayer; the distribution of rate-support grants from the Treasury to different local government districts; and the type and quality of local government services.

Rates were assessed on the net annual value of land and buildings in their existing condition. This was a tax on fixed real property, occupation of which was the sole measurement of ability to pay. It ignored personal 'movable' wealth, the contents of property; and it ignored income, the profits and losses of trade and employment. The rate was thus an insensitive impost, oblivious of periods of industrial distress. Notoriously rates and rents lay heaviest, in relation to profits, on small retail establishments and workshops, which was why the lower-middle class was so prominent in ratepayers' economy movements. Certain big land-users among large-scale industry suffered the incidence of rates too, which was why a trend away from central-city sites was beginning. As for house-occupiers, the rate was regressive in tendency because though rich people generally occupied more valuable houses, they did not do so proportionately to income. Then there was the case of neighbours in the same type of house placed in different personal circumstances: one household might contain several wage-earners, another only a pensioner or person living off savings.

The want of uniformity and professional standards of valuation within and between districts was an additional source of discontent. The 640 Boards of Guardians constituted the assessment committees until the Rating and Valuation Act, 1925, transferred the responsibility to the county and municipal borough councils and urban and rural districts, which were obliged to prepare regular quinquennial revaluations subject to Inland Revenue supervision. The model for this was Goschen's Valuation of Property (Metropolis) Act, 1869, but every attempt to extend its principles to cover the whole country floundered before 1925. By the 1925 Act the number of rating areas was reduced from 14,330 to 1,770 and assessment committees from 640 to 340. Of course, the hypothetical nature of calculating rateable value still roused dissatisfactions; but before 1925 assessments were riddled with antiquated and inconsistent procedures and more than a hint of favouritism, particularly under-assessment of wealthy districts. The Town Clerk of Hull represented the Association of Municipal Corporations on this question to the Royal Commission on Local Taxation in 1896. He pleaded for the overhaul of rating laws.

No branch of the law is of greater every day importance to the citizen . . . but no part of our statute law is in greater state of perplexity. There is a series of statutory enactments, beginning with the 43rd. Eliz., heaped one on the other, with no attempt at logical sequence, order, or arrangement; while many provisions which have been practically superseded remain on the statute book. Others, which were originally designed only to apply to a particular subject-matter, have had to be stretched and applied by judicial construction to subject-matter not in contemplation at the time when the enactments were originally framed. . . .

The incidence of rates was criticized also in respect of unoccupied land or buildings. These were assessed on their existing rentable condition, not capital or saleable value. Hence the ground landlord or urban speculator, holding unbuilt land, escaped tax on his unearned increment, that increased property value which resulted from a town's enterprise and from public amenities financed by other ratepayers. To rectify this was the urban component of the Radical Liberals' land programme. By taxing owners they would force unoccupied land on to the market for building, simultaneously easing urban congestion and unemployment and transferring power from a parasitic landowning class to a proprietary democracy. Perhaps, too, by relieving existing heavy ratepayers – small retailers and businesses which were large land-users – benefits might devolve to consumers in reduced prices.

The unwarranted escape from rate-liability of urban landlords was a Radical refrain which gathered to a crescendo from 1880 with the publication of Henry George's *Progress and Poverty*. This American tract against the concentration of landownership was subtitled: 'An Inquiry into the Cause of Industrial Depression and of Increase of Want with Increase of Wealth'. The remedy was a single tax of land, confiscating the unearned increment. Issued in cheap editions, *Progress and Poverty* outpaced popular novels, selling 60,000 in England in its first three years. Everywhere single-tax converts announced themselves, from future MPs like J. C. Wedgwood and C. P. Trevelyan, to humble labourers like Fred Jeffs of Tysoe, who burnt 'hundreds of candles' studying the Georgite gospel. Another devotee was John Burns, the trade unionist, who saw in the Georgite recipe a means to pay off municipal debts. Later, as minister for local government, he was less enthusiastic.

The accolade was conferred by the Catholic Church, which placed *Progress and Poverty* on the Index. Economists were sceptical from the start. J. A. Hobson thought George's work injured the progress of genuine collectivism: it focused on the injustice of landownership and ignored the injustice of capital. Indeed it extolled the industrial economy whose only fault was that it was fettered by the landed interest. Hobson concluded: ' "A single-taxer" is free to take every economic advantage he may enjoy as capitalist, employer, investor, in dealing with weaker bargainers. While the landowner's income is wholly unearned, his own business gains are the product of his skill, industry, foresight!' Hence, the most ardent land-tax disciples were 'middle-class townsmen affected by personal knowledge of local cases of land-increments'.

The single-taxers were not alone in courting urban ratepayers.

There was A. R. Wallace's Land Nationalization Society; Joseph Chamberlain, who advocated greater municipal purchase of land; and the leasehold enfranchisement movement, which demanded legislation to entitle leaseholders to buy freeholds. Each was voluble but it was always the more modest case, that which sought to extend the rate to include site values, which had the best chance of political acceptance. The plight of leaseholders, real enough where landlords jacked up rents and extracted substantial premiums upon the renewal of leases, fell on deaf ears in largely freehold towns. The Liberals' Land Inquiry of 1914 reckoned the proportions of dwelling tenures thus:

Substantially more than one-half of the urban population of England is living under ordinary freehold tenure; about one-twentieth under freehold subject to some form of perpetual annual payment; somewhere about one-tenth under long leasehold; and rather under one-third on short leasehold.

Politicians were not going to upset property contracts on behalf of a dispersed minority of suffering leaseholders. In any case London leaseholders did not elicit the same sympathy as distressed miners. On the contrary they were allegedly even more flagrant property speculators than aristocratic urban landlords. Small tradesmen were exposed in the campaign against the vestries in the 1870s and 1880s. They formed a substantial section of that group of middlemen who acted as rack-renters (having taken on and exploited the fag-ends of leases) or as 'house-knackers' (sub-letting rooms within properties). Asquith opposed the Leasehold Enfranchisement Bill of 1891 for this reason, that he 'saw no advantage in substituting for a small body of large landowners who . . . are more or less amenable to public opinion, a large body of small landowners who . . . were absolutely unrestrained by any public authority'.

The propriety of rating site values was debated by several official inquiries. The Royal Commission on Working-class Housing, 1884–5, recommended that land in the vicinity of populous towns – that is, actual or prospective suburbia – should be rated at 4 per cent on selling values. The Select Committee on Town Holdings, 1886–92, laid a different emphasis, as did the majority of the Royal Commission on Local Taxation, 1896–1901. Mere taxation of ground rents would be inequitable. Furthermore, site valuations would be complex, even impracticable, and provoke expensive litigation. But a minority of five commissioners, including the chairman, Lord Balfour of Burleigh, was impressed by the need to redistribute some rate burden from buildings, which were ultimately perishable assets, to sites, whose values generally rose. They also accepted that a site-value rate might mitigate inner-city overcrowding by releasing cheap suburban land for building. Accordingly local authorities of densely populated districts should have optional power to impose an additional, moderate, site-value rate, levied initially upon leaseholders who, upon termination of existing contracts, would exact a moiety from the owners by deduction from the rent. This concession, they hoped, would sap the agitation for extreme measures – land nationalization, confiscation, or single-tax doctrines – by removing public doubts about an untapped source of revenue and by reducing inequalities between districts and between landlords.

Bills were presented to Parliament to advance these ends. Glasgow Corporation's promotion of private Bills in 1899, 1900, and 1901 was defeated; but its ambitions were shared by several hundred urban authorities, represented by the Association of Municipal Corporations. Their commitment was keen in the late 1890s, chiefly for two reasons. One was that rising urban land values had greatly stimulated anti-landlord feeling; another that the municipalities' need to derive additional revenue was sharpened as municipal debts rose from their expanded investment in public utilities and ordinary works. On their behalf the Liberal MP, C. P. Trevelyan, moved a Rating of Site Values Bill in each year from 1902 to 1905. The Unionist Government was unenthusiastic, though a second reading was passed on two occasions. Trevelyan execrated the existing rating system as 'a universal burden on enterprise, industry and building', 'as heavy as the bread tax was in the bad old days'. Liberal ministries were strongly memorialized on the question from 1906. At length some progress was made in Lloyd George's 1909 Budget.

In his intentions and methods, Lloyd George differed from those who proposed a straight rate on site values. His priority was to raise revenue for national purposes – armaments as well as pensions – not to expand the local authority rate base. His land-tax proposals alienated former friends by annexing revenues which they claimed for local authorities. Furthermore, he avoided a simple, comprehensive tax on site values and imposed a range of modest duties – an increment value duty, reversion duty, undeveloped land duty, and a mineral rights duty – charged only on select categories of land. The local authority interest was hardly appeased by Section 91, which prospectively assigned half the yield to them, because everything would wait upon the new Land Valuation Department. In May 1911 the Government was petitioned to allow local authorities to levy rates on the same basis, and to establish an equalization fund from the proceeds of the land taxes, to be allocated in grants-in-aid for services such as education, police, main roads, poor relief, and hospitals. Disappointment faced them as the Land Valuation Department proceeded with painful slowness, bogged down in the complexity of its task. There was additional disappointment in the Land Inquiry Committee which reported in 1913. This Committee gave priority to the rural aspects of land reform, to stimulate agriculture and to raise the wages of rural labour. Its urban report was not expected to appear until 1914. Thus Lloyd George's Limehouse rhetoric ultimately spelled bunkum to local authorities: his Budget not only failed to deliver what the urban authorities wanted, it even deepened their plight by the depression of rateable values that followed the blow to property-owners' confidence.

We may conclude this section by recapitulating the reasons why successive governments resisted the urban-rating reform lobby. The site-value rate was intrinsically unattractive. Ministers were reluctant to grasp this nettle, with its stinging political consequences for the security of property in general. The case in equity against the owners was unproven. Practical difficulties, too, were formidable, in assessing capital and original site values. Respected rating experts, like the economist, Edwin Cannan, himself a borough councillor, were opposed to it. The existing rate was not indefensible, enabling local authorities to exercise some freedom of action while schooling the citizenry in responsible self-interest. The regressive quality of rates for the lower-middle classes was mitigated in the context of the total tax structure, income tax and indirect taxes. Regarding the working classes, Arthur Collins, onetime City Treasurer of Birmingham, later Financial Adviser to Local Authorities, asserted that 'every working class house produced less in the way of contributions to the rates than was sufficient to enable the responsible Local Authorities to meet the demand for services attributable to the occupants of the house'. He calculated that, before 1914, every house with an assessable value of under £18 a year constituted a dead loss to the local authority, increasing its liabilities. That was why so many borough authorities, containing a high percentage of working-class housing, were straitened unless they could offset this by rate-remunerative commercial and industrial premises or by incorporating more valuable house-property. This explains the contest between county and county-borough authorities for control of the suburbs; but, rather than embark upon a wholesale reconsideration of areas after the 1888 fiasco, and rather than recast the rating system by transferring the weight from buildings to sites, governments were convinced that local authority malcontentment was best treated by other methods. Especially they favoured the grant-in-aid system. Ideally, by this they could support desirable local expenditure, achieve some minimum standard in the local provision of national or quasi-national services, and moderate inequalities of rate burden between localities.

IV

The grant-in-aid system by 1914 was more than a palliative to soothe sorely tried ratepayers. In *Grants In Aid* (1911), Sidney Webb argued that it was increasingly 'the pivot on which the machine [of local government] really works'. The mechanics, however, were inordinately complex. It is discouraging to discover Webb's bureaucratic brain reeling from the effort to comprehend the operative principles. In the course of describing how education grants were dispensed, he wrote: 'I hope that I have got all these complications right; but it is impossible to feel sure!' The austere and methodical Edwin Cannan made similar animadversions in the 1912 preface to his *History of Local Rates in England* (1898).

The grant-in-aid was introduced, effectively, in 1846 as part of Peel's corn-law repeal package. The first grants were sweeteners to the agricultural interest, to compensate it for the withdrawal of protective tariffs by defraying some costs of rural poor-law administration, criminal prosecutions, and prisons. Following the depression in cereal prices in the 1870s, the agriculturalists' appeals were insistent. Various concessions were made, capped in 1896 by the Agricultural Rates Act. That relieved, or 'de-rated', agricultural land by one-half of its liabilities as regards the poor rate and three-quarters of the general district rate. This deficiency the exchequer made up in grants to the appropriate authorities. Urban leaders, particularly Liberals but many a Conservative too, disliked this strategy. Allegedly it was a dole to Conservative rural interests; certainly it was unselective. The recent depression in profits, and unemployment, in some industries seemed equal to the plight of agriculture; moreover, not all sections of agriculture were suffering – not market-gardening, not dairy-farming or indeed any land held near a town and liable to be built on. The

Association of Municipal Corporations was decidedly upset by these rate exemptions.

The professed ambition of the Government in 1896 was to reduce inequality of burden between agricultural and urban land; but that was not all. The Government was also acknowledging through the grant system another principle, that local government was administering quasi-national services for which the taxpayer should support the ratepayer. This was a principle only gradually admitted and fitfully applied in the nineteenth century. In the case of prisons, from 1878 the exchequer took over the entire costs, thus converting the service into a national one. Most commonly it contributed grants conditional upon the attainment of a certain level of efficiency: in 1856 with respect to police, in 1870 education, in 1873 medical officers of health and sanitary inspectors, in 1874 care of pauper lunatics, in 1875 registration of births and deaths, in 1876 industrial schools, in 1882 disturnpiked and main roads, in 1891 the educational fee-grant and so on. But the grant-in-aid was an instrument for both good and ill, encouraging desirable expenditure or inciting extravagance, relieving ratepayers or subsidizing party supporters. Hence, the motive which inspired grants-in-aid was not the same in every instance, nor was its distribution between local authorities equal. Furthermore, as demands on the imperial exchequer grew through the increasing use of grants-in-aid, so pressure was placed on Westminster politicians to expand *national* sources of revenue. Thus local needs were one forcing agency of the party controversy in Edwardian England over the introduction of indirect taxes (tariffs) or the extension of direct taxation (on personal income and real property).

Webb observed that the main growth of exchequer subsidies occurred after 1874 'and the really startling increases after 1900'. The sum amounted to about £0.8m. in 1868, £2.7m. in 1880, £6.5m. in 1890, £12.2m. in 1900, £20.9m. in 1910. This exchequer contribution to local authority accounts had the effect of reducing the rates, on average, by about 2s. 4d. (12p) in the £ by 1910. Subventions to local authorities accounted for 6.7 per cent of national revenue in 1890, 11.6 per cent in 1913. Ratepayers, however, were hardly comforted. In the same period the proportion of total local authority receipts raised by rates was practically constant, around 43 per cent; but the toll was greater since local government was undertaking wider, more expensive, responsibilities. In 1890 local government expenditure accounted for 38 per cent of total government outlay, in 1913 47 per cent. To appreciate ratepayer dissatisfaction we should now examine some of the circumstances under which grants-in-aid grew and some of the conditions under which they were dispensed. Through the grant-in-aid system the conception of local government as organically locked into central government was reinforced. Until 1888, however, governments were reluctant to recognize this. Their priority was to maintain the pecuniary self-interest of ratepayers in economical local government and to minimize the scale of central bureaucracy. Subventions to local government were petty, annually voted and a fixed proportion of the amount which a local authority spent on certain services. The expediency of local management and, so far as possible, local funding, was axiomatic. The president of the Poor Law Board (forerunner of the Local Government Board) in Gladstone's first ministry, Goschen, refused any grant-in-aid for poor relief, lest this 'open the floodgates' on the exchequer. Goschen, however, was one politician with comprehensive ideas of reform. It was he who described local government as 'a chaos as regards Authorities, a chaos as regards rates, and a worse chaos than all as regards areas'. Goschen was not unfeeling towards the agricultural interest, but his strongest beliefs were that urban occupiers suffered unduly and that relief would best be administered by dividing rates between occupiers and owners. He was also of the opinion that personal property should take some strain off real property in local finance. He conjured with the idea of an extra penny on the income tax, assigned for local purposes. This would ease the local authorities' circumstances and rid government of their mendicant appeals and of bothersome wrangles over subsidies.

Goschen's thoughts did not chime with those of the Prime Minister. Gladstone's great design, having reduced income tax to 3*d.* in the £ in 1874, was to extinguish it. We should not be too critical of Gladstone's sense of the politically possible and desirable. Income tax was not viewed as a social instrument. It was considered an emergency tax, chiefly required in war-time. Its contribution was relatively unimportant in ordinary times. In 1874 it produced £5.6m. out of a total exchequer revenue of £75.5m. Gladstone was then wrestling with Cardwell, his Secretary of State for War, with a view to effecting such armed services economies that income tax could be dispensed with altogether. He was, therefore, intolerant of demands on the local government side. Income tax he mistrusted for its potentially damaging economic effects. It might squeeze personal savings and arrest capital formation, a not absurd fear when the typical business was the family firm. Higher rates of income tax or lower thresholds, furthermore, might reduce the incentive to work, distort prices, and inspire compensatory and inflationary wage demands. Together with these presentiments Gladstone weighed certain benefits. First, income-tax abolition would end the clamour for differentiation between categories of income-tax payers, the professions, tradesmen, industrialists, and farmers, whose feuds duplicated the ratepayers' controversy and threatened schism between the governing classes. Second, it would make government economy inescapable. Without income tax governments would have to trim their spending to match 'real' market activity, when revenue was derived solely from customs and excise and from commodity taxes. Income tax, Gladstone wrote grimly in 1887, was 'an engine of public extravagance'. An easy and limitless source of revenue, it destroyed effective public economy.

Gladstone's ambition was never realized but, having seceded from the Gladstonian ranks over Home Rule, Goschen drifted with the Liberal Unionists towards association with the Conservatives and, in 1887, found himself Chancellor of the Exchequer with a part to play in the financial arrangements of the Local Government Act of 1888. Instead of certain annual grants, whose renewal and accountancy were fussy, he assigned what he thought moderately expansive revenues to local government: 40 per cent of the probate duty, some new beer and spirit duties, and the yield of certain licences, on dogs, carriages, pawnbrokers, auctioneers, game-shooting, etc. Goschen hoped by this reform to satisfy the economizers by setting a maximum to the appetites of local authorities, and at the same time to appease the local authorities by conceding revenues which would steadily appreciate in value. In fact he alienated most opinion.

In the first place, the Goschen scheme applied to fewer than half the existing grants-in-aid. It discontinued annual grants for police, pauper lunatics, roads, criminal prosecutions, and some items of poor-law administration; but it left alone the education grants, which even in 1888 cost more than the rest together. The grant-in-aid system, far from being dissolved, in the next few years grew hugely – in 1891 when elementary education was freed of fees, and in 1896 when agricultural land was partially de-rated. Thus the projected separation of local and national accounts and functions never materialized. Secondly, the Treasury disliked the loss of control which the assigned system entailed. It complained that it was impotent to check local authorities' imprudent spending. The Royal Commission on Local Taxation, 1896–1901, dealt severely with the Goschen scheme:

> Experience shows that Grants do not reduce the rates, these being, as a rule, as high now as before such Grants were in operation. Grants should be given for special purposes, and not in aid of rates generally. . . . At present they are too much given to regard these Grants in the light of doles.

Finally, the allocation of the assigned revenues was determined by an unfortunate principle, frozen in proportion to the existing grants of 1887–8. Here was the chief objection to the entire grants system, that little attention was paid to the means of different authorities. It did not compensate most those with the highest expenditure in relation to ability. Only a fraction of the education grants had regard to variable local means. This amounted to under 1 per cent of total grants in 1900 although, after the county and borough councils assumed responsibility for education in 1902 and further special grants were added, the proportion rose to nearly 13 per cent by 1911–12. Broadly, however, the grant system failed to incorporate variable criteria – population, rateable value, and desirable expenditure – in order to obtain a just estimate of local authority needs. Neither efficiency nor equity was achieved in these circumstances.

The police grant is one example. This was a percentage grant (25 per cent between 1856 and 1874, 50 per cent afterwards) towards the cost of pay and uniforms. The qualification was essentially ratio of police to population: about one per 1,000 was the Home Office's working rule. In 1857 120 boroughs or counties received no police grant; in 1860 seventy-eight, in 1870 fifty-six, in 1880 thirty-two. By 1890 every force (except the City of London which, out of pride, refused to apply) received a grant. By then, if not earlier, the original objective of encouraging local authorities to establish a force was satisfied; and it was time to set more exacting standards, regarding buildings, organization, pay and conditions. The towns' special problems required recognition, with their variable commercial and residential property and traffic hazards. This change in the conditions of the grant did not occur and the modernization of the police in training and equipment was retarded. In 1912 the rating expert, Edwin Cannan, concluded that what efficiency obtained in the police service was due more to the local Watch Committees than to the pecuniary stimulation or penalty of the grant. Likewise he argued that more scandals were uncovered by local public spirit than by the Government's inspectorate.

The prejudice against a national force persisted; but the percentage grants disbursed among umpteen authorities weakened the Government's ability to foster an efficient and united system of local forces. In 1918 186 separate police forces existed, 128 of them borough forces. Three county and twenty-one borough forces contained 25 or fewer men, four county and twenty-one borough forces between 25 and 50 men. Their independence was not just ceremonial. They differed markedly in recruitment, organization, and pay, and to all intents and purposes worked in isolation. The 1890 Police Act, permitting local authorities to lend each other men in emergencies, was mostly inoperable because few could spare men or agree about expenses. The merger of small forces into larger was only tentatively advanced. The Municipal Corporations Act, 1882, disallowed the establishment of separate forces in boroughs of under 20,000 people; and the 1888 Act insisted upon the merger into county forces of existing forces in boroughs with under 10,000 population in the 1881 census. In fact each category of force contained defective species: 18 out of 58 county forces were without trained detectives in 1918, and others were insufficiently equipped. The Desborough Commission, 1919–20, judged 100,000 population the ideal minimum for a separate borough force; but its chief recommendations concerned Home Office standardization of procedures and conditions. That a co-ordinated service did not obtain was due to a combination of respect for local authority independence and an inept grant-in-aid system.

The police service was not the only area in which government grants operated to perpetuate rather than weed out inefficiency. D. N. Chester, in *Central and Local Government* (1951), cited the misgivings of the 1914 Committee on Local Taxation, that the community's interests slipped from sight as local authorities were seized with the object of receiving as much financial aid as possible. The most obnoxious example was the 1874 grant of four shillings per week towards supporting pauper lunatics in hospitals or asylums. Given with a view to relieving poor-law administration, its effect was to spur local authorities to classify paupers as lunatics and place them in asylums.

Several education grants also gave cause for anxiety. The value of the state grants is not so jauntily estimated by historians now. Partly, this is due to a fresh appreciation of the part-time education available before 1870, through religious and other agencies. Modern estimates of literacy suggest that around 80 per cent of men and 70 per cent of women had achieved this bare condition (signifying some ability to read rather than write) by 1870. Regional, as well as town–country, differences were evident; still, the state- and rate-supported service after 1870 did not effect a revolutionary transformation. Quality of education was not promoted by grants based on average attendance; and the 'payments by results' system which operated until 1890 produced alarming evidence of cramming. To be fair, it was essential first to compel school attendance by law, then to stimulate accommodation and basic tuition by grant. By 1880 73 per cent of the school-age population was subject to attendance by-laws. In the boroughs the figure was 97 per cent, but practical difficulties in the way of fulfilling the law were immense. In London, for instance, there was accommodation for fewer than 500,000, and an average attendance of only 373,701, out of an estimated 740,377 school-age population.

The minimum age for school-leaving was progressively raised, 10 in 1876, 11 in 1893, 12 in 1899. In 1900 School Boards were permitted to raise the age to 14; but exemptions were allowed in respect of child employment in agricultural and textile districts, and the 1903 Employment of Children Act enabled local authorities to make by-laws licensing street-trading by children aged over 11. In the 1911 census 98,000 boys and 50,000 girls aged under 15 were recorded as occupied. Astonishing though this sum might seem to modern eyes, it was almost certainly less than at any other time in English history. Few would be younger than ten years old. There had been 41,926 so recorded in 1851, 36,515 in 1861, 21,836 in 1871. After 1881 this category of child employment practically ceased. Of course, an untold amount of illicit employment would remain, even more part-time employment beyond school-hours. The official Return on Wage Earning Children (1899) estimated that about 300,000 schoolchildren engaged in paid work, about 50,000 of them working twenty hours and more per week. These considerations need to be held in mind when evaluating the number of those employed between the ages of ten and fifteen. Still, that record was demonstrably one of improvement. The proportion of that age group who worked fell from 26 per cent in 1871 to 14 per cent in 1911.

What is clear is that educational reformers prospered most when swimming with prevailing economic and demographic tides. The proportion of the population aged under fifteen continued to rise until 1881, when it peaked at 36.5 per cent. By 1911 it had fallen to 30.6 per cent, a trend which has persisted so that in contemporary England children constitute fewer than a quarter of the total population. It is hardly coincidence, therefore, that public education expanded at this time. The economy was able to carry a heavier burden of non-workers (children and elderly), and the adult labour force was growing at a rate which made the children's contribution less vital. As the child part of the labour force contracted in size, it also changed in character. While for girls domestic service, textiles, dressmaking, laundry work, and child-minding remained significant occupations, for boys agriculture lost importance. Mechanization and the 1867 Gangs Act exercised the strongest persuasion away from agriculture: meantime the towns threw up umpteen blind-alley occupations – as paper-sellers, milk-sellers, messengers, minders and helpers in works, warehouses, shops, and transport.

The economy had not ceased its call upon child labour. In other respects, too, educational progress was not straightforward. Education was not emancipated from clerical management. The churches' schools were supplemented, not supplanted, by local authority provision; and on the School Boards, which were promoted after 1870 to supply schooling in areas where the churches were deficient, religious interests secured a significant presence. In the light of this we can appreciate the cool appraisal of S. G. Checkland, in *The Rise of Industrial Society in England, 1815–1885* (1964): 'The failure to renovate the nation's system of education, involved as it was in a tangle of attitudes and obstructions, was one of the most striking examples of the difficulties involved in remaking a traditional society.'

Nevertheless, the indictment of central government sluggishness remains substantial. Education was a national as well as parental responsibility and, even if local administration was preferred, the Government had the duty to set proper standards. It also had the ability to exert control, because education was the most expensive of social services and local authorities could not function without grants. Instead, successive governments opted for financial assistance, not control. According to the Prime Minister in 1902, this produced an educational system which 'is chaotic, is ineffectual, is utterly behind the age, [and] makes us the laughing stock of every advanced nation in Europe and America'. Practical training in the workshop remained the customary form of education in industrial skills; but by the late nineteenth century its defects were exposed, as Britain began to feel the neglect of formal technical education in the advanced sciences, with a shortage of chemists, physicists, engineers, and managers of a sophisticated type. The quantity of elementary education provision was sufficient. Its quality was poor. The quantity of secondary and higher-grade technical education was insufficient. Its quality was poor also. The 1902 dismantling of all 2,560 School Boards did not effect a scientific solution. The county councils, boroughs with populations over 10,000, and urban districts with populations over 20,000, were made education authorities. The result was 350 new authorities crazily distributed. Fourteen counties contained no other education authorities within their shire; 16 counties contained one such area, 10 counties two areas, 10 counties three. The other 11 counties contained four, five, six, seven (2 counties), eight, nine, twelve, thirteen, sixteen, and twenty-seven autonomous areas. Lancashire was the extreme case of patchwork authority.

One criterion, only, makes the urban elementary education system sparkle gem-like. By comparison with rural schools, urban schools in general had better qualified teachers, superior equipment, more effective attendance enforcement, more public support, and at least a glimpse of wider horizons which might be achieved through educational progress. In 1900, Roger Sellman writes in G. E. Mingay (ed.), *The Victorian Countryside* (1981), 'the gap between urban and rural standards was still widening'. Officially, however, the priority was still getting children to school, in tolerable physical shape. In 1906 local authorities were empowered to provide meals for elementary pupils by voluntary contributions or a halfpenny rate; and a grant covering half the cost of meals was forthcoming after 1914. A specific grant from 1912 aided the development of school medical services. This was overdue. By compelling school attendance the authorities had risked the spread of infectious diseases. When school medical services began under the Education (Administrative Provisions) Act, 1907, there remained an evident need to correct unwholesome conditions. In 1910 30 per cent of children in rural, and 50 per cent in urban, elementary schools had verminous heads. But, with respect to the quality of elementary education and the need to expand secondary education, the Government failed to use the grant system to best effect. From 1907 grants of nearly half the costs made available more free places in secondary schools. There were 5,500 such scholarships in 1900, and nearly ten times that number by 1912; but the competition was intense, and children from working-class backgrounds failed to benefit proportionately. Fewer than 5 per cent of all children went on to secondary schools. There was a general conspiracy – entered into by most members of government and industry, by many schoolteachers and working-class parents too – not to educate children above the level of work which they were almost predestined to do and above the social class in which they were almost predestined to stay.

Some upward social mobility was generated through education; but this was almost in spite of, rather than because of, the system of schools. A comparison of the Victorians' railway and education networks is suggested. Each was divided into first-, second-, and third-class compartments, but with a difference. On the railways the comfort of the third-class passengers was dramatically raised, and second-class carriages progressively eliminated, by most companies between 1874 and 1910; and whatever their circumstances passengers always travelled to the same stations. In the educational system those in first- or second-class accommodation, the various ranks of fee-paying independent schools, achieved privileged destinations never glimpsed by the third-class passengers in the public elementary schools, who were frequently detained in dark waiting-rooms, shunted into sidings, or derailed by inadequate staff and resources.

V

Through studying the maladjustment of local authority areas to services and the grant-in-aid system, we have evidence of the shortcomings of central direction of local government. We should now consider the executive departments, to explain why their performance was such a poor parody of government.

The supervision of local affairs was divided between several departments, the Poor Law (from 1871, Local Government) Board, Home Office, Board of Trade, Board of Agriculture (established 1889), and Board of Education (1899). The Treasury should be included too: according to Lord Salisbury in 1900, 'by exercising the power of the purse it claims a voice in all decisions of administrative authority and policy'. But because the Local Government Board was the most directly involved, it is sensible to concentrate upon that. The Local Government Board united the Poor Law Board (1847) and the Medical Department of the Privy Council (1858). Union was advised by the Royal Commission on Sanitation, under the chairmanship of C. B. Adderley, 1869–71. Since, however, the cardinal feature of

Central and local government

English government was 'local administration, under central superin-
tendance', their object now in proposing a new state department was
'not to centralize administration, but on the contrary to set local life in
motion . . .'.

Formidable centralizing power was the last thing contemplated by
the Adderley Commission. It is true that it regretted that too much
legislation was permissive rather than binding; but the fundamental
defect of local administration was 'the smallness of the parochial unit
of area [which] minimizes the material for public officers'. This was
best corrected by the transfer of sometimes multiple sanitary jurisdictions to a single authority (in boroughs, the town council), and by
the availability of central advice and expertise. Here was that Victorian optimism in the liberating, dynamic power of mere information. This trust was not entirely quixotic. We should acknowledge
the influence of William Farr, who persistently drew lessons from the
tables of comparative sickness and mortality which he issued from the
Registrar-General's Office for over forty years from 1838. Farr's
emphasis was wrong – he bolstered the miasmatic theory of disease –
but his belief was right, that statistics were 'an arsenal for sanitary
reformers to use'. Without effective legislation to act upon, however,
statistics were as useless as ammunition without weapons to fire it.
Hence, it was mischievous of the introducers of the Public Health Act
of 1872, practically the first issue of the Local Government Board, to
boast that – apart from an insistence that sanitary authorities appoint
medical officers – no new centralizing power was embodied in their
legislation. The ineffectualness of public health they explained by the
confused rather than defective state of the law. Consolidation and
clarification would supply the inspiration to local authorities. It was a
shallow vision.

This meekness in the public health ambitions of the Local Government Board was joined with a severity in poor-law supervision, a
character inherited from the Poor Law Board. 'Divided between a
health Jekyll and a pauper Hyde', is K. B. Smellie's pungent description. This combination made the ministry unattractive to the
ambitious statesman, a circumstance compounded by Gladstone's
decision to pay a salary of £2,000 instead of the £5,000 enjoyed by the
Chancellor of the Exchequer, First Lord of the Admiralty, and Secretaries of State. Not until 1910 was this indignity removed, and it was
suffered by other departments vital to domestic well-being – Trade,
Agriculture, and Education. An official inquiry, under Lord Jersey, in

1903-4 pressed that the President of the Board of Trade should rank with the Secretaries of State, but feebly concluded that no change was required in the constitution of the Local Government Board. Politicians reacted accordingly. The post had a low appeal, at best a stepping-stone to higher office. Some determined not to touch it at any price. When Asquith was forming his ministry in 1908, Winston Churchill pleaded not to be lumbered with the Local Government Board – 'There is no place in the Government more laborious, more anxious, more thankless, more choked with petty and even squalid detail, more full of hopeless and insoluble difficulties.'

The Local Government Board's presidents before 1914 were not altogether undistinguished; but what distinction they achieved was rarely earned in that office. With few exceptions, they were ignorant of urban requirements. James Stansfeld was the first president, 1871-4; and he resumed the post briefly in 1886. Stansfeld was born at Halifax (which he represented in Parliament), the son of a County Court judge. He himself was a non-practising barrister and, a curious combination, a Nonconformist whose main source of income was a brewery in Fulham. A radical individualist, Stansfeld was content with the Adderley Commission's prescription of the Board's humble role. His main concern was to tighten poor-law administration, especially to curb the extent of outdoor relief. When Gladstone's ministry fell in 1874, Stansfeld was replaced by George Sclater-Booth. A Winchester- and Balliol-educated lawyer, Sclater-Booth belonged to that club of 'mediocrities with double-barrelled names' whom Randolph Churchill strafed. As president he was not even in Disraeli's cabinet; and this was the summit of his ministerial career. Another dullard, J. G. Dodson, followed him upon the change of government in 1880. The abilities of this Eton- and Christ Church-educated lawyer 'did not appear on the surface', wrote Algernon West in his *Recollections* (1899), 'and many people were puzzled at the success he attained'. Nevertheless, we can surmise why Gladstone appointed him. Dodson was an authority on parliamentary procedure, especially private Bill legislation; he had a nose for accounts; and he was remote from those urban interests which might aspire to adventuresome finance. Later he was first chairman of East Sussex County Council.

Dodson was replaced in 1882 by Sir Charles Dilke, whose commitment to London government reform was noticed in Chapter 2. Joseph Chamberlain also occupied the post, briefly between February and

April 1886; but what prospects this opened – for instance, he circularized borough councils to accelerate public works programmes in order to keep skilled and customarily independent workmen from the workhouses – were closed conclusively by the Home Rule glaciation. The intermediate Conservative administration lowered the tempo. Arthur Balfour, the Prime Minister's nephew, made a lustreless ministerial debut in this office. In Salisbury's caretaker ministry, and in the first year of his second ministry, the president was excluded from the cabinet. Henry Chaplin refused the post on this account in 1886; but C. T. Ritchie was accorded cabinet status in 1887, in anticipation of the local government reorganization which was finalized in the 1888 Act. Ritchie, a London MP, had merchant and manufacturing interests; but the Conservatives' inclination to advance county over urban causes was manifest, and Ritchie's Parliamentary Secretary, Walter Long, was their champion. Long was himself president, 1900–5, having succeeded that other rugged exponent of county Toryism, Chaplin, in whose time the Agricultural Rates Act was passed. The last Conservative tenant of the office was Gerald Balfour, in the final months of his cousin's government. Balfour personified that wariness of municipal enterprise which generally actuated the Conservative benches. He moved to the Local Government Board from the Board of Trade, where he was considered a 'company man' from his efforts to remove the municipal veto over company provisional orders for electricity and tram supply and by his use of discretionary authority to tighten the terms of municipal loans.

In the Liberal administrations, 1892–5, the post was occupied by two men, Henry Fowler and G. J. Shaw-Lefevre, each experienced in local government questions. Fowler it was who carried the Parish Councils Act, to invigorate rural radicalism; but, though he was that rare creature, a president who had been a town councillor and mayor (of Wolverhampton), he was well known to be antipathetic to new departures, such as the programme of the London Progressives. Altogether his heart was not in the job. According to his daughter, Fowler felt insulted by Gladstone's appointment, and he was avid for the promotion, which eventually came, to the India Office in 1894. Apart from Herbert Samuel, who conducted the ministry in the months before the Great War, there remains only John Burns in this dispiriting catalogue.

Burns surpassed every president in length of office, December 1905 to February 1914. As the first working-man to enter the cabinet, a former trade-union official and LCC Progressive, he aroused high expectations. His subsequent poor performance was attributed to want of education and ability or want of class authority and confidence, such that he became the puppet of permanent officials. This implies that Burns was bubbling with intitiatives which others then numbed. The record does not bear this out. His commitment to public economy was inbred not transplanted. His unsympathetic response to reports of the Royal Commission on the Poor Laws, 1905–9, which aimed to re-shape the administration, stemmed from a proper suspicion that these ambitions would consume public money and engender a bureaucratic leviathan. Burns's thoughts on how to tackle poverty and unemployment were not too distant from the orthodox character-building school: root out drinking and gambling and do not cushion the work-shy. Public works relief schemes he viewed hopelessly: not only wasteful but injurious, because they perpetuated the immobility of labour.

Burns had risen by his own efforts and was not averse to recommending a similar exertion to the rest of the world. We should not disregard this opinion as attributable merely to vanity. Burns was not untypical of his class in his fierceness towards malingerers. The economist Alfred Marshall argued before the Royal Commission on Aged Poor, 1893, that the Poor Law would be strengthened by the inclusion of working-class people in its administration.

I am convinced that the leaders of the working men would be as firm as anyone in insisting that the scamps and lazy people should be put to a severe discipline; that they would be in many ways sharper than people not in the same rank of life in seeing through a fallacious story, and would have no sympathy at all with the tramp; in fact I believe that probably the professional tramp is even more odious to large classes of the working men than he is to the rest of society.

It was with this conviction that property qualifications for guardians were abolished in 1894.

The case against Burns and the Local Government Board thus requires careful framing. Burns was not shackled by his officials. The problem was that his officials did not break his shackles. They did not broaden his and their own vision. The key officials were schooled on the poor-law side of the department's work. They fretted that the principles of 1834 were being eroded, with good reason since, as recent historical studies have shown, many unions (in the north especially) resisted the central pressure to uniformity and worked out policies in the light of their own interpretations of local business cycles and social needs. Each permanent secretary between 1871 and 1919, John Lambert, Sir Hugh Owen, Sir Samuel Provis, and Sir Horace Monro, was steeped in the Chadwickian and Charity Organization Society traditions, as was the inspectorate, led by such as J. S. Davy. On the public health side the Board attracted several enlightened officers, like Sir John Simon, George Buchanan, Sir Richard Thorne, Sir William Power, and Sir Arthur Newsholme; and their efforts, in conjunction with sympathetic spirits in urban districts, brought significant improvements in the treatment of the pauper sick and physically infirm. More boards of guardians came to build and equip hospitals and dispensaries which were detached from workhouses; and in 1885 the disfranchisement was ended of men who received only medical assistance from poor-law sources. Similarly more boards of guardians transferred pauper children from workhouses to separate 'homes' or foster families, and showed more consideration to elderly couples. Workhouse diets improved too. But most medical officers at the Local Government Board (as in the local authorities) bewailed an unequal contest. Theirs were peripheral duties: the Board's chief ambition was to prevent relaxation in policy towards the able-bodied poor, and the increasing tendency of local guardians to dole out relief only stiffened its obstinacy.

Below the Board's departmental heads was a staff generally inferior to other ministries'. Treasury control was blamed for this, pegging their salaries and prospects on a lower rung, just as the minister himself was paid less and treated more lowly than some of his colleagues. The Board's staff grew with its expanding duties. Between 1900 and 1914 alone its number of civil servants more than doubled, from 425 to 963. But that staff was not reclothed in imagination; and for this reason reformers argued that new social services – pensions, health insurance, labour exchanges and so forth – should be placed under the jurisdiction of departments other than the Local Government Board.

We have noted that the Board's work expanded. This was not a novel feature of the early twentieth century. It was true of one of the Board's forerunners, the Local Government Act department of the Home Office, whose work has been studied by Royston Lambert. Though the department was unambitious about extending its influence, its annual correspondence increased threefold, from under 10,000 letters in the late 1850s to just under 30,000 in 1864. This was caused mainly by smaller boroughs seeking advice about sanitary codes. The origin of many a central intervention was this local initiative. Here, apparently, was a fulfilment of Mill's precept: 'Power may be localised, but knowledge to be most useful must be centralised.' We may question how knowledgeable central departments were. They were, no doubt, exemplary in legalism; but 'knowledge to be most useful' requires more than that. The Board conceived of its function as primarily one of restraining, the motive force residing in the local authorities. It subjected the accounts of first the Boards of Guardians, then (from the 1870s) sanitary authorities and (from 1888) county councils, to a searching audit, but in a purely negative way, with a view to disallowing expenditure.

The Board's unenterprising strategy can be illustrated by its statistical work. Some effort was made by the medical department in the 1870s to standardize the classification of infectious diseases and causes of mortality; but the returns relating to local rates and public expenditure were a mess, as the LCC's statistical officer, G. L. Gomme, deplored in 1897. And of statistics to comprehend unemployment, or statistics to foster efficient local management of services by tabling comparative unit costs, the Local Government Board knew nothing and had no desire to know. By contrast, the Board of Trade, especially Llewellyn Smith's labour department from 1893, took steps to remedy the unreliability of its returns and to utilize them in the formulation of policy. It was eager to codify the causes of industrial disputes and to exercise its influence, by measured use of data of wage relativities and working practices, whenever formal collective bargaining procedures had broken down. The state of the Board of Trade before 1893 was that of the Local Government Board throughout. As the Board of Trade economist Robert Giffen described it, this was the publication of 'statistics for statistical purposes alone, the statistics not being required for daily administration'.

The unpopularity of the Local Government Board should not surprise us. Enterprising local authorities complained about the Board's grudging sanction of loans, suffocating red tape, and hostility to new departures. Local experiments in numerous matters were repressed. The surcharges laid by the Board's district auditors on benevolent or daring poor-law guardians are only the best known examples. The Board seemed determined to render local government not just accountable but devitalized.

With regard to the corporate purchase of land, the Board was excessively timid. T. C. Horsfall, of the Manchester and Salford Sanitary Association, argued before the Inter-departmental Committee on Physical Deterioration in 1903–4 that it was essential for local authorities to control their outskirts and regulate building there. Many suburbs came under rural sanitary administration, which had less exacting standards than its urban counterpart. Though suburban house-building was generally an improvement upon older inner-city accommodation, there were enough examples of over-building, eliminating green spaces, and of jerry-built properties, ill-supplied with essential services, to substantiate an indictment of uncontrolled suburbia. Town corporations lamented their inability to plan suburban developments, and were fearful that they would ultimately be saddled with the cost of correcting faults which should have been avoided in the first place. These townsmen spoke from experience of the dreadful cost of repairing their own past negligence and impotence. A survey conducted by the Association of Municipal Corporations in 1907 indicated that three-quarters of the expenditure undertaken on street-widening and open spaces in the previous decade would have been spared if they had had legislative power to control development at the time. No one could quantify the wasted money with precision, but it was reckoned as over £14 million, possibly as high as £22 million. Hence, we can appreciate Horsfall's exclamation:

No intelligent anticipation of a town's growth is allowed to dictate municipal policy in regard to the extension of borough boundaries, with the result that when these are extended the areas taken in have already been covered with the normal type of cheap and squalid dwelling houses, which rapidly reproduce on the outskirts of a city the slum characteristics which are the despair of the civic reformer in its heart.

The Physical Deterioration Committee agreed with Horsfall, and recommended that 'it would be expedient to secure the co-operation of Local Authorities in contiguous areas that are becoming rapidly urbanized'. But the Local Government Board persisted with its earth-worm vision. In 1906 it roused Sheffield City Council to organize a joint protest with other municipalities, petitioning for remedial legislation, when the Board checked it from purchasing lands with a view to controlling suburban housing. The Sheffield representation fell on deaf ears, the fate of similar deputations led by William Thompson and his colleagues on the National Housing and Town Planning Council (1900). The Association of Municipal Corporations prepared a draft town-planning Bill along these lines in 1907, to which the Local Government Board responded with its modest 1909 Act; but this sequence of events puts the Board in a poor light. The Local Government Board was depressing, not inspiring. It would not readily initiate new legislation, and it would not always enforce existing legislation. In certain health matters the Board had power to compel a defaulting authority to fulfil its duties, by writ of *mandamus*. It might even undertake these responsibilities itself and charge the expenses; but this procedure was administratively unwelcome, hence rarely adopted.

The conclusion is this: the Local Government Board – and central government as a whole – insufficiently stimulated negligent authorities and fastidiously dampened enterprising authorities. Why this was the case should now be plain. There was a lack of coherence and nerve in determining the distribution of authority between central and local government. A 'correct' classification of national and local duties, however, seemed neither theoretically nor practically feasible, since the relationship of perceived needs and means was changing all the time. Moreover, government had always to work within the limits of consent.

7 Municipal councils and municipal services

This chapter complements the previous chapter in its concern for local government. Here attention will be directed more closely to the urban localities. It has been suggested in chapter 6 that certain municipalities, over a range of matters, possessed imagination and technical ability not at all inferior to Westminster departments. This chapter enlarges upon that argument, while acknowledging that the picture is discoloured by extreme diversity.

I

It is suitable to begin with the officials, that apparently 'ever-increasing class'. Here was reason for anxiety. The sociologist Max Weber prophesied that 'the dictatorship of the official and not that of the worker is on the march'; and the medieval historian T. F. Tout believed that it was 'the demure and obscure gentlemen in neat black coats and tall hats' who really ruled, not the voters or 'vote-hunting politicians'. Generally, though, observers distinguished between Whitehall and local government officials. The central civil servant roused fears about a New Despotism: that this factotum was neither civil nor servile, an arrogant and irresponsible trespasser on policy who thwarted democratic initiative and self-government. Local government officials, on the other hand, were estimated genially, as the origin of most local good. This view is expressed by E. L. Hasluck, in *Local Government in England* (1936; revised 1946): since public opinion was undiscerning and councillors were 'mostly conspicuous for stupidity', the 'real credit for the efficiency of the Local Government services in the vast majority of areas should be given to the Medical Officers of Health, the Sanitary Inspectors, the Directors of Education, the Surveyors and the Clerks of the Councils'. In the same way an American observer of English cities, A. L. Lowell, imagined in 1908 that 'the excellence of municipal government was very roughly proportional to the influence of the permanent officials'.

By Edwardian times there was not the same suspicion of the influence of local government officials as of Whitehall, because demonstrable benefit might be traced to their actions, and because their relationship to the elected councillors was differently perceived from that of civil servants to ministers or MPs. The boundary between advice and policy-making was admitted to be fluid in local government. Its officers were expected to be creative figures, not simply agents obeying orders and executing routine work. Nonetheless, the degree of independence and initiative conceded to local officials was hotly debated. Accountability was not mere form.

The Whig authors of the Municipal Corporations Act, 1835, took a jaundiced view of the chief corporate officer, the Town Clerk. Many had conspired in the abuses of unreformed corporations and fought the Royal Commission of Inquiry. The Whigs intended to shackle the clerk by subjecting his tenure to annual review by the borough council, until Tory opposition argued that no able or self-respecting man would serve under such terms and that it was undesirable to license party political caprice. The Tory counter-proposal was that the clerk should hold office during 'good behaviour'; but the outcome was a formula nearer the Whig than the Tory nostrum, namely that the clerk 'hold his Office during Pleasure'. This placed town clerks on a par with magistrates rather than with judges. Less consideration was given to defining the clerk's business and qualifications. It was accepted that a lawyer's training was necessary to expedite the technical affairs of a corporation. Otherwise there was no prescription. T. E. Headrick, in *The Town Clerk* (1962), explains that 'the era of the full-time official was just dawning'. The authors of the 1835 Act did not conceive of the need to carve out a substantial place for the expert in local government; indeed, according to R. C. K. Ensor, this same omission can be held against the authors of the 1888 Local Government Act as well.

It was left to the town clerks and colleagues in other departments to express themselves. Several did so in unmistakable fashion. The oft-cited names are Joseph Heron, Town Clerk of Manchester from 1838 to 1877, and, among late-nineteenth-century town clerks, Samuel Johnson of Nottingham or Harcourt Clare of Liverpool. According to their eulogists, these outstandingly able men became in effect city managers; and their ostensible masters in the council were dummies to their ventriloquism. Indeed there is evidence of Heron and Johnson actively participating in council meetings; not just neutrally elucidating a complex point of law, but forcefully intervening to check councillors who, in their view, advocated wanton or mistaken policies. The textbooks note the Herons and generally overlook the likes of Thomas Pierce, Town Clerk of Bootle, who fled abroad in 1883, having embezzled £24,000 from the corporation. In fact there were few Herons and few Pierces; but we should not be satisfied by an estimate of the officials' influence which attributes the variety chiefly to personality. This discounts the authority of the council, the significance of politics, the size of townships and public opinion.

The larger towns were the first to appoint full-time officials. Manchester converted Heron from part-time in 1846; York did not do the same for its town clerk until 1886. Part-timers remained common in medium and small boroughs. The same applied to other officials. The first Medical Officer of Health, Dr Duncan in Liverpool in 1847, was full-time, but Manchester did not appoint an MOH until 1868, Birmingham until 1875. Many corporations practised what Sir Arthur Newsholme execrated, that 'extravagant parsimony' which refused to spend what was needed to secure communal health. Preventive medicine could not develop in small boroughs where the medical officer remained in private practice, or in large boroughs where the full-time officer was starved of adequate staff. Only twenty-two of sixty-four county boroughs in 1900 were receiving the grant-in-aid of half the salaries of their medical officers and sanitary inspectors. This was not a sure index of inefficiency: several municipalities preferred to pay full salaries from principle, to retain entire control over their executive officers. Still, the Onslow Commission in 1928 concluded that progress towards full-time appointments had been 'indefensibly slow'. Only about a quarter of MOHs were full-time in 1873, and slightly above one-third by 1920. York, with 76,000 people, had no full-time MOH before 1900. The Board of Trade was equally disappointed by local authority administration of the weights and measures and food and drugs Acts. Smaller boroughs again were most culpable, failing to appoint full-time or qualified inspectors. It was also observed that difficulties arose where councillors were tradesmen, since the inspector was 'dependent on their good will for his advancement, or even for the continuance of his appointment'. Larger boroughs had a scarcely superior record. In relation to population and area, their staff of inspectors of weights and the number of samples of food taken for analysis were unimpressive.

Hence, local self-government, according to Frederic Harrison in

Order and Progress (1875), might stand for 'local mis-government and local no-government'. The conspiracy to keep local government in this state encompassed many parties – not just miserable ratepayers who understood that reduced staffs meant low rates, or interested councillors who wanted to restrict meddlesome inspectors. Working-class people were invariably hostile, in the cherished cause of liberty and privacy. We should not belittle this as the freedom to be filthy, the suffrage of the stinkard. When borough health departments were tiny the police were used to enforce sanitary legislation. The Torrens Act, 1868, seeking to check overcrowding, gave inspectors right of entry into bedrooms at night. Sir John Lubbock, with Thomas Huxley, accompanied the police on one of their night inspections in Liverpool when the British Association met there in 1870; and, though he adjudged the police as considerate as circumstances allowed, Lubbock was worried about the principle. Materially, too, the poor suffered. Property and possessions were damaged by official disinfection and fumigation procedures wherever infectious diseases were suspected or known. Provision for compensation existed in legislation from 1875 but was rarely used. Mostly, we can only guess at the opinions of those on the receiving end of these invasions, though a Bethnal Green cabinet-maker, George Acorn, born around 1885, wrote in his auto-biography in 1911 how his family feared the tread of the health inspec-torate: 'To our minds at that time they were soulless inhuman "powers", mysterious inquisitors, whose one object was to get us all into the workhouse.' Gradually, the habit of inspection was learned and borne, but a grievance remained. This was explained to R. H. Tawney by two miners in his WEA class at Longton in 1912; that 'inspection and so on does not press upon every one equally . . . because it's applied to one class and not to another'.

Slum clearance, even more than inspections, aroused bitter resis-tance. Communities were broken and dispersed by health authorities. The dispossessed were often left to their own resources; and both they and those dependent on them, small tradesmen especially, bristled with resentment. Schoolteachers and clergy often spoke out on their behalf against insensitive officialdom; and politicians, mindful of their public, were inclined to curb the sanitarians. Not that this check always needed to be administered. Since local authorities could dismiss officers at pleasure, fear of incurring disfavour usually kept initiatives within modest limits. Conformity also resulted from the political patronage which influenced appointments, although no party before 1914 was as blatant as the controlling Labour group in Walsall whose electoral manifesto in 1980 proclaimed an intention not to employ Conservatives in key positions in the corporation. A candidate's chief qualification, they specified, was 'a social awareness akin with our philosophy'.

The most powerful officials were those whose outlook coincided with influential opinion in a town or its council. There were few possibilities in a head-on fight, some possibilities in artful persuasion, most of all in moving in the direction in which politicians and people were going anyway. These officials enjoyed a position not unlike royal favourites or Byzantine eunuchs in time past. Heron's reputation in Manchester was unimpeachable among the Liberal majority because he had been a staunch member of the original charter committee. Clare later was a force in Liverpool because, as the architect of the consolidated rating system and boundary extensions of the 1890s, he was expressing the will of the ruling party. Certainly the clerk was in a strategic position, as go-between or by-pass of cumbrous machinery. His office recorded the minutes of the council and its committees, distributed their directions to the departments, and conducted the corporation's external correspondence. But most clerks were content or compelled to occupy themselves with routine work and refrain from active generalship. Indeed the prevailing fault of local government was not the number of Napoleons (in the person of the town clerk or whoever), but the lack of co-ordination between departments.

It was this deficiency which emboldened many to suggest that, in larger authorities at least, the choice of head official should not be restricted to the legal profession. It might be advisable to separate the duties of legal consultant and chief administrator, with the latter freed from routine, elevated into corporate management, and recruited from industry, the universities, or local government service. This suggestion was canvassed before the Royal Commission on Local Government, 1923–9, but not endorsed until the Redcliffe-Maud Report of 1969. One or two cities encouraged the development notwithstanding. Clare in Liverpool delegated most legal work to the deputy town clerk precisely in order to achieve this overall supervision, though this was hardly personal rule. His superintendence was designed to stimulate the elected councillors, for Clare, like the town clerks of Birmingham and several cities, had to issue a weekly or monthly epitome of committee proceedings, so that subjects should not escape the notice of councillors. Party caucuses or an informal cabinet system supplied another impetus towards coherence. In many corporations joint committees were established on an *ad hoc* or formal basis; and nearly everywhere finance and general purposes committees strove to survey the business and accounts of the spending departments. But generally the committee structure was arranged vertically not horizontally, and an excessive departmentalism prevailed. Too many decisions were taken in isolation. The check upon a committee by the Finance Committee or whole council was often merely formal. Financial waste was rampant, with duplicated staffs and the failure to exploit bulk or central purchasing. Worse was the blindness as to how policies of one committee or department affected others. This distortion and disintegration disabled borough councils from realizing and grappling with problems. Beatrice Webb's diary for 9 September 1899 contains a searching criticism of Manchester City Council on this score. This same deficiency was felt by E. D. Simon when he published *A City Council from Within* in 1926.

The dominant science was muddling through. Most councils got only what they paid for. The distribution of local government officers' salaries in 1914 showed 4 per cent being paid above £450 p.a., 2 per cent £450, 6 per cent between £260 and £450, and 88 per cent below £260. The average in 1898, according to the Municipal Officers Association, was something over £100 per annum; but this is hardly revealing when the range was so extensive, from town clerks, treasurers and medical officers, to school-attendance officers, rent-collectors, veterinary inspectors and their subordinates. In 1899 Banbury, with under 13,000 population, paid its town clerk £300, and Sheffield, with nearly 400,000 people, paid £1,150. Liverpool, with a population around 650,000, paid Clare £1,650 on appointment in 1895. It was important not to be niggardly. Joseph Chamberlain told the Birmingham Council in the 1870s that, unless they were prepared to pay handsomely for professional services, they might as well not commence municipal trading. He returned to this theme as a minister in 1897, warning that local government would be corrupted if higher officials were paid less, and lower ranks more, than their market value merited.

That Chamberlain made this appeal at this time was not accidental. Though councils were always prone to economize on salaries, wage differentials excited lively controversy in the late nineteenth century when Labour parties emerged in many boroughs. The first to experience Labour control, West Ham, saw the introduction of an eight-hour day, thirty-shillings minimum wage, and paid holidays for municipal employees. Elsewhere Labour parties pressed generally for 'fair-wages' clauses in corporation contracts, and to raise the wages of most ordinary grades – labourers, refuse collectors, gas workers, tramway employees. These groups manifestly could bear improvement. Less justifiable was Labour's tendency to dismiss the claims of higher officers. It was nothing new for the salaries of town clerks and their colleagues to be used as a party football; but now the game seemed more like class warfare. In 1913 the Conservative boss in Liverpool, Salvidge, discountenanced pay rises for the corporation's chief officials solely in order to deny Labour 'a popular electioneering cry'. Not surprisingly the Royal Commission on Local Government, in 1929, was impressed by the damage public debate caused to 'the salary and promotion of individual officers'. E. D. Simon declared that it was notorious how head officials were paid less than in comparable private enterprise undertakings. The best municipal officers were occasionally attracted away to private companies, 'whereas the reverse process is unknown'.

Local government workers made their own efforts to improve conditions of service through professional associations or trade-union combination. Others, too, recognized the need of local government to establish adequate qualifications and training for technical and administrative staff, and to rid appointments and promotions of personal favouritism, political patronage, and parochialism. The last, that bias against 'foreigners', was rampant. In the 1920s the general secretary of the National Association of Local Government Officers (NALGO) reported that 95 per cent of local authority staffs were recruited from within their areas. How widespread other abuses were we can only guess. One expert, W. A. Robson, told the Onslow Commission, 'within his knowledge there were five or six Local Authorities where a large proportion of the staff were relatives or friends of the local councillors'.

NALGO, founded in 1905 from several local guilds of municipal officers, aimed to raise the quality and independence of the service by encouraging members to aspire to certificated standards and by using the examinations as a negotiating instrument regarding pay and conditions. Uniform superannuation and salary scales were seen as indispensable for making local government an attractive career and, though a national agreement was not won before 1946, NALGO made headway in some areas before 1914. Professional associations and journals, too, did much to improve the expertise of senior officials, thus arming them in two directions, against the blinkered outlook of their borough councils and against the relative failure of central government to supply suitable encouragement, assistance, and research. Pre-eminent here were societies of medical officers, sanitary inspectors, municipal treasurers and accountants, civil engineers, surveyors, and librarians; and magazines like the *Municipal Journal* and *Local Government Journal*. Finally, we should mention, both in this respect and as an introduction to a wider context, the Association of Municipal Corporations, established in 1872. Drawing town clerks, mayors, and councillors (some of whom were MPs) to its assemblies, this Association by the 1890s was the most important representative body of urban opinion, wherein views were exchanged and policies formulated on vital matters – municipal trading, rating and taxation, and parliamentary strategies.

II

We should now consider the borough councillors themselves, before reviewing the services which they authorized. The size of councils varied by the Edwardian period, from nine in the smallest boroughs to over 130 in Liverpool and London. Varied too was their quality, an issue which raises evergreen debate.

J. S. Mill, in *Representative Government* (1861), was not the first to disparage councillors, but his observations will furnish us with a start in this question. The 'greatest imperfection of popular local institutions', he wrote, 'and the chief cause of the failure which so often attends them, is the low calibre of the men by whom they are almost always carried on.' In Mill's view both 'the local representative bodies and their officers are almost certain to be of a much lower grade of intelligence and knowledge than Parliament and the national executive.' We have argued already that, comparing local government officials with their central civil service counterparts, this judgement is presumptuous; now the same will be argued in a comparison of local councillors and Westminster politicians. Though the criteria by which critics passed judgement have not always been explicit, we can discover the recurrence of several issues. Amateurism, inferior social standing, rising political partisanship, public apathy, and the structural defects of local government itself – each was reflected in the failure of councils to attract able representatives. That some able men did enlist in local government was usually conceded but always the paucity is emphasized.

Joseph Chamberlain is commonly upheld as the first statesman to have served an apprenticeship in local government but, with the exception of several Labour politicians, the list invariably begins and ends here. The LCC was known to have attracted *already* celebrated individuals – peers like Rosebery, Hobhouse and Monkswell, and assorted talents such as Sir Arthur Arnold, Sir Thomas Farrer, Sir Reginald Welby, and Sir John Lubbock. But, like councils elsewhere, it made fewer reputations: John Burns, perhaps, from one generation, Herbert Morrison from another. The relatively infrequent cross-breeding of councillors and parliamentarians constituted a grave indictment of local government, which was failing, so the argument ran, as a nursery of statesmen. Some even denied that local government service could ever fulfil this mission and suggested that local government, schooling men in a narrow outlook, should be considered a positive disqualification for national leaders: *vide* Lord Hugh Cecil's opinion that the trouble with Neville Chamberlain as Prime Minister was that he remained 'no better than a Mayor of Birmingham, and in a lean year at that'.

We should not be precipitate in conclusions. It is sensible to start with arithmetic. Parliament ideally required 1,300 talents (670 MPs and 622 peers, eligible to attend the Lords, in 1910). Local government required many times that quantity. Even with first tap of the nation's genius Parliament was not overflowing with Solons. The House of Lords was dense with hereditary incompetents. Rosebery believed its effectiveness as a second chamber could be enhanced by an elected element from, among others, borough and county councillors. The Commons' composition too was not irreproachable. The tendency to cabinet and departmental rule was seen as a consequence and confirmation of the Commons' deterioration. However, we should recognize that the severest strictures followed upon franchise extensions. Implicitly many critics of both the House of Commons and local councils questioned not merely the failure of the popular representative system to elect sufficient candidates of quality but its ability to do so at all.

On the other hand, amateurism – one charge persistently levelled against councillors – was surely a shortcoming of the pre-democratic regime which lingered into the modern. MPs received a salary of £400 per annum from 1912, but local councillors remained unpaid, recompensed only for certain expenses. The German system of paid, professional mayors appealed to such as Thomas Horsfall, a proponent of town planning in Edwardian England. His was a minority conviction, yet few were satisfied with the existing 'happy-go-lucky amateur system' (Winston Churchill's phrase) which allegedly produced councillors who knew nothing worth paying for. Councillors, Herman Finer has remarked, resembled casual labour: they lacked 'preparation, skill, purpose, and regularity of application'.

Before 1914 the leisured, educated amateur was widely revered, in occupations as diverse as cricket and burglary, pursuits in which Raffles demonstrated effortless superiority. In the civil service professionalization made progress; but the generalist controlled the specialist and technician as he controls him still. The Webbs before 1914 derided this system. Nonetheless, it was not mandatory. Local authorities were permitted to co-opt experts who might be deterred from seeking election either from distaste for the hustings or from an inability to give much time. Co-option was most common on education, health, arts, and library committees, but altogether infrequent. There were good reasons for caution. There was danger in enlisting individuals who had no direct financial accountability to the electorate; and there was temptation for parties to play politics by co-opting defeated colleagues. Mostly co-option was not practised because it was not needed. Many councillors became specialists through the committee system; and the aldermen, though often selected by party preferences and containing not a few extinct volcanoes in their ranks, possessed a valuable stock of experience. These were not negligible resources, and many a departmental official discovered that a committee chairman had a thorough grasp of the business.

Certainly there were defects in the councils' constitution which might be traced to amateurism. Absenteeism was a besetting problem; and council meetings tended not to challenge committee decisions. Here Parliament appeared livelier; yet, according to E. D. Simon, who had experience of both Parliament and city council, MPs talked more but to less effect. With more rigid party lines, parliament had little to show for its longwindedness and bluster, since most ministerial Bills achieved the statute book. The councils' ability to command an overall vision would arguably not be improved by the substitution of the 'expert' for the 'amateur'.

The councillors' social status excited wider comment. Mill again can be cited to open the account. Council membership, he wrote, was not 'in general sought by the higher ranks'. The assertion is that councils did not attract, and the implication is that it was detrimental that councils did not attract, the community's 'natural' social and economic leaders, those in French jargon called 'élites' or 'notables'. In *Fit and Proper Persons* (1973) E. P. Hennock reflects these views when he argues that, because the financial basis of local government between the 1850s and 1880s was increasingly limited in relation to its expanding activities, ratepayers' revolts tended to replace the wealthy élites with representatives of the parsimonious lower-middle class. Further broad changes occurred subsequently. One was the admission of a 'new' professional element – accountants, surveyors, and school-teachers. The last group, from 1902, were council employees, demonstrably interested in a particular public service. Another new party was the specifically working-class representative, with an interest group or power base in the expanding ranks of council menials, street cleaners, tramwaymen, gas workers and the like. As for the miserly middle classes, who had initially displaced the substantial industrialists or old-fashioned oligarchy, these were less active as Treasury subsidies relieved their burdens. Altogether councils became more mixed socially.

The issue is whether we can correlate changes in council policy with changes in the councillors' social composition. In *Coal Metropolis: Cardiff 1870–1914* (1977) M. J. Daunton argues that the economic élite never were the 'natural' council leaders because their substantial interests were not specific to a city, rather regional, even international, in character. Well-to-do businessmen were not gifted with a more enlightened outlook or committed to more expansive policies with regard to council affairs. In any case theirs was never a conspicuous presence in Cardiff because the docks belonged to the Bute estate and the council was relatively powerless to direct the city's economic affairs. The same would apply to most towns without substantial corporate estates. In general, then, Daunton explains the cycle of economy and expenditure in Cardiff council policy by party political rivalry, initially between Liberal and Conservative, later between proponents and opponents of municipal trading, lastly from the internal tensions of Liberalism as Labour made headway.

We can adduce many reasons for the absence of élite participation in borough councils, more pressing perhaps than an alleged small

tradesmen's revolt. It was commonly asserted that the dignity and significance of council affairs were insufficient to attract local notables.
Local government was subdivided between too many *ad hoc* authorities. The separation of boards of guardians and school boards from
town councils was the most glaring instance of this; on the other hand
improvement commissions were gradually wound up, and by 1879
only fourteen of 240 municipal boroughs had a sanitary authority
separate from the town council. Later, as the councils became larger,
compendious, multi-purpose authorities, adding education and
welfare services to their business, they began to lose some trading
functions. The emphasis shifted from municipal to national public
ownership; and local government seemed no more than a branch
office of central government. The scope of council work thus discouraged socially or intellectually eminent candidates.

The community's élite might also be deterred from council work
because they were jealous of their time or disenchanted with party discipline and the process of popular election. Absorption in business
was alone sufficient excuse for avoiding the council; increasingly, too,
the traditional élite was buffeted by upstarts or it moved from town to
country. The Webbs observed this of late-nineteenth-century
Leicester, where factory organization in the boot trade brought to the
fore 'a new and somewhat rough class of employer'. Gradually 'the old
families of Paget, Whetstone, Ellis, Johnson, etc., dropped out of
municipal life – becoming MPs and semi-county people – if
remaining in Leicester, tending to become an aristocracy'. It may be
argued, *a priori*, however, that the élite could not enhance their status
by becoming councillors. Their 'natural' leadership and social
position might thereby be underlined, but less certainly than by
participation in chambers of commerce, trade and professional
associations, or voluntary societies with a religious or philanthropic
appeal. This last was generally the preferred leisure pursuit of local
notables. It was esteemed above council work because practically less
demanding and socially more rewarding. It also wore a non-partisan
appearance. A distaste for council politics was rife, because this sub-
stituted debate for deference. That instinct was compounded with the
emergence of Labour. A. L. Lowell indeed correlated the increase in
Labour members with the declining quality of councils. Finally, we
may speculate that the élite did not require council membership to
influence council decisions. They had access through numerous
channels, business, private, and social, to make opinions known to

councillors and officials, to organize mutual protection, and to challenge or modify the adoption of policies which might disturb their interests. A check to this surreptitious influence might be administered by party organization. The Webbs argued this from Newcastle, where until the late nineteenth century most elections were not subject to party contests. As a result the leading local capitalists exploited the corporation, obtaining favourable terms as 'buyers and lessees of its land and port facilities, and in their arrangements for the composite payment of town dues, and in the control of the gas works, water works and tramways'. The strength of party control everywhere was various; but Newcastle notwithstanding, the bigger the city the tighter the party domination was the rule. The caucus operations in Birmingham and Liverpool after 1867 epitomize this, although we should heed Derek Fraser, in *Urban Politics in Victorian England* (1976), when he advises that late Victorian caucuses constituted, not a new departure, rather 'the formalization, systemization and perhaps exaggeration of a political structure which had existed in English towns for half a century'. Fraser points to the politicization of most local government institutions – vestries, boards of guardians, school boards and improvement commissions, as well as borough councils – fairly consistently from 1835; but until the 1880s the contest for urban power was essentially middle-class in nature. The variables which made for different intensities of conflict were family (newcomers versus establishment), personality, religion, party ideology, organization and patronage, and the financial relations between town and county, borough and government, and central and suburban zones. Leeds, Manchester, Liverpool, and Birmingham furnish Fraser with the bulk of his evidence, though Leicester, Nottingham, Salford, Bradford, Gateshead, Sheffield, and Preston feature in supporting roles. Other historians' work corroborates this picture. Robert Newton's *Victorian Exeter* (1968) revealed persistent party politics in that council, as did G. W. Jones's *Borough Politics* (1969), a study of Wolverhampton Council, 1888–1964, though there party conflict was tepid before the advent of Labour.

National party forms, however, did not fit snugly into borough politics and administration. There was less blind adherence to party tickets in elections; and party politics might disappear in council and committee proceedings, in the absence of agreed programmes of municipal action, in the rousing of the wards' sectional interests or individuals' vested interests, and in the excitement generated by a big local question, like the Rivington Pike water scheme which blasted party-voting in Liverpool in the 1840s and 1850s. All party majorities in borough councils were prone to fracture. Cross-voting in the council chamber was commonest when issues of 'economy' or temperance were raised; party-voting was commonest when municipal interference with private enterprise and the establishment of new services were debated as matters of principle, and when a Labour group arose. Party discipline was always liable to waver when party domination was complete: in Exeter where the Conservatives held power for sixty-four years between 1835 and 1914, in Leeds where the Liberals were the largest single council party for sixty-six years, or in Liverpool where the Conservatives controlled the corporation for all but nine years.

Altogether the presence of party in borough government was a beneficial force. Able candidates might be debarred for purely party reasons; and, where a party supremacy existed without effective opposition, corruption and cronyism might flourish. But, generally, what George Brodrick asserted in 1875 seems sound, that 'where local party spirit runs high, there is much less danger of public interests being neglected, than where a non-political local oligarchy rules supreme'. A. L. Lowell, an American, was qualified to put this issue in perspective. He judged in 1908 that 'English towns have, as a rule, been singularly free from corruption'. Bribery and treating occurred in municipal as in parliamentary elections: less after the secret ballot than before but occasionally luridly still, as at Shrewsbury in 1902. The corruption of council members and officers was sometimes uncovered also with regard to brewers, publicans and the licensing laws, and property-owners, building contractors, and corporation improvements; and the expansion of municipal employment brought instances of illegitimate personal and political patronage and, more rarely, falsification of accounts.

The law was not indifferent to this problem. The Municipal Corporations Act, 1882, provided that 'a member of the Council shall not vote or take part in the discussion of any matter before the Council, or a Committee, in which he has, directly or indirectly, by himself or by his partner, any pecuniary interest'. There were difficulties and loopholes in its operation. Councillors who were trade-union officials in a sense represented both sides, the council itself as an employer, the gasmen or whoever as council employees. Equally problematical was the spread of limited liability companies to embrace a wider investing public. It was important for interests to be known where public contracts were involved; it was undesirable for a council to be deprived of the advice of all who held shares in companies with which a corporation might deal. It was not the interest itself, however sizeable, rather its concealment, which was fraught with danger. Where party spirit, leaky individuals, and journalists were active the scope for dishonest dealings was limited. In E. D. Simon's opinion, it was 'almost universal experience that a committee cannot be trusted to keep a secret'. The public had been permitted to listen to council debates since 1835, and the press fed upon this facility to provide extensive discussion of council affairs. The statutory right of the press to attend council meetings was formalized in 1908. By special resolution a council might exclude reporters when sensitive committee business was discussed. The opposite applied to the committees themselves: the press was normally excluded, though it might be invited.

How well did the press fulfil its vigilante function? Many journalists regretted the libel laws which gagged disclosure or speculation, and the dependence of the press on profits from advertising which exercised subtle persuasion in favour of business interests. George Bernard Shaw argued limpidly, 'No censorship on earth could be more complete than the simple practice of the British Press in private hands.' By the 1870s about £100,000 was thought necessary to found and operate a London daily with any chance of success; about £20–30,000 for a local paper. These requirements had doubled by 1900. A steady if uneven tendency to concentration of ownership followed.

Some syndicates ran newspapers for party political, not commercial, reasons. A. J. Lee's *The Origins of the Popular Press, 1855–1914* (1976) notes the number of councillors and MPs among newspaper proprietors and influential shareholders. From J. Christie-Miller's *History of the Stockport Advertiser* (1972) we can trace developments in one locality. Founded by James Lomax in 1822, the *Stockport Advertiser* remained in the family, as a paper of independent Tory hue, until 1873, when it was sold to William Swain and Alfred Bearby. Bearby was the editor, but Swain as business manager was the decisive force. He launched or purchased seven other *Advertisers* in ten years, extending their presses over south Manchester and east and central Cheshire. Swain was not a political partisan. He was not a good businessman either, and he over-extended. The scale of operations, however, attracted local Conservatives. They took over the presses as a limited company in 1888. Among the shareholders were the Sykes family, leaders of the Tory interest in Stockport, Sir William Brooks (MP for Altrincham), and W. J. Legh (first Lord Newton). No dividend was paid on ordinary shares; and subsidies were obtained from Conservative funds in 1892, two years after the price of the *Stockport Advertiser* was reduced from 2*d.* to 1*d.* This was not a commercial decision. Circulation, even at financial loss, was vital for political purposes.

Impartial inquiry was hardly rampant in these conditions. Politicians everywhere brandished personal megaphones, like J. J. Colman and J. H. Tillett in East Anglia, or Joseph Cowen and Samuel Storey in Newcastle and Sunderland. But higher standards existed too. The *Manchester Guardian, Liverpool Daily Post, Birmingham Daily Post,* and *Yorkshire Post,* though sporting party favours, all beamed searchlights in the public interest and claimed circulations above 20,000 daily by the late 1880s. Moreover, the number of towns having more than one daily paper rose from 16 in 1868, to 50 in 1885, and 71 in 1900. Though this number fell to 57 by 1910, competition discouraged conspiratorial concealment.

The electorate rather than the press was the ultimate umpire of the politicians. It exercised its powers fitfully. In the 1840s and 1850s, in any given year, half the boroughs had no contested elections; later, in 1899, Lowell's random survey of 103 boroughs and urban districts disclosed under half the seats contested, including thirteen places without any contests. Appreciative or apathetic, it seems that democracy was more dumb than vocal. This is misleading. Aggregated figures conceal the state of the parties in different towns. Take Bristol, Leeds, Liverpool, and Nottingham, four substantial cities, in 1893. Each city comprised sixteen wards, but there were six contests in Bristol and Nottingham, twelve in Liverpool, and fifteen in Leeds. The explanation is that recent elections in Leeds had placed the Conservatives in a position to wrest control from the Liberals, as they had not been since 1872–4; and in Liverpool the Conservatives were ardently seeking to recover the council control which they had lost in 1892. Had another set of municipal elections been taken, the political temperature would vary again – for instance, six years earlier, in 1887, there were only two contested elections in Liverpool. Most places had moments of passion as well as of passivity; and, though polls were generally lower than in parliamentary elections, this was not always by a large margin. In Wolverhampton in the 1890s, for instance, few wards were contested but those that were brought out 65 to 75 per cent of voters.

George Jones concluded about Wolverhampton that most citizens had no continuous or profound interest in local government: 'very few people keep the system going'. Certainly averages of election turn-out suggest that the public's attitude to local government was lukewarm and grudging; but because these figures disguise extreme fluctuations of indifference and commitment, from place to place and from time to time, this depressing overall conclusion may not be warranted. Another point may be made in this connection. It was often alleged that, though a larger (county or regional) authority might deal more competently with issues arising, it would sacrifice that electoral intimacy which the smaller (parish or borough) unit of local government possessed. But, since the case for a persistent correlation between electoral participation and the sizes and/or powers of local government units cannot be sustained, there would appear to be no democratic principle at stake which would prevent the determination of local government units according to other criteria, of resource capacity and service efficiency. That questions of popular interest and local government structure should be considered separately was argued by those who faulted the electoral system itself.

All adults were not legal citizens because all were not enfranchised. For most of our period the voting qualifications were determined by the Municipal Franchise Act, 1869. Rate-paying remained fundamental, but the period during which a person must pay rates in order to qualify as a voter was reduced from the two-and-a-half years prescribed by the 1835 Act to one year in 1869. The 1869 Act also confirmed the franchise of compounders, that is, occupiers of cheaper property who compounded their rate-paying in the rent they paid to their landlords. This had two results: it expanded the overall electorate and it made more uniform the percentage of voters in boroughs everywhere. Before 1869 the size of municipal electorates varied markedly, owing to the disputed eligibility of compounders and to the levels of rentals below which compounding occurred. The 1869 Act additionally enfranchised women who fulfilled the rate-paying qualifications. This meant widows or spinsters, not married women since their property was legally their husbands'. Broadly the 1869 revision resulted in municipal electorates which comprised 18–20 per cent of *total* borough populations. Because of the inclusion of women in the municipal roll, and plural voters in the parliamentary roll, it is difficult to correlate municipal and parliamentary electorates. Probably the municipal electorates were more extensive between 1869 and 1885; thereafter they were more evenly matched, around 60 per cent of adult males, though the generally low parliamentary franchise levels of big cities make this supposition hazardous.

Here we should emphasize one implication of these franchise restrictions for municipal government. It is clear that historians must judge the level of citizen interest in local government, and the level of services furnished by local government, within the perspective of the electoral system. The provision, and especially the distribution, of local government services will not remain the same under a fully democratic system as under a limited franchise. Democratic politics portend more social politics. However, without a single day for polling in all areas, it was hard to present local government as a national concern. When only one-third, at most, of councillors were seeking re-election in any one year, and when the aldermanic system might neutralize that, the electorate was discouraged by the difficulty of achieving political change. Invariably only a popular majority sustained over several years could alter the political complexion of a council.

III

It has been argued in the foregoing section that, since both the interest shown by the electorate and the scrutiny undertaken by the press lacked sharpness, it was mainly up to the politicians and their officials to drive themselves forward and to monitor their progress. What type and quality of services did they provide, and what considerations governed their supply? Before the mid-nineteenth century the priorities were public order, street maintenance and lighting, and the provision of basic sanitary services. There was some investment in gas and water supply; but the scale of public utilities and municipal trading subsequently was altogether grander. What accounts for this? According to Lowell, the party political side was unobvious. Municipal trading, he wrote in 1908, though 'more controversial than any other English question, [was] not strictly a matter of party politics'. Many councils embarked upon municipal trading without fully reckoning the political implications. This was improvisation, in a common-sense manner. So R. C. K. Ensor thought: 'They were simply empirical Englishmen facing public needs, and trying to meet each of them specifically in what appeared the most practical way.' In fact the exercise was not devoid of principle. Always the spectre of socialist collectivism caused unease. A Whig authority on local government, George Brodrick, writing in the *Nineteenth Century*, April 1884, denied that the Public Health and Education Acts were socialistic. They were 'founded on reasons of public utility, and not on the principle of equalizing the lots of the higher and lower classes in the community'. Yet this same authority, in the same journal five months earlier, argued that socialism was already established in English legislation. It was probably introduced by the 1834 Poor Law Amendment Act, Brodrick wrote; certainly by the 1881 Irish Land Act. Legislators were susceptible to socialist contamination because of 'the presence of one party to bid against the other for democratic support'.

Other politicians evinced comparable confusion. In 1881 John Morley thought it peculiar 'that in the country where Socialism has been less talked about than any other country in Europe its principles have been most extensively applied'. Joseph Chamberlain seemed even wilder when he proclaimed at Warrington, on 8 September 1885, that he was undeterred that the Radical programme was thought socialist.

The Poor-Law is Socialism, the Education Act is Socialism, the great part of our municipal work is Socialism; every kindly act of legislation by which the community recognises its responsibility and obligations to its poorer members is socialistic, and it is none the worse for that (cheers). Our object is the elevation of the poor (hear, hear) of the masses of the people – a levelling up which shall do something to remove the excessive inequalities in the social condition of the people, and which is now one of the greatest dangers as well as the greatest injury to the State (hear, hear and cheers).

Actually, in that sentence where he talked of levelling, and further when he advocated 'graduated taxation . . . which is proportioned to the superfluities of the taxpayer', Chamberlain flirted with socialism; but generally he used the term indiscriminately. At Manchester on 16 January 1895 A. J. Balfour grasped what was intended. He extolled 'social legislation' as the 'direct opposite and . . . most effective antidote' to socialist legislation. 'Social legislation' was designed to raise the standard of life and to reduce public inefficiency without endangering the continuity of institutions, without inaugurating class confiscation, and without confining individual enterprise.

State or municipal ownership of production, direction of trade and industry in a planned economy, and redistribution of wealth by socialist taxation, were anathematized. That is why, in the system of social security established before 1914, the contributory principle was embodied in the National Insurance scheme, and old-age pensions were set at a level inadequate for subsistence unless supplemented by personal savings or family assistance. Individualism was to be stimulated by the collectivism of 'social legislation', not enfeebled and displaced by coercive socialism and regimented egalitarianism. The prevailing philosophical model of society was the organic, evolutionary concept. This postulated no abrupt discontinuities, no irreconcilable conflicts. It was perfectly expressed by a subsequent Master of Balliol, A. D. Lindsay, who was raised in this tradition: 'I am a conservative, a liberal, and a socialist.'

It is in this philosophical perspective that the growth of municipal trading and public services should be viewed. If there was a distinct ideology about it, it was rather municipal capitalism than municipal socialism. This was how one leading exponent saw it, the Tory Democrat, A. K. Rollit, who from 1890 to 1906 was President of the Association of Municipal Corporations. The municipality should do what individuals 'cannot do, or do so well, for themselves'. By 'wise Collectivism' the *civis* would become a focus of loyalty and source of inspiration to its citizens. Socialism was a point of reference in the conception, but hard-headed municipalists were clear about their relation to it: 'the adoption of what is good [in socialism] is the best preventive of what is bad.' Expenditure on schools, hospitals, roads and slum clearance, and the operation of water, gas, electricity, and transport undertakings, were in the nature of social investment capital to maximize the product of private enterprise. This was consonant with Bentham's dictum: 'All government is a great evil, nevertheless when by the exercise of that evil a greater evil is prevented such action takes the name and character of good.' And it tuned with J. S. Mill's opinion that government had the right to operate, or to control by taxation, services of general utility or necessity which were monopolies or were managed incompetently by private enterprise. Here was an amber light to nose ahead, though the junction of municipal and private enterprise was not traversed without commotion or recrimination.

Mill indicated water and gas companies as proper cases for municipalization because, 'though perfect freedom is allowed to competition,
none really takes place, and practically they are found to be even more
irresponsible and unapproachable by individual complaints than the
Government'. Regarding water supply, Chadwick's Report on the
fifty largest towns in 1842 had implacably condemned private enterprise. Only in six instances were the arrangements deemed good;
thirteen were styled indifferent, and thirty-one 'so deficient as to be
pronounced bad'. Legislation in 1847–8 permitted municipalities to
establish their own, or to transfer privately owned, water companies.
Some had done this already, by private Bill procedure. Additional
legislation in 1870 and 1875 cheapened and speeded the process.
Nevertheless, municipalization was not uninhibited. Local authorities might not oust companies which supplied water 'proper and sufficient for all reasonable purposes', unless by agreement. An onus lay
upon the municipality to prove mismanagement or failure by a company. Upon this test authority was given or withheld and terms of
compensation were slight or generous. Permission was refused to
Eastbourne and Southampton in 1897, Hartlepool and Norwich in
1898, Cambridge in 1911. The assumption of water supply by local
authorities was irregular. By 1871 250 of 783 urban districts provided
some supply; by 1879 413 of 944 urban districts were doing so, while
290 were supplied by companies. In most cases the authorities had
constructed the waterworks themselves. Where they were purchased,
more transactions were by agreement than arbitration.

It is worth pausing to notice the number of urban districts (not all
were municipalities) which still lacked piped water. Most places suffered some restriction in supply: either turned off during certain times
or fed through a common stand-pipe instead of directly into the home.
Not until the late 1890s and after did urban domestic water supply
become practically universal. In 1879, however, 241 urban districts
were without any piped supply. Generally, these were not towns of
enormous size, though Portsmouth was one with over 120,000 people
and the Pottery conurbation of Hanley, Longton, and Stoke was
another. Still, the striking feature of the list is that, so far from
dominating, the maligned northern industrial towns were little represented. There was a cluster of smaller townships, Colne, Haslingden,
and Rawtenstall in Lancashire, Dewsbury and Heckmondwike in
Yorkshire, and the mushroom towns of Birkenhead and Crewe in
Cheshire; but the most conspicuously negligent were older

established towns. There was Chester in the north; otherwise the offenders were all in the south: Exeter, St. Albans, Hitchin, Guildford, Salisbury, Ashford, Beckenham, Chatham, and Gravesend. Several extra-metropolitan growth areas featured too, Kingston upon Thames, Epsom, Barnet, Ealing, and Hornsey; so did some resorts, Bournemouth, Torquay, Folkestone, and Tunbridge Wells, which evidently bargained on attracting visitors more by external show than fundamental services.

The position in 1897 was as follows:

Type of authority	Means of water supply			
	1	2	3	4
	by the local authority itself	*by another local authority*	*by private companies*	*by 1 + 2 or 1 + 3*
County boroughs	44	1	19	0
Municipal boroughs	121	26	78	11
Urban districts	223	199	249	23

By 1914 two-thirds of the population were supplied by a public authority. Fifty-one county boroughs, 151 municipal boroughs, and 298 urban districts then managed their own waterworks; in addition there were 35 joint authorities. Even by 1903 – that is, before the formation of the Metropolitan Water Board – the capital outlay totalled almost £57m. This constituted the largest item in municipal trading accounts and practically half of the loan indebtedness.

In previous centuries water supply was one of several environmental factors which set limits to urban growth. Now, by sophisticated technology and enlarged wealth, this confinement was broken; but for the larger cities the massive cost of extending supplies brought political turmoil. In Liverpool the Rivington Pike scheme unhinged council party alignments from 1847 to 1857, as did the Lake Vyrnwy scheme four decades later, when new supplies were sought fifty miles away in Montgomeryshire. Birmingham too looked to Wales for its water, above 70 miles to the rivers Elan and Claerwen; Manchester tapped Thirlmere, 80 miles away in the Lake District; and Leicester, Nottingham, and Derby drew upon the Derwent Valley, respectively 60, 40 and 35 miles away. The problem was aggravated not merely by population growth but by rising standards of life and the multiplication of amenities. Between 1850 and 1900 Manchester's population doubled, and its daily supply of water quadrupled, from 8 to 32 million gallons. Eighty per cent of Manchester homes had their own tap by 1876; but, regarding sewerage, Manchester's ashpit system was inferior to towns which had introduced water-closets. As for fitted baths, an engineer reckoned in 1931 that the average number of houses which possessed this amenity, in various northern and Midlands industrial towns, was 5 per cent in 1894, 10 per cent in 1904, and 20 per cent in 1914. Public swimming-baths and wash-houses increased the demand for water; so did industrial use. One new application was the water-pumped lift in tall buildings. Birmingham used 30,000 gallons daily for this in 1885, 90,000 gallons in 1890.

Supply was not the sole problem. Purity mattered, and here the municipalities' record was less satisfactory. Many rivers were seriously polluted, not only by industrial waste but by untreated sewage which the municipalities themselves discharged or allowed others to dump. Waterborne diseases were not yet eliminated. Typhoid outbreaks were common into the 1870s, and isolated epidemics occurred thereafter in places with particularly inadequate systems of sewerage and water supply, as at Cambridge in 1887 and at Maidstone and King's Lynn in 1897. Still, by the late nineteenth century English cities were relatively immunized from the cholera epidemics whose visitations inflicted heavy mortality in European cities. The last severe cholera epidemic to visit England was in 1866. Some 15,000 people died, mostly in concentrated poor working-class zones like London's East End or Liverpool's dockside district. The number of deaths, nevertheless, was half that of the previous visitation, in 1853–4, and a quarter that of 1848–9. It was to prevent contamination as much as to ensure supply of water that co-ordination between local authorities was required. But there were few regional schemes under way before 1914, despite the urging of several public inquiries, the latest being a Joint Select Committee in 1910 which recommended the establishment of a Central Administrative Authority, with representative regional boards, to supervise the allocation of the country's water resources.

The municipalization of gas contains some different features from the municipalization of water, though Mill considered the principle the same. In both, and again in the case of tramways, the disturbance to public highways from the laying of services roused the municipal authorities' interest. Then there was the important or essential nature of these services, and the de facto monopoly conditions enjoyed by most private gas companies. Some towns were served by more than one company but, through amalgamations, price-fixing, and agreed territorial spheres, argued H. E. Finer in *Municipal Trading* (1941), 'competition practically ceased in the provinces, by 1850, and in London by 1860'. Nine municipalities assumed control of their gas supply before 1850; another 18 did so in the 1850s, 22 in the 1860s, 76 in the 1870s, 24 in the 1880s, 50 in the 1890s, and 25 between 1901 and 1910. Over two-thirds were northern and Midlands towns, but several large cities, Liverpool, Sheffield, Newcastle, and Bristol, as well as London, remained in the grip of private companies. By Edwardian times local authority gas sales comprised 37 per cent of the total. Their consumers, though falling from 47 to 41 per cent between 1885 and 1913, rose in aggregate from 980,000 to 2,888,000. The vast increase in domestic users was due chiefly to two inventions: the gas mantle and the slot meter.

Municipalities were not given compulsory powers to supplant private gas companies any more than water companies; but the incentive to purchase was different, as Joseph Chamberlain instructed Birmingham Council in the 1870s: 'When the purchase of the Water Works comes before you it will be a question concerning the health of the town; the acquisition of the Gas Works concerns the profits of the town.' In modern circumstances, Chamberlain added, gas was as much a necessary of life as water; and private companies should not hold communities at ransom. The pricing policy of publicly owned gas companies subsequently was not such as to win unmixed gratitude from consumers; but it may be that, without local authority intervention, the private companies would have exploited their position more. By 1906, on average, local authorities charged 2*s.* 8*d.* and private companies 2*s.* 11¼*d.* per thousand cubic feet of gas. The difference was explained partly by local authority reluctance to take over unprofitable concerns.

The profitability of gas roused arguments which were absent over water supply. Councils were sometimes torn over the application of these profits. In Birmingham Chamberlain argued that, since the corporation possessed no extensive estates, essential town improvements would be deferred unless some revenue other than the rates was found. Gas profits were his salvation but this course did not commend itself to every municipalizer. An alternative was to reduce gas charges or relieve the rates, while resisting new public works.

The municipalization of gas, therefore, aggravated political controversy. It also had far-reaching industrial consequences. A deceleration in the movement towards municipal ownership in the 1880s will be noted from figures on page 304. This hesitation was due to commercial possibilities now apparent in electricity. A number of private houses, theatres, railway stations, offices, and public buildings installed electric lighting in 1880–1; and street arc lamps appeared in select areas. Several corporations, led by Manchester, expressed anxiety about the establishment of another private monopoly, or fear for their investment in gas; and they lobbied the Government for some security. Their reward was the 1882 Act, which limited an electricity company's licence to operate to twenty-one years, after which a local authority might purchase the plant at its existing structural value. That meant that no compensation would be made for goodwill, past or future profits, or compulsory purchase.

Apparently, this legislation so discouraged the infant industry that another Act was required in 1888, enlarging the company licence to forty-two years. Whether municipal hostility was primarily responsible for checking the electricity industry in those years, as opponents of municipal trading alleged, is difficult to judge. Private investment too was wary of newfangled enterprises, and technical as well as statutory circumstances inhibited supply. When the industry did develop, from the 1890s, municipal undertakings accounted for two-thirds of the organization and distribution. By 1914 municipal capital indebtedness on electricity works totalled over £30m. Nevertheless, the scale of plant and service was disappointing. The inherent possibilities for relocating industry and for reviving rural resources were barely explored. The early history of this utility betrays the towns' narrow conception of their interests and obligations. But the towns alone should not be censured. Government imagination was dim. The first report of the Central Electricity Board, 1929, blamed the failure to attain economies of large-scale production on 'a strong tendency to relate the generation of electricity to local government areas'.

The same criticism could be made of an allied municipal undertaking, transport. Technical economies and regional services were hindered by too rigid adherence to local government boundaries. The Stalybridge, Hyde, Mossley and Dukinfield Tramways and Electricity Board (1901) was a rare example of four corporations combining before 1914. In the absence of joint boards traffic agreements between contiguous authorities were the minimum necessary; but even in the conurbations there was little progress towards through-running or the standardization of stock and fares. Municipal independence lay behind this quarrelling; but a suburban interest, which believed the exclusion of tramways would preserve property values, also conspired against integrated networks. In Bradford and Leeds, where a difference in tram gauges obtained, trolley-buses were introduced in 1911 as a partial answer to the problem. However, since both municipal and private tram companies were legally inhibited from speculative land development, there was no incentive to plan a strategy of suburban building and transport in any region.

These comments cast a cloud over municipal transport in retrospect, though it was not until Edwardian times that local authorities owned and managed the majority of tramways. The 1870 Tramways Act chiefly licensed private enterprise. Municipalities might build and lease tram systems, but not operate them. However, they were empowered to purchase private systems after twenty-one years, at their existing structural value, and, because of their interest in highways, to regulate the amount and course of traffic. H. E. Finer commented: 'the situation was satisfactory to neither, for a twenty-one years' term was not long enough to stimulate a sense of continuous enterprise in private firms, while local authorities had, in effect, been warned off the direct administration.' An exception was allowed in 1882 when Parliament authorized Huddersfield Corporation to run a tramway in default of a private company willing to take on the task; but not before the 1890s were other local authorities similarly favoured, when the original leases expired. In 1895 33 of the country's 124 tramway systems were local authority built, representing under £2m. capital. In 1905 161 of 276 systems were local authority owned and run, representing nearly £28m. capital. The dramatic rise in investment had two causes: systems were extended, from 264 to 1,196 miles of line; and systems were electrified. In Manchester, for instance, where the system was completely renovated over a five-year period from 1898, when the corporation bought out the Manchester Carriage Company, the cost of electrification alone was £1½m.

By 1913 about 1,500 miles of local authority line existed. Municipal ownership embraced 63 per cent of lines, 71 per cent of capital expenditure, 73 per cent of vehicles, 75 per cent of car miles run, 80 per cent of passengers carried, and 81 per cent of electricity consumed. This last item indicates a fundamental limitation about municipal conceptions. Electricity undertakings were developed mainly to supply tramways, not to rival gas in industrial or domestic consumption: hence they remained tiny and localized. But the tramways' electrification only redoubled forces of inertia and inflexibility in transport, confining traffic areas to inappropriate frontiers, and engendering stubborn corporate opposition to more mobile motor-bus services. In the modern age the municipal area as an economic unit increasingly lacked feasibility. Public ownership, if it was to rival privately owned combines in economies of scale or in the ability to renovate plant, needed regional or national organization.

Of more urgent concern before 1914 was the municipalities' financial strategy. Their aggregate capital indebtedness on utilities was as follows:

Year	Water	Gas	Transport	Electricity
	£m.	£m.	£m.	£m.
1879–80	19.06	9.43	–	–
1884–5	30.33	13.77	1.17	–
1889–90	37.73	14.85	1.28	–
1894–5	43.97	16.93	1.47	1.38
1899–1900	53.4	19.82	5.78	7.85
1904–5	114.7*	23.83	23.31	25.64
1909–10	126.98	23.25	35.97	29.54
1914–15	131.8	22.54	37.9	31.5

* From 1904 the Metropolitan Water Board is included.

The prudence of the municipalities' loan funding and debt repayment policies was a major controversy of the late Victorian and Edwardian periods. Once thought 'practical progress', Municipal Socialism now seemed a rake's progress as debts increased faster than amortization. Total local indebtedness – this includes all services, public health and street improvements as well as municipal trading – increased from £173,208,000 in 1884–5 to £435,545,000 in 1905–6. This represented £1. 3s. 4d. per £ of rateable value in 1884–5, £2. 2s. 10d. in 1905–6. The amount raised in rates at the same dates was £25,667,000 and £56,048,000 respectively. In other words, the debt increased 151 per cent, the yield from rates 118 per cent, and rateable value 37 per cent.

Much of the debt incurred by municipalities, it was argued, was 'wasteful', spent in purchase and compensation of private companies whose undertakings were transferred to municipal ownership. Thus ratepayers were literally paying for a principle, since this money was not used for new investment. Furthermore, municipalities disguised the real costs of their services. Bowing to electoral pressure to maintain low charges, they succumbed to the temptation to 'live on posterity', failing both to tackle debt redemption and to reckon the depreciation of plant. Water supply, essential for public health, was generally exempt from these strictures and a rate-subsidy of prices was forgivable. But the rate-subsidy of uneconomic transport was not; likewise the transfers of gas and electricity profits in aid of rates was thought tantamount to malversation, for these should have been managed on commercial principles. Municipalities also pursued philanthropic policies as regards prices to consumers and wages to employees, this social aim taking precedence over business practice. Once competition from private enterprise was eliminated, the municipalities fell into bad ways, making do with deteriorating equipment rather than offend the electorate by levying higher rates and ploughing back profits to renovate their undertakings.

That there was cause for complaint cannot be doubted; but, without a statutory form of accounts, comparisons between different municipal utilities were stymied. The Joint Select Committee on Municipal Trading (the Crewe Committee), reporting in 1900 and 1903, advocated the discontinuance of the amateurish borough audit; but, since the Government persisted in its respect for borough independence and in its distaste for a central audit, irregular and superficial accounting prevailed. As Arthur Collins, one-time City Treasurer of Birmingham, wrote, the borough auditors' reports were 'more spectacular than practical. Items which disclose any incident of civic feasting or expenses paid to members of the council were emphasized, whilst important matters, such as the adequacy of reserves or depreciation allowances, are seldom dealt with.'

The absence of proper budgeting and auditing of municipal trading deprived friends and critics alike of effective ammunition in their struggle. Monopoly conditions, too, made the judgement of efficiency difficult. Still, political and business interests conspired to raise a storm over the subject, which raged most violently when the Crewe Committee invited depositions in 1900 and *The Times* published a series of hostile articles, from 19 August to 11 November 1902. Prominent on one side were the Liberty and Property Defence League and Industrial Freedom League, and on the other side a miscellany of Municipal Socialists.

Municipal trading's critics complained chiefly about municipal debts rising more steeply than the value of rateable property; about the municipalities' obstruction of technical progress by private firms; about excessive responsibilities crushing elected councillors and officials; and about 'political' interference with market 'laws' governing prices for goods and labour, which would pave the path to socialism. The author of *The Times* articles against municipal trading, Edwin A. Pratt, connected this question with the long-standing controversy about railway freight rates, which affected the country's commercial and industrial welfare. One reason for the railways' rising charges was heavy working expenses and one cause of that, Pratt argued in *Railways and their Rates* (1905), was 'the dead-weight of local taxation', the 'policy of plunder', the 'abnormal', 'iniquitous' and 'extortionate' sums which railway companies had to pay in local authority rates.

Still, even Pratt was not inclined to blame the railways' costing problems entirely on local authority taxation. There was disingenuousness and misdirection in the onslaughts of others, too. Many a slum-owner, for instance, profited from the Housing of the Working Classes legislation, under which local authorities were compelled to pay exaggerated prices and substantial compensation to acquire properties for clearance. There were also numerous property-owners whose land and buildings inflated in value through local authority improvements and amenities. Subsequent increases in rateable value invariably fell short of the real appreciation to the owners; but Parliament would not concede the local authorities' claim to levy a betterment tax. This account does not exhaust the list of private interests which directly or indirectly profited from public action. About 23 per cent of poor-law expenditure on medical relief in 1904 was consumed in 'administration'. Numerous lawyers, doctors, builders, contractors, and suppliers were locked into the system; cheap energy and lighting subsidized big business more than poor people; and cheap workmen's fares on trams both supplied industry with ready labour and advanced the social good by deconcentrating housing. Hence, we should not be surprised to discover that more than principles moved the Liberty and Property Defence League and Industrial Freedom League. First Edward Bristow, in 'The Liberty and Property Defence League and Individualism' (*Historical Journal*, XVIII, 4, 1975), then Avner Offer, in *Property and Politics, 1870–1914* (1981), emphasized the financial backing given to these protest groups by electricity trusts, which writhed under local authority curbs on the extension of their generating and tramway networks. Here was a sinister aspect; but the tactics which the companies employed should not tempt us summarily to dismiss their case. This was that lower prices would result from economies of scale if they were permitted to build huge generating plant at pitheads to supply electricity to entire regions. Furthermore, many heeded the critics of municipal trading when they drew attention to the increasing army of civic dependents.

The size of municipal employment, more obvious than the deficiencies of municipal book-keeping, roused general fears. The ability of municipal employees to inconvenience the public, and thereby press upon politicians, was prefigured nationally by the postal workers' unionization. R. W. Hanbury, Financial Secretary of the Treasury, declared in 1898: 'We have done away with personal and individual bribery, but there is a still worse form of bribery, and that is when a man asks a candidate to buy his vote out of the public purse.' Controversy over post-office workers' wages and conditions punctuated late Victorian and Edwardian politics and necessitated frequent inquiry, the Tweedmouth Royal Commission of 1897 and the Bradford, Hobhouse and Holt Committees of 1903–4, 1907, and 1913.

An official report of earnings in the public utility sector in 1906 hardly supplied proof of municipal extravagance. Average annual earnings were £78 per man in gas supply, £70 in water supply, and £62.5 in road and sanitary services. These were unexceptional. Nevertheless the rise of Labour representation seemed likely to speed the municipal employees' claims for preferential treatment. Many, not only Labour councillors, believed that local authorities should, from common justice, behave as model employers; but few had confidence in their ability to avoid becoming indulgent employers. It was true that municipal gas and water workers were forbidden, under the Conspiracy and Protection of Property Act, 1875, to imperil their service to the community by strike action, and the same penalty was extended to electricity workers in 1919. Nevertheless, trade unionization in the municipal service was troublesome, particularly in public transport; and everywhere councillors began to count their electoral influence. Not all would be voters, and they could not swing elections alone; but Birmingham Corporation, for instance, had 7,000 municipal employees in 1903 and reckoned another 1,500 when the tramways were municipalized. The general public shared these alarms if the disfavour which befell the LCC's Works Department is a guide. The

Progressives who established this staff in 1892 argued that they were driven to it from the expensiveness and shortcomings of a system of contractors; but allegations about spendthrift and slack administration influenced the electorate to dismiss the Progressives in the 1907 elections. Provincial borough councillors concluded that the best way to fulfil their fiduciary responsibility in regard to ratepayers, and to maintain their seats, was to restrain the size of the corporate service.

The proponents of Municipal Socialism were not without excitement either. In *The Commonsense of Municipal Trading* (1904) George Bernard Shaw felt that 'the political struggle over it may come nearer to a civil war than any issue raised in England since the Reform Bill of 1832'. Keir Hardie, in *The Co-operative Annual* (1901), employed similar language:

The battle now waged around Municipal trading is but the renewal of a struggle carried on for two hundred years against king, cleric, and lordling ere yet there was a Parliament in being. The issues remain the same, however much the methods may have changed. As the burghers triumphed then, so will they now. Already property of the estimated value of £500,000,000 has passed from private to public ownership. The citizens of our time are beginning to realize the benefits which follow in the train of common ownership. On every side can be seen the dawning of the idea that were the means of producing the fundamental necessaries of life – food, clothing, shelter – owned communally, as many of the conveniences already are, the problem of poverty would be solved.

The ideologues and faddists comprised a minority among the general public, probably also among borough councillors. An undoctrinaire pursuit of those elusive targets, efficiency and economy, moved most citizens. The comprehensive municipalization of housing, banking and pawnbroking, harbours, telephones, transport, hospitals, restaurants, milk, bread, meat, clothing, alcoholic drink, and coal retailing remained far from practical politics. Though municipalities experimented in the supply of many of these, they were limited in their impact and did not constitute a monopoly. Local authority housing, for example, contributed less than 2 per cent of housing stock before 1914. No socialist imperative moved the majority of councillors who acted in the housing question. The sanitary aspect was paramount. Slum clearance work was hampered by rising land prices and by the excessive sums required to compensate owners; nevertheless, fierce battles were waged over private legislation like the Liverpool Act of 1864 or the Government's 1875 and

1890 Housing Acts, to determine equitably public and private interests. Few advocated council housing as an end in itself. Where it was supplied it was supplied reluctantly, in default of provision by private builders. The socialist case for council housing was the just use of the public purse to furnish the needy with decent accommodation. By contrast, correct political economy still prevailed in those councils which embarked upon housing provision. They generally insisted that rents should cover the interest on the loans. Without exchequer subsidies until 1919, council housing failed to accommodate those most in need.

Restrictions hedged other municipal adventures. Thus a Municipal Savings Bank, founded in Birmingham in 1916, was confined by a stipulation that its borrowing should reflect current banking rates. Hull and several other towns established municipal telephone services. Resort towns ventured into the entertainments industry (Bournemouth and Bexhill even sponsored municipal orchestras). Doncaster managed a racecourse, Worcester a dairy, Wolverhampton a cold store, Sheffield a printing plant; and Liverpool organized a supply of sterilized milk. Each instance of municipal activity was a special dispensation. Though their miscellaneous spread worried many politicians and caused them to think that the pass might have been sold, altogether they did not presage that transfer of control from private to municipal enterprise which socialist zealots demanded. R. H. Tawney summed up the position harshly in his Commonplace Book, in November 1914:

The *motive* of nearly all these developments has been a purely utilitarian consideration for the consumer. They have not been inspired by any desire to introduce juster social arrangements, nor, in particular, by any consideration for the wage-earner. They have been inspired simply by the desire for cheap services akin to the free trade agitation. In fact the two movements appealed to much the same classes. Manchester manufacturers want cheap gas and electricity for exactly the same reason that they want cheap cotton and machinery. Clearly there are no germs of a revolution here.

Two years earlier, in 1912, the first academically reputable survey of the subject had been published, Douglas Knoop's *Principles and Methods of Municipal Trading*. His conclusions brought no comfort to municipal adventurers. Services which were natural monopolies, he affirmed, might be managed municipally, with least disadvantage. Otherwise he believed that 'municipal trading in itself cannot be regarded as a desirable institution' and 'the management of industrial undertakings is not really a suitable sphere of activity for a local authority'.

Knoop's opinion was commonly held. The municipal provision of services was a *pis aller*. Progress was particularly limping in respect of supererogatory, non-profitable services. Voluntary provision was preferred, because this postulated individual effort and class harmony growing through personal contact and charity. Consider public libraries, their finances limited by a maximum rate of a halfpenny under an Act of 1850, and from 1855 to 1919 by a penny rate. In the late 1870s eighty-six rate-supported libraries existed, but the economist W. S. Jevons, in the *Contemporary Review*, March 1881, preferred not to applaud these towns but rather to castigate those without a service. Arguing that every town of 20,000 people should have a rate-supported library, Jevons compiled a 'formidable' list of defaulters. This included most districts of London, Accrington, Ashton, Barnsley, Bath, Batley, Burnley, Burton, Carlisle, Chatham, Cheltenham, Colchester, Croydon, Darlington, Dewsbury, Devonport, Dover, Dudley, Gateshead, Gravesend, Grimsby, Halifax, Hastings, Huddersfield, Hull, Lincoln, Portsmouth, Rotherham, Scarborough, Shrewsbury, Stalybridge, Stockton, Torquay, Wakefield, Yarmouth, and York. This was not an exhaustive list.

Following the 1870 Education Act, the public-library movement developed more momentum. By 1900 about thirty towns had presented local Bills to exceed the penny-rate limitation; but unenthusiasm was not overcome generally. Since free libraries were conceived as a service to the working classes foremost, the question had to be argued whether those classes were impervious to improvement. 'Oxfordshire people don't want to read,' it was confidently proclaimed during a debate in that council, which rejected the offer of a Carnegie grant to establish a library whose maintenance would fall on the rates. Oxfordshire did not adopt the Public Libraries Act until 1923. Too many urban authorities echoed its feelings about an inessential and unwanted service. Not that it was unreasonable to be sceptical of those who descanted upon the miraculous physic of books for the people. The first free library in Southampton started in 1889, according to A. Temple Patterson, 'in two rooms over a stable in St. Mary's Street, from which the librarian had sometimes to be escorted home by a policeman to prevent him from being molested or manhandled by the roughs of the neighbourhood'. The enterprise progressed only after new premises were made available in 1892. Suspicion of the working-class public was not dead, however, for it was not until 1894 that one library, Clerkenwell, gave borrowers open access to its shelves; and controversy surrounded the extension of this practice in other places. In Edwardian times a sizeable reading public at last emerged. United Kingdom library loans doubled between 1896 and 1911, from 26,225,000 to 54,256,000 book issues; and expenditure on the public-library service rose from £286,000 to £805,000. But fewer than 5 per cent of the population were registered borrowers.

Broadly, then, the public-library movement scarcely gave cause for unstinted satisfaction about the willingness of municipalities to furnish the community with scintillating amenities. By 1919, 91 boroughs and 550 urban districts still had not provided a library, and those that existed were invariably poorly stocked and organized. Without benefactions, such as the Carnegie Trust, which injected large doses of money, or the Mechanics' Institutes, whose collections of books provided the nucleus of many public libraries, the local authority service would have been even more attenuated. Generally libraries struggled, to gain proper staff and books and to establish branches, for the penny-rate was shared between municipal museums and art galleries as well as libraries. Though the libraries tended to receive the greater part of these funds, this was (and remains) a cinderella service, normally under-supplied and in financially stringent times squeezed even more.

A review of municipal services inevitably results in a mixed account. It is easy to scale down achievement, but an irreducible substance survives. Civic pride had genuine foundations. This was expressed in the craze for historical pageants, mounted in several towns between 1905 and 1909. Liverpool celebrated the septencentenary of its charter in 1907; Bury St. Edmunds, Colchester, Coventry, Oxford, St. Albans, and Warwick were others whose citizens re-enacted ancient battles and royal visits, and melodramatized key episodes in their civic past. Innocent of real historical sense though these pageants may have been, they emphasized the continuing honour and fulfilment of civic life. This was richer in the modern city than in the past. No one was going to stage a morality play about the municipalization of a gas works but, as the companies of amateur actors perambulated about their public parks in 1907, it could not be gainsaid that modern citizens enjoyed more tangible benefits than their forebears.

The strongest testimony to this was that, while a greater proportion of the country was being urbanized, life expectancy was improving. It was a feat to have held the crude average death-rate at between 22 and 25 per 1,000 population in a peak period of industrialization and urbanization, 1840–75. Thenceforward, this fell to below 15 per 1,000 in the years before 1914. Certainly, the toll of infant life was heavy – approaching half of all deaths were of children under five years of age – and infant mortality remained fairly constant before 1900, that is a generation after the general death-rate fell. It was also the case that towns with the highest population densities generally returned the worst mortality rates and that large disparities existed between the death-rates of wealthy middle-class districts and poor working-class districts in cities; but indirectly, by furnishing means by which working-class real earnings rose, and directly, through sanitary services, English towns enhanced the living standards of the nation. This can be underlined by international comparison. In the late nineteenth century it was better to be the citizen of an English city than one of almost any other in the world.

By 1914 England could boast some remarkable civic creations. Consider Greater Birmingham, that formal creation of 1911 which meant that Birmingham overtook Liverpool in size, succeeding to the title of 'second city in the Empire' with a population of 840,000 in an area of 68 square miles. Birmingham City Council, now expanded from 72 to 120 members, had already invested extensively in gas, water, electricity, and tramway undertakings. It had spent £6m. to drink Welsh water, and of its income of £1½m. about one-third resulted from municipal trading profits. The corporation had moved keenly to establish a university and bishopric. On the other hand there was a good deal wanting, in respect of housing and town planning especially. Administratively, the framework of operations remained tangled and unwieldy and if that applied to Greater Birmingham how much more inadequate was the position of smaller boroughs?

In the mid-Victorian period it was plausibly argued that the municipalization of essential services was a sound way to achieve efficiency and economy. By 1914 the current of opinion flowed in reverse, and municipalization (though not yet nationalization) laboured under doubts from which it has never since been freed. Technical, more perhaps than ideological, factors were responsible for this movement out of favour, as they were chiefly responsible for the movement into favour in the first place. Right up to 1914 an extraordinary range of experiments in municipalization had occurred, the span being widened to comprise 'desirable' as well as 'essential' services; and a great stock of goodwill was built up for municipalities as a result. Nonetheless, the belief grew that the existing distribution of municipal areas and type of municipal management could not survive. Major reconstitution was necessary if they were to provide public services appropriate to modern requirements. Considering the outlook for further municipal advances in *A Century of Municipal Progress 1835–1935* (1935), W. A. Robson was emphatic: 'It would be difficult, indeed, to name a single municipal service of any importance in regard to which the areas of administration are such as to satisfy competent expert opinion.'

Hence this review of municipal endeavour ends on a note of frustration; but that fairly summarizes the sixty years of civic activity before 1914. Always it seemed that half the citizenry was wanting the municipal authority to do what it could not do, and the other half was wanting it to stop doing what it could do.

Conclusion

In the high Victorian era, the period which bulks largest in this book, English towns and cities expanded in striking fashion. They also collapsed in spirit, according to popularly held opinion. It is right, however, to rehearse the charge before reaching a verdict. Here is Thomas Sharp, in *Town Planning* (1940):

First there came the degradation of the town: utter black and hopeless degradation. In foul slums and in deserts of dreary byelaw-standardised streets, in the sun-obscuring murk of factory chimneys, the very conception of the town *as a town* disappeared from English minds. By the end of the 19th century, so vilely had the English towns been built in the period of their greatest extension, the whole conception of the town as a home, as a utility for collective living of a good life, as a place where beauty might be created, whence enlightenment might emanate, had vanished into the anything but thin contemporary air. The town was no longer any of these things. It was a mere multiplication of that object of Victorian hate and fear – the workhouse: a hateful prison-workhouse, sordid, brutal, mean. The town should be an object of love and loyalty. The Victorian town was an object of indifference at best, of hatred and loathing at worst.

This book has argued a different case and seeks another judgement, not despondent and denunciatory like Sharp, but not Panglossian either. One repeated emphasis of the book is that we must pay more than lip-service to variety and change among Victorian and Edwardian towns. There was no monolithic and monomorphous Victorian and Edwardian town which emerged complete and then endured, a rigid, relentless manufacturing slum. Towns were of many sorts and there were many sorts within towns. Slums were not a Victorian invention though the Victorians may have been the first to mass-produce them. The housing question, then as now, is partly a matter of aesthetics, mostly a matter of law, politics, and economics. The presence of slums denotes fundamental inequalities of wealth and opportunity as much as malevolent landlords and builders or degenerate and irresponsible tenants. To observe this is not to absolve slum-production, merely to look at it differently.

It returns us to the most pointed lesson of this book. As with slums, so with towns as a whole: they are social, political, economic, and legal compositions. The shape towns take reflects certain geological predispositions but, very properly, it is the human ecology that interests urban historians most. Towns display the economic standing, the social relations, the cultural appreciation, the governmental dynamic, of the people who inhabit them. Towns summarize civilization.

This is why English towns differ from foreign towns. This is why English towns differ from each other. Thus, the response to the question first posed in the Preface – is it worth studying towns? – is plainly an affirmative. History is concentrated there quite as obviously as in courts, cabinets, and parliaments. The history is there: it is another matter to extract and interpret it. The purpose of this book has been to restrain readers from arbitrary conclusions, to encourage them to contemplate the variegated character of their immediate urban past. The anti-urban tradition will not be expelled easily from English historiography, still less from common opinion. But it is a travesty of the evidence to portray Victorian urbanization and its allied industrialization as the principal articles of a Bleak Age of human suffering. Not only does such a view implicitly romanticize earlier times as a Merrie England, it does less than justice to the manner in which Victorian towns and cities and Victorian industry enlarged the material welfare and social satisfactions of most English men and women.

Guide to sources and further reading

Many sources used in the composition of this book are cited in the text. Some are repeated here, together with suggested further reading. Unless otherwise stated, place of publication is London.

Urban history has been well supported by bibliographical collections. The best service that an introductory book like this can do is to point the zealous reader in their direction rather than survey the area in a more superficial manner. The leader is G. H. Martin and Sylvia McIntyre, *A Bibliography of British and Irish Municipal History*, volume I: *General Works*, published in 1972 by Leicester University Press. This is a comprehensive guide to modern publications in urban history, defined as works which were issued subsequent to those listed in Charles Gross, *A Bibliography of British Municipal History* (1897). A second edition of Gross appeared in 1966, under the imprint of Leicester University Press, with a preface by G. H. Martin. Modern urban historians may also profitably use the massive general *Bibliography of British History 1851–1914*, compiled by H. J. Hanham and published by Oxford University Press in 1976. The late H. J. Dyos was adept at making critical surveys of past literature and current trends in urban studies. His essay, 'Agenda for Urban Historians', in H. J. Dyos (ed.), *The Study of Urban History* (1968), acted as a searchlight for the subject; and his summary articles in *Victorian Studies* (1966) and in *British Book News* (1973) may be read with equal interest. It was owing to the enterprise of Professor Dyos that the *Urban History Newsletter* appeared in 1963. Twenty issues followed before the *Urban History Yearbook* supplanted it in 1974. The *Yearbook* has been published annually by Leicester University Press ever since. Both the *Newsletter* and *Yearbook* are essential for the reader who wishes to keep abreast of urban history, for the modern period and any other.

From bibliographical surveys we should turn to general studies of urban history in our period. Three works stand out. One is the aforementioned *Study of Urban History*, edited by H. J. Dyos in 1968, which contains essays first delivered as conference papers. Dyos was co-editor, with Michael Wolff, of a further collection, *The Victorian City*, in two volumes in 1973. This was a more ambitious and altogether less successful project, but no urban historian can fail to be stimulated by some of the essays. Unequal performance is an occupational hazard of works which embrace contributions by many hands. That a single author not only will escape this disadvantage but may soar above the summit of collective enterprise is attested by the achievement of Asa Briggs in *Victorian Cities* (1963, revised 1968). This is justly regarded as a classic; and it was owing to his admiration for that work that this author ventured upon a new arrangement which would avoid comparison with Briggs. Both the Dyos collections and Briggs contain useful select bibliographies.

We may now isolate a small number of works for recommended reading in connection with particular chapters of this book.

Chapter 1

David Cannadine and David Reeder (eds.), *Exploring the Urban Past: Essays in urban history by H. J. Dyos*, Cambridge, 1982.

B. I. Coleman (ed.), *The Idea of the City in Nineteenth-Century Britain*, 1973.

Oscar Handlin and John Burchard (eds.), *The Historian and the City*, Cambridge, Massachusetts, 1963.

J. H. Johnson and C. G. Pooley, *The Structure of Nineteenth-Century Cities*, 1982.

Emrys Jones, *Towns and Cities*, Oxford, 1966.

C. M. Law, 'The growth of the urban population in England and Wales, 1801–1911', *Trans. Instit. Brit. Geogr.* 41 (1967), pp. 125–43.

Peter H. Mann, *An Approach to Urban Sociology*, 1965.

B. R. Mitchell and Phyllis Deane, *Abstract of British Historical Statistics*, Cambridge, 1962.

J. Douglas Porteous, *Canal Ports*, 1977.

Harry W. Richardson, *Urban Economics*, 1971.

Henk Schmal (ed.), *Patterns of European Urbanization since 1500*, 1981.

Murray Stewart (ed.), *The City*, 1972.

Adner F. Weber, *The Growth of Cities in the Nineteenth Century*, New York, 1899; reprinted 1963.

Max Weber, *The City*, 1921; translated and edited by Don Martindale and Gertrud Neuwirth, New York, 1958.

W. D. C. Wright and D. H. Stewart (eds.), *The Exploding City*, Edinburgh, 1972.

Chapter 2

Walter Besant, *South London*, 1899; *East London*, 1901.

Charles Booth, *Life and Labour of the People in London*, 1889–1902.

John H. Davis, 'The Problem of London Local Government Reform, 1880–1900', Oxford D. Phil. thesis, unpublished, 1983.

A. G. Gardiner, *John Benn and the Progressive Movement*, 1925.

Gwilym Gibbon and R. W. Bell, *History of the London County Council*, 1939.

Henry James, *English Hours*, 1905; edited by A. L. Lowe, 1960.

Donald J. Olsen, *The Growth of Victorian London*, 1976.

Gareth Stedman Jones, *Outcast London*, Oxford, 1971.

Paul Thompson, *Socialists, Liberals, and Labour*, 1967.

Anthony S. Wohl, *The Eternal Slum*, 1977.

Ken Young, *Local Politics and the Rise of Party*, Leicester, 1975.

Chapter 3

E. H. Phelps Brown, *The Growth of British Industrial Relations*, 1959.

A. K. Cairncross, *Home and Foreign Investment, 1870–1913*, Cambridge, 1953.

H. A. Clegg, Alan Fox, and A. F. Thompson, *A History of British Trade Unions since 1889*, volume 1, *1889–1910*, Oxford, 1964.

Peter N. Davies, *Henry Tyrer: A Liverpool Shipping Agent and his Enterprise*, 1979.

Robert E. Dickinson, *City Region and Regionalism*, 1947.

T. W. Freeman, *The Conurbations of Great Britain*, Manchester, 1959; revised, 1966.

E. D. Hunt, *British Labour History 1815–1914*, 1981.

Jane Jacobs, *The Economy of Cities*, 1969.

Patrick Joyce, *Work, Society and Politics*, Brighton, 1980.

Tony Mason, *Association Football and English Society, 1863–1915*, Brighton, 1980.

C. A. Moser and W. Scott, *British Towns*, 1961.

A. E. Musson, *The Growth of British Industry*, 1978.

A. Temple Patterson, *A History of Southampton*, volume 3, *1868–1914*, Southampton, 1975.

P. L. Payne, *British Entrepreneurship in the Nineteenth Century*, 1974.

Henry Pelling, *Social Geography of British Elections, 1885–1910*, 1967.

J. B. Priestley, *English Journey*, 1934.

Robert Roberts, *The Classic Slum*, 1971.

Brian T. Robson, *Urban Growth*, 1973.

John Ruskin, *Fors Clavigera*, 1871–84.

Michael Sanderson, *The Universities and British Industry, 1850–1970*, 1972.

Bernard Semmel, *Imperialism and Social Reform*, 1960.

John B. Sharpless, 'Intercity Development and Dependency: Liverpool and Manchester', *Stanford Journal of International Studies*, vol. 13, Spring 1978.

P. J. Waller, *Democracy and Sectarianism: A Political and Social History of Liverpool, 1868–1939*, Liverpool, 1981.

Chapter 4

William Ashworth, *The Genesis of Modern British Town Planning*, 1954.

David Cannadine, *Lords and Landlords: the Aristocracy and the Towns, 1774–1967*, 1980.

Geoffrey Crossick (ed.), *The Lower Middle Class in Britain, 1870–1914*, 1977.
H. J. Dyos, *Victorian Suburb: A Study of the Growth of Camberwell*, Leicester, 1961.
H. J. Dyos and D. H. Aldcroft, *British Transport*, Leicester, 1969.
A. G. Gardiner, *The Life of George Cadbury*, 1923.
A. B. Granville, *The Spas of England*, 1841.
J. R. Kellett, *The Impact of Railways on Victorian Cities*, 1969.
Peter Mathias, *Retailing Revolution*, 1967.
J. A. R. Pimlott, *The Englishman's Holiday*, 1947.
Thomas Sharp, *Town Planning*, 1940.
Eric M. Sigsworth (ed.), *Ports And Resorts in the Regions*, Hull, 1981.
Anthony Sutcliffe (ed.), *Multi-Storey Living*, 1974.
Anthony Sutcliffe, *Towards the Planned City*, Oxford, 1981.
John K. Walton, *The Blackpool Landlady*, Manchester, 1978.
John K. Walton, 'The Demand for Working-Class Seaside Holidays in Victorian England', *Economic History Review*, 2nd ser., xxxiv, no. 2, May 1981.

Chapter 5

George Ewart Evans, *From Mouths of Men*, 1976.
Alan Everitt (ed.), *Perspectives in English Urban History*, 1973.
Alan D. Gilbert, *Religion and Society in Industrial England*, 1976.
H. J. Hanham, *Elections and Party Management*, 1959.
Pamela Horn, *Labouring Life in the Victorian Countryside*, Dublin, 1976.
Richard Jefferies, *Hodge and His Masters*, 1880.
David Jones, *Crime, Protest, Community and Police in Nineteenth-century Britain*, 1982.
J. M. Lee, *Social Leaders and Public Persons*, Oxford, 1963.
Hugh McLeod, *Class and Religion in the Late Victorian City*, 1974.
G. E. Mingay (ed.), *The Victorian Countryside*, 2 vols., 1981.
Margaret Penn, *Fourteen Miles from Manchester*, 1947.
Enid Porter (ed.), *Victorian Cambridge: Joseph Chater's Diaries*, 1975.
B. Seebohm Rowntree, *Poverty: a Study in Town Life*, 1901.
Raphael Samuel (ed.), *Village Life and Labour*, 1975.
George Sturt ('George Bourne'), *Change in the Village*, 1912.
Audrey M. Taylor, *Gilletts, Bankers at Banbury and Oxford*, Oxford, 1964.
F. M. L. Thompson, *English Landed Society in the Nineteenth Century*, 1963.
Martin J. Wiener, *English Culture and the Decline of the Industrial Spirit, 1850–1980*, Cambridge, 1981.
Raymond Williams, *The Country and the City*, 1973.

Chapter 6

George Brodrick, *Local Government in England*, 1875.
Kenneth D. Brown, *John Burns*, 1977.

Edwin Cannan, *History of Local Rates in England*, 1898.
Joseph Chamberlain *et al.*, *The Radical Programme*, 1885.
D. N. Chester, *Central and Local Government*, 1951.
Herman Finer, *English Local Government*, revised, 1945.
A. Lawrence Lowell, *The Government of England*, 2 vols., 1908.
John Stuart Mill, *On Liberty*, 1859; *Considerations on Representative Government*, 1861.
Avner Offer, *Property and Politics, 1870–1914*, Cambridge, 1981.
Josef Redlich and Francis W. Hirst, *Local Government in England*, 2 vols., 1903.
K. B. Smellie, *A History of Local Government*, 1946.
Gillian Sutherland (ed.) *Studies in the growth of Nineteenth-century Government*, 1972.
Sidney Webb, *Grants In Aid*, revised, 1920.
Brian D. White, *A History of the Corporation of Liverpool, 1835–1914*, Liverpool, 1951.

Chapter 7

M. J. Daunton, *Coal Metropolis: Cardiff 1870–1914*, Leicester, 1977.
Eric J. Evans (ed.), *Social Policy, 1830–1914*, 1978.
Herman Finer, *Municipal Trading*, 1941.
Derek Fraser, *Urban Politics in Victorian England*, Leicester, 1976.
Derek Fraser (ed.), *A History of Modern Leeds*, Manchester, 1981.
T. E. Headrick, *The Town Clerk*, 1962.
E. P. Hennock, *Fit and Proper Persons*, 1973.
G. W. Jones, *Borough Politics*, 1969.
J. R. Kellett, 'Municipal Socialism, Enterprise and Trading in the Victorian City', *Urban History Yearbook*, Leicester, 1978.
Harold J. Laski, W. Ivor Jennings, William A. Robson (eds.), *A Century of Municipal Progress*, 1935.
A. J. Lee, *The Origins of the Popular Press, 1855–1914*, 1976.
William A. Robson, *The Development of Local Government*, 1931.
Royal Commissions on Local Government: the Onslow Commission, 1923–9, and Redcliffe-Maud, 1969.
E. D. Simon, *A City Council from Within*, 1926.
F. B. Smith, *The People's Health, 1830–1910*, 1979.

Index

Finnegan, Frances, 198
fires, and fire brigades, 59, 61, 236–7, 243
Firth, J. F. B., 57
fish, consumption, 52; ports, 4, 96–7, 120, 135–6, 139
flats, 146–7
Flaubert, Gustave, 35
Fleetwood, 139
fogs, 43, 48, 99, 186
Folkestone, 139, 302
food, and food distribution, 41, 52–3, 71, 84, 89–90, 104, 149, 155, 157–8, 195–6, 202, 206, 283, 311
football, *see* sport
Ford, Henry, 146
foremen, 44, 125, 150–1
Forster, W. E., 110
Fountains Abbey, 134
Fowey, 78
Fowler, Henry, 275
Fowler, Sir John, 162
franchise, *see* municipal elections *and* parliament
Fraser, Derek, ix, 187, 293
Fraser, James, 224
Freeman, T. W., ix, 29, 75–7
free trade, 54, 58, 87, 91, 120
Frith, W. P., 82, 131
Fulham, 3, 274
Fuller, John, 210
Furness Railway Company, 98
furniture manufacture, 24, 41, 46, 194

Gainsborough, 4
Galsworthy, John, 144
gambling, 51, 106
garden cities, 176–83
Gardiner, A. G., 53, 61, 175
Garvin, J. L., 111
gas, 12, 18, 20, 24, 63, 72, 85, 158, 179, 193, 235, 243, 291, 293, 300, 303–5, 307–8, 310, 312, 314–15
Gateshead, 3, 9, 73, 244, 293, 313
Gauldie, Enid, 147
Geddes, Patrick, 73, 176, 181, 214
geography, and urban studies, vii, 11, 229–30
George III, King, 133
George IV, King, 133, 142
George, David Lloyd, 111, 163, 261–2

George, Dorothy, 40
George, Henry, 61, 176, 259
Gervis, Sir George Tapps, 138
Giffen, Robert, 278
Gilletts, bankers, 234–5
Gillingham (Kent), 3, 219, 244
Gissing, George, 43–4, 149, 213
Gladstone, W. E., 58, 207, 210–11, 265–6, 273–5
Glasgow, 95, 161, 261
glass manufacture, 4, 18, 71
Glastonbury, 174
Gloucester, 5, 19, 209, 219, 224
Gloucestershire, 194, 233
glove-making, 193–4, 214
Glover-Kinde, John, 131
Godwin, George, 50
Gomme, G. L., 278
Goole, 97
Gore, Charles, 180
Goschen, G. J., 60, 256–8, 265–7
Gott, Benjamin, 19
grain trade, 6, 98; *see also* milling
Granby, Lord, 205
grant-in-aid system, 22, 250, 252–3, 255, 257, 263–72
Grantham, 200
Granville, Dr A. B., 133
Gravesend, 302, 313
Great Central Railway, 159
Great Crosby, 9
Great Eastern Railway, 24, 40, 132, 160, 209
Great Northern Railway, 219
Great Western Railway, 4, 6, 136, 160, 164, 209, 219, 220
Greenaway, Kate, 186
Greenwich, 42
Gretna, 183
Grimsby, 4, 97, 144, 313
Grimshaw, Atkinson, 99
Gross, Charles, 319
Grossmith, George and Walter Weedon, 148
Grundy, Revd G. D., 225
guardians, boards of, *see* poor law
Guildford, 302

Hackney, 3, 40–1, 59, 156
Hadfield, Charles, 17
Haldane, R. B., 83

Martin, Geoffrey, 236, 319
Marylebone, 50, 59
Maryport, 172
Marx, Karl, 128, 147
Mason, J., 82
Masterman, C. F. G., 31, 148, 152–3, 206
Matcham, Frank, 142
Mather & Platt Co. Ltd., 89, 112
Matlock, 133
Maude, Sir John, 167
Mayhew, Henry, 51, 116
mayors, 21, 55, 59, 82, 289
Maypole Dairy Co., 72, 156
Meakin, J. E. B., 172
Mearns, Andrew, 32
Mechanics Institutes, 102, 314
medical facilities, 12–14, 47, 114, 127, 133–5, 158, 181, 206, 223, 230, 236, 243, 246, 251, 268, 271, 273, 277–9, 300, 309, 315
Medical Officers of Health, 57, 264, 281, 283–5, 288
Melbourne, 11
Melton Mowbray, 232
Mersey Docks and Harbour Board, 88, 92, 244
Merseyside, 74
metal work, *see* iron, steel, and metals manufacture
Metropolitan Board of Works (MBW), 25, 30, 54, 59–61
metropolitan boroughs, 30–1, 51, 58, 60, 62–5
metropolitan culture, 22, 36, 185–7
Middlesbrough, 3, 11, 100–1, 104, 108, 121, 169
Middlesex, 153, 194, 210
Midland Railway, 160, 219, 227
Midlands, 17, 20, 73–4, 79, 94, 100, 104, 114, 125, 143, 147, 174, 193–4, 213, 232, 242, 250, 303–4
migration, 26–7, 31, 47, 101, 125, 145, 192–4, 197, 215
Mile End, 42, 59
milk trade, 26, 52–3, 189, 311–12
Mill, John Stuart, 58, 121, 254, 278, 288, 291, 301, 303
Millais, Sir John, 82
milling, 89, 200, 233
Millthorpe, 180

Milner, Alfred, 112
Minehead, 132
mining and miners, 71, 84, 97–8, 100, 113–14, 116–17, 121, 125, 129, 135, 172, 203, 212, 219, 260
Mingay, G. E., 271
mobility, 12, 16–20, 26–30, 115, 149–52, 173, 272, 276
Monet, Claude, 99
Monkswell, Lord, 289
Monro, Sir Horace, 277
Morecambe, 142
Morley, John, 58, 108, 222, 299
Morris, William, poet, designer, and critic, 21, 81, 100, 109, 128–30, 171–2, 176, 184, 204
Morris, William, car manufacturer, 20, 234
Morrison, Arthur, 35, 141
Morrison, Herbert, 59, 63, 289
mortality, 28, 238, 273, 277–8, 315
motor vehicles, 4, 20, 38, 94, 97, 125, 146, 155, 163–4, 170, 179, 192, 203, 205–6, 230
Mumford, Lewis, 10, 147
Munby, A. J., 161, 203
municipal boroughs, 2, 242–6, 302
Municipal Corporations Acts, 1835 and 1882, 57, 59, 64, 241–6, 268, 282, 294
Municipal Corporations, Association of, 258, 261, 264, 288, 300
municipal elections, 61–2, 245–6, 251, 296–8
municipal socialism, municipal trading, and municipalization, 20, 60, 84–6, 121, 235, 243, 256–7, 261, 275, 286, 292, 298–316
Municipal Reformers (LCC), 60, 62
museums, 39, 84, 314
music, concerts and societies, 102, 138, 156, 179
music-halls, 38–9, 101, 204
Musson, A. E., 69
Myerscough, John, 131

National Association of Local Government Officers (NALGO), 287–8
national culture, growth of, 22–3, 36, 239, 254–5